THE PATIENT
ASSASSIN

THE PATIENT ASSASSIN

A True Tale of Massacre,
Revenge and the Raj

ANITA ANAND

**SIMON &
SCHUSTER**

London · New York · Sydney · Toronto · New Delhi

A CBS COMPANY

First published in Great Britain by Simon & Schuster UK Ltd, 2019
A CBS COMPANY

Copyright © Anita Anand, 2019

The right of Anita Anand to be identified as the author
of this work has been asserted in accordance with the
Copyright, Designs and Patents Act, 1988.

5 7 9 10 8 6 4

Simon & Schuster UK Ltd
1st Floor
222 Gray's Inn Road
London WC1X 8HB

www.simonandschuster.co.uk
www.simonandschuster.com.au
www.simonandschuster.co.in

Simon & Schuster Australia, Sydney
Simon & Schuster India, New Delhi

The author and publishers have made all reasonable efforts to contact
copyright-holders for permission, and apologise for any omissions or errors
in the form of credits given. Corrections may be made to future printings.

A CIP catalogue record for this book
is available from the British Library.

Hardback ISBN: 978-1-4711-7421-6
Trade Paperback ISBN: 978-1-4711-7422-3
eBook ISBN: 978-1-4711-7423-0

Typeset in Sabon by M Rules
Printed and bound by CPI Group (UK) Ltd, Croydon, CR0 4YY

MIX
Paper from
responsible sources
FSC
www.fsc.org   FSC® C020471

For my mother and father.
And in memory of my grandfather,
Ishwar Das Anand.

No guilt in survival.
I wish I could have told you that.

CONTENTS

'Vengeance and retribution require a
long time; it is the rule.'

CHARLES DICKENS,
A Tale of Two Cities

PREFACE

In February 2013, David Cameron became the first serving British prime minister to visit Jallianwala Bagh, a stone's throw from the Golden Temple in Amritsar. The dusty walled garden was the site of a brutal massacre on 13 April 1919 and, for Indians at least, it has come to represent the worst excesses of the Raj. On that day, a British officer, Brigadier General Reginald Dyer, hearing that an illegal political meeting was due to take place, ordered his men to open fire on around 20,000 innocent and unarmed men, women and children. The youngest victim was a six-month-old baby; the oldest was in his eighties.

The lieutenant governor of Punjab, a man named Sir Michael O'Dwyer, not only approved of the shootings, but spent much of the rest of his life praising the action and fortitude of his brigadier general. Sir Michael's attitude, coupled with the behaviour of British soldiers in the weeks that followed, created a suppurating wound in the Indian psyche. The scar is still livid in the north of India to this day.

The number of people killed at Jallianwala Bagh has always been in dispute, with British estimates putting the dead at 379 with 1,100 wounded and Indian sources insisting that around 1,000 people were killed and more than 1,500 wounded. By his own admission, no order to disperse was given and Dyer's soldiers fired 1,650 rounds in Jallianwala Bagh that day. He instructed them to aim into the thickest parts of the crowd, which happened to be by the perimeter, where desperate people were trying to scale walls to escape the bullets. The configuration of the garden and the position of the troops meant civilians were trapped, much like fish in a barrel.

The bloodbath, though appalling, could have been so much worse. Dyer later admitted that he would have used machine guns too if he had been able to drive his armoured cars through the narrow entrance to the Bagh. He was seeking to teach the restive province a lesson. Punctuated by bullets, his message was clear. The Raj reigned supreme. Dissent would not be tolerated. The empire crushed those who defied it.

Ninety-four years later, laying a wreath of white gerberas at the foot of the towering red stone Martyrs' Memorial in Amritsar, David Cameron bowed solemnly as India watched. In the visitors' condolence book he wrote the following message: 'This was a deeply shameful event in British history – one that Winston Churchill rightly described at the time as "monstrous". We must never forget what happened here. And in remembering we must ensure that the United Kingdom stands up for the right of peaceful protest around the world.'

Though sympathetic, Cameron's words fell short of the apology many Indians had been hoping for. The massacre was indeed monstrous, and I have grown up with its legacy. My grandfather, Ishwar Das Anand, was in the garden that day in 1919. By a quirk of fate, he left Jallianwala Bagh on an errand minutes before the firing started. He remembered Brigadier General Dyer's convoy passing him in the street. When he returned, my grandfather found his friends, young men like him in their late teens, had been killed.

According to his children, Ishwar Das Anand suffered survivor's guilt for the rest of his relatively short life. In his late forties, he would lose his sight, but tell his sons never to pity him: 'God spared my life that day. It is only right that he take the light from my eyes.' He never managed to reconcile why he had lived while so many others had not. He found it excruciatingly painful to talk about that day. He died too young. I never got the chance to know him.

The story of Jallianwala Bagh is tightly wound round my family's DNA. Ironically, it is also woven into my husband's family history, a fact we only realised years into our marriage. His forebears were pedlars from Punjab who came to settle in Britain in the 1930s. Bizarrely, one of them found himself living with a man named Udham Singh. The happy-go-lucky Punjabi would turn out to be the 'Patient Assassin' of this book, deified in India, the land of my ancestors, but largely unknown in Great Britain, the land of my birth.

Speaking to descendants of the pedlar community, which came to Britain in the early 1920s, helped me to understand their experience. They also helped to bring Udham Singh to life.

Thanks to my parents, I grew up knowing the names of Reginald Dyer and Sir Michael O'Dwyer, but of course Udham Singh loomed larger still. According to legend, he, like Ishwar Das Anand, was in the garden on the day of the massacre. Unlike my grandfather, he was not crushed by survivor's guilt, but rather consumed by violent rage. We, like many Punjabis, were told how Udham, grabbing a clod of blood-soaked earth, squeezed it in his fist, vowing to avenge the dead. No matter how long it took him, no matter how far he would have to go, Udham would kill the men responsible for the carnage.

Twenty years later, Udham Singh would fulfil at least part of that bloody promise. He would shoot Sir Michael O'Dwyer through the heart at point-blank range in London, just a stone's throw away from the Houses of Parliament.

The moment he pulled the trigger, he became the most hated man in Britain, a hero to his countrymen in India, and a pawn in international politics. Joseph Goebbels himself would leap upon Udham's story and use it for Nazi propaganda at the height of the Second World War.

In India today, Udham Singh is for many simply a hero, destined to right a terrible wrong. At the other extreme, there are those who traduce him as a Walter Mitty-type fantasist, blundering his way into the history books. The truth, as always, lies somewhere in between; Udham was neither a saint, nor an accidental avenger. His story is far more interesting than that.

Like a real-life Tom Ripley, Udham, a low-caste, barely literate orphan, spent the majority of his life becoming the 'Patient Assassin'. Obsessed with avenging his countrymen and throwing out the British from his homeland, he inveigled his way into the shadowy worlds of Indian militant nationalism, Russian Bolshevism and even found himself flirting with the Germans in the run-up to the Second World War. Anybody dedicated to the downfall of the British Empire had something to teach him, and he was hungry to learn.

Ambitious, tenacious and brave, Udham was also vain, careless and callous to those who loved him most. His footsteps have led me on a much longer, more convoluted journey than I ever anticipated. The diversity of sources and need to cross-reference hearsay has been challenging, but not the hardest thing about writing this book. I have also had to consciously distance myself from my own family history. For a while, the very names O'Dwyer and Dyer paralysed me. We had been brought up fearing them.

Only when I thought of O'Dwyer as 'Michael', the ardent Irish child growing up in Tipperary, or Dyer as 'Rex', the sensitive boy who cried over a dead monkey he once shot by accident, could I free myself to think about them as men, and even start to understand why they did the things they did. It was the only way I could empathise with the situation they faced in 1919 and the years that followed.

The same goes for Udham Singh. He had always been one of the pantheon of freedom fighters who had fought against tyranny. I blocked out the statues and stamps dedicated to his memory in India and refused to watch any representations of his legend in popular culture till my own work was complete. I needed to find the man beneath the myth and marble, and I knew I would not be able to do that if I became dazzled. Thousands of original documents guided my way, and my search for the real Udham Singh led me to people who either had first-hand knowledge of him, or were repositories of stories from their parents and grandparents.

I found myself left with a surprisingly contemporary story, which resonates with the news I cover today. Udham's is a story of dispossession and radicalisation, of 'Russian interference' and a realigning of world powers. It speaks of failures in the seemingly infallible security services. It is also the story of buried facts and 'fake news'. I was left with a picture of one man's very personal obsession wrong-footing some of the world's most powerful players.

As to whether Udham really was in the garden the day of the massacre, a source of fierce contention in some quarters, only he knew for sure. What I can say with absolute certainty is that the British authorities were desperate to separate Udham's assassination of Sir Michael O'Dwyer from the Jallianwala Bagh massacre. The attendant propaganda surrounding a 'revenge killing' was the last thing they needed with so many Indian troops engaged on the side of the Allies in the war.

Whether he was there when the bullets started to fly or not, the massacre in Jallianwala Bagh was transformative for Udham Singh. He was both forged and destroyed by the events of 13 April 1919. The massacre became the catalyst turning him from a hopeless, faceless member of India's oppressed masses into a man who would strike one of the most dramatic blows against the empire. Udham Singh dedicated his life to becoming a hero to his people, to freeing his country from the British.

He would go to the gallows thinking he would lie forever forgotten in an unmarked grave in a foreign land. Though he would never know it, seven years after he was hanged, India would be free and his countrymen would declare him one of their greatest sons. They would fight to have his remains returned to them.

In 2018, a statue of Udham Singh was unveiled outside Jallianwala Bagh. It shows a man with a clod of presumably blood-heavy earth in his outstretched palm. Udham will forever stand watch over the garden. All who come to pay their respects in the garden will be forced to look up to him and remember what he did in their name.

PART ONE

CHAPTER 1

THE DROP

LONDON, 30 JULY 1940

Albert was in an odd state of mind. Not frightened, nor angry, nor particularly depressed, just not himself somehow – out of sorts. The 35-year-old, plain-speaking Yorkshireman had been shaken out of his habitual good humour even before he boarded the juddering train from Manchester to London. Though the job waiting for him in the capital would have turned the stomachs of his fellow passengers, it was not the cause of his mood. Albert was on his way to kill a man, and he was fine with that.

He had done it before, and, if the fates were kind to him, he would do it many times again. No, something else was troubling him, something he had no control over. He, Albert Pierrepoint, junior executioner for His Majesty, might die in the next few days. Winston Churchill had told him so.

Albert had been at home the previous day, packing his bags, when Churchill's jowly voice crackled through the wireless. The war was going to be long and bloody, and London, Albert's destination, was the Nazis' imminent target. Simultaneously hectoring and seductive, Churchill's words filled Albert's bedroom and his head: 'The vast mass of London itself, fought street by street, could easily devour an entire hostile army.'

With his next breath, somewhat less reassuringly, Churchill addressed the potential cost to his people: 'We would rather see London laid in ruins and ashes than that it should be tamely and abjectly enslaved.'[1]

The words were vivid in Albert's mind as he hauled his suitcase off the train and made his way through the press of people on the platform. London might feel like a sprawling, crawling, sooty mess to most of his fellow northerners, but Albert always found magic in the grime. Now, heading towards Pentonville Prison, he looked at his surroundings with different eyes: 'Newly aware that [the war] might be fought street by street while I was in it.'[2] Churchill's words had resonated somewhere deep in his patriotism. The voice from the radio, carried on waves of static, had been clear. Britain would give no quarter: 'Any traitors that may be found in our midst – but I do not believe there are many ... will get short shrift.'[3]

Albert knew all about retribution. He embodied it every time he adjusted a noose.

Men like Albert, who devoted their lives to the penal system, referred to Pentonville Prison as 'the Ville', making it sound like a provincial hotel or a friendly local pub. A Victorian brick building of imposing size and colour-draining drabness, the Ville had taught Albert Pierrepoint all he knew about killing. He had learned his trade there eight years before, practising the hangman's silent walk past the condemned cells, learning the art of measuring, coiling and tightening a rope. The Ville had helped him perfect his lightning-quick 'capping' technique, the action of whipping out a white cotton bag from a pocket and pulling it over 'Old Bill's' head before neck-lacing him with the noose.

Old Bill was the name given to the heavy dummy that trainee executioners used for practice: 'Cap noose pin lever drop. You've got to get it right. *There's no allowance for error.* Haul him up and do it again.'[4]

Posted to Armley Gaol in Leeds, Albert showed himself to be a natural hangman. It wasn't long before people were comparing him to his uncle, the great Thomas Pierrepoint – a legend among executioners. The two became a team; 'Uncle Tom and Our Albert', as the Armley staff liked to call them. Together, uncle and nephew were responsible for most of the hangings in the north of England and in Ireland. Tom led while Albert assisted. There was much praise for the calm efficiency with which they despatched condemned men and women.

Itching to take the lead, Albert thought he might have finally got his chance when Pentonville's usual executioner received his call-up papers. Many men were being yanked out of professions to fight at the Front, their spaces providing opportunity for those left at home. It was a macabre way to make your way in the world, but Albert would have seized the chance with both hands.

Much to his disappointment, Albert's move proved to be sideways rather than up. Pentonville's own regular assistant hangman was getting the job. To make matters worse, he was someone Albert knew well, and for whom he had scant regard.

Stanley William Cross had trained with Albert at the Ville. As apprentices Albert had seen Cross up close, gone to the pub with him, swapped stories and compared notes. Their friendship was never more than superficial. Albert found his fellow trainee's temperament unsuited to the 'art'. Careless and boastful, Cross had a habit of turning 'jobs' into entertaining yarns in exchange for free drinks. That kind of behaviour made Albert wince, and for Cross to get his chance before him was galling.

It was therefore with a mixture of satisfaction and alarm that Albert greeted the scene at Pentonville Prison when he arrived. Cross was in a state of total panic, 'suffering a bad attack of nerves'.[5] Though the execution was slated for 9 a.m. the next morning, things were in total disarray. That Cross had allowed himself to get into such a mess for this of all hangings was hard to believe.

Executions were like pulses of energy through a prison population at the best of times, with a great machinery swinging into action around the intimacy of the actual killing. Hangings as important as this one required even more meticulous care than usual. Plans were in motion to move the rest of the prison population far from the condemned wing in the morning, setting inmates to work before they even had the chance to have their breakfast. This would give Albert and Cross the time and space they would need to do what they had to do.

Busy prisoners were calm prisoners, but there was an added incentive for distraction this time round. The doomed man had a habit of making speeches at the last minute – incendiary, treasonous speeches – and that was the last thing the authorities needed. They had worked so hard to keep the prisoner's words out of the press, they did not need some dying diatribe to undo all that.

Though Albert was trained to regard every hanging with the same dispassionate professionalism, he knew the execution of Udham Singh, or 'Prisoner 1010' as the chalkboard outside his cell identified him, was the most important in his career. From India to Great Britain, this man had dominated headlines for weeks. His grinning face had been splashed over countless front pages, and his crime had shaken an already unstable world.

Despite acres of coverage, analysis and condemnation, most remained incredulous that this brown-faced foreigner had, at a time of heightened wartime paranoia, simply sauntered into a meeting in the heart of Westminster, close to the Houses of Parliament, and emptied his pistol into some of the most important men of the realm. His victims had included the secretary of state for India himself, but it was the slaying of one man, a former lieutenant governor of Punjab called Sir Michael O'Dwyer, that had dominated the news. Shot straight through the heart at point-blank range, there seemed to be something almost operatic about the murder.

For some, the shooting of Sir Michael was merely the callous murder of an old and defenceless man. To others, it threatened the very foundation of the British Empire. Sir Michael was a stalwart defender of the Raj, and many in Britain agreed with his hardline policies towards India.

Conversely, millions in India itself regarded the murderer as an avenging angel, who, after twenty-one long years, had settled a terrible score. Thanks to Udham Singh, the name 'Jallianwala Bagh' was being spoken all over the world once again. It was a name the British would rather have forgotten – a portal into a nation's shame at a time when the country needed to be both shameless and fearless.

The Home Office, Special Branch, the Secret Intelligence Service (SIS), MI5, the Indian Political Intelligence (IPI), as well as the prison and prosecution services, all knew the importance of Prisoner 1010. They agreed he had to die quickly, with as little fuss as possible. Cross must have known all this. How had he managed to mess things up so badly?

Instead of taking his own measurements, Cross appeared to have relied heavily on the prisoner's paperwork. According to 1010's file, he was 'stocky', 'heavy built' or 'well built'. It described a man 5 feet 8 inches tall, 'weighing 172 lbs' and 'generally sound and healthy'. The man Albert saw through the spyhole in the cell door seemed like a different person entirely. Udham was thin, sallow and sickly, nothing like the iconic picture of him that had run in so many newspapers.

Udham had been held on remand at Brixton Prison for months before his transfer to the Ville's condemned wing. There, the senior medical officer, a man called Dr Hugh Grierson, had been tasked with keeping the prisoner alive long enough to hang him. Udham had not made it easy. From the moment he arrived at Brixton, he had been trying to kill himself. When his attempts to slit his wrists or take poison were discovered, he pushed his food tray away. Udham had tried to starve himself to death. Weeks of hunger striking did terrible things to the human body.

Grierson found it objectionable that Udham refused to die the way the British had planned, and talked about him as if he were a stubborn animal or errant child in dire need of training. Udham was 'uncooperative' and 'responded badly to authority'.[6] In his notes, Grierson observed: 'There was always an undercurrent of antagonism to everyone, sometimes bordering on dumb insolence. He was untruthful, and I could not rely on anything he said.'[7]

Adamant that Udham Singh should not escape the hangman's noose, Grierson ordered a regime of force-feeding. Three times a day in the weeks leading up to his trial, warders entered 1010's cell and pinned his body to a gurney. They forced a feeding tube into his mouth, down his throat and into his stomach. His teeth clenched on the rubber gag that prised his jaws apart. Denounced as a form of torture for decades, ever since harrowing accounts of the procedure had been made public by the suffragettes, force-feeding was rarely used in Britain by 1940. Prisoner 1010 was subjected to ninety-three of these brutal acts during his time at Brixton.

Grierson had been at pains to play down the impact on his prisoner, insisting that he had taken it all surprisingly well. Even if the true horror of the experience had been made known, few would have cared. Udham Singh was one of the most hated men in Britain. Most were counting the days till he dangled from the end of a rope.

Grierson's troublesome prisoner only decided to eat again after the judge passed the death penalty on him, but by that time his weight had plummeted. As he accepted meal trays again, he slowly put the pounds back on, but Stanley William Cross had no idea what he actually weighed at this moment, on the eve of his execution. To Albert's disgust, Cross had ignored the hangman's code, drilled into them both all those years ago when they had trained at this very prison. Nothing should be left to chance. Preparation was key:

> Take your time all the time ... Choose your rope the afternoon before. And that's the time you test that the drop works smoothly, to your complete satisfaction, when you've got word that the prisoner is at exercise, or in the chapel, or wherever they've put it in his mind to go. You don't want to have him hear it, he's only next door.[8]

Udham was right in front of them now, playing cribbage with a guard, passing the hours till the moment appointed for him to die. Albert knew that, at this late stage, there was no way discreet measurements could be taken. The governor and the sheriff of London were hovering outside Udham's cell, talking nervously among themselves, showing no sign that they were going to leave. There was no way the two executioners could now breeze in and ask the Indian to step on a set of scales. Not without disgracing themselves entirely.

Cross looked at Albert in desperation. Speaking out of the corner of his mouth, and hoping nobody else could hear, he begged for help: 'Eh, Albert! What drop shall we give?'[9]

Not entirely displeased by his colleague's plight, Albert replied: 'You should know. You're the boss.'[10] A more spiteful man would have left it there, let Cross's career go hang with the convict, but his Uncle Tom would not have approved. Besides, Albert was not a man who liked to see needless suffering. If the hangman's drop was too short, this man would strangle slowly, legs kicking in the space beneath the trap door. If the sandbag attached to his feet was too light, his spine would fail to sever cleanly and painlessly, and the end would also come slowly. If it was too heavy, his whole head might rip off. Albert understood that this was no time to gloat:

> I took the paper out of [Cross's] hand and a pencil from my pocket. The truth was that I had already worked out in my mind an approximate drop from the details of the prisoner's height and weight which I had heard, and from my inspection of the condemned man. I put the paper up against the wall of the execution chamber, made a fast check that my memory of the weight was right and wrote down a figure. I didn't bother to look at the Home Office table, because I was already using my own experience.[11]

Congratulating himself on his superior skill, Albert took a last look at the man they were going to kill in the morning. It was hard to believe that this crumpled creature had caused so much trouble.

But people had been underestimating Udham Singh all his life.

There is no record of how long it took 1010 to die. In his memoirs, Albert Pierrepoint would only say: 'We duly carried out the execution next morning, took the body down, stowed the gear and reported to the governor.'[12]

Confidential prison files indicate that Udham Singh's last moments were anything but easy, suggesting that Cross either misunderstood or ignored Albert's advice. Details, deemed so potentially embarrassing they were ordered sealed in perpetuity, forcibly opened by Freedom of Information requests, hint at the gross incompetence of the execution. Blame was laid firmly at Cross's feet: 'I have to report for the information of the Commissioners, that in my opinion this man [William Cross] is unsuitable for the post of executioner . . . the whole method in which he carried out the execution was such as to bring me to the opinion that it would not be safe for him to be employed again.'[13]

Stanley William Cross never did work as an executioner at the Ville again, but Albert Pierrepoint went on to become Britain's longest serving hangman. He would pull the lever on 400 men and women during his long career. Keeping his cool while Cross lost his won him his longed-for recognition. In death, Udham Singh had inadvertently set Albert Pierrepoint up for life.

Hanged men get no headstones. Bodies, cut down and loaded into a wooden cart, were rolled into a small nondescript space round the back. The space reserved for bodies was so small that Pentonville's executed had to be buried one on top of another. After the burial party had dug its hole and lowered in the new incumbent, guards threw layers of chalk dust onto the plain wooden boxes before covering them with dirt. It was a tried and tested way to avoid putting a spade through some old murderer's skull. The soil round the back of Pentonville was striped like a grisly gateau, white lines showing where one man ended and another began.

Udham Singh's line lay close to Roger Casement's, an Irish aristocrat who had been hanged as a traitor, and Dr Crippen, a notorious wife-killer. Only Pentonville's governor knew for sure where all these men lay. Gathering dust in his desk drawers, he had a chart with names, depths and steps away from the wall. It was important to keep a record, just in case anyone wanted to dig up any of these wretched specimens. Of course, it rarely happened. This patch at the back of Pentonville was filled with the forgotten and the damned.

CHAPTER 2

THE GOOD SON

Michael O'Dwyer had always loved the loamy richness of Tipperary earth. It was good, wholesome and it grounded a fellow. To his mind there was no nobler profession than tilling the soil, making things grow and going to sleep exhausted after a long, hard day. Michael was a sentimental man.

Born on 28 April 1864, close friends described him as 'Irish to the backbone'.[1] The land of his forefathers, filled with folklore, music and poetry, meant everything to him. In later years, Michael devoted much of his time tracing his *sept* – a Celtic term for a large and influential family within a clan. Historically, the O'Dwyer *sept* was one of the most powerful in Tipperary, and his family even had its own coat of arms: a rearing red lion, or 'lion rampant', pawing the air on a background of white ermine. The Latin motto beneath reads: '*Virtus sola nobilitas*' – 'virtue alone ennobles'.

To his delight, Michael found that his ancestral roots were entangled in hundreds of years of Irish history. As he would later write, his clan had witnessed the very birth of his beloved country: 'The O'Dwyers emerged from the Celtic twilight of tribal conflicts and struggles against the Danes at the Battle of Clontarf, AD 1014.'[2]

Even Barronstown, where Michael grew up, an inconspicuous parish of 33 square miles, was described by him in terms of epic poetry. Lying in 'the heart of the "Golden Vale"' and 'under the shadow of the Galtees'. He described a land of 'blue mountain and the rushing river'.[3]

Michael was one of fourteen children, the sixth of nine sons born to Catholic John O'Dwyer and his wife Margaret. The family farmed an 85-acre holding,[4] and from childhood the somewhat wild boy gained a reputation as a ferocious rider, pelting over fences and pushing both his riding companions and his mounts to their absolute limits. He was courageous, careless and sometimes callous with his horses.

Surrounded by siblings of similar age, Michael preferred the company of adults, particularly his own father, of whom he said: 'It is no filial exaggeration to say that he possessed the best traits of the Irish character.'[5]

In Michael's doting eyes, John O'Dwyer had 'an unselfish devotion to his family, partly concealed by an austere demeanour, loyalty to his friends, fortitude in times of trouble, and a genial spirit of hospitality'.[6] Margaret, his mother, was no less adored. In his memoirs Michael described a woman with saint-like patience: 'She kept the family together in her own loving, unobtrusive and efficient manner till all were launched in the world or provided for at home, no easy task in those days of agricultural depression.'[7]

Economic downturns were merciless in Ireland, and Catholic Ireland suffered most of all. The Great Famine gripped the country for years, beginning with an outbreak of potato blight in 1845. It wiped out an entire harvest; crops were left to rot as the disease laid waste to acres of fields. Since potatoes were the mainstay of the Irish diet, widespread starvation was inevitable.

Despite describing parents who valiantly struggled against the odds, Michael's family were immune to the horrors faced by their neighbours. His father not only owned land and stables, but also made money from a modestly sized herd of cattle. The O'Dwyers of Tipperary were by no means rich, but business was good enough for John to pay for the education of all fourteen of his children. Michael's family never knew a day's hunger in their lives.

Other things set the O'Dwyers apart, too. Though staunchly

Catholic, Michael's father could not stand the tenor of nationalism among his co-religionists. While they detested the English and called for full Irish independence, John O'Dwyer was more convinced by the arguments of Daniel O'Connell, an Irish political leader who, in the first half of the nineteenth century, campaigned for the right for Catholics to sit in the Westminster Parliament. O'Connell believed the only way to improve the lives of his countrymen was to come to some power-sharing agreement, working within Parliament.

In contrast, groups like the Young Ireland movement demanded nothing less than full independence. These men, who later morphed into the Irish Republican Brotherhood, or Fenians, were despised by the O'Dwyers. They referred to them as 'thugs' and 'hotheads'. John O'Dwyer placed more faith in the men in Westminster than those seeking to overthrow them. Michael was therefore weaned on the belief that Parliament's might was right. Nationalists embodied chaos. His later responses to men like Gandhi were rooted in these early attitudes.

At the age of seven, Michael O'Dwyer was sent to St Stanislaus boarding school in Tullamore in central Ireland. Miles away from the warmth of his family, he would endure an austere school regime run by Jesuit monks. Though they were known to wield a cane with enthusiasm, Michael never expressed any regret at being sent away at such a tender age. The Jesuit brothers' benign despotism was to be admired. Michael was an unusual boy in many ways.

While other Stanislaus pupils were preoccupied by books or the first XI cricket team, he saw his future in the Indian Civil Service, or ICS. An administrative elite never exceeding 1,200 in number, the ICS ran the Raj in the name of the monarch. Drawing from a pool of the best British talent, ICS men were given enormous power and responsibility and chosen by fiercely competitive exams. For young men born without title or fortune, the ICS was one way they could really make their mark on the world.

One of the first British civil administrators in India was the legendary John Lawrence, every schoolboy's hero. Born in 1811,

Lawrence owed his fortune and his considerable fame to Punjab, a province in the north of India. Lawrence was viceroy of India by the time Michael was born, and his meteoric rise fired up many a schoolboy's imagination:

> A hard, active man in boots and breeches, who almost lived in the saddle, worked all day and nearly all night, ate and drank when and where he could . . .
>
> Heat, sun, rain, climatic changes of all sorts were to be matters of indifference to him. There was no place for drawing room niceties as an officer who made the mistake of taking a piano with him to the Punjab discovered. 'I'll smash his piano for him,' Lawrence declared and moved the officer five times from one end of the province to the other in two years.[8]

Men like Lawrence were heroes to boys like Michael.

The competition to join the ICS in the late 1800s was tremendous, and a market for 'Educational Crammers' burgeoned as a result. One of the most famous was run by a Mr Wren in London's Powis Square. Michael O'Dwyer cantered through the curriculum as if he were riding one of his family's horses, but his gusto failed to impress Wren. As O'Dwyer would later observe, he 'used to say that our batch of thirty was the rottenest that had ever passed through his hands'.[9]

Emerging from the 'rotten' bunch, Michael passed his ICS exams with flying colours. It was an especially notable achievement because news of two murders in Ireland had threatened to derail his studies altogether. On 6 May 1882, Lord Frederick Cavendish and Thomas Henry Burke, the chief secretary and permanent undersecretary for Ireland respectively, were stabbed to death in Dublin's Phoenix Park. It had been one of the most audacious acts of nationalist violence for years. Alarmed, Michael's thoughts flew to his father. The Phoenix Park murders made him 'ashamed of being an Irishman'[10] for the first time in his life, he said. If the nationalists could kill powerful statesmen, what hope was there for a farmer like John O'Dwyer?

Michael O'Dwyer's worst fears came true seven months later: 'Our home was fired into in December 1882, and my father and sister had a narrow escape.'[11]

The family received police protection, but the episode took an unexpected toll on his colossus of a father nevertheless. When Michael returned home for the Christmas holidays, John O'Dwyer suffered a stroke, which he believed had been brought on by the stress of recent months. It seemed mild at first, leaving him lightly paralysed, but another stroke was on its way. On Christmas Day, 'one of those soft mild winter days the south of Ireland is often favoured with',[12] John asked Michael to drive him around his fields.

'It was to be his last look,' recalled the devastated son. 'Soon after his return, he had a fresh seizure and passed away early the next morning.'[13]

Michael never forgave the nationalists for what they had put his father through. He would loathe their kind for the rest of his life.

Young ICS candidates were expected to complete a two-year probationary period at an English university. Balliol College, Oxford, had a reputation in the late 1800s as a leadership factory. Recent graduates included George Nathaniel Curzon, Alfred Milner and Herbert Henry Asquith, men who would go on to serve as viceroy of India, secretary of state to the colonies and prime minister of Great Britain respectively. After Michael won his coveted place, he studied with his customary intensity, passing out fourth among all ICS candidates that year.

This result was good enough to catapult him into a prime Indian posting, however the young Irishman did not yet feel ready to start his working life. Still in mourning, Balliol, with its rigorous demands, provided him with just the diversion he needed. He asked for permission to remain a while longer. The India Office agreed to fund a year-long extension, on the condition that he completed an honours degree in that period. This left Michael with little time to wallow in his sadness, because he had to squeeze a three-year course into just one. Jurisprudence was one of the most challenging degrees Balliol had to offer, and though predicted to get only a third-class degree, he came away with a First.

Qualifications in hand, emotions mastered, Michael O'Dwyer now felt ready for India.

The intense Indian humidity that greeted Michael O'Dwyer in the winter of 1885 could not have contrasted more with the chill he had left behind. When the ship dropped anchor in the port of Karachi, Michael was forced to navigate his way, marshalling trunks and cases, through a sprawling quayside of bawling dock-workers, hawkers and hard-palmed lascars, the Indian sailors who crewed Raj ships. There was barely enough time to take it all in before he had to get the train north. Michael's orders would take him to the capital of Punjab, the city of Lahore. His posting put him right in the heart of John Lawrence country.

Though Lawrence had died in 1879, everywhere Michael looked he could feel his presence. The impressive Lawrence Hall, conspicuously white inside and out, held concerts exclusively for European audiences. Lawrence Gardens stretched out before him, where dark-skinned ayahs wheeled pink-cheeked charges, the children of the Raj. While it did not bear his name, Lahore railway station, Michael's link to the rest of the world, was John Lawrence's greatest legacy.

Work for the grand, red-brick terminus began two years after the Indian Mutiny of 1857. To inaugurate the enterprise, Lawrence had broken earth with a silver shovel engraved with the Latin motto 'tam bello quam pace' – 'better peace than war'. His railway station was ready for both.

With its pretty turrets, Lahore station looked like a fairy-tale castle, but it was more of a fortress. Great steel doors slid across the ends of train sheds and over platforms, turning the station into a massive makeshift bunker for the British should there be a repeat of the violence of 1857. Attractive round bastions were cannonproof. Narrow, decorative slits in the walls were specifically designed to accommodate 'Maxims', the world's first recoil-operated machine guns. Lawrence had wanted those who came after him to feel safe.

The Indian Mutiny of 1857 had shaped Britain's attitude towards her Indian natives. In the years that preceded it, the country had been battered by British economic exploitation. In pursuit of profit, the East India Company had squeezed both the land and the people who lived on it unsparingly. The peasant class, forming the majority of India's population, found itself either starved off ancestral lands or reduced to the status of indentured labour, thanks to a system of punitive taxation. Farmers that continued to work the land were forbidden from growing edible crops. Instead, they were forced by their new foreign overlords to produce cotton and indigo, vital for Britain's lucrative and growing textile industry.

On an individual level, working men could no longer feed their families. In a wider context, self-sufficiency in rural India was all but destroyed. The poor now had to buy their food and clothing at inflated prices. Many were forced to take loans secured against their property to pay for goods and were later crushed by astronomical interest on their repayments. It was a perfect recipe for poverty, hunger and despair, yet the British kept taking.

William Bentinck, the governor-general of India in 1834, admitted: 'The misery hardly finds a parallel in the history of commerce. The bones of cotton weavers are bleaching the plains of India.'

Soon after, famine swept through British-controlled territories, killing almost a million people. In July 1840, news of unprecedented hardship reached London and a select committee of MPs convened to examine the conduct of British traders in India. When called to give evidence, Thomas Cope, a successful silk merchant from Macclesfield, did not deny that his Indian workers were starving. Instead, he insisted that it did not matter: 'I certainly pity the East Indian labourer, but at the same time I have a greater feeling for my family than for the East Indian labourer's family. I think it is wrong to sacrifice the comforts of my family for the sake of the East Indian labourer because his condition happens to be worse than mine.'[14]

In addition to the suffering of the poorest, the British policy of territorial annexation had led to the displacement of a large number of rulers and chiefs. They too began to organise against the British. The spark that lit the tinder came when sepoys, the Indian soldiers serving under the British, were told to use a new type of rifle where cartridges greased with animal fat would have to be bitten before pouring the gunpowder into the gun. Muslims were forbidden pork; Hindus and Sikhs were forbidden beef. Rumours spread that both were being used to provide the fat.

Sepoys first mutinied in Barrackpore near Calcutta. Their rebellion quickly spread to Meerut in the north and spilled over into Delhi, the capital of the former Mughal Empire. Sepoys in Lucknow, Bareilly, Kanpur, Jhansi, Central India and Bundelkhand joined the uprising, overthrowing and killing British officers.

Not since the loss of the American colonies a century before had Britain felt such a threat to its national interests. If India was to slip her bonds, economic collapse at home would follow.

By the middle of June, the whole of northern India was in open revolt. Rebels rampaged across the region and a minority committed unspeakable atrocities against British civilians. Kanpur, or Cawnpore as it was then known, saw some of the worst of the bloodlust, culminating in the massacre of 204 British women and children on 27 June 1857. The slaughter at the Bibighar had a devastating effect on the relieving British forces. Expecting to find the female hostages alive, they instead found floors 'ankle deep' in blood, and rooms littered with bonnets, children's shoes and hair, matted in gore.

Retribution was swift and ruthless. The British government poured men and logistics into the region. Sepoys were rounded up and, whether they had taken part in the uprising or not, were summarily executed. By his own account, Frederick Cooper, the deputy commissioner of Amritsar, shot to death no less than 237 captured sepoys at the end of July 1857. A further forty-five suffocated in cells as they awaited the firing squad.

Within four months, the British had executed around 100,000 sepoys, most of whom had played no part in any atrocity. The manner of their killing exemplified the vengeance that drove the British. Sepoys were tied to the mouths of cannons and blasted to pieces for sport. Their brother soldiers were forced to stand in the splattered blood and tissue, reinforcing the British message: This is how we deal with defiance.

Thousands more were hanged from makeshift gallows in trees. On occasion, their still-breathing bodies were used for bayonet practice to improve morale among British troops. The sweeping brutality, which included the slaughters of tens of thousands of innocent civilians, became known in India as 'The Devil's Wind'.

There is an old Punjabi saying, '*Jinaay Lahore nahi veak'aya oou jum'aya eei nahi*', which loosely translates as: 'If you haven't seen Lahore, you ain't seen nothing.' Lahoris are rightly proud of their city. The Mughals were first to lavish attention on it during a reign that lasted more than two centuries. Emperor Akbar (1542–1605) created the city's mighty fort, a 20-hectare walled enclosure filled with mirrors, mosaics and marble. It was dotted with beautiful palaces, harems and gardens. Akbar's architectural taste married Hindu and Muslim traditions, melding intricate Persian calligraphy, precise Arabic geometry and ostentatious Hindu-temple flourishes. The Shalimar Gardens, with their 400 fountains and pools of tranquillity, were mankind's attempt to mirror the gardens of paradise.

The Sikhs had left their own aesthetic too, including the *samadhi* or mausoleum to Lahore's Sikh maharajah Ranjit Singh. Its great golden dome catches the light of the rising and setting sun.

Young Michael noticed none of this. Lahore was disappointing, and his first impressions were far from good: 'There was a pervading sense of dust and disorder, relics of the rough Sikh dominion.'[15]

The presence of 'the brilliant Kipling family' was Lahore's

saving grace, providing much-needed relief from the overwhelming foreignness: 'I think it was in 1886 that Mr and Mrs Lockwood-Kipling, with their son (Rudyard) and daughter, combined to bring out a Christmas Annual which was full of humour and sparkle. Rudyard Kipling at the age of twenty was already mounting the ladder of fame.'[16]

Michael, somewhat blind to the accomplishments of Indians, would always seek out and admire his own kind.

Michael O'Dwyer's first assignment was something of a sink-or-swim experience. He found himself despatched to the rural areas of Punjab for a 'winter tour' armed with only a canvas tent, some utensils and a few boxes of stationery.

A *munshi*, an Indian secretary, and an orderly were his only staff. Neither spoke a word of English and Michael knew only a handful of words in Hindi, Urdu or Punjabi. Despite the obvious language barrier, Michael was expected to render British justice to the natives. He felt eminently qualified, even if he could not yet understand a word they said.

British mastery over the natives was both necessary and inevitable according to Michael, with his unassailable belief in the superiority of his race: 'The Indian of whatever class and way of thinking, even the rabid anti-British agitator ... prefer[s] that his case should be decided by a British official rather than by one of his own people.'[17]

For Michael, life was at its best when the Indians knew their place.

Though Michael O'Dwyer talked of the intrinsic and incorruptible justice of the British Raj, he himself could be almost callously capricious. On one occasion, while he was posted to the district of Shahpur, Michael was called upon to judge a grisly killing:

The case came before me in 1889 ... in which a young Awan, jealous of his young wife who was a local beauty, in a moment of passion cut off her nose with a razor so that she might not be able to attract other men again. Having done the cruel deed he ran away in fright and the poor girl died of shock. Husband gave him-self up soon after, admitting his guilt, expressing his penitence, and explaining that evil tongues had made bad blood between him and his dead wife, who had really been quite innocent.[18]

Michael showed the man an inexplicable level of leniency that even outraged the white *memsahibs* back at the club. He saved the Awan from hanging, transporting him instead to the Andaman Islands.

Some six years later, while serving in Gujranwala, another Punjabi district, a curious, beaming man approached him: 'When I asked who he was, he looked disappointed and said, "Don't you remember whom you were so kind to? You only gave me seven years when I expected to be hanged for killing my wife."'[19]

The Awan killer, let off early for good behaviour, had brought gifts of gratitude. These included seashells upon which he had engraved Michael's name, and a dried-out Andaman shark's tail. Michael accepted these tokens with delight, and the story became one of his entertaining anecdotes. The 'true north' on his moral compass was far from constant. Where in Shahpur he had shown mercy, elsewhere in Punjab he would show none.

Michael moved steadily from post to post and up the ICS ladder. Just when his ascent seemed unstoppable, at the end of 1895 some-thing happened to temporarily wrong-foot him. Michael took sudden leave from India and decided to use an unusually long fur-lough to travel around Europe. His grand tour lasted a year and a half, and took him to Egypt, Greece, Turkey and Russia. Wherever he went he sought out enclaves of British expats: 'One feels drawn to one's own folk in a foreign country.'[20]

Moscow was particularly convivial, because it was here that Michael met a slender, dark-haired young woman from the Channel Islands. She, like him, had travelled to Russia in the hope of learning the language.

Eunice Bond, or Una as she preferred, would become the centre of Michael's world. Their courtship was short and intense, and the pair married just weeks after they met. Throughout their long marriage, Michael would rarely talk about his wife in public, but when writing his memoirs many years later would describe her as 'the source of all my subsequent happiness'.[21] With Una at his side, Michael O'Dwyer felt ready to tackle India again. They left England in December 1895 and arrived in Lahore just before Christmas.

CHAPTER 3

Birth of the Upheaval

December was a busy time for the servants in British India. Overseas deliveries, quite mystifying to the brown fingers that unwrapped them, had been coming in for weeks. Swaddled in distinctive department-store paper, these included great wheels of pungent Stilton, brightly boxed sweets and mysterious cured meats. Realising how much it meant to their *sahibs*, Indians referred to Christmas Day as '*Burra Din*' – 'The Big Day', and those in domestic service did all they could to make their masters feel special: 'All the natives know and respect the sahib's *Burra Din*. The *mali* (gardener) wreathes your gate posts with scarlet poinsettia and yellow marigold, and all the servants don their cleanest and best attire, salaaming to the *sahib* and *mém*, hoping to receive a "*burra din ka baksheesh*", i.e. a Christmas present.'[1]

Temperatures tipped 30 degrees Centigrade, yet turkeys and potatoes roasted in kitchens all over the Raj. Fruit puddings sat in puddles of flaming brandy, while the *sahibs* and *memsahibs* sat in puddles of perspiration, laughing, eating and singing carols. It was every bit as traditional as Christmas 'back home'.

On Boxing Day, cantonments fell into whispers as masters and mistresses of the house nursed heads and bellies. Servants took advantage of lulls and leftovers with quiet gatherings of their own. Boxing Day was a time of sated tranquillity for the Raj. To the rest of 'native' India, it meant nothing at all.

Some 130 miles south of Lahore, in the *mohalla* (neighbourhood) of Pilbad in Sunam,[2] the smells and sounds of normal Indian life were augmented on 26 December 1899[3] by the cries of a woman. They got steadily more regular and urgent. Narain Kaur was in labour. She was about to give birth to her second child, and while Tehal Singh, her husband, waited anxiously for news, soothing his two-year-old son, he might have been forgiven for uttering a silent prayer: 'Let the child be healthy and let him be a boy.' Boys were breadwinners; they took care of their families; they lit their parents' funeral pyres. Boys were also much cheaper to bring up than girls.

Daughters ate and drank in their fathers' houses, only to be married off as soon as they became useful. They needed dowries for good matches. Sweets were distributed on the birth of sons. Daughters came with commiserations.

When the faint mewling of his son finally reached his ears, Tehal Singh might have allowed himself a moment of relief, but nothing more. He could barely feed his existing family, let alone this new mouth. His little one was blissfully unaware that his tiny wriggling body was saddled with an invisible burden from the moment he arrived in the world. Like his parents, he was 'Kamboj', one of the lowest castes in India.

The suffocating and hierarchical caste system predates written history, and according to ancient Hinduism, a cycle of karmic reincarnation governs its strict rules. If a person is good and decent in this life, they can come back as a high-caste member of society in the next. Those who prove exemplary gain *moksha,* a release into a higher spiritual plane. Those found wanting are reborn in the lower castes. Those who are abhorrent return as animals. A dogged belief in karmic justice meant there was little pity for those who needed it the most.

Low- and high-caste families lived parallel lives when Tehal Singh's youngest son was born. They were often forbidden from drinking at the same wells or worshipping at the same temples. Low-caste children did not play with high-caste youngsters. Intermarriage could be punished by brutal violence or even death.

As Narain Kaur held her baby in her arms, she must have known how hard his life would be. She had little more to offer the infant than the bravest name she could think of. Sher Singh was perhaps an attempt at double indemnity. Both 'Sher' and 'Singh' mean 'the Lion'. A big title for such a tiny boy.

Two years earlier, his mother had attempted the same nominative determinism for her elder son, naming him Sadhu, or 'the sage' – one who is close to *moksha*. Any optimism in their naming was outweighed by the boys' crushing reality; the mortality rate among low-caste babies was high. They were the first to suffer from hunger when the harvests failed and the first to die when disease rampaged through the country. The future for Sher Singh and his brother looked bleak.

Defying statistical probability, the children survived. However, their mother would not be so lucky. Though the exact date is unknown, Narain Kaur died when her boys were only about three and five years of age.[4] The cause of death is unrecorded, but given the time and place where she lived it is likely that she was swept up in one of the waves of pandemic washing over the subcontinent. In 1896, bubonic plague, originating in China, entered the ports of India on ships belonging to the British Empire. In the heat and the sprawl of densely packed cities, it spread swiftly and without mercy. In just a couple of years the disease took the north and west of India firmly in its grip and stubbornly refused to let go.

It is estimated that during the next three decades some ten million people would die of plague in India.[5] To add to the misery of this medieval disease, the early 1900s saw cholera spread through Punjab too, a waterborne disease that hit the stagnant, poverty-stricken areas hardest. At the turn of the century, one in ten deaths in India was blamed on cholera alone.[6] With its canals and open sewers, in Sher Singh's hometown of Sunam the stench of death was never far away.

Tehal Singh did his best to raise his children alone. Their home, a single, windowless room made of tiny kiln-fired mud bricks, stood near an almost barren tract of land.[7] Tehal grew what few vegetables he could coax out of the ground and took them to sell in nearby villages. The income barely kept his family from starvation, so he was forced to look for other work. Many low-caste men were already working for the British as labourers carving out Punjab's canal system. The hours were long, and the work dirty and back-breaking. It was hardly a place to drag two small children, but Tehal had few options.

The Nilowal canal lay less than 5 miles south of Sunam, and the canal overseer was a man called Baba Dhanna Singh.[8] He was a religious man, well respected, as demonstrated by the honorific people used to address him: 'Baba' or 'father'.

Originally Dhanna was a Sunam man and, presuming on the hometown connection, Tehal turned to him for help. Thanks to Baba Dhanna's recommendation, Tehal joined legions of dirt-encrusted men carrying wet mud from the newly carved waterways. Dhanna also took Tehal to work for him as a part-time servant,[9] boosting his income a little.

After barely a year, Baba Dhanna was transferred from Nilowal to another canal site on the other side of the province.[10] The departure spelled disaster for the young Kamboj family. With his benefactor gone, Tehal Singh lost his job and only sources of income. Bundling up his family, he looked for work further afield.

Low-skilled, low-paid work was available on the Raj's railways. Tehal was posted to a village called Upali, some 60 miles west of Sunam. His home, a hut even more rudimentary than the one he had left behind in Sunam, was surrounded by dense jungle scrub. The job involved raising and lowering Upali's main railway barrier for passing trains[11] – long, hard, mind-numbing work, and the beating sun was relentless. Tehal kept his infant children close, feeding them milk from a goat he tied to the crossing.[12]

The jungle was home to many predators, and years later local people would tell an apocryphal story about Tehal's youngest boy, Sher Singh. At no more than five years of age, he was left unattended and tethered to the barrier with the goat. A wolf emerged from the scrub, attracted by the smell of boy and beast. As it prepared to leap, Sher Singh supposedly picked up his father's axe and swung it wildly, wounding the wolf and forcing it back into the jungle.[13] Some stories replace the wolf with a leopard.[14]

The very idea of a small boy picking up a heavy axe and wielding it at a snarling animal seems so far-fetched that it is more than likely that this story attached itself retrospectively to the man this young boy would one day become.

The pressure of work and raising his children by himself eventually took its toll on Tehal Singh. In October 1907, he became too ill to operate the Upali crossing. Tormented by an exhaustion that never seemed to leave him, fearing for his boys, the widower packed his meagre possessions again and set off for Amritsar, home of the Golden Temple, the most holy shrine of the Sikhs.

There is a saying in Punjab that, loosely translated, means: 'Even the most troubled soul finds peace at the Golden Temple.' Tehal was not merely troubled; he was desperate when he started the 150-mile trek from Upali. The main arterial route into the city, the Tarn Taran road, was busy at the best of times, a hectic current of carts filled with produce and pilgrims. Too poor to afford a donkey, let alone a cart, Tehal and his family travelled on foot. The usual flow of people was significantly swollen thanks to the impending festival season.

Diwali, the Hindu festival of lights, and the Sikh festival Bandi Chhor Divas were fast approaching. Punjabis from all over the province would converge on the city[15] for days of fasting, feasting and festivity. On Diwali night itself a moonless sky would fill with fireworks. Millions of little clay lamps would freckle the earth.

Tehal Singh forced one foot in front of the other knowing that Amritsar would be bursting with visitors during the religious month. People would need their bags carried, clothes washed and latrines cleaned. A man like Tehal might find work in the city, yet every step took its toll on his feverish body.

Somewhere on the Tarn Taran road, too tired to go on, Tehal

Singh sat down to rest near a *bhainswala* pond,[16] a watering hole where buffaloes stop to drink. He never got up again. Drawn by the cries of his frightened children, a group of holy men rushed to help.[17] They took the unconscious Tehal Singh to the nearby Ram Bagh hospital, but he never opened his eyes again. The actual cause of death is unknown. Such details were rarely recorded for lower-caste deaths.

With nobody left to look after them, seven-year-old Sher Singh and his nine-year-old brother were taken under the wing of the same travelling priests who had helped their father. They knew of an ashram in Bhatinda,[18] not far from Sunam. One of the men even claimed to know a member of the orphaned boys' family, a distant relative called Chanchal Singh.[19] Grief-stricken and alone in the world, the children had no choice but to wait with strangers for an uncle they barely knew.

In India, blood ties are supremely important, and when Chanchal Singh heard about his cousin's death and the plight of his two boys, he tried his best to meet his obligations. Chanchal was poor, too, and it soon became clear that he could not feed the extra mouths, nor could any of his Kamboj clan. With a heavy heart Chanchal took the children to the Central Khalsa Orphanage in Amritsar[20] and begged them to take them in.

The superintendent of the orphanage, established and run by observant Sikhs, was a man called Sohan Singh. His father had also once worked on the railways, and that awoke a sense of kinship in him. He took the boys in and told Chanchal they would have all that they needed for as long as they needed it.[21]

The admissions ledger for the orphanage shows Tehal's sons formally accepted on 28 October. From the courtyard of their new home, during their darkest hour, they would see the skies light up above them as the rest of Amritsar rejoiced.

The orphanage saw fit to baptise the children soon after their arrival, washing them clean of their past and caste. Born again, Sher and Sadhu were given new names. Sahdu became Mukta, which means 'one who has escaped the cycle of reincarnation'. Sher Singh became Udham Singh. Whether the name was inspired by his behaviour, it would certainly prove to be prophetic. 'Udham' translates into English as 'the upheaval'.

Home to around a dozen children, the Khalsa orphanage fostered strong bonds of brotherhood between its children. Udham became known affectionately as Ude by his friends and, despite the rigorous and repetitive regime, he thrived. Boys rose at four in the morning, bathed in cold water, and recited prayers for two hours every day.[22] After a simple breakfast, lessons began, both in the classroom and the workshop. By filling their days this way the orphanage hoped to give their charges both discipline and a trade.

By all accounts, although not very taken with reading and writing, Udham showed an early aptitude for carpentry. People remembered seeing him around the orphanage, holding his brother's hand.[23] Shared tragedy had made the boys inseparable.

As Udham Singh got used to his new life, one of the most powerful men in the world was trying to do the same. Born during the reign of his grandmother Queen Victoria, Prince George Frederick Ernest Albert was never supposed to be king. Both his father, Albert Edward, and his elder brother, Prince Albert Victor, stood ahead of him in the line of succession; however, when his brother died unexpectedly at the age of only twenty-eight, the course of George's life altered irrevocably. His father, King Edward VII, died in May 1910, and George was named King Emperor. Overnight, he became arguably the most powerful man in the world.

King George V's coronation was marked by an enormous pageant in London. 'The Festival of Empire' was epic in scale and described as 'a Social Gathering of the British Family', exemplifying 'those invisible bonds which hold together the greatest empire the world has ever known'[24]. Holding on to that empire would become the single greatest challenge of George V's reign.

The new king's first major engagement was to be Ireland, where members of the 'British Family' had been struggling to break free of it for years. The Irish turned out in droves to welcome George, despite Palace fears that the nationalists might hijack the affair. One British newspaper called the visit a breakthrough in Anglo-Irish relations: 'Half the great fog of misunderstanding and suspicion that has brooded so long over the relations between England and Ireland has been cleared away in the seven-mile roar of welcome.'[25]

Basking in Irish success, Palace officials were now looking forward to the next leg of George V's coronation tour. Like Ireland, India, too, had been growing increasingly unruly of late. A visit from the new monarch, it was thought, might calm those waters as well.

In anticipation, the viceroy, Lord Hardinge, declared he would hold a great *durbar* in His Majesty's honour. The word *durbar* usually refers to the courts of Indian emperors, but when Hardinge used it he promised a proxy coronation, an unforgettable ceremony that would show off the full might and splendour of the British Raj. December 1911 would be divided between Christ and Crown.

DELHI, DECEMBER 1911

The moment the king accepted the viceroy's invitation, Michael O'Dwyer's social calendar was saturated. The *durbar* promised a heady mix of Western pomp and pageantry coupled with exotic Eastern opulence. Though the balls, concerts, polo matches and hunts would not disappoint, they would pale in comparison to the event itself. The coronation *durbar*, due to take place on 12 December 1911, would surpass even the wildest imaginations. Logistics were epic in scale – epic and expensive.

Almost a million pounds was spent, worth more than a hundred times that amount today.[26] Thirteen villages next to the city had been cleared and flattened in order to create an area vast enough to accommodate the 25,000 VIPs. Maharajahs, princes, nawabs, aristocrats, noblemen and tribal chiefs had been summoned to Delhi from all over India. For weeks they had been arriving, accompanied by vast retinues of soldiers, horses and elephants.

Each potentate was allocated a space reflecting his importance. These they filled with temporary canvas palaces, complete with harems, stables and in some cases entire pleasure gardens replete with statues and miraculously plumbed fountains. Each tried to outdo the glory of his neighbours.

Michael O'Dwyer must have received his invitation with sheer delight. He had spent the past fifteen years working hard to earn his place at the top table, impressing his superiors in a series of diverse postings. He spent time in the craggy wilds of the North-West Frontier Province, settled land claims and collected revenues in the lush rural belt of Punjab, and dispensed British justice in the arid deserts of Rajputana. More recently, Michael had won the trust of the nizams of Hyderabad, showing the viceroy he could call upon diplomatic skills, not immediately obvious to those who knew him and his plain-speaking ways.

As Michael's reputation had grown, so too had his family. Una had given him two children: a daughter in 1898, also named Una, then two years later a son, called John after Michael's beloved father.

Michael kept his family close, though this affection sometimes put them in harm's way. Once, while settling a boundary dispute in Rajputana's Alwar district, his wife and little girl, barely two years old at the time, came out to meet him. While he looked through maps and wrangled with bickering bureaucrats, his little girl had somehow toddled off: 'When I finished she was not to be found.'[27] Icy panic set in as Michael tore up and down the river bank hoping to find her tiny footsteps in the mud: 'After some search the tracks were found leading upstream, and the people were horror-stricken as they told me they led up into the favourite haunts of the local tigers.'[28]

Fiercely fond of his daughter, Michael caught up with her before the tigers did. He would have done anything to protect his Una. The bond with her was far closer than any he would be able to forge with his only son.

John Chevalier O'Dwyer, more reserved than his sister, was

chronically short-sighted. Bottle-thick glasses ruled him out of the riding and hunting pursuits his father loved so passionately. Without these shared interests the two had little to bring them together. For months at a time John was sent back to boarding school in England, and though these long separations were hard on him, the days he spent by his father's side were not much easier. John Chevalier was nothing like his namesake, and the difference weighed heavily on the boy.

Perhaps sensing his failure to live up to expectations, young John elected to go by the name of Jack as soon as he had some choice in the matter and would go by that name for the rest of his life.

The *durbar* of 1911 fell during the children's Christmas holidays, so it is more than likely that Jack and Una were with their mother and father to see the arrival of their new king, and to hear the momentous news that would change their lives for ever.

Some 80,000 army troops were drafted to Delhi for the coronation *durbar*, both to march in endless parades and to provide security for visiting dignitaries. The Raj's police force also found itself significantly bolstered for the event, a slew of new recruits hastily inducted into the ranks. Among the new intake was a fresh-faced 21-year-old Irishman named Philip Vickery.

Vickery was given the seemingly mundane task of guarding the king emperor's bedroom during his stay.[29] It was not the job any thrusting young officer would have picked for himself, yet despite his rather soft induction into Imperial security, Vickery would go on to become one of the most hardened men in British colonial intelligence.

Michael O'Dwyer had always been an immensely social creature, with an uncanny ability to hold both a room and his liquor. Once, when facing arrest in Russia for travelling on the wrong documents, he had managed to win his freedom by drinking the arresting officer, an old Muscovite general, under the table. The *durbar*, with its ceaseless pace and endless good cheer, was just the kind of occasion where Michael could shine.

Those with weaker constitutions must have suffered terribly on 12 December, when soon after dawn they were herded into Coronation Park. It would prove to be a swelteringly hot day, and they were forced to wait for hours, heads pounded by the sun and the sound of brass bands.

At precisely midday, just as the sun was at its highest, the royal couple arrived. Resplendent in their heavy coronation robes, they ascended the high dais to a deafening fanfare of trumpets. To add to the weight of the occasion, the king emperor had chosen to wear his Imperial Crown of India, containing 6,170 diamonds, sapphires, emeralds and rubies. Head held high, King George acknowledged the slow and steady stream of men who stepped forward to bow before him. Whites went first.

The viceroy, Charles Hardinge, 1st Baron Hardinge of Penshurst, led the way. He was followed by the commander-in-chief of the army and members of the governor-general's executive council; a litany of lieutenant governors; senior members from a variety of government-departments; judges and clergy. Only when the last of these had returned to their seats was it the Indians' turn to genuflect.

One after another, maharajahs, rajas and nawabs weighed down by jewels came forward to the sound of tailored gun salutes. The importance of each man could be measured by the bone-jarring blasts accompanying their bows. A complicated diplomatic formula had awarded gun salutes based on the wealth and strategic impor-tance of their kingdoms. The greater the number of bangs, the more important the potentate.

To gasps of astonishment, a man worth a significant number of cannon blasts, the maharajah of Baroda, otherwise known as Sayajirao Gaekwad III, broke every single rule he had been instructed to follow: 'He arrived at the amphitheatre in full dress and covered in the historic Baroda jewels, but removed them all just before the moment came for him to approach the king.'[30] By appearing plainly before the king emperor, he was in effect dressing him down. 'On reaching the *shamiana* [dais] he made a cursory bow from the waist, stepped backwards and then, wheeling around, turned his back on the royal couple and walked from their presence nonchalantly twirling a gold-topped walking stick.'[31]

The calculated insult was designed to show that even those who prospered under the Raj chafed at its existence. The Gaekwad resented the enforced gilded grovelling and wanted his people to know it. He was seen laughing all the way back to his seat. The British would punish him for his impudence for years to come.

Homage and humiliations complete, the king emperor rose to make his address. Even the most jaded were forced to sit up and take notice. Had their artillery-battered ears heard right? Had George V just announced the reunification of Bengal?

Bengal had been partitioned six years earlier, in 1905, by the then viceroy, Lord Curzon. In cleaving the province in two, Curzon had separated the largely Muslim eastern areas from the largely Hindu west. The Congress Party, a nascent nationalist organisation that would one day have the likes of Gandhi and Nehru at the helm, was growing particularly strong in Bengal. The old 'divide and rule' adage guided Curzon's hand, as he explained to the then secretary of state for India, St John Broderick:

> Calcutta is the centre from which the Congress Party is manipulated throughout the whole of Bengal, and indeed the whole of India. Its best wire pullers and its most frothy orators all reside here ... Any measure in consequence that would divide the Bengali-speaking population; that would permit independent centres of activity and influence to grow up; that would dethrone Calcutta from its place as the centre of successful intrigue, or that would weaken the influence of the lawyer class, who have the entire organisation in their hands, is intensely and hotly resented by them.[32]

Curzon's partition ripped through neighbourhoods, dividing Hindu and Muslim communities, upending a harmonious co-existence that had stood for generations. Curzon knew the people of Bengal would object, and advised the secretary of state to block his ears: 'The outcry will be loud and very fierce, but as a native gentleman said to me – "my countrymen always howl until a thing is settled; then they accept it."'[33]

Bengal never accepted its mutilation. From the moment the province was divided, a campaign of resistance erupted. The mass boycotting of British goods – *swadeshi,* as the Indians called it – spread from the newly created rift. Like burning lava it oozed from Bengal and into the rest of India, spreading hatred against the British.

Some of the more extreme Bengali nationalists disappeared underground after 1905, only to surface later to commit acts of targeted violence. Sir Andrew Fraser, the lieutenant governor of Bengal, despised for his own role in Curzon's partition, was lucky to escape with his life on three separate occasions. In 1907, two attempts were made to blow up his official train; one used so much explosive it left a five-foot-wide crater where his carriage had been moments before. The following year an Indian student tried to shoot Fraser at close range and was foiled only when his weapon misfired.

The ambition of the anti-colonialists grew with each blast. In November 1909, two bombs were thrown into the open carriage of Curzon's successor, the new viceroy Lord Minto. He had been travelling with his wife through the streets of Ahmedabad. A combination of quick thinking and sheer dumb luck saved them. One bomb bounced off a parasol; the other was swatted into the sand by a soldier with an outstretched sabre.[34]

Two British women were not so lucky. The explosive thrown into their carriage detonated on impact, killing them both.

The decision to reunify Bengal, as detailed in the king's proclamation, was Hardinge's attempt to calm an escalating situation. He knew his plan would not be universally popular. Some of the senior ICS cadre, Michael O'Dwyer among them, would undoubtedly see reunification as a capitulation to nationalist violence. While the crowds attempted to make sense of the words and their implication, a second proclamation stilled their chatter. His Majesty's Indian government would be moving its capital from Calcutta to Delhi. The words sent a shockwave through both the British and Indian enclosures. Nobody had seen this coming.

From 1793, when the East India Company first abolished *Nizamat*, indigenous rule, in the region, Calcutta had served as the nerve centre of British control. Now, after more than a hundred years, the intricate machine of government bureaucracy was to be uprooted and transported almost a thousand miles away.

Hardinge's plan 'was one of the best-kept secrets in history'.[35] No more than twelve people had known about it, and nothing had leaked. Having the king emperor make the announcement at his own *durbar* made it a fait accompli. There was no room for debate.

Hardinge's third major decision would only become public days later, and though it would pale in significance to the news about Bengal and Delhi, it had a profound effect on one particular man in the *durbar* audience. Michael O'Dwyer must have spent the entire ceremony struggling to keep his expressive face from giving the game away.

At one of the plethora of parties in the run-up to the *durbar*, Lord Hardinge had drawn him aside for a confidential chat. The lieutenant governor of Punjab, Louis Dane, would be stepping down soon, and Hardinge had decided to name Michael his successor.[36] The promotion catapulted the Tipperary boy into the highest echelons of Indian colonial rule, leaving him well placed, one day, to succeed Hardinge himself. The job was prestigious, but also fraught with challenges: 'In informing me of my selection the viceroy made it clear that the Punjab was the province about which the government was then most concerned; that there was much inflammable material lying about, which required very careful handling if an explosion were to be averted.'[37] Against a backdrop of growing civilian unrest, Michael accepted the position, hungry for the chance to prove himself.

Oblivious to the reshaping of his country and the appointment of a new lieutenant governor in his province, Udham Singh continued his quiet existence, thankful just to have a roof over his head. His young life, so defined by chaos and loss, had finally settled down. The Khalsa orphanage in Amritsar had given him peace and stability. It would not last.

CHAPTER 4

RISES AND FALLS

With news of his promotion still sinking in, an explosion on 23 December 1912 shook Michael O'Dwyer out of his private reverie. It targeted the very man who had just anointed him lieutenant governor of Punjab.

Lord Hardinge, in full viceregal splendour, had been taking part in a parade through the streets of his new capital, Delhi. The king's visit had been a huge success. *Burra Din* was just around the corner, so there was every reason to keep the party going.

Riding on the back of an elephant, Hardinge took in his new capital city. Seated behind a *mahout* (elephant handler) in a gilded *howdah* – the kind of open carrier once favoured by sultans and maharajahs – Hardinge, with his wife at his side, smiled and waved at cheering crowds.

Suddenly, just as they reached Chandni Chowk, the old bazaar district of the city, a man ran out of the mass of spectators and lobbed a bomb. It landed squarely inside the elephant's *howdah* and exploded, sending screaming bystanders running for cover. Hardinge and his wife were left covered in blood. Some of it belonged to the viceroy himself, but most of it came from his Indian elephant handler, killed instantly when the bomb went off.

As hands reached up to calm the frantic elephant and pull survivors from the carrier, the ringing in his ears would have drowned out the vicereine's screaming. One look at her face would have told Hardinge how badly he had been hurt. Shrapnel from the home-made device had torn through the flesh on his back and shoulders. It could have been so much worse, but in taking the full force of the blast, the *mahout* had undoubtedly saved the viceroy's life.

Michael O'Dwyer knew that a similar bomb had recently exploded in Lahore's Lawrence Gardens, just in front of Governor House. The building would become his home in a matter of months. That device had also been intended for British targets, but, like the Hardinge device, it had missed its mark. An innocent Indian *chaprassi* (secretary) was killed instead.

Punjab police had been working hard trying to trace the bombers and the source of their ammunition. Such were the similarities of the Lawrence Gardens and Hardinge blasts, detectives were convinced they were dealing with one specific group of increasingly confident, capable insurgents. All fingers pointed at Bengali nationalists, but further investigations threw up a Punjabi name, too. The master-mind of both bomb plots was believed to be a young North Indian called Har Dayal.

Born in the Punjab on 14 October 1884, Har Dayal was an unlikely terrorist. He had been a clever, bookish boy with a special aptitude for Sanskrit. Such was his ability, it earned him a coveted scholarship to St John's College at Oxford University. Though it sounded like the opportunity of a lifetime, the experience of living and learning in England both broke and remade Har Dayal.

Har Dayal was made to feel inferior by his English peer group and tutors. He worked hard and did well, but the realisation quickly dawned on him that no matter how much he tried, no matter how much he achieved, he would never be anything but a second-class citizen when he returned to his own country.

All he could hope for was a lowly administrative job, grunt work for the Raj. White candidates would always be promoted ahead of him, even if he was far more capable. Frustration swept over him and pushed open a gateway into a world of underground militant anti-colonialism.

Initially, Har Dayal only vented his rage in words. The *Indian Sociologist*, a radical newspaper published in London, gave him his pulpit. It claimed to be 'An Organ of Freedom and of Political, Social and Religious Reform', as its first issue described:

No systematic attempt has, so far as our knowledge goes, ever been made in this country by Indians themselves to enlighten the British public with regard to the grievances, demands, and aspirations of the people of India and its unrepresented millions before the bar of public opinion in Great Britain and Ireland.[1]

The brainchild of an Indian named Shyamji Krishna Varma, the *Indian Sociologist* became a conduit through which virulent anti-colonialists could find each other. Krishna Varma was also the proprietor and landlord of a terraced residential building in the leafy suburb of Highgate in north London.

'India House', as it became known, offered lodgings to Indian students enrolled at London's colleges. However, along with accommodation, India House also provided a regular diet of anti-British venom to any who had the appetite. The place became a magnet for the disaffected. Marxists, anti-colonialists and anarchists from all over Europe were invited to speak at India House seminars. Young, discontented Indians were encouraged to meet and mix, developing networks in the process. By 1905, India House had become a de facto radicalisation factory.

Among those who made a pilgrimage to India House in the early 1900s was Mohandas Karamchand Gandhi, years before anyone would call him 'Mahatma'. Gandhi had been a practising lawyer in South Africa, butting heads with the authorities in his adopted home of the Transvaal. New and racist pass laws were being used to victimise the Indian population there, and Gandhi was determined to fight them. On a visit to London in 1906, Gandhi made his way to Highgate and the place where he had heard Indian intellectuals could meet and swap ideas. However, what he heard at India House appalled him. The sheer violence of the rhetoric only reinforced

Gandhi's own developing belief in passive resistance. To men like Har Dayal, in contrast, India House's rage felt like a balm.

Three years after Gandhi's visit, India House would yield an assassin named Madhan Lal Dhingra, who would, in 1909, outrage British society by shooting a British official dead on British soil. Even before Dhingra shot Sir William Hutt Curzon Wyllie dead in London, the police were waking up to the danger of India House. Such domestic terrorism would never be allowed again.

Special Branch, the British police's national security wing, placed tails on several Indian students frequenting the Highgate hive. Their efforts were not entirely successful at first, since the white detectives stood out at the radical meetings. As the British police persisted in their efforts and became more sophisticated in their methods, more and more Indians found themselves being watched. Not all took the intrusion well. One Special Branch officer, Harold Brust, was badly beaten up when his 'mark' realised he was being tailed.

Brust, despite his bruises, admired the idealistic Indians he had been ordered to shadow: 'Most of us SB [Special Branch] men held a sneaking admiration for the ardour of these lads who mistakenly believed themselves to be appointed "saviours" of their "down-trodden country".'[2]

Har Dayal, who had established a lively correspondence with Krishna Varma while at Oxford, unsurprisingly earned himself unwanted SB attention. By 1908, the echoing footsteps and inter-cepted letters became too much for him. Without warning, he ditched his studies, quit England and disappeared, surfacing in Paris a year later. Safely in France, Har Dayal stepped up his activities.

Establishing a newspaper, *Vande Mataram*, or 'I vow to thee oh Mother [India]', Har Dayal slammed the inequity and oppression of British rule, but his Paris writing was beginning to betray a new obsession: Germany.

Anglo-German relations were at an all-time low in 1908. The countries had been embroiled in a naval arms race for more than a decade, accelerated by a series of German navy bills rapidly increasing the rate of naval construction. The British political and military leadership responded with escalation of their own, and as trust between the countries evaporated, the sea filled with battleships.

Two years before the outbreak of the First World War, Britain's domestic counter-intelligence agency, MI5, became convinced that German agents were secretly manipulating both the English working class and Indian nationalists. Har Dayal's Paris publication only confirmed suspicions, particularly when he wrote an editorial pinning his hopes for a free India on Berlin – 'the capital of the country which at present is most hostile in spirit to England'.[3] Har Dayal wrote that 'the cultivation of friendly relations with the powerful German nation will be of great advantage to the cause of Indian independence'.[4]

Britain may have had 'divide and rule' as its guiding principle, but the nationalist relied on the adage: 'My enemy's enemy is my friend.' The French seemed untroubled by his activities and he was left alone to write and disseminate his paper. Then, one day, as suddenly as he had arrived, Har Dayal disappeared again.

LAHORE, 1913

Sitting behind his desk in Lahore, the new lieutenant governor of Punjab read through his papers with Lord Hardinge's warning still fresh in his mind: 'Punjab was the province about which the government was then most concerned.'

Michael now had a new title to go with his new job. Knighted in the king's New Year's Honours list, Sir Michael O'Dwyer assumed his role as the scars on Lord Hardinge's back were still healing. The name Har Dayal kept coming up in his security briefings, mostly in conjunction with two other names: Kartar Singh Sarabha and Sohan Singh Bhakna. Both were Sikhs, originally from his province.

A new word, 'ghadar', also peppered the reports. The word, he knew, meant 'revolt', and under its aegis it seemed Har Dayal and his new friends were creating a rebel army. They even had a newspaper, also named *Ghadar*. Its intentions were made abundantly clear from the very first publication. Under the masthead, writ large, was the movement's credo:

Today there begins '*Ghadar*' in foreign lands, but in our country's tongue, a war against the British Raj. What is our name? Ghadar. What is our work? Ghadar. Where will be the Revolution? In India. The time will soon come when rifles and blood will take the place of pens and ink.

These Ghadars were frustratingly out of Sir Michael's reach. By 1913 Har Dayal, who had left France for America, was firmly ensconced in San Francisco, California, where he had ostensibly taken up a job at the University of California, Berkeley, working as a lecturer in Indian philosophy and Sanskrit.

Unable to arrest Har Dayal for his suspected role in the recent outrages, Sir Michael looked again at those who had been successfully rounded up by his police. Frustratingly, the man who had actually thrown the bomb at Hardinge, a known Bengali terrorist called Rash Behari Bose, had fled the scene, detectives believed, dressed in a burqa. He was still at large, however police had managed to capture two of his co-conspirators: fellow Bengalis accused of transporting the bombs for him from Calcutta to Delhi and Lahore.

Another man, a petty official who worked at the Dehra Dun postal office, was also charged with 'aiding the traffic of explosives'. He claimed that he was just doing his job and had no idea what was in the parcels he rubber-stamped through transit. The judge believed him and let him walk free.

Of the two Bengalis found guilty by the courts, only one was sentenced to death. The other, a seventeen-year-old boy named Basanta Kumar Biswas, was deemed 'less intelligent'[5] by the judge, who thought the older man might have manipulated him. Smooth-cheeked and small of frame, it was easy to believe. Biswas looked much younger than his years. He was sentenced to transportation for life. An alternative punishment to hanging, transportation saw convicted criminals taken on prison ships to far-flung corners of the colonies. There they were expected to serve out their time working in chain gangs till they dropped. Biswas was destined for a maximum-security prison in Burma, where disease and hard labour resulted in high rates of mortality. It was an appalling prospect for one so young. For some, however, it was not harsh enough.

Sir Michael's irritation at the 'leniency' shown to Biswas was exacerbated when he read that the exonerated postal worker was now petitioning to get his old job back. This was not how Sir Michael wanted to start his term in office:

> After going through the papers I decided, contrary to the opinion of my legal advisers, that government should also appeal and ask for the death penalty on the Bengalis, and for the conviction and adequate punishment of the petty official. The honourable judges accepted the appeal on both points. The petty official, who might have escaped justice had he kept quiet, was sentenced to transportation for life, and the Bengalis were sentenced to death.[6]

Thanks to Sir Michael's intervention, Basanta Kumar Biswas became one of the youngest people to be executed by the Raj. A photograph of him, perhaps taken at the time of his arrest, shows what looks like a wide-eyed child with neat hair in a side parting, and ears that stuck out so much he must have been teased in the playground.

Sir Michael had set the tone for his tenure as lieutenant governor of Punjab. He would take the hardest line, overrule judges, fellow civil servants and Westminster politicians if he had to. Those who brought chaos to his province could expect the severest penalties.

A man of fastidious habit, Sir Michael rose at the same early hour every day and never worked beyond seven o'clock at night. He took his meals punctiliously, favouring the same few dishes he had loved since childhood. A maharajah had once invited him to a banquet and had paid Sir Michael the ultimate honour of preparing some of the food with his own hands. The gesture merely irritated the honoured guest. 'In culinary matters I am a strong Conservative,' Sir Michael wrote later, 'almost a "Die Hard".'[7] He had no taste for foreign fare, even if it had been cooked by a king.

The term 'Die Hard' was loaded with a meaning that went well beyond the plate, as Sir Michael was well aware. Die Hards were arch-Conservatives who believed in the racial superiority of the British and the vital importance of the Raj. At the maharajah's banquet, Sir Michael had, as had become his custom, brought his own lunch in a basket. The question was how to utilise its contents without offending his powerful host? Diplomatic incident was averted, not by any compromise on Sir Michael's part, but by sleight of hand: 'Being an orthodox Hindu he could not sit and eat with us; so the chicken and ham were skilfully disposed among his innumerable dishes.'[8]

Sir Michael was suspicious of all Indians, but the Hindu majority most of all. He loathed the educated 'Hindu Bourgeoisie' as he liked to call them, believing they had been coddled and needlessly empowered thanks to the recent Morley-Minto reforms. The 1909 Act of Parliament had brought about a limited increase in the involvement of Indians in the governance of British India.

Indians coming forward to take advantage of Morley-Minto were overly ambitious and treacherous in Sir Michael's opinion. Brahmins, India's highest caste, were the worst of the lot: 'The Brahmin or Kayasth, with his advocate's training, may make a brilliant speech in faultless English. But it is purely critical and barren of any constructive proposal, for he has behind him neither traditions of rule nor administrative experience.'[9]

Since his arrival in India, the new lieutenant governor had been categorising Indians like a botanist documenting interesting but potentially poisonous specimens. He would later share his classifications with the world, and uncharitable generalisations about Brahmins figured repeatedly: 'The Mahratta Brahmin is from diet,

habit and education, keen, active, and intelligent but generally ava-
ricious and often treacherous.'[10]

The Sikhs, the group that had once united and ruled the province
he himself now governed, were 'Virile and enterprising but often
of overweening conceit, and unless firmly and tactfully handled
obstinate to the point of fanaticism.'[11]

Sir Michael simply could not understand why his masters in
London failed to see the deficits in the natives that he did. It mad-
dened him that greater autonomy was being given to inferior races.
Step by step Britain would lose the entire Raj unless men like him
stopped it from happening.

On Sunday 28 June 1914, at 1.45 p.m. Lahore time, a shot rang out
in the far-off Austro-Hungarian city of Sarajevo. The assassination
of Archduke Franz Ferdinand by Gavrilo Princip, a Serbian with ties
to the secretive military group known as the Black Hand, propelled
all major European military powers into war. Just over a year into
Sir Michael's term in office, one man, with one bullet, changed the
course of human history.

When Britain formally entered the war in August, the repercussions were felt as keenly in India as they were in the Home Counties
of England. From Sir Michael's province, the 47th Sikhs, a regiment
comprising an initial 10,000 men, became one of the first infantry
divisions to be sent into the French trenches. Most of the men had
never left their home villages and had no idea of the icy conditions
they would face in France's harsh, long winter. Such was the rush
to move them to the front line that many men did not have boots or
uniforms to suit the climate. In consequence, they found themselves
battling both the Germans and the elements. Both exacted a heavy
body count.

One million Indians would be sent to Europe to fight between
1914 and 1918. Some of the letters they sent home painted a grim
picture: 'Do not think that this is war. This is not war. It is the
ending of the world,'[12] wrote one who found himself wounded in
the filthy and freezing trenches.

Sir Michael made it his private crusade to send more men to war than any of the provincial lieutenant governors of India. He toured Punjab, insisting the young had a moral duty to fight in 'defence of their hearths and homes'.[13] He took great pride in his efforts and successes.

At the outbreak of war, half of the Indian army was drawn from Punjab, and as these early deployments suffered the heaviest casualties, the need for replacement troops grew urgent. Sir Michael described his Punjab as 'the Shield ... the Spearhead ... and the Sword-hand of India'[14] and made it his mission to replace the dead as fast as they fell. Indians were supposedly a willing force, yet the experience of some Punjabi villagers suggested that not all were as inclined to fight in the foreign war as Sir Michael would have the generals believe. Officials in the Punjab were told to produce a given number of men from each particular district. In response, they used a mixture of bribery and threat to get what they needed.

At first there were promises of land and financial reward for those who enlisted, but as the war dragged on and the trenches grew hungrier, inducement gave way to coercion. Stories of press-ganging began to stir in the local population. In Gujranwala, the city of Maharajah Ranjit Singh's birth, young men fled their homes one night after hearing that twenty blacksmiths and carpenters would be rounded up and deported to the front line in the morning.[15]

Despite such stories, the vast majority of troops from Punjab signed up of their own volition. Some joined up because they came from families where their fathers had served; others because they wanted to make a better life for their own kin. No matter what their motivation, all who fought believed Britain would be grateful for their sacrifice. Their gratitude might even force them to allow Indians to govern their own country.

CHAPTER 5

NAME, RANK AND SERIAL FAILURE

While the world was tearing itself apart, Udham Singh found his own small corner of it in tatters. His brother, Sadhu Singh, the only person who truly knew him, was taken from him in 1917. The exact cause of death was not recorded, or perhaps even known, but according to orphanage records, Udham's brother contracted an illness and died quickly.

Such was the closeness of the two boys, it is almost certain that Udham, barely sixteen at the time, watched his brother die. Being so young when his mother and father were swept away, their loss would have been an abstract horror. The death of his brother, however, must have been viscerally real and unbearably painful. It explains perhaps why, later in life, one of his favourite aliases would be 'Sadh', a diminutive of the word 'Sadhu', his brother's birth name. Only those who were fondest of him would know and use that name. Perhaps when he heard them say it, he felt his brother was still close.

While Udham Singh grieved, most of his orphanage family were leaving. They were old enough to find apprenticeships or places in the army. The orphanage's credo was and remains to this day: 'Be a man. Make your way. Make us proud.'[1] In 1917, Udham was in no fit state to do any of those things.

The orphanage was compassionate enough to let him stay.

While he struggled to find his feet, Sir Michael tirelessly toured his province driving young men just like Udham into the arms of the recruiters. With the government promising to set aside 178,000 acres for those who served with greatest valour, it was hard for the poor to resist.[2]

If the carrot failed to work, Sir Michael had a number of different sticks, including pitting Punjabis against each other. In the Montgomery district, not far from Amritsar, Sir Michael turned signing up into a matter of tribal honour. Could the Muslims of the area stand to be humbled by the Muslims in the mountains? Failure to sign up would be tantamount to cowardice and an insult to their faith.[3]

In Karnal, where scripture said an Iron Age Hindu king once shredded his own flesh to please his gods, O'Dwyer told men they were unworthy of their lineage, outdone by others in neighbouring areas.[4]

His message did not need to be consistent. It just needed to be convincing. In Ludhiana, he talked of 'Sikh tenacity and heroism'.[5] In Ferozepur, he called Sikhs cowards: 'You have seen how races hitherto unaccustomed to arms have responded to the call.'[6]

Sir Michael weaponised friendly rivalries, particularly those that had always existed between Lahore and Amritsar. He taunted the young men of the capital for being outshone by their neighbours in Punjab's 'second city': 'On the 1st January, if Lahore had done its duty in the way Amritsar has, it should have had 10,000 fighting men in the army; actually, it had less than 3,000.'[7]

He threatened Lahore's status as provincial capital: 'Perhaps some future Lieutenant-Governor will revive the scheme of Maharajah Ranjit Singh to remove the capital of the Punjab from Lahore to Amritsar because the people of Amritsar have shown such splendid loyalty and sprit of service for their King and country.'[8]

It was not an empty threat. The British had moved capitals before.

The busiest recruitment kiosk in Amritsar lay just outside Hall Gate, one of the twelve fortified entrances into the old city. Its distinctive clock face and crenelated red-brick turrets towered over, but was largely ignored by, Punjabis as they bustled in and out of the narrow gullies of Hall Bazaar. Amritsar was a city of the senses, of noisy commerce, garish colours and delicious food. Its inhabitants prided themselves on their lust for life.

The main army recruitment kiosk was manned by a man named Mela Singh, a civilian whose job it was to out-shout the hawkers around him and sell the war. Some eight months after his brother's death, Udham heard Mela's promises of honour and riches to the brave. Sometime late in 1917 he approached Mela Singh and asked to enlist.[9]

During the First World War, the official minimum age for recruits was nineteen; however, demand at the fronts in both western Europe and the Middle East had become so overwhelming that younger boys often slipped through the net. Mela Singh ignored the fact that Udham was a few months under age and told the eighteen-year-old to go home, pack his bags and come back in a few days, when a rail ticket would be waiting for him. Udham was to travel to the capital, where he would be officially processed.[10]

In Lahore, the enlistment officer, a man named Rai Sahib,[11] apparently had more scruples than Mela Singh. He took one look at Udham and told him to go away and come back in a year when he was old enough.[12] Udham begged him to change his mind,[13] arguing that, as a member of India's low-caste poor, the army was his best chance to change his life. Terrifying as the fighting might be, the army guaranteed food on his plate, clothes on his back and, for the most part, a roof over his head.

Udham, even then, had a gift for persuading people to do things against their better judgement. Reluctantly, Rai filled and stamped forms, committing the boy to a war from which he knew many did not return. Handing over the documents, he instructed Udham to make his way to the Mian Mir cantonment, where he would be required to present himself to undergo a medical examination.[14]

Two miles from the lieutenant governor's residence, Mian Mir was the historic home of the 32nd Sikh Pioneers. The regiment had been raised after the mutiny/rebellion of 1857 and was made up largely of Mazbhi and Ramdasia[15] Sikhs, low-caste Hindus who had converted to the newer religion. Though Sikhism supposedly abjured the caste system, old hierarchy still made itself felt, often in nuanced ways. Marriages rarely crossed the old caste divides, and Mazbhis and Ramdasias worshipped in their own gurdwaras. The British followed these dotted fault lines in the faith and reinforced them, composing regiments along caste lines.

The regimental motto of the 32nd Pioneers, '*Aut inveniam viam aut faciam*' – 'Find a way or make a way', suited their fiercely dogged reputation. At the time Udham was signing up, Indians were desperately needed to shore up British forces in the Middle East, where losses had been catastrophic.

Young Udham, still with the long, uncut hair of his Sikh faith, waited in line to be weighed, measured and prodded by a doctor. Only then was he issued with a regimental badge: a metal circle capped with two ominously crossed axes, capped by a crown. New identity pinned to the front of his turban, uniform hanging off his tall, rather gangly frame, the teenager waited for mobilisation.

Mesopotamia lay at the heart of the old Ottoman Empire, nestled between the Tigris and Euphrates rivers. Thanks to an eastern border with Persia, it had immense strategic significance. In 1908, a large oil field was discovered in the fields of Masjed Soleiman in the south-west of what is now Iran.

Within a few years, that same oil was fuelling the British Empire. The British knew that if the enemy were to cut them off from these reserves, its navy would be left dead in the water. Now Germany was threatening to do just that.

Even before the declaration of war, while accelerating its own ship-building programme, Germany had been busy establishing close relations with the Ottomans. At first, ties were defined by trade, designed to further their '*Drang nach Osten*' – 'Thrust towards the East'. Before long, bilateral agreements morphed into acts of blatant infiltration. By the time Udham found himself on a ship headed towards the region, the Ottoman army was already firmly under the influence of German 'advisors'. Encouraged to think of the British as their enemy, and the war against them as a *jihad*,[16] the Ottoman army was fully committed to the British Empire's destruction.

Britain needed men from India to keep the oil flowing. At the start of the war, in November 1914, the 104th Wellesley's Rifles and the 117th Mahrattas of 16th Brigade of the Indian army's 6th Division were among the first to arrive in Mesopotamia. Their successful capture of Basra provided one of the only glimmers of light in an otherwise desperate time, nonetheless it was only the beginning of a protracted and bloody campaign that would claim the lives of more than 40,000 British and Indian soldiers.

The commander-in-chief of the Mesopotamian expeditionary force, Lieutenant General Sir Stanley Maude, outlined the situation he was facing. In Baghdad and Basra, his men had been under relentless assault and were exhausted.[17] Maude reserved particular praise for the camaraderie between his British and Indian soldiers: 'British and Indian troops working side-by-side have vied with each other in their efforts to close with the enemy, and all ranks have been imbued throughout with that offensive spirit which is the soldier's finest jewel.'[18]

To maintain communication and supply lines in his hard-won territory, Maude ordered the construction of a field railway, running up from the coast all the way to Basra. The lieutenant general also had a small flotilla of armoured boats at his command, ensuring supplies and communication got through in the event that on-land logistics were cut.

It was to Basra that Udham Singh was sent and ordered to keep Maude's railway running and his boats afloat.[19] The carpentry skills he had learned at the orphanage should have made Udham useful, but youth, lack of experience and temperament made army life very difficult for him. He exhibited insolence and an inability to deal with authority, which his commanding officers found intolerable.

Deemed immature and unreliable, after less than six months of what should have been a year-long tour, Udham was declared unfit for service and sent back to India.[20] In a place where his fellow countrymen were hailed as heroes, not only had Udham Singh failed to make his mark, he had managed to disgrace himself.

On his return to Punjab, and at a loss as to what to do next, Udham Singh returned to his birthplace of Sunam and stayed with a maternal uncle, Jiwa Singh. The older man was fond of his hot-headed relative,[21] and only too aware of the tragedy of his youth. He also perhaps understood his recent experiences better than most. Jiwa had served in the army as a *subedar*, the second-highest rank an enlisted Indian could attain.

Despite Jiwa's reservoir of sympathy, for some unknown reason Udham left the *subedar*'s home as suddenly as he had arrived, after only a short stay. He returned to Amritsar and his old orphanage. There he was granted temporary residence, further testament to his charm and powers of persuasion.[22] The war had created many fatherless children and the orphanage would undoubtedly have been facing more need than it could accommodate. Nonetheless, it would always find space for Udham.

Though Khalsa orphanage had been the only real home he had known in his life, Udham appears to have found it impossible to settle down here either. Perhaps the absence of his brother was too hard, but after less than a month he decided to re-enlist and try the army once again. Udham sought out Mela Singh, the rule-bending Hall Gate recruiter, once more.[23] The Great War was in its final throes and haemorrhaging men. Mela did not turn him away.

So many of the records pertaining to Indian servicemen at this time have been lost or destroyed, so one cannot be certain how Mela Singh managed it, but somehow, and despite Udham's ignominious and curtailed first tour, Mela got him out to Mesopotamia once again.[24]

Udham was sent to Basra and then later to Baghdad, where he

appeared to have kept his head down and his hands busy, working as a carpenter for Three Works Company.[25] His labour unit, among the lowest ranking in the Pioneers, was tasked with general maintenance of vehicles and machinery. A lowly, motor oil-covered grunt, far away from the fighting, Udham may not have appreciated that he had a ringside view on history.

Events unfolding around him were changing the face of the world map for ever, and while he hammered nails and planed down planks, the Ottoman Empire came crashing down around him. The Allies carved up what was left.

Having served a full year this time, Udham Singh returned to India in early 1919. He barely had 200 rupees to his name and, despite the promises of the British, not one square inch of land to call his own.[26]

CHAPTER 6

BLACK ACTS, RED LINES

Disillusioned but alive, Udham Singh was home. Thousands of his countrymen would not be so lucky. Left to rot in mass graves in foreign lands,* their distraught families would never be able to pray over their pyres, or stand by freshly draped burial plots, palms face up to the sky. Punjab had sent its boys across an ocean. Waves of grief rolled back.

As Udham unpacked his dirty kit bag wondering what to do next, Gandhi, the *mahatma* or 'Great Soul' as he was now known, was sick. So sick that many believed he might die. It was as if the war had broken the very spirit of the man.

Mohandas Karamchand Gandhi, the same South African lawyer who had visited London's India House years before, had returned to his native India four years earlier in 1915. In that time he had

---

* According to the Commonwealth War Graves Commission, Basra Memorial commemorates more than 40,620 servicemen of the British Empire who died in Mesopotamia and have no known grave. More than 33,250 of those commemorated served with the Indian Army.

Baghdad (North Gate) War Cemetery contains the graves and memorials of more than 6,880 British Empire servicemen of the First World War, of whom more than 2,720 remain unidentified.

Amara (Left Bank) Indian War Cemetery commemorates some 5,000 servicemen of the Indian Army, of whom only nine are identified. No comprehensive records of the burials were kept by military authorities.

turned the political situation in India upside down, becoming both the greatest hope and greatest disappointment to the national-ist movement.

Gandhi had travelled to India in 1915 on the insistence of one par-ticular man: a soft-bodied, bespectacled former clerk named Gopal Krishna Gokhale. A prominent member of the infant Congress movement, Gokhale knew great tracts of Thomas Paine and John Stuart Mill off by heart and would quote them to any who would listen. The problem was that, after the hurt of the war, people did not want to listen to him anymore. The gratitude that so many had expected from the British was not forthcoming. Wartime emergency powers, in the form of the Defence of India Act, had granted men like Sir Michael unprecedented powers, which he seemed to be using too enthusiastically for the Indians' liking. The laws allowed preventive detention and internment without trial; people could be lifted from their homes and jailed without even knowing what their offence had been. It also restricted freedoms of speech and movement.

Moderates and radicals within Congress were tearing each other apart around Gokhale, fighting over the best way to fight the Raj. Struck by the non-violent way in which Gandhi had defeated the pass laws of the Transvaal, he begged him to come home and help. Gandhi was his last and best hope to win concessions for his fellow Indians without losing lives in the process. Gokhale hoped he might at least teach them how to use passive resistance in the wake of the new oppression.

Gandhi obliged, causing a throb of almost constant consternation in the higher echelons of the British Raj. Soon after his arrival, he had successfully agitated on behalf of impoverished indigo farmers in Bihar's Champaran, shaming landlords forcing them to grow the inedible crop even while their families starved to death. Later, in the flood- and famine-devastated area of Kheda in Gujarat, Gandhi demanded that the British cease all tax collection until the natural disasters released his people. Though they hated him for it, the British were forced to give in.

Wise to his growing influence in the country, and even though he was still in the midst of his vexing Kheda agitation, the new viceroy of India, Hardinge's successor Lord Chelmsford, invited Gandhi to a war conference in 1918 in Delhi. During two days of talks between 27 and 29 April, the viceroy put the case forward for greater Indian participation in the war effort. He told delegates he was under enormous pressure to send more men to the Front and India had a moral obligation to respond:

> I do not claim, no one claims, that the British Government is infallible. But if you agree that the Empire has been, on the whole, a power for good, if you believe that India has, on the whole, benefited by the British connection, would you not admit that it is the duty of every Indian citizen to help the Empire in the hour of its need?[1]

Not only did Gandhi listen patiently to what Chelmsford had to say, but on the way back to Kheda, he wrote a letter to the viceroy's secretary, John Maffey, saying: 'I would love to do something which Lord Chelmsford would consider to be real war-work. I have an idea that, if I became your Recruiting Agent-in-Chief, I might rain men on you. Pardon me for the impertinence.'[2]

Confounding his former Indian political allies, Gandhi devoted the rest of his time to weaving his way around India, stitching together the argument for his countrymen to sign up. It had not been an easy sell. Gandhi had always preached *ahimsa* (non-violence), and had declared on numerous occasions that he would gladly give up his own life before taking another. By 1918, however, his message had morphed into something alien, unrecognisable and ugly to many Indian ears. Some of the words coming out of Gandhi's mouth could have come from Sir Michael O'Dwyer:

> I have been travelling all over India these days and I tell you, from what I have seen for myself, that India has altogether lost the capacity to fight. It has not a particle of the courage it

should have. If even a Tiger should make its appearance in a village, the people would not have the strength to go and kill it and so they petition the collector to have it killed ... Can a nation, whose citizens are incapable of self-defence, enjoy *swaraj* [self-government]?[3]

Gandhi turned the war effort into a test of honour:

How can people who are incapable of defending their lives, their women and children, their cattle and their lands, ever enjoy *swaraj*? ... When the people become physically fit and strong enough to wield a sword, *swaraj* will be theirs for the asking ... My experience during the last three months, I know we are utterly timid.[4]

The Mahatma was met by a barrage of fury. He was accused of betraying India and was warned repeatedly not to trust the *firangi*.* Gandhi remained resolute, arguing that, if India helped, it would surely be granted Dominion status by a grateful nation. Autonomous but still bound to the empire, everyone would win. As he continued to push his message, Gandhi was pilloried. Those who had once looked up to him now called him a British stooge, and a fraud.

The criticism stung, but it was nothing compared to Gandhi's internal struggle. Was it really acceptable to abandon *ahimsa* in order to obtain a greater good for the majority of his countrymen? Gandhi seemed to be coming apart under the strain of the argument, making different and eventually peculiar lines of reasoning as to why it was right for men to join up.

First, it was that the war was just. Then it was that India would earn her freedom through earning the gratitude of her colonial masters. Sometimes he said the war was a test, to prove his people were worthy of governing themselves; other times he argued it was the will of the gods.

---

* Slang for white man – particularly used pejoratively for the British.

At one point, perhaps wounded by claims he had betrayed his own non-violent beliefs, Gandhi claimed he wanted Indians to travel to Europe, face the enemy and lay down their guns, just so their piling bodies could justify their superior morality:

> Supposing that the response to my call is overwhelming and we all go to France and turn the scales against the Germans ... [Supposing] further that I succeed in raising an army of fearless men, they fill the trenches and with their hearts of love laid down their guns and challenge the Germans to shoot them – their fellow men – I say that even the German heart will melt.[5]

As India reeled from the rising numbers of casualties, Gandhi's health began to fail. He confessed to his closest friend, a Scottish clergyman named C. F. Andrews: 'This hard thinking has told upon my physical system.'[6] In autumn 1918, while Udham was trying again in Basra, the Mahatma took to his bed wracked with fever. It did not look as though he would make it to the New Year.

Punjab bristled as Gandhi faded. Why were they fighting a war that they did not understand for a power that treated them like second-class citizens? Sir Michael recognised the growing dissent, however it seemed as if that was all that he saw. The sacrifices of the men who had rallied to his call, the great numbers who were fighting for Britain, dying for Britain, were pushed to the back of his mind as he made it his mission to crush those who defied him. In punishing them, Sir Michael seemed to forget about the debt of gratitude he owed to those, the majority, who had stayed loyal to the empire in its time of need. For the rest of his time in office he would use a blunt instrument in dealing with his Punjabi insurgents, and did not seem concerned about collateral damage. His view went no further than his own desk, which was covered with worrying intelligence reports.

Thousands of miles away in America, the Ghadars were fully exploiting the misery war had brought the province. Har Dayal and his small cadre of Punjabis in San Francisco, once regarded as a terrorist cell, now appeared to have an army of their own at their disposal. They had made concerted attempts to raise a mutiny among Indian soldiers fighting for the British on multiple fronts. Their most audacious plot, had it worked in February 1915, might have dislodged the British from India altogether. According to the plan, at an appointed time the 23rd Cavalry in Punjab was meant to turn its weapons on its British officers. Peasants and city dwellers alike would take up arms in support of their soldiers, realising that this was the start of a wider action.

While chaos reigned in India, soldiers based in Singapore were supposed to mutiny, killing their officers and releasing German prisoners of war held in the stockade. The Ghadars assumed that the grateful Germans would fight shoulder to shoulder with those who set them free.

The plot never got off the ground. Sir Michael's Punjab Crime Investigation Department successfully infiltrated the conspiracy in India, rounding up scores of men and detaining them under the Defence of India Act. Though some of the men arrested claimed to have nothing to do with the conspiracy, forty-two would be sentenced to death, 114 would be transported for life, and ninety-three would find themselves serving varying terms of imprisonment.

In Singapore, only four of the eight companies making up the 5th Light Infantry mutinied. The others, mostly Pathan sepoys, wanted nothing to do with the uprising and ran away. The Germans not only refused to join the mutineers; they refused to leave their cells.

Having headed off trouble in Punjab, Sir Michael fired off a volley of angry missives to London, accusing Westminster of being out of touch with the dangers he was facing. He told politicians they risked losing the whole empire unless they took stronger action against those who agitated against the Raj, either in word or deed.

November 1917 proved particularly trying for Sir Michael. Five Germans and eight Indian Ghadars living in America were indicted by a US federal grand jury on a charge of 'Conspiracy to Form a Military Enterprise against the United Kingdom'. The trial, known as the Hindu–German Conspiracy, lasted for five months. It was a tense affair, with defendants seizing repeated opportunities to condemn British tyranny before a packed press gallery. Thanks in part to these 'freedom speeches' from the dock, American reporters began to draw parallels between the Indian struggle and the American War of Independence.

The Hindu–German trial had everything. There were accusations of bribery and threats made against witnesses. Court proceedings were regularly disrupted by shouting and the slamming of fists into polished wood. Defendants claimed their statements were being deliberately mistranslated by their own legal teams in a bid to incriminate them, and the name Michael O'Dwyer was never far from the lips of those being tried. Sensationally, one of the accused even shot and killed another defendant while in court, having somehow managed to smuggle a pistol into the dock. As the *New York Times* reported: 'Ram Chandra arose and started across the room. Ram Singh also arose. He raised his revolver and began firing. Ram Chandra staggered forward and fell dead before the witness chair, with a bullet in his heart and two others in his body.'[7]

Public drama was the very last thing Sir Michael had wanted. He had tried to get the Americans to return his troublemakers quickly and quietly, so he might hang them at home; however, such was the colourful coverage that American public opinion started to swing behind the Indian defendants. Though they were ultimately found guilty of conspiracy, the US Department of Justice refused to send the men back to Punjab. The prisoners had done enough to persuade the Americans that they would never receive due process on Sir Michael's watch. Most were quietly released after relatively short periods of incarceration.

With one eye on his vexing Ghadar problem in America, Sir Michael continued to drive young men in his own province towards the war effort. Though publicly he celebrated the Punjab's loyalty and sacrifice, behind the scenes he was petitioning Westminster for yet more powers to supress their freedoms.

Some of his peers worried he might be pushing his province too far. The governor of Madras, Lord Willingdon, the governor of Bombay, Sir George Lloyd, and the secretary of state himself, Edwin Montagu, would later admit that they thought Sir Michael's actions in Punjab might cause his province to revolt.[8] If he heard their concerns, Sir Michael ignored them. He was fighting for the empire against enemies at home and abroad. If that left him standing alone, so be it.

Udham Singh was feeling similarly isolated. A nineteen-year-old war veteran with no home, no family, and only a dull ache of failure where others had tales of battles won and comrades lost, Udham would never know what it was to be a part of the 'band of brothers'. Even in the army he had been insignificant, a low caste among low castes.

Desperately needing to belong to something more, in 1919 the Kamboj orphan found what he was looking for. The Ghadars were pumping seditious pamphlets into Punjab and needed an army of errand boys to collect the bundles and take them to every corner of the province. The very possession of such literature could lead to lengthy terms of imprisonment, and those who spread the Ghadar message risked far worse.

Udham was no coward, though he had never been able to prove that in the army. Hiding wads of sedition under his shirt, he became one of the lowliest members of the Ghadar family, running their pamphlets from the narrow gullies of his city into the wide countryside that surrounded it. To many, this would have made him a local hero.[9] Sick of being a creature to be pitied and pushed around, he was fighting for something they could understand. He was fighting for his country's freedom.

Udham's battleground had changed, but Sir Michael's remained the same. Even before the outbreak of war and his liberal use of the Defence of India Act, he had found judicial processes needlessly irksome:

In the Punjab the task of maintaining order was becoming increasingly difficult owing to three main causes, the weakness of the police, the failure of the public to assist in the prevention and detection of crime, and the tendency of the courts – the personnel of which 90 per cent was Indian – to take too technical and narrow a view of evidence.[10]

Sir Michael's 'wider' view of justice created a swifter and more draconian due process. During the war, in Punjab, forty-six men were executed on Sir Michael's watch. In contrast, in the whole of Great Britain and Ireland only three men were hanged: one was a serial killer responsible for the notorious 'Brides in the Bath' murders; one was an army deserter who would later be pardoned; and the last was an Irish nationalist who had once worked for the British Foreign Office. Sir Roger Casement was convicted of conspiring with Germany to incite insurrection in Ireland and mutiny among Irish soldiers in the British army. Udham and Casement would one day meet in the dirt behind Pentonville Prison.

After the armistice on 11 November 1918, it looked as if the lieutenant governor might lose his Defence of India Act. However, while he had been sending Punjabis to war, he and his peers in the Bengal government had been busy laying the groundwork for a new set of laws to keep the natives in check.

The Anarchical and Revolutionary Crimes Act of 1919, more commonly known as the Rowlatt Act, indefinitely extended and, in some cases, augmented the Raj's wartime powers. Thanks to Rowlatt's 'Black Bills', as the Indian nationalists referred to them, he retained the right to detain men indefinitely without trial. He had the right to close down newspapers and imprison journalists who wrote things he disapproved of. He had the power to ban people from entering or departing his province without giving them any leave to appeal. He could prevent Punjabis from speaking in public if he deemed what they might say could be seditious.

The parameters of sedition were set so wide that anyone critical of the Raj might fall foul. The police were free to search homes without warrants. Courts could try defendants *in camera* without the defendant knowing what evidence was held against them, or where it had been obtained.

Punjabi soldiers came back from the war to find they were less well-off than when they had left. The gulf between what they felt they had been promised and the reality Sir Michael presented on their return caused bewilderment and resentment, even in places where there had once been blind loyalty.

Gandhi was a lawyer at heart and had always respected the British rule of law. Rowlatt was such an illiberal piece of legislation that it roused him from his sickbed. His fever broke just as a bitter realisation dawned: he had been entirely wrong to trust the British. All the pretty words had meant nothing. All his loyalty meant nothing. Instead of reward, the Raj now tightened its grip on his country.

Gandhi rose, and in doing so became what Sir Michael O'Dwyer had always accused him of being, namely the Raj's worst nightmare. Cooperation with the British was no longer an option. They had to leave, and his people – all Indian people – would need to unite to force them out. Though Gandhi had radically shifted his perspective on power-sharing, on some things he was constant. His revolt would be bloodless. Not one shot would be fired in anger or retribution. His soldiers' only weapon would be their total, unwavering non-cooperation.

Trains would stop on tracks, letters would stay in sacks, telegraphs would fall silent, shutters on shops would remain down. Indians had always outnumbered their British masters. It was time they felt the strength of those numbers.

The message of resistance tore around Allahabad, Madras, Bombay, Delhi and Madura, but found nowhere a more receptive audience than in Punjab. Pamphlets littered the province like seditious confetti. The date for the mass civil disobedience was set for 30 March 1919. As tirelessly as Gandhi had criss-crossed the country for the war effort, he now travelled around India gathering support for his '*satyagraha*'. The term, invented by Gandhi himself, literally translates as 'force of the soul'. What it really meant for the Raj was complete and utter paralysis.

Between 30,000 and 40,000 people gathered in Amritsar on 30 March in answer to Gandhi's call. The organisers of Amritsar's *satyagraha* were a Hindu doctor and a Muslim lawyer. Both committed Gandhians, they believed passionately in their leader's doctrine of *ahimsa*, or non-violent resistance. Aged thirty-three, Dr Satyapal had a thriving practice in the heart of the old city. During the war he had held a viceroy's commission as a lieutenant in the Indian Medical Service and served with distinction. He was a reserved, thoughtful man with a dry sense of humour, and not naturally comfortable in the spotlight.

His friend, Dr Saifuddin Kitchlew, on the other hand, was a showman. Two years younger, innately charismatic and bombastically erudite, he was far happier to take to a stage. Kitchlew had studied at the University of Cambridge and had qualified as a lawyer after leaving Peterhouse College. The experience had not been a happy one for Kitchlew. Like Har Dayal before him, he too had faced lonely isolation and peer-group condescension.

When Gandhi visited Cambridge in 1909, it changed Kitchlew's life. Sitting around a table, the two lawyers talked about Gandhi's developing belief that only non-violent struggle would work against seemingly unassailable powers.[11] Little did the idealistic young men realise that, one day in the not so distant future, they would be putting the theory to the test against the mightiest empire in the world.

Three hundred miles away from Amritsar, Delhi had also ground to a halt in response to Gandhi's call to inaction. Amid the paralysis, however, scuffles broke out when some food stalls around the main station refused to join the strike. According to British reports, an angry mob gathered round the 'offending' stalls and demanded they shut up immediately to show solidarity. Two of the loudest protestors were arrested at the scene and taken to the local police station.

Fearing the pair might be deported or hanged, crowds gathered outside the police station where they had been taken. They were greeted by police and infantry with guns raised. This only increased tension, and what had started as a noisy demonstration degenerated quickly. A barrage of stones flew at the police. According to the British, men with *lathis* (long sticks) appeared among the demonstrators. Then, someone gave the order to open fire. Irregular volleys hit the crowd. Two men died instantly. An unknown number were wounded.

As the crowd panicked and ran, news of the shooting scattered with them and pockets of violence flared up around the city quicker than the troops could be deployed to deal with them. Within a matter of an hour, Delhi was in the grip of a major riot. At the town hall, a large crowd gathered near the Western Gate, where the additional superintendent of police, a man named Jeffreys, ordered his men to open fire. Bodies fell by the dozen. Jeffreys would later say that he had ordered his men to fire into the depth of the crowd because the front row of the crowd was 'simply thick with boys'.[12] Not being able to see who they were shooting, and therefore not knowing whether they were armed, or indeed even adults, Jeffreys nevertheless insisted that his orders had been humane. His superiors later congratulated him on his 'great restraint ... in a very sudden and awkward situation'.[13]

When news of the shootings reached Gandhi, he reacted with horror. This was not meant to happen. This was not what he had planned. He blamed the British for the heavy-handed policing that he was convinced had precipitated, and even provoked, the violence. It was a 'slaughter of the innocents',[14] he said, and he vowed not to let it go unanswered.

Gandhi declared that the entire country would show its solidarity with the fallen seven days after the Delhi shootings. The day would be called 'Black Sunday'. It would become one of the greatest general strikes the world had ever witnessed.

All around Punjab, illegal handbills were printed off in their thousands, brazenly in defiance of the Raj. Ink barely dry, boys in short trousers grabbed bundles and were sent scurrying to every corner of the city. Gandhi-ji needed them and they spread the word. 6 April would be the day of reckoning, when all India would say 'no more' to the British. After the shootings in Delhi, there was even more impetus behind this day of action. If they sang with one voice, the British would have to listen.

There is no way to know if Udham Singh carried some of those pamphlets, but if, as some say, he was in the city at that time, it is likely that he was involved.[15] The 'Black Acts' had motivated men with less of a grievance than Udham. The Ghadars had already used him as a leaflet boy, so there is no reason to believe that he would not have helped spread the word for Black Sunday, too.

The anti-British resentment reached its highest point in Punjab at the time of Gandhi's call to action. Not only did people object to Rowlatt, but a post-war hike in taxes was squeezing the province, too. Punjab had already paid the Raj in blood; there was little appetite to pay in coin as well. In addition, new ordinance banning the sale of 'platform tickets' to Indians was also causing a level of fury that astonished the authorities. It effectively cleared Indians from their own train stations, preventing them from receiving or sending off their loved ones. The thought of women and children, as well as the elderly, struggling off trains and across densely crowded platforms enraged the family-oriented Punjabis on the deepest level.

Rail travel was indispensable to most urban Indians, and nowhere more so than Amritsar, where people travelled to and from Lahore regularly. The reaction was angrier than anything Miles Irving, the district commissioner, could have predicted. Black Sunday had every sign of being much bigger than Gandhi's first *satyagraha*.

BOMBAY, 6 APRIL 1919

The first rays of sun crept along the sands of Chowpatty to reveal thousands hoping to catch a sight of the Mahatma. Still weak from the fevers that had gripped him for months, Gandhi appeared at exactly eight o'clock, as promised. Leaning his skeletal frame on two volunteers, he hobbled down towards the sea to bathe before beginning his 'day of prayer and fasting'. Thanks in part to an editorial in the *Bombay Chronicle* that said: 'If you value your freedom, you will join,' the crowds surpassed even Gandhi's expectations. The press described the turnout as 'a solid mass of humanity gathering strength on the way'.[16] Undeterred by the violent outbreaks in Delhi the previous week, families brought their small children out to pray with Gandhi and show solidarity with those who had been shot dead. The wall of white cotton-clad men gathered around Gandhi was punctuated by a colourful ruffle of saris, blowing in the sea breeze.

Too weak to deliver his own speech, one of his followers read from a piece of paper Gandhi had penned in his characteristically chaotic handwriting. In it, Gandhi rejected the official account of the events in Delhi, describing the actions of the British against an unarmed and peaceful crowd as 'vindictive'. His audience listened in reverential silence. Gandhi brought Bombay to a complete standstill.

PUNJAB, 6 APRIL 1919

In Punjab, the action spread beyond the towns and cities, with rural areas also answering Gandhi's call. Lawyers, labourers, farm and factory workers, teachers and students all downed tools to join the protest. One journalist, particularly struck by how many women joined the strike in otherwise ultra-conservative areas, commented: 'In one village called Sanghoi, women joined the protest with a religious zeal, fasting and chanting Gandhi's name, and deploring the Rowlatt Act.'[17]

The Amritsar strikers were heartened when news reached them that, in Lahore, the home of the *sirkar* (government) and Sir Michael O'Dwyer, tens of thousands of their brothers and sisters had rallied to Gandhi's call. Despite an overwhelming military presence, Muslims and Hindus had joined together to bathe in the river Ravi before sunrise and together they had recited prayers. According to press reports, their religious mantras were peppered with political slogans.[18]

The fact that these 'prayers' could be heard from Governor House and not one bullet was fired as a result led protestors to believe that the British had learned from the mistakes of Delhi and 30 March. The massive *hartal* in Punjab passed off without a single report of violence. The worst that could be said was that crowds in Lahore 'hissed' and 'hooted'[19] at the British.

Indians might have believed that the lieutenant governor was similarly impressed with their restraint, but Michael O'Dwyer was seeing a very different picture. He saw before him only mutiny: 'The orders regarding public meetings were openly defied, menacing crowds with black flags paraded the streets, and only the presence of a large body of British and Indian troops, including cavalry, with machine-guns prevented them from forcing their way into European quarters.'[20]

The unity between Hindus and Muslims shook him most of all. 'Divide and rule' was a tried and tested policy of colonial governance. If Indians now refused to be divided, how should they be ruled?

CHAPTER 7

ELEPHANTS AND TWIGS

Sir Michael, a lover of Persian poetry, had a particular fondness for one couplet:

> *Sar-i-chashma ba bayad firiftan b'a mil*
> *Chi pur shud na shayad guzushtan ba fil.*

> You can stop a spring with a twig.
> Let it flow unchecked, and an elephant cannot cross it.

In other words: act early, act decisively, show strength, or risk being swept away.

On 4 April, two days before the spectacular defiance across India, Sir Michael had attempted to lay his twigs ordering Gandhi to be banned from entering his Punjab. In direct defiance of his order, on 9 April the Mahatma was on his way, invited by Satyapal and Kitchlew.

The north had been clamouring to hear from the Mahatma for months, and Satyapal and Kitchlew had begged him to come to explain his doctrine of non-violence directly to the masses. Without him, they worried the outpouring of emotions unleashed by the two days of action might morph into something they could not control. From his rocking compartment on the train, Gandhi reviewed the speeches he intended to give. One was aimed at the people of Delhi, the other for Amritsar; both would encourage participation but preach restraint. As the train pulled into Palwal station, a relatively small, rundown place on the border of Punjab province, the police, on Sir Michael's orders, were waiting: 'I was served with a written order to the effect that I was prohibited from entering the boundary of Punjab, because my presence there was likely to result in a disturbance of the peace.'[1]

Gandhi had no intention of turning back. In his reedy but uncompromising voice, he told the police he was going to Punjab no matter what their warrant said: 'I want to go to the Punjab in response to a pressing invitation not to foment unrest but to allay it.'[2]

An officer placed his hand on Gandhi's shoulder. 'Mr Gandhi, I arrest you,' and with that he was forced off the train, escorted across the platform and onto another back to Bombay. Armed escort would accompany him for the rest of the journey, just in case he got off again and tried another way in.

News of the arrest rippled out from Palwal in a matter of hours, causing disruption as far afield as Ahmedabad, almost 600 miles away. A city of textile production, as soon as residents heard news of Gandhi's arrest, men downed tools, mills closed, and the streets filled with rage. Ahmedabadis were overwhelmingly ethnic Gujaratis, like Gandhi himself. He was their greatest son.

Rumours swirled: Gandhi had been hurt by the police; Gandhi had been deported; Gandhi was to be hanged. Predictably, the situation turned very ugly very quickly. The Bombay presidency despatched armed reinforcements as widespread reports of violence flooded in. But the tide was rising faster than the British could have dreamed possible.

By lunchtime, Ahmedabad's cinema was on fire and two British mill supervisors named Sagar and Steeples had been pulled from their vehicles as they attempted to cross town. The men were stoned and pursued on foot as they ran for cover. Though they escaped, an Indian policeman trying to protect them was thrown from a balcony, his broken body beaten to death.[3]

By three o'clock, the entire city was in chaos. Pockets of police found themselves besieged, saved only when armoured vehicles came to their aid. By 5 p.m., thousands of protestors had surrounded a mill at the Prem Gate in the north-east of the city. Indian barristers and pleaders, followers of Gandhi and members of his non-violent *satyagraha* movement rushed to the worst scenes, putting themselves between the mob and the trapped, begging their countrymen to stop.

They read out a statement by Gandhi himself, pleading with the crowds to stay calm. He was fine. There was no need for this. He did not want this. The words seemed to have the desired effect and the crowds dispersed by dusk. Although Ahmedabad cooled, sparks had already been thrown thousands of miles away, and Sir Michael appeared to be fanning them into an inferno.

Even before the first signs of violence in Ahmedabad on 9 April, Sir Michael ordered the arrest and deportation of Dr Satyapal and Dr Kitchlew, the very men who had ensured that protests in his province had been peaceful. He would later claim that he had been forced to act on reports from his man on the ground, the deputy commissioner Miles Irving. In truth, Sir Michael had been a tightly coiled spring ever since Lord Hardinge had first appointed him, whispering words of congratulations and warning in his ear.

Usually a 'gentle and quiet man',[4] Irving 'spent most of his working life in the Punjab, living and breathing its ideals of paternalism and tradition',[5] but his unease in Amritsar had been growing exponentially since the *satyagraha* on 6 April. Though the day had passed peacefully, a religious festival was fast approaching his city – Ram Naumi on 9 April – which Irving believed might be the flashpoint. The festival marked the birth of Lord Rama, one of the pantheon of Hindu gods. It was usually celebrated by peaceful, saffron-clad processions, which marched good-naturedly through the streets as Muslims and Sikhs looked on from the sidelines. However, something unnerving was happening in Amritsar that Irving could neither stop nor understand. The creeds were uniting.

There was talk of Muslims, Sikhs and Hindus joining together for this year's Ram Naumi parade, and this, in his view, made the situation incendiary.

On 8 April, Irving had written to Lahore warning of his 'very grave concern' that Amritsar was on the brink of disaster. The level of Hindu–Muslim unity was new to his city. He described Satyapal and Kitchlew as troublemakers. Kitchlew in particular, Irving said, was a 'local agent of very much bigger men'.[6] Irving asked for immediate reinforcements. Motor-machine gun units, too, if Lahore could spare them:

> I think that we shall have to stand up for our authority sooner or later by prohibiting some strike or procession which endangers the public peace. But for this a really strong force will have to be brought in and we shall have to be ready to try conclusions to the end to see who governs Amritsar.[7]

The letter confirmed what Sir Michael already believed. A mutiny was brewing, and it was showing every sign of starting in his province. This was his problem to solve and he was more than up to the task.

Just as Irving predicted, on Ram Naumi day, Hindus, Sikhs and Muslims walked with their arms entwined. To Irving's horror they even drank out of the same water vessels, usually an anathema to both religions, and one that Hindus historically believed compromised their place in the cycle of karmic reincarnation.

Making matters worse, amid the usual singing and clapping Irving had clearly heard cries of 'Hindu Mussalman ki Jai' and 'Gandhi-ji ki Jai' – 'Long live the Hindu–Muslim brotherhood' and 'Long Live Gandhi'. Though the processions passed entirely peacefully, Irving was convinced this was the calm before a terrible storm. Sitting in Lahore, Sir Michael felt the same way. With Gandhi's deportation already being taken care of, Irving was given permission to arrest Satyapal and Kitchlew.

AMRITSAR, 10 APRIL 1919

Ten o'clock was a civilised hour to hold a morning meeting. It gave a man time to wake up, wash and have his breakfast leisurely. It allowed food to be digested in an acceptable fashion and left the rest of the day to parley in a reasonable way. Civilised men met at ten o'clock.

Satyapal and Kitchlew were still bathing in the success of the Ram Naumi marches when they arrived at Miles Irving's bungalow, a smart, whitewashed building nestled within well-tended gardens in Amritsar's Civil Lines cantonment. The men were in good spirits. They thought they had been called to discuss the ban on Gandhi and hoped to convince Irving that the Mahatma's message of non-violence was precisely the kind of intervention he should welcome. It would help them in their continued efforts to keep the peace.

When an officer politely asked Satyapal's and Kitchlew's two companions to wait outside on the veranda, neither objected. They were guests; to do so would have been rude. They watched their leaders go in, not knowing that as soon as the door closed behind them, the solicitous smiles disappeared and Satyapal and Kitchlew were handed warrants for their immediate arrest and deportation. They were taken to waiting cars outside, which had their engines running.

An armed escort sped Satyapal and Kitchlew towards Dharamshala in Nepal, where they would be detained until further notice. No trial, no appeal, not even the opportunity to inform their friends on the veranda.

Still waiting patiently, Satyapal's and Kitchlew's companions had no idea that the vehicles racing away from the cantonment had anything to do with them. Only after Satyapal and Kitchlew were far enough away did an officer, less polite than the one who had welcomed them, come out. He handed them hastily penned notes from their leaders, intended for their families, and told them to get off the property and leave the cantonment without delay.

In a state of shock, the pair raced back to the old city to spread

the word. The British had tricked them: their leaders had been kid-
napped, and for all they knew, they might be hanged by nightfall.
As news of Satyapal's and Kitchlew's arrest spread, crowds gathered in front of Hall Gate, more in incredulity than anger. Lawyer
colleagues of Kitchlew suggested a deputation should go and ask
Irving what had happened. He was a reasonable man; there must be
an explanation. Perhaps they would be released later. Perhaps they
were still inside talking. Hundreds fell in line behind the pleaders
and a crowd made its way towards Civil Lines.

The cantonment could only be reached by two bridges crossing
the railway tracks and Irving had already posted men at both. As a
growing number reached the first narrow bridge, they found a company of twelve British and Indian soldiers on horseback blocking
their path. The sight of their picquet caused the first ripple of rage.
This had been premeditated. Satyapal and Kitchlew were nowhere
in sight. They were gone, and the men who had done this were now
hiding behind horses and guns.

By 11.30 a.m., vast crowds gathered at Aitchison Park started
streaming towards the second bridge. As Miles Irving recalled:
'They were very noisy, a furious crowd; you could hear the roar of
them half way up the long road; they were an absolutely mad crowd,
spitting with rage and swearing and throwing stones.'[8]

Indian eyewitnesses tell a very different story. They con-
cede that the crowds grew rapidly, but insist they were, at first,
entirely reasonable. A tense hush descended on Hall Bridge as
people strained to hear the lawyers arguing with the magistrates
and soldiers.

Mian Feroz Din, one of the lawyers at the front of the impromptu
Indian delegation, told a later inquiry that 'The people were bare-
footed and bareheaded and unarmed, without even sticks in their
hands.'[9] Violence came suddenly, without warning, and without
Satyapal and Kitchlew to stem it.

The pleaders at the bridge found themselves pushed forward by
the growing crowds pressing from behind. Irving ordered his picquet to withdraw by about 100 yards, but the horses, pawing the

air with their hooves, were clearly distressed by the building noise and numbers.

Irving's refusal to speak to the delegation only exacerbated the anger behind them. Nobody knows who threw the first stone, but a hail of objects followed. Almost simultaneously, a party of reinforcements arrived at the bridge, led by a Lieutenant Dickie. One of the pleaders, a High Court lawyer named Maqbool Mahmood, and his friend Mr Salaria turned to the crowd and begged them to drop their stones and stay calm: 'Salaria and I shouted out to the deputy commissioner and the officers to get back and not to fire, as we still hoped to take the crowd back.'[10]

Dickie either did not hear, or was not listening: 'Oh, for God's sake send reinforcements,'[11] he cried, as he ordered his men to open fire, straight into the body of the crowd. Rounds hit the protestors in quick succession. Maqbool Mahmood later described the scene from his vantage point near the front; he was extremely lucky not to be hit in those first few seconds: 'The soldiers at once opened a volley of fire without any warning or intimation. Bullets whistled to my right and left.'[12]

When the firing finally stopped, Maqbool stood up from where he had thrown himself on the ground, pushed his way forward and begged the soldiers to let the medics past. There were none to send. In desperation, Maqbool pushed his way back across the bridge, stepping over the dead and dying, intent on reaching the nearest hospital so he could get help, but soldiers prevented him from reaching the hospital. Maqbool would always remember the sight of Irving watching everything in silence. This was a man he had trusted. A reasonable man. A civilised man, 'The Deputy Commissioner himself was present when the fire was opened,' Maqbool recalled. 'He knew that Salaria and I were members of the Bar and were trying to get the people back to the city . . . I still believe, if the authorities had a little more patience, we would have succeeded.'[13]

Between twenty to thirty people were shot at the bridge; fifteen of them would die from their injuries. Maqbool was heartbroken; he had devoted his life to British due process. What he had just seen felt like summary execution: 'I believe some of the wounded might have been saved, if timely medical assistance had been forthcoming. After the first few shots, the crowd rushed back, but the firing was continued even after they began running away.'[14]

The pattern of firing told Maqbool all he needed to know about the British intent at the bridge: 'Most of the wounded were hit above the belt, or on the head.'[15] Word spread – the British had learned nothing from the Delhi shootings. They were doing it again. Amritsar erupted in response.

The terrified manager of Amritsar's National Bank, a man named Stewart, was stabbed and battered to death and his body was burned along with his office furniture. Stewart's deputy manager, a man called Scott, was overpowered next and brutally murdered. The city was falling into violent chaos and nobody seemed able to stop it.

At the Alliance Bank, the manager there, Thompson, was able to get to the pistol he kept in his drawer, but he too was murdered. As men ransacked his offices, trying to force their way into the safe, others peeled off and made towards the town hall and post office. In no time at all, it felt like the whole city was on fire. Some of the rage was political, driven by the scenes on the bridge, but lawless opportunists inevitably also took advantage. The situation was made worse when the telegraph wires connecting the city were cut. Now nobody outside had any idea what was going on in Amritsar, although those nearby could see the smoke.

A troop train of 270 Gurkha soldiers, just passing through Amritsar, was flagged down by the district superintendent and ordered to defend the railway line. Other soldiers were ordered to keep the mob from Civil Lines at all costs. White families were trapped there. This was not going to be another Cawnpore. Wives and children would never be subject to the violent slaughter of 1857.

Within the cantonment, the British could hear the guns and screaming from their homes. Finally, an armed convoy arrived to pick them up and take them to the safety of Amritsar fort. Those

British scattered about the city could not be reached in time, because nobody was quite sure where they were.

Amritsar was in the hands of rumours and rage: a British female doctor named Ms Easdon was said to have laughed in the faces of wounded Indians who had been dragged, bleeding, from the bridge. She supposedly looked at their bullet-riddled bodies and refused to treat them. Whether it was true or not, the mob came for her, but by the time they reached the hospital, Ms Easdon was nowhere to be found. She had been hidden by brave hospital colleagues who told the mob she had already run away. In reality, Ms Easdon would remain in the hospital till later, fleeing the city dressed in a burqa.

Still on their crazed mission to hunt down and punish the 'heartless woman' Ms Easdon, a gang of thugs happened upon a missionary school teacher instead. Miss Marcella Sherwood was making her way innocently through a narrow Amritsar street near the hospital when they found her. They dragged her from her bicycle, beat her savagely, and left her for dead in the dirt.

Miraculously Miss Sherwood survived, and after her assailants moved off looking for more victims, she managed to drag her barely conscious body across the threshold of a house. News that they had not managed to kill her eventually reached the mob and they returned to finish her off.

Miss Sherwood would have been murdered that day had it not been for the courage of an Indian family into whose house she had crawled and collapsed. At great risk they refused to give her up when the lynch mob came back, telling them that she had dragged herself to a neighbouring area, sending them racing off on a wild goose chase.

Sir Michael, trying miserably to get up-to-date reports from his cut-off city, believed Lahore would be next. He would later write in his memoirs that he was convinced Amritsar's banks would burst and trouble would flow directly towards him and his own family: 'We in Lahore, who knew what had happened at Amritsar a few hours before and what was likely to happen on an infinitely greater scale in Lahore if military aid was delayed, went through some hours of the most terrible suspense.'[16]

As news of what had happened in Amritsar spread to Lahore, by around 6.30 p.m. crowds began to gather in the city. As far as the authorities were concerned, this gathering was the precursor to a riot, and it was dealt with accordingly: 'A crowd collected in the bazaar. It rapidly grew and started coming down Anarkali. Thence the mob, which had assumed an ugly aspect and equally ugly proportions, proceeded down the Mall. By this time the police were out in force and a party of them stopped the demonstrators, now surging along the road, near the O'Dwyer Soldiers' Home.'[17]

Sir Michael could hear the sound of unrest building from his doorstep:

> From my veranda I could hear their ominous cries, one and a half miles off, and there was only a small body of armed police to block their way . . . I ascertained that the police were armed with buckshot, and I said that if they had to fire there was to be no firing in the air. We could afford to take no risks with the safety of thousands of women and children at stake.[18]

The Easter holidays had brought his children home to Lahore. He had saved his daughter from tigers once; he was not about to let the mob take her now.

In Amritsar, Miles Irving felt like he was staring into an abyss. Before the last of the telephone lines went down, his staff managed to get a call out to Lahore. The message was short but unequivocal: send infantry and gunners. Send an aeroplane, too, if you have one. Send them now or all will be lost.

Brigadier General Reginald Dyer had only recently taken command of armed forces in Jullundur. Though he would later tell his son that he had expected to deal with trouble, he had not expected it to come so soon. He had also noticed the increasing camaraderie between

Hindus and Muslims, and it left him bristling. It was proof, as if he needed it, that *they* were planning something. Dyer waited to see what would happen. He was a man who hated waiting. The call from Lahore must have been almost a relief. Dyer was to send troops to Amritsar immediately. He was also to reinforce his own city.

Immediately he set to work, calculating how many men he could send without leaving Jullundur unprotected. While briefing his staff in Lahore's divisional headquarters, Dyer received another worrying situation report. Trains were on fire; routes in and out of Amritsar were blocked and burning. Lahore would be sending a special train to Jullundur to push his reinforcements through the smouldering barricades and into the city.

Dyer was advised to send a company comprising '100 British and 100 Muhammadan troops',[19] the assumption perhaps being that Hindus and Sikhs, who together made up 60 per cent of Amritsar's population, would be less likely to open fire on their own kind.

Dyer arranged for twice as many troops as had been asked for.[20] Despite Lahore's concerns about the ethnic mix of his force, he had complete faith that his men, all his men – whoever they were and no matter what God they prayed to – would obey him without question. Dyer's company comprised 100 rifles from A Company, the 1/25th London's, 100 rifles from the 2/151st Infantry and 100 rifles from Frontier Force Regimental Depots in Jullundur.[21]

The special troop transport arrived in the small hours of the morning, as promised, and Dyer's men boarded and were on their way. They would reach Amritsar within hours. He watched the train disappear into the distance. Rex Dyer would be joining them very soon. He was never a man who led from the back.

The next day, at around 6 p.m., after leaving orders that he believed would secure and defend Jullundur, Dyer packed his kit bag and prepared to leave for Amritsar – but not before he took his son to one side.

Twenty-four-year-old Ivon Dyer was a serving soldier like his father, and though the idea of fighting with his son beside him appealed, Dyer was relieved Ivon was going to stay back this time: 'There is a very big show coming,'[22] he warned his son gravely. 'I must leave your mother and Alice in this house, although there is the same danger from Jullundur city. You will sleep under a tree beside the veranda near your mother and cousin.'[23]

With that, Dyer jumped into his waiting motorcar and sped off. Dyer's biographer, Ian Colvin, writing shortly after his death, would claim that the brigadier general was ordered to Amritsar by his superiors in Lahore: 'If the situation permitted, General Dyer should himself proceed to Amritsar and take charge,'[24] but there is little in the way of hard evidence to suggest that such a call was placed. Either Colvin was right and the official record was changed in light of what was to follow, or Dyer had done what was in his nature. He had jumped into the fray.

CHAPTER 8

REX

Reginald Dyer, 'Rex' as he preferred to be known, had always been a soldier's soldier. A man of action rather than letters, one of his colleagues had once said of him: 'He does not know what fear means and is happiest when crawling over a Burmese stockade with a revolver hanging from his teeth.'[1]

Fifty-four years of age in 1919, he looked much younger. Tall, well-built and dapper, his face and neck were brick red thanks to hours in the sun. The steel grey creeping though his neatly side-parted hair and well-groomed moustache seemed to be his only concession to age. Dyer had a reputation as a vivacious man and a courageous soldier, striding among his troops with his shirtsleeves rolled up and a lit cigarette dangling from the corner of his mouth. He demanded, and got, absolute loyalty from his men. They talked about him with genuine affection.

Rex was Raj to his bone marrow. His grandfather, John Dyer, was first to leave his native Dorset in the 1820s, travelling thousands of miles to the eastern reaches of the empire to fight pirates for the East India Company. Life in India agreed with him so much, the buccaneer decided to stay.

Rex's father, Edward Dyer, was born in Calcutta. Traditionally, Dyer men joined the army, but Edward saw opportunity in Kasauli, a snow-capped hill station in what is now called Himachal Pradesh.

India was hot, the Raj was thirsty and Edward found the perfect climate in Kasauli to grow hops for beer. Dyer's Breweries with their lion insignia did roaring trade, so much so that Rex's father was able to open other breweries in Shimla, Murree, Rawalpindi, Quetta and Mandalay. His enterprising spirit made him a fairly wealthy man.

In the 1850s, John met and fell in love with a 'back home girl', Mary Passmore, who came from the village of Barnstaple in Devon. After they were married, he brought her out to India just in time for the 1857 mutiny/rebellion. Though they were far away from the bloodbath, safe in their hill station enclave, one of Mary's first experiences of India was that of sheltering refugees, 'English women escaping trembling and aghast, from the smoke and carnage of the Plains below to the safety of the Hills.'[2]

Born seven years later, Rex Dyer lived most of his childhood in Simla, one of the most fortified zones in all British India, yet his mother's vivid memories of the mutiny were tightly woven into his own consciousness.

Rex started out as a particularly sensitive little boy, and, according to his family, was utterly at ease with the 'natives': 'Hindustani was Rex's nursery tongue.'[3] An early experience, it was said, betrayed Dyer's true nature: 'An unhappy little accident gave him a lifelong distaste for killing in sport. Once when shooting at a bird, he heard a cry from the foliage beyond, and looking more closely saw a small monkey with drops of bright blood on her grey fur.' Horrified that he had missed his mark and hit an innocent creature, Dyer was seized with grief as he looked at the female monkey he had just shot: 'Tears streamed down her cheeks as she tried to wipe herself clean with a handful of leaves and catching sight of the boy she looked at him so reproachfully that her eyes haunted his dreams for months afterwards.'[4]

It is hard to reconcile the image of the grieving child with the incident which would later define Dyer. It does, however, suggest that Rex was a man who could be tortured by the consequences of his actions.

Brigadier General Dyer reached Amritsar around 9 p.m. on the night of 11 April. Miles Irving gave him a situation report of a city now quiet but still taut with tension. In Dyer's opinion, the civil administration had allowed a bad situation to spiral out of control. It could no longer be trusted.

Rex was most unimpressed at the administration's decision to allow funerals to take place for those killed at the bridge. Mourners had come out en masse and Irving allowed them to do so on condition that all civilians vacated the streets by 2 p.m. If anything, the local population had been more than compliant, returning to their homes a full hour before he had asked. The silent streets were a testament to their desire for peace.[5] Nevertheless, on the night of 11 April, Irving still felt the need, or was persuaded, to hand his city over to the military.

Funerals had already been planned and given permission to take place on 12 April; there was little the brigadier general could do to stop them. The next day, when Dyer stepped on the thick carpet of petals left in their wake, he thought it insane that so many people had been allowed to congregate so soon after the disturbances.

He was not alone. The day before Dyer's arrival, Sir Michael had despatched a trusted colleague from Lahore, a senior ICS man named A. J. W. Kitchin, commissioner of police, to travel to Amritsar in order to appraise him of the situation.

Kitchin described a city on the edge of a precipice. Writing to Major-General Sir William Beynon, the divisional commander in Lahore, Kitchin requested the immediate despatch of a man 'who is not afraid to act'. Beynon had sent Lieutenant-Colonel M. H. L. Morgan, but Dyer arrived hours later. Eclipsed in rank and personality, Morgan now faded into the background.

Dyer established his own command centre at the Ram Bagh gardens in the north of the city. Choosing to sit far from the offices of civilian administration, he had established de facto martial law.

At best Dyer's was an act of extraordinary hubris, at worst it was downright illegal. When Sir Michael heard about the confusion in Amritsar, instead of issuing precise instructions to clear up the mess, he chose to say nothing, letting the situation unfold on its own. His civilian government had been benched and Dyer was now unarguably calling the shots. Nevertheless, Sir Michael allowed him to carry on as he saw fit.[6]

Rex rolled up his sleeves and unrolled maps of Amritsar. He would bring this city to heel. This was a war. And he knew how to win wars.

Why was Sir Michael content to leave both Amritsar and Rex Dyer in legal limbo, caught between civil and martial law? It could be that Dyer was precisely Sir Michael's kind of man: a creature created in the Lawrence, piano-smashing mould; a man who had little truck with courts and committees. This brigadier general would get things done while others sank in quagmires of bureaucracy.

Amritsar, as far as Dyer was concerned, was a disaster. For a start, the natives here no longer stopped and *salaamed** British superiors. Some even had the temerity to spit at the feet of his men. Such insolence was intolerable.

When he encountered a noisy knot of demonstrators at the Sultanwind Gate, shouting '*Hindu-Mussalman ki Jai!*', extolling the unity between the two faiths, Dyer was torn over whether he should open fire or merely arrest the ringleaders. In the end, he somewhat grudgingly opted for the latter.[7]

He needed to shake up this rebel nest. Issuing orders to limit the supply of water and electricity, Dyer reasoned that if the natives struggled with day-to-day existence, they would think twice about making trouble. Amritsar had forgotten its place. He was there to remind them.

---

* The traditional salute of respect – a hand is raised to the forehead, with the head slightly bowed.

Most history books about this period dwell on the plight of the Europeans in Amritsar during the riots and their aftermath. They fail to acknowledge the experience of Indians caught up in the violence. Most Amritsaris were as terrified as those white women and children who had cowered in Civil Lines at the height of the disorder. They, too, had families caught in the crossfire, but no troops came to ferry them to safety.

Amritsar was filled with innocent civilians, yet Sir Michael and Dyer regarded them as complicit. They were either rebels or rebel sympathisers. It made the idea of collective punishment so much easier to peddle if lawyers and law breakers were painted with the same brush.

Though it would never have occurred to an innocent street vendor in the Hall bazaar to apologise for the actions of the mob, Sir Michael and his Brigadier General Dyer expected nothing less. Amritsar was the author of its own developing misfortune according to Sir Michael, and he wanted contrition: 'Amritsar City, far from showing any signs of repentance, was still on the 13th in a state of tumult and revolt ... The rebels had practically isolated General Dyer.'[8]

It was an odd way to characterise the situation. Dyer was surrounded by Amritsaris, it was true, but where else were they meant to go? This was their city, and the day after Dyer's arrival they were as grateful as anyone that the trouble appeared to have burned itself out.

Almost all the dead had been buried or cremated. None had taken up arms against Dyer's men since their arrival. His troops might have been spat at, but despite the hurt of the past forty-eight hours, nobody on the Indian side had fired a shot.

As if to reinforce the feeling of normalcy, Punjabis from neighbouring areas were even starting to trickle in to the city again. A big festival was about to break over Amritsar, the most important in all Punjab. How could they know that the lieutenant governor and brigadier general saw these visitors as reinforcements for a rebel army in an imminent battle?

Ishwar Das Anand's journey to Amritsar had been long and convoluted. The nineteen-year-old had been travelling for a week and was tired and covered in dust by the time he arrived in the city, late in the afternoon of 12 April. The only inkling he had of trouble came when the trains to Amritsar stopped running two days earlier. He did not think much of it at the time. Trains stopped without warning in India all the time. It was a fact of life and Ishwar Das did what most poor Indians did: pocketed his ticket and started to walk. He had come such a long way, turning back was not an option.

Ishwar Das's whole family was counting on him, and this propelled him forward even though it was hot and the journey was long. He felt blessed whenever a bullock cart heading his way let him jump on the back: 'I always felt as if God had one hand on my shoulder,' he would later tell his sons. 'If he wanted me to be somewhere he would show me a way.'[9]

Kala Bagh, Ishwar Das's home, lay just over a hundred miles north in the newly created administrative area of the North-West Frontier Province. On the border with Afghanistan, it was a place filled with spaces and silence. Slopes covered in densely packed evergreen foliage gave the place its name – Kala Bagh, 'the Black Garden'.

Ishwar Das's family were traders and he had been raised around the sparse conversation of the Pathans: tall, fair-skinned men who had perfected the language of the nod and hand gesture. Though ethnically Punjabi himself, Ishwar Das felt more kinship with the Pathans of the mountains than noisy Amritsaris or proud Lahoris.

He and his mother had watched the camel trains since his childhood, passing by in a constant stream as the snow of the Khyber Pass melted away. The Pathans made their way towards the cities, beasts laden with rolled-up carpets and shawls – goods to sell in the busy city markets. Ishwar Das's mother would always leave a *mutka* (a traditional clay pot) of buffalo milk or cold water outside her boundary wall, knowing the camel drivers would be thirsty. The rules of hospitality meant one should never wait to be asked.

Ishwar Das's mother was a quiet woman, one who could convey meaning with just an *ishaara* – a look, or tilt of the head. He had grown up saying everything he needed in the fewest words possible. Amritsaris, in contrast, never seemed to stop talking, or so Ishwar Das thought when he finally arrived after two days of walking. The city thrummed with chatter, grunting livestock and rattling carts. He was witnessing a city coming back to life after forty-eight hours of enforced hibernation, but for all he knew, these people were always like this.

One of Ishwar Das's uncles had given him the names of two Frontier families who had recently relocated to the city, and he was looking forward to meeting some familiar faces in this foreign and intimidating place. Finding them was almost as challenging as his journey from Kala Bagh had been: the city was a maze; Ishwar Das got horribly lost, walking and walking only to find himself back where he started. Confused and exhausted, he cursed Amritsar and everyone in it.

Finally, one of the addresses on his battered piece of paper was in front of him, and behind the door he found the warmest of Punjabi welcomes. The family had received his uncle's letter and knew he was coming. He shared a meal with them, heard something of the recent troubles, though he failed to understand the scale and importance of what his friends had just lived through. In return he gave them news from back home, told them about his family and the births and deaths they had missed. The afternoon slipped into evening and he was shown to a good guest house nearby. There were unmarried girls in the family's home; it would have been disrespectful to stay and he did not expect an invitation.

The sons of the household arranged to meet him the next day. They had played together as children in Kala Bagh and Ishwar Das was relieved that they still had some connection.[10] However, city life had changed them a lot. They were 'smarter' than he remembered, and very proud. Amritsar seemed to have seeped through their skins.

Excited by the timing of Ishwar Das's visit, on the eve of Baisakhi, the harvest festival, the boys had promised him a day of '*musti*' (irresponsible fun) as they dropped him and his bags at the guest house. Come tomorrow they would show their country cousin how to have a good time in Punjab's 'best city'. He might never want to go back.

Baisakhi was a time of feasting and thanksgiving after months of hard labour. The most important festival in the region, it celebrated the fertility of the land as men brought their wheat, corn and sugarcane to market. For Sikhs, the day had added religious significance. It marked the foundation of the *Khalsa*, the brotherhood of orthodox Sikhs upon whom the religion was built.

Ishwar Das had grown up hearing so much about Baisakhi in the big city. He had only left his home and attached 'factory' – his father's fanciful name for the corrugated metal shed where he and his uncles repaired and refurbished European sewing machines – twice before. Previous trips had been minor local errands where he was expected to collect late payments and make deliveries to nearby Frontier towns. Tall and strong, with a good head for figures, Ishwar Das was good at prying payments out of reluctant hands. Now the teen had been sent on his first important business trip. The harvest festival might have been a good time to pray, but it was also the best time of the year for a man to make a deal. The place would be teeming with visitors. Men would have money in their pockets.

He had repeated his father's instructions so often they were ingrained. Ishwar Das was to buy a consignment of second-hand, largely broken German Pfaff sewing machines from a merchant in the bazaar, but not before he checked them thoroughly, ensuring none were beyond repair. He was then to sort out transportation to the 'factory' in Kala Bagh, ideally using Pathans travelling back home to the mountains. Pathans never liked to travel with empty paniers and they would be cheaper and less likely to chisel for more money at the end of the trip. A Pathan's word was his bond.

Ishwar Das had touched his pocket so many times, checking to see if the bulge of cash was still where he had put it, that he looked forward to the moment he could hand it over to the merchant. If he did this job well, his father might trust him to come back again. The second time was bound to be much easier than the first.

CHAPTER 9

NO WARNING, NO WAY OUT

BAISAKHI MORNING, 13 APRIL 1919

The sun rose just before 6 a.m. with the promise of a bright
Baisakhi day. Rays of sunlight cutting through the mist prodded
the sleepy city, nudging it gently to its senses. The threat of violence, like the haze of a typical Punjabi morning, promised to lift
completely. Although there were rumours of continuing clashes
elsewhere in the province, Amritsar had been peaceful for more
than two days. The worst was over. The city unclenched.

In contrast, after three nights of poor sleep, with thoughts of
mutiny never far from his mind and people entering the city all the
time, Dyer's nerves, in contrast, were stretched taut. He was on the
streets again that morning with an armed force at his heels. Summary
floggings, handed out to the insolent, had discouraged disrespect,
nevertheless Rex had a new set of edicts for the city. They were to be
obeyed immediately and without question: 'It is hereby proclaimed to
all whom it may concern that no person residing in the city is permitted or allowed to leave the city in his own private or hired conveyance
or on foot, without a pass from one of the following officers.'[1] A long
list of names and locations where such documents could be applied
for followed. Then came news of a rolling curfew: 'Any person found
in the streets after 8 p.m. is liable to be shot.'[2]

Dyer also banned groups of more than four people congregating on the streets: 'No procession of any kind is permitted to parade the streets in the city or any part of the city or outside of it at any time. Any such processions or any gathering of four men will be looked upon and treated as an unlawful assembly and dispersed by force of arms if necessary.'[3]

From its birth in the seventeenth century, the old walled city of Amritsar had spread, untroubled by town planning. Two centuries of growth saw its web of alleys and winding streets reaching into the surrounding fields. Dyer's new rules were read out at nineteen different locations by town criers, accompanied by the beat of a military drum. The 'drum proclamation' was repeated in English, Urdu and Punjabi; nevertheless, in a place of noise, high walls and general convolution, a drum proclamation was the worst way imaginable to spread the word of such far-reaching changes.

Relying on maps to identify the most important locations where they could read out their drum proclamation, Dyer's men missed many of the city's key congregation points. The day was also far hotter than usual. Dyer had told them that Amritsar was infested with rebels, and with the combination of blistering sunshine and trepidation, it comes as no surprise that Dyer's men were in a hurry to read out their proclamations and get back to the shady safety of their headquarters at the Ram Bagh.

With his scattered drum proclamations, Dyer dropped pebbles into a vast and choppy pool. The expectation that his message would ripple out and reach every nook and cranny of the city was wholly unreasonable. At 12:40 p.m., news reached Dyer that confirmed his view that collective defiance bubbled just under the surface of the city. Despite his new edicts, a political meeting, he was told, was going to take place at a nearby garden called Jallianwala Bagh.

He could have acted to stop it, posted guards at the site, plastered prohibition posters on the walls in the neighbourhood, but Dyer did nothing. If he was going to teach the natives a lesson, Jallianwala Bagh might as well be the classroom.

Jallianwala Bagh, or 'the garden of the Jallah-man'*, had a name that suggested greenery and flowers, and perhaps it had been that way once. The well at the centre of his eponymous garden certainly gave every indication that things once grew, were tended and watered here. Those days were long gone.

Over the years, Jallianwala Bagh had dried up and become run down. Amritsaris used its dusty seven acres as a recreation ground. The garden was tightly bound by high tenement buildings on its perimeter, and apart from a handful of tiny, tapering gullies where the buildings did not quite touch, there was only one real entrance/exit to the Bagh. It was so narrow that three men walking shoulder to shoulder could just about pass through.

Pilgrims on their way to or from the Golden Temple, a mere ten minutes' walk away, would often use Jallianwala Bagh for respite, and though nobody could accuse the place of being beautiful, the garden was undeniably popular, well-placed and well-used, so much so that grass struggled to grow under the constant footfall. Dust swirled under sandaled feet, as children played and adults escaped the noise of the streets.

The meeting at Jallianwala Bagh which so irritated Dyer that afternoon had been arranged the day before by a man named Hans Raj. It promised much: the chance to respond to the Mahatma's exclusion; the deportation of Satya Pal and Kitchlew; and the Rowlatt Act.

The organisers had called the meeting in the name of a respected and aged High Court lawyer. Lala Kanhyalal Bhatia had put together an agenda and its four resolutions read more like dull minutes of a meeting than a call to arms. He also openly and unequivocally condemned violence:

---

* Sardar Himat Singh, one of Maharajah Ranjit Singh's generals in the early 1800s, had come from the village of Jalla and he and his family had simply been known locally as the Jalle-walleh – the people from Jalla. The garden was his legacy to the city.

This grand meeting of the inhabitants of Amritsar looks with extreme indignation and disapproval on all those revolutionary actions which are the inevitable result of the inappropriate and inequitable attitude on the part of the Government and entertains apprehension that this despotic conduct of the Government might prove deleterious to the British Government.[4]

If Rex Dyer even saw the agenda for the meeting, he was reading something very different between the lines.

The Golden Temple had been welcoming a steady flow of worshipers since daybreak. By midday, the heat thinned the lines and the skies filled instead. Children took advantage of the hot breeze above the city, flying their brightly coloured paper kites. Baisakhi filled the earth and the sky with colour.

Ishwar Das Anand lay on his back watching the kites duel with each other from a string cot he had pulled out into the courtyard of his guest house. He had allowed himself a late and lazy morning, well-deserved after the wearing journey of the day before. After a rich breakfast, he had fallen asleep again, all good intentions of visiting the Golden Temple evaporating in the heat. He had nowhere to be and nobody to tell him what to do and savoured the time he had stolen for himself, a bit of peace in this crazy city.

Ishwar Das's *musti* friends had arranged to have a late lunch with him at Jallianwala Bagh just after three. It was not far to walk to the Bagh from his guest house, so it left him plenty of time to doze, wash, dress, meet his friends, and still get to the market in time to do his deal. The scrap dealer with his sewing machines had agreed to meet him between four and five. He would conclude his business and the evening would be his, free to do whatever his friends had in mind – the perfect plan.

When Ishwar Das reached the Bagh later that afternoon, he could

seehe *satyagrahi** volunteers were out in force. A makeshift platform
of cobbled-together planks, surrounded by busy-looking men in
white *khadi*† greeted him as soon as he passed through the narrow
alleyway. They bustled with such a sense of self-importance he
half expected Gandhi to turn up. When it became clear that would
not be happening, Ishwar Das drifted, bored and hungry, towards
the shade of the perimeter wall, where his friends and his lunch
were waiting.

Many had come to Jallianwala Bagh that afternoon in response
to the political handbills, but others, families with children, worshippers from the Golden Temple, people taking a break from the
city, had come to the garden with the same idea as Ishwar Das. They
wanted to meet and eat. The food vendors had been particularly
exuberant that day, anxious to make up for the lack of sales during
recent disturbances and curfews. Ishwar Das would remember
years later that the ground was covered in greasy translucent paper,
discarded wrappings from the food that made Amritsar famous
throughout the province.

Baisakhi in Amritsar usually involved an enormous livestock
fair, but after the recent trouble the British had cancelled both the
horse and cattle market. News had not managed to reach everyone, however, and some poor souls had travelled miles, dragging
unwilling animals behind them. Left with no place to sell them,
several brought their bullocks into the Bagh, resigned to the fact
that the hulking beasts would be returning with them at the end
of the day.

Amid the feet and hooves, some still managed to stretch out and
sleep, worn out by heat and heavy lunches. Ishwar Das marvelled
at their ability to doze in the filth, as he irritably pulled yet another

---

* Follower of Gandhi's non-violent doctrine
† Homespun white cotton. *Khadi* had been turned into a political statement by those,
including Gandhi, who believed in *swaraj* – the notion that Indian goods should be
produced for Indian people by Indian people. This was a direct attack on the more
expensive textile imports from Britain. The flag of modern India has a spinning
wheel at its centre.

piece of sticky paper from his freshly polished shoes. Laughing at his discomfort, his friends dragged him to sit down in the dust with them. Nobody would be starched and clean on Baisakhi day, they assured him, least of all a scrap-metal dealer. Who exactly was he trying to impress? Ishwar Das relaxed into their laughter, kicked off his uncomfortable shoes and ate. The food really was as good as he'd heard. It was almost good enough to make him forget why he had come to the city in the first place.

At 4 p.m., Brigadier General Dyer was on the move. It had taken him all of fifteen minutes to summon his men and muster them behind his two machine-gun-mounted cars. The soldiers carried Lee–Enfield rifles and around thirty-three rounds of ammunition each. The Gurkhas, who made up half of his force, were also armed with traditional *kukris,* curve-bladed machetes. Amritsaris jumped out of their way, making space for the convoy to pass through the crowded Baisakhi streets.

As a distant clock struck four, Ishwar Das realised with a start that he was going to be late. Brushing dust from his clothes, spitting on a handkerchief and trying to clean his now-detested shoes, he did his best to smarten himself up again. Shouting over his shoulder, he told his friends to save his place and get him something sweet to eat. Hopefully he would not be long and he was sure to be hungry again soon. Pushing his way through the crowds to the narrow exit, he was barely aware that the speeches were about to start.

Desperately trying to remember the way, Ishwar Das ran past a column of soldiers coming towards him. He flattened himself against a wall to let them pass.

Ishwar Das had become accustomed to the massive presence of soldiers since his arrival. He believed this was just how it was in the big city and thought nothing more about the soldiers as he pushed his way into the bazaar, thinking only of broken sewing machines. He was going to make his father proud.

Dyer knew what he was going to do even as he passed the skinny young man in the uncomfortable shoes. The natives were daring him just by being there: 'My mind was made up as I came along in my motor car – if my orders were not obeyed, I would fire immediately.'[5]

An estimated 15,000 to 20,000[6] people were inside Jallianwala Bagh by the time the armoured column pulled up outside. Getting out of his vehicle, Dyer was met by a sight that irritated him greatly: the alleyway leading into the gardens was too narrow for his vehicles. Instructing his drivers to wait outside, blocking the main exit, Dyer ordered his riflemen to unsling their guns and quick march into the Bagh.

The dramatic entrance of the soldiers had an immediate effect on those inside. Expecting an imminent order to disperse, some started to pack up their picnics as the soldiers spread out along the northern wall on a raised bank of earth. Others stood rooted to the spot, watching as the uniformed men dropped to one knee and took aim. Hans Raj stood on the podium and screamed at all who could hear him to sit down where they were. When they heard him, they believed, perhaps as he did, that the soldiers would not shoot.[7]

It happened so fast it did not feel real. Dyer gave the order. His second in command, a man named Captain Crampton, repeated it, shouting out for all to hear. Whistles rang out from the line of uniformed men. They took aim, squeezed their triggers and fired.

Sergeant Andrews, who was standing right at the side of Dyer, described the scene as if it unfurled before him in slow motion:

> The whole crowd seemed to sink to the ground, a flutter of white garments . . . I saw no sign of a rush towards the troops . . . After a bit, I noticed that Captain Briggs was drawing up his face as if in pain and was plucking at the General's elbow . . . Dyer seemed quite calm and rational. Personally, I wasn't afraid. I saw nothing to be afraid about. I'd no fear that the crowd would come at us.[8]

Men and children fell clutching their faces and chests, tearing flesh and ripped organs, creating a red mist over the places where they lay. The sight of children having their limbs shattered by bullets and their eyes shot out before him[9] was too much for Amritsar's superintendent of police, John Rehill, who had been asked to show Dyer's men the shortest route to the garden. After a few moments witnessing the scene he could stand it no more and walked out of the Bagh as the soldiers continued to swivel and fire. He would be so traumatised by what he had seen that he would never be able to speak of it.[10] He would become a rampant alcoholic in the years that followed.

From the Indian side, numerous eyewitnesses gave disturbingly similar accounts of what Rehill could not bear to watch: 'At first the soldiers fired high, but the Sahib ordered them to fire straight and low. There was a short interval after the first firing. Then the second firing began. All fire was directed towards people who were running away. The second firing ceased; and soon after the third firing began.'[11]

Troops swivelled, following swarms of terrified, screaming Indians, running for cover that did not exist. They shot, again and again, deliberately and methodically, into the thickest parts of the crowd. Parents wailed for their children, men cried out and fell, clasping at their backs. Bodies piled near the tiny gullies in the perimeter wall. Those who realised they had nowhere to run tried to shield the ones they loved. Some jumped into the well.

Several retired Jat Sikh soldiers, who had served with the British during the Great War, shouted for people to lie down, but their voices were drowned out by gunfire and the screaming. No discrimination was made between targets. The son of the local doctor, a thirteen-year-old boy named Madan Mouhau, used to visit the garden every day to play with his friends. A bullet, aimed at his head, found its mark and shattered his skull.[12]

Wherever there was hope, there was death. A fanning *peepul*, an indigenous tree with a broad trunk, became a shelter for dozens of screaming people. Dyer directed his men to aim at the tree. Splinters flew with blood and flesh. Nathu the *dhobi*, or laundry man, was in his eighties. Nathu Kamboj was an eight-year-old boy from the same peasant caste as Udham Singh. Both were killed instantly.

Knots of people were massed in the corners of the garden, desperately trying to clamber over the high walls. Dyer ordered his men to aim at them too. Dozens fell with bullet wounds to the face, head and chest. Most were shot in the back as they tried to run away. Many were trampled in the panic: 'There was not a corner left of the garden facing the firing line where people did not die in large numbers ... Blood was pouring in profusion.'[13]

'The worst part of the whole thing was that the firing was directed towards the exit gates through which the people were running out. There were three or four small outlets in all and bullets were actually rained over the people at all these places.'[14]

Bharpur Singh was only four years old on 13 April 1919 but would remember events vividly for the rest of his life, relating them to anyone who cared to listen well into his old age. He had been taken to the Bagh by his grandfather, and when the firing started, the old man picked him up and ran towards the wall furthest from the soldiers. Realising there was no way out, Bharpur's grandfather threw him over a seven-foot wall, breaking his arm in the process. Fear of further 'punishment' prevented either of them from getting medical aid for days.[15]

Watching the carnage from his roof, Mohamed Ismail knew some of his family was down in the Bagh below, and he could do nothing to help them. Later, he would have to sift through corpses looking for his cousin. The dead were once his friends and neighbours: 'At several places, the corpses were ten or twelve thick. I saw some children lying dead. Khair-Ud-Din Teli of Mandi had his child, six or seven months old, in his arms.'[16]

The shooting lasted for ten long minutes, during which time the soldiers managed to fire 1,650 rounds of ammunition. The death toll would have been so much higher if the entrance to the Bagh had been wide enough for machine-gun-mounted cars.

When the order to cease fire finally came, the soldiers left as suddenly as they had come. Dyer jumped back into his car and was driven off towards the Ram Bagh, his men following at a trot. No medical aid would be allowed in that night; nor would people be permitted to carry their dead and wounded out. In those ten minutes of sustained gunfire, between 500 and 600 people were most likely killed. Three times that number are estimated to have been wounded.[17]

Children identified among the dead included: Sohan Lal (9), Gian Chand (15), Mohammed Shariff (12), Abdulla Baksh (15), Nand Lala (12), Mohan Lal (12), Harnam Singh (15), Guru Brahman (15), Nikmu Mal Girdhari (14), Sundar Singh (15), Sohan Singh (15), Tara Singh (15), Labhu Ram (14) and Murli Mal (12).[18]

There were certainly more fatalities than we have names of the dead. Any attempt to collate names would only be made much later, by which time Amritsaris were too scared to admit that they, or anybody they had loved, had been anywhere near the Bagh.

Ishwar Das was still deep in the bazaar, on his hands and knees looking at the underside of half-mangled machinery, haggling with the salesman, when the sound of wailing reached him in waves. 'Jallianwala Bagh.' 'Guns.' 'Soldiers.' The words pounded in his head as he raced back, hoping to find his friends among the living. He never made it as far as the Bagh. He was greeted by an armed policeman who lowered his gun muzzle and screamed at him: 'Get off the streets! Now!'

Terrified, the teenager ran as fast as he could to his guest house. He thought of his mother. He thought of his father. He thought he was going to die. Then he thought of the friends still in the garden. He wept. He prayed. He wept again. He was ashamed. Ishwar Das would have to wait till morning to find out what had happened to his friends. As he would tell his own sons, years later, it would be the longest night of his life.

Ratan Devi's home was close enough to the Bagh that she heard the firing from her bedroom. She, like many that day, had escaped the heat for a siesta: 'I got up at once as I was anxious, because my husband had gone to the Bagh. I began to cry and went to the place accompanied by two women to help me.'[19]

Ratan Devi found a place filled with twisted corpses and the outstretched hands of the wounded and dying. There was so much blood in the dust: 'I saw heaps of dead bodies and I began to search for my husband.'[20]

Pulling bodies off other bodies, she finally found him beneath a pile of corpses: 'The way towards it was full of blood and of dead bodies. After a short time both the sons of Lala Sunder came there; and I asked them to bring a *charpai* [wicker bed] to carry the dead body of my husband home.'[21]

Though they promised to help her, the young men never came back. Perhaps armed patrols similar to the one that had terrified Ishwar Das off the streets prevented their return. As Ratan Devi waited in vain, she tried to drag her husband out of the carnage herself. Everywhere she looked she saw people, some of them familiar, riddled with bullets: 'I entreated a Sikh gentleman to help me in removing my husband's body to a dry place, for that place was overflowing with blood. He caught the body by the head and I by the legs and we carried it to a dry place and laid it down on a wooden block. I waited till ten o'clock but nobody came.'[22]

Ratan Devi could do nothing but wait for morning and the lifting of the curfew. With the head of her dead husband in her lap, she endured a night filled with unimaginable grief and horror:

> I found a bamboo stick which I kept in my hand, to keep off the dogs. I saw three men writhing in agony, a buffalo struggling in great pain; and a boy about twelve years old, in agony, entreated me not to leave the place ... I asked him if he wanted any wrap, and if he was feeling cold, I could spread it over him. But he asked for water.[23]

There was no water, and nothing she could do. Ratan Devi listened as his whimpers faded away. Distant chimes marked the passing of the night. Hundreds trapped within the same walls counted the bells with her.

THE LEGEND OF UDHAM SINGH

And he tried to help the dying, but could do nothing for them, his water all spilled in the dust, a bullet in his arm. He waited out the long night, trying to bring comfort to those whose lives seeped out in the darkness. Blood like water spilt in the dust ... And with the first light of morning, he saw the truth. Piles of bodies, their silence harder to bear than their cries had been ...

He took a handful of blood-soaked earth in his hand, heavy and black, and rubbed it against his forehead ... and he swore a terrible vow ... No matter how long it took, no matter how far it took him ... he would track down the dogs who did this to his people and he would kill them ... with as little mercy as they had shown his countrymen.[1]

Only Udham Singh knows the truth of where he was on the day of the massacre, and during his life he told so many people so many different versions of events that it is impossible to know which, if any of them, is true. Some say he swore he was there in the Bagh when the shooting began.[2] Others say that he told them his 'brothers and a sister were killed'[3] and that the need to avenge them had almost driven him mad. Though we know Udham had only one real sibling, a brother who died in the orphanage, in the Indian tradition we often refer to close friends as 'brothers' and 'sisters', so it is possible he knew some of the dead and cared for them deeply.

Some in India, including local historians, have placed Udham at the side of Rattan Devi, insisting he was the 'Sikh gentleman' who helped her move his bloodsoaked corpse from a pile of bodies, although there is no evidence to support this.

It has also been claimed that Udham was not even in India at the time of the massacre. That now often-repeated assertion can be traced to one author, the medal collector Roger Perkins, who first made the case in his 1989 book, *The Amritsar Legacy*.

In it, Perkins writes: 'I happened to purchase two medals which seemed to be related to each other. Both were of the India General Service series. The first bore the clasp Afghanistan NWF 1919 and the name impressed upon the rim was that of Lieutenant J. C. O'Dwyer, Indian Army Reserve of Officers. The other had the clasp Waziristan 1919–21 and was named to an Indian, Udham Singh Railways.'

I have spoken to Roger Perkins, and whereas I have no doubt that he bought the medal pair in good faith, believing that they belonged to Udham Singh and John Chevalier O'Dwyer, the son of Sir Michael O'Dwyer, a cursory search of the 'Forces at War' database yielded four Udham Singhs during the relevant period, and the National Archives more than thirty different medal cards for Udham Singhs in the same time frame. These records are far from exhaustive. So many service files were destroyed after independence, but even the few that survive raise question marks over Perkins's assertion.

British intelligence documents[4] from the 1930s state categorically that Udham Singh, the Kamboj orphan, served in Basra and Mesopotamia. They make no mention of Waziristan. Moreover, we cannot even be sure that Udham signed up for military service under his orphanage name. He frequently used his birth name, 'Sher Singh', for official documents, and a host of other aliases besides. If, as looks likely, the recruiters fudged his date of birth to allow him to sign up, not once but twice, it is entirely possible they changed his name, too, at least once.

As we will later see, if the British service record could have proven that Udham was far from Jallianwala Bagh at the time of the massacre, the authorities would certainly have published the information in 1940. It was in their interest to do so. Perkins may have been indulging in understandable but wishful thinking to believe that both the O'Dwyer medal and Udham's medal had come to him in a grisly coupling.

One particular story told to me in the course of my research rings truer than most, purely because it is so mundane. It says that Udham *was* in Punjab at the time of the massacre, but he was not at Jallianwala Bagh, rather in neighbouring area of Majah, spreading seditious leaflets, just as he had done in Amritsar before Gandhi's *satyagraha*.

If that was true, it paints Udham's obsession in hues of human frailty. He would have had to live with the fact that he had personally encouraged many of his countrymen to go to that doomed Baisakhi meeting. They died, but he had lived. It would haunt him.[5] Survivor's guilt can be a terrible thing.

What we *can* say is that the massacre transformed Udham Singh. Vengeance took over his life, and for the next twenty years, though he would be given numerous chances to live a happy and fulfilling existence, he would continue his quest, travelling thousands of miles, meeting a variety of people, learning what he needed, trying to become the avenging angel for his people. A man born with so little, who wanted to be so much more.

PART TWO

CHAPTER 10

I REPENT, I REPENT, I REPENT

The first news of the massacre reached Lahore in trickles. Miles Irving telephoned in a report at around midnight, but Sir Michael kept the information to himself, waiting for official written confirmation. That report arrived at 3 a.m. on 14 April, more than ten hours after the first shots had been fired. Though it made for alarming reading, still Sir Michael did not pass the report on to London:[1]

At Amritsar yesterday, Brigadier-General Dyer and Deputy-Commissioner read proclamation in city forbidding all public meetings. Prohibition proclaimed by beat of drum and read and explained at several places in city. In spite of this, meeting attended by six thousand was held at 4-30 contrary to Deputy-Commissioner's expectation. Troops present under command of General Dyer fired, killing about two hundred. Deputy-Commissioner not present. Military report not yet received. City quiet at night but political effect on Manjha (Sikh tract around Lahore and Amritsar) and troops uncertain. In view of possibilities General Officer Commanding is arranging to draft into Lahore more troops, British and Indian.[2]

Irving's report vastly underestimated both the number of people who had been in the Bagh and also how many had been hurt and killed. He warned Sir Michael that trouble was headed his way: 'Early this morning large mob attacked railway station at Wagha (between Lahore and Amritsar); rail was removed by skilled hands and signaller bolted. Armoured train went out from Lahore and two cars were derailed and left on line under guard. Assistance being sent. Line cutting and attacks on trains becoming frequent.'[3]

Brigadier General Dyer's own account arrived after Irving's, and when it did, it was surprisingly bloodless. It also dramatically under played the number in the Bagh and the results of the shooting: 'I saw a dense crowd, estimated at about 5,000; a man on a raised platform addressing the audience and making gesticulations with his hands.'[4]

'I realised that my force was small and to hesitate might induce attack. I immediately opened fire and dispersed the mob. I estimate that between 200 and 300 of the crowd were killed. My party fired 1,650 rounds.'[5]

Rex Dyer, a man who prided himself on his straight talking, was either being obtuse or blind to what he had just done. His men had made no effort to survey the scene, count bodies or treat the wounded, so in truth he had no idea of casualty or fatality numbers when he wrote his report. For him to suggest that he had successfully 'dispersed the mob', when they had in truth trapped them and shot at them, was extraordinary. Dyer, a stranger to Amritsar, did not know if there were other exits to Jallianwala Bagh, or how narrow some of the channels between tenements were. He was well aware that he had turned his guns on knots of people at the wall. He also knew that he had left many seriously wounded in his wake.

In a later inquiry, Dyer would be pushed to give a fuller explanation of his actions and state of mind,[6] and asked why he had failed to provide any medical help to the wounded. His reply bordered on belligerent: 'It was not my job. Hospitals were open, and they could have gone there.'[7]

The boy who had once supposedly cried over a wounded monkey would take years to show a shred of compassion for the hundreds of men, women and children he gunned down in cold blood on 13 April 1919 at Jallianwala Bagh.

In Lahore, General Beynon was completely supportive, insisting that 'Dyer had crushed the rebellion at its heart in Amritsar.'[8] Sir Michael agreed: 'My own view, based on my knowledge of the people and the opinions of competent judges like the Commissioner Mr Kitchin, was that not only did Dyer's action kill the rebellion at Amritsar, but, as the news got round, would prevent its spreading elsewhere.'[9]

Anxious to reassure Dyer, Beynon asked whether he might add Sir Michael's support to his own in writing. The lieutenant governor's initial hesitation would be taken by some in the Indian National Congress as an admission that he knew he would be rubber-stamping a massacre.

Sir Michael denied that, insisting he hesitated because he thought the action was a military matter, not civilian. It was for the army to pass judgement, not him. Beynon reminded Sir Michael that Amritsar was still under civilian government and therefore he was beholden to say something, so he agreed for a message to be sent to Dyer on his behalf.

The telegram sent from Lahore by Beynon to Dyer was simple but reassuring: 'Your action correct and Lieutenant-Governor approves.'[10]

News of the massacre reached the far corners of Punjab within hours. The response was predictable. From Gujranwala, 45 miles north of Lahore, desperate messages started to pour into Governor House. The deputy commissioner rode as fast as he could to a communications hut, 8 miles away from his city, and tapped out a message steeped in panic: '*Hartal* [strikes] and disturbances going on. Mob active, more expected. Bridges on either side of station burnt. Police insufficient. Military arrangements required.'[11]

Sir Michael's troops were too thinly stretched to deploy to Gujranwala without leaving their own jurisdictions unguarded. One military commander in Rawalpindi, some 200 miles away from Gujranwala, summed up the logistical position: 'He had not troops to send, and even if he had them to send, there was no means of sending them owing to the communications being cut.'[12]

Sir Michael had been thinking about mutiny for so long, he already had contingencies drawn up, even before the first shot was fired at the Bagh. Acutely aware that the massacre might unleash a tsunami of rage, he decided to act pre-emptively. Men on the ground were one thing, but Sir Michael had already made plans for the sky:

> General Beynon and I had discussed with Captain Minchin, the Officer Commanding the Air Force, the conditions under which aeroplanes might drop bombs or use their machine guns. The suggestion I then made, was that as a rule, no bombs should be dropped in cities or towns, and machine guns might be used in the circumstances in which troops on the ground would fire.[13]

On the afternoon of 14 April, British planes took off for Gujranwala, a highly populous civilian centre. Sir Michael would later paint a sanitised picture of their mission in his memoirs:

> The military authorities at once dispatched a few aeroplanes which arrived in the nick of time – about 3 p.m. – to save the Treasury building (in which the few European women and children had taken refuge) and the jail, which the rebels – having destroyed all other public buildings – were threatening. The aeroplanes speedily dispersed the rebellious mobs by bomb and machine gunfire – causing some dozen death casualties, and restored the situation pending the arrival of troops from the North late that night.[14]

The truth was far more chilling, and just as in Jallianwala Bagh, innocent men, women and children were killed in cold blood. In one incident, 150 peasants, making their way home after a long day in the fields, suddenly felt the shadow of a plane flying low over their heads. One of the planes despatched by Sir Michael made a pass and then wheeled back. Without warning, the pilot opened fire with machine guns. The screaming of the civilians was drowned out by the engines of the plane. Those who could ran for their lives, the others fell onto the road where bullets strafed them in the back. One woman, a child and two men were cut to pieces by automatic fire there on the dirt road. Bullets ricocheted off the ground around them, kicking up dust like raindrops in the monsoon.

The lucky ones fled into their village, but to their horror found themselves pursued by Major Carberry in his First World War BEX bi-plane. He turned his machine guns on them again, shooting many in the back. Even the ones who managed to reach their homes found no sanctuary. Carberry continued to fire through their roofs and walls, with no idea who was inside.

As far as Carberry was concerned, all the people of Gujranwala and the surrounding area were rebels or rebel sympathisers. To him, anyone on the road that day was fair game. Like Dyer before him, he was intent on teaching Punjab a lesson. As well as machine-gunning civilians that day, he also dropped eight 20-pound bombs on and around Gujranwala.

When later challenged about his actions, Major Carberry was entirely unrepentant:

Q: Those bombs you dropped on particular crowds that you saw there?

A: Yes.

Q: Where were the crowds, in the streets or outside the village?

A: They were on the road outside the village.

Q: That crowd consisted of how many people?

A: I reported 150, I cannot tell you exactly.

Q: How many miles was this village from Gujranwala.

A: About two miles north-west of Gujranwala.

Q: What was this crowd doing?

A: They were going towards Gujranwala.

Q: How were you able to ascertain they were coming to Gujranwala?

A: They were walking in the direction of Gujranwala.

Q: And you dropped three bombs on them?

A: Yes.

Q: And you say in your report that you fired a machine gun into the village itself?

A: Yes.

Q: That firing was not at any particular crowd?

A: It was the people on whom I dropped the bombs and who ran back to the village.

The lines between war and peacetime, civilian and combatant, were entirely blurred in 1919. In Delhi, the senior commanding officer, Brigadier-General D. H. Drake Brockman, a man who would also give an order to fire indiscriminately on crowds in his city that same year, gave voice to the new morality. Indian men, women and children were lesser humans. Collective punishment had become the unofficial doctrine of the men giving the orders:

> Composed as the crowd was of the scum of Delhi city, I am of firm opinion that if they had got a bit more firing given them it would have done them a world of good and their attitude would be much more amenable and respectful, as force is the only thing that an Asiatic has any respect for.[15]

Two full days after Jallianwala Bagh, on 15 April, Sir Michael O'Dwyer finally declared martial law and officially handed over control to the army. Everything that had happened up to date – the deportation of Gandhi, the arrests of Satyapal and Kitchlew, the massacre, the use of war planes against civilians – had all taken place on his watch. Though Sir Michael would argue that he did not know about the worst of the military excesses that followed the massacre, it later emerged that, even before he formally handed power to the army, Sir Michael gave the order to build gallows in public spaces. As far as he was concerned, Indians needed to see how they would be dealt with if they challenged the *sirkar*, the government. The terror that continued after 15 April may not have been under his supervision, but he had laid the foundation for its architecture.

It would take the secretary of state himself to intervene and veto the idea of public executions. Edwin Samuel Montagu was becoming convinced his lieutenant governor had lost all sense of proportion.

One of the most dogged critics of Sir Michael O'Dwyer and his soldiers was a British journalist named Benjamin Guy Horniman, editor of the *Bombay Chronicle*. Born in Sussex and educated at a military academy, young Horniman had no interest in joining the army and chose instead to work for newspapers. For twelve years he worked for a variety of titles before he decided to venture east towards India.

Horniman joined the *Bombay Chronicle*, a newspaper founded and owned by an Indian, and worked his way up to the editor's job.[16] The imposition of martial law after the massacre imposed a news blackout, and even though he was hundreds of miles away in Bombay, Horniman was one of the only men with the courage to defy it.

Using C. F. Andrews, the clergyman confidante of Gandhi, who travelled to Punjab to see with his own eyes what had taken place, Horniman collected testimony and photographs of the wounded. British newspapers were busy congratulating Sir Michael and his brigadier general when Horniman unleashed his tirade against the Raj. The barbarity of what had been done in its name turned his stomach. So did the way his countrymen were effectively whitewashing the story.

Benjamin Horniman was arrested for his efforts and deported back to England. One of his reporters, an Indian, was sentenced to three years' hard labour for sedition. Horniman's newspaper was shut down. However, even in exile in London, Horniman continued to savage Sir Michael and his men:

The public are asked to believe that this promiscuous dropping of bombs or the firing of altogether 255 rounds of a machine gun, apparently at close quarters, into crowds of people, resulted in the killing of nine and wounding of only about sixteen people! Can anyone who remembers the work of the German aeroplanes in England during the war, doubt that the popular assertion of many more casualties is well founded?[17]

Horniman was particularly scathing about Carberry, the pilot who had strafed villagers from the sky:

Major Carberry, RAF, was the gentleman who bombed a party of people, because he thought they were rioters going or coming from the city. These wretched people fled after the bombs were dropped and he then pursued them to a village with a machine gun. He 'could not say if any casualties were caused by the machine gun firing'. Major Carberry's account in this evidence of the bombing and machine-gunning in the city differs even from the Official Report ... He was at a height of feet 200 and could see perfectly what he was doing.[18]

Horniman reminded readers that, until recently, Punjabis had been fighting side by side with British Tommies in the trenches:

Let it be remembered that these operations were conducted not against a city or villages in a hostile territory of a country with which Great Britain was at war; they were not reprisals for similar acts against ourselves. They were inflicted on an unarmed civilian population of a province, whose loyalty and sterling assistance of the Empire in the war was Sir Michael O'Dwyer's constant boast, when it suited him to 'boost' his own achievements as a Lieutenant Governor.[19]

In England, Horniman's voice was drowned out by others in Fleet Street. They, like Sir Michael, 'approved of the action'.

The brutality in Punjab continued for weeks. Two men, Lieutenant Colonel H. McRae and Captain A. C. Doveton, showed particular enthusiasm. Despatched to Kasur, 45 miles south-west of Amritsar, they assembled the city's schoolboys, pulled six out at random, and had them whipped in front of their classmates. The boys had committed no offence. The youngest was just thirteen years of age.[20]

Soldiers raided homes and dragged out hundreds of people who found themselves arrested without being told what they were accused of, or what evidence was held against them. One elderly and well-respected lawyer was detained for forty-six days in Lahore's notorious Central Jail. He was released without ever being told what he was supposed to have done.

Captain Doveton, who 'did not like to go through the formalities of trial and sentence',[21] invented special punishments for Punjabis in his jurisdiction. Those who failed to *salaam* a white man or woman with sufficient humility were forced to prostrate themselves on the ground, with their foreheads and lips pressed to the dirt.[22]

Others, no matter what their age or infirmity, were required to perform acts of pointless hard labour. Many were sent to the railway station and forced to lift heavy bales, carrying them from one end of the yard to the other for no particular gain. Those who were not up to the task were forced to skip on the spot, without break, or to 'mark time'[23] by climbing up and down ladders. Educated prisoners were forced to write poems in praise of martial law and their British masters. All these 'fancy punishments', as they were called, were designed to debase and humiliate the Indian population.

In Amritsar, Rex Dyer and his men remained busy. They erected large wooden triangles around the city – 'flogging triangles', which struck fear into the heart of the civilian population. Though only six people were flogged in public (twenty others were whipped *in camera*), the incidents were so horrifying that entire neighbourhoods were left traumatised.

Wrists tied to the apex, legs splayed and fastened to the base, the six young men suspected of taking part in the brutal attack on Miss Sherwood were given summary punishments of thirty lashes. According to one resident of Kucha Kaurianwala, some were no more than boys. With her house right opposite one of the triangles, Ishwar Kaur had no escape from the sound of their screaming:

> Sometimes, I stood up to see the flogging; sometimes I sat down, not being able to bear the sight. The first Sikh boy was whipped with his clothes on, and then his clothes were taken off, and he was flogged naked. Then all the boys were whipped naked. The third boy became senseless three times. Each time, he was unbound, laid flat in the street, and water was poured down his throat. [The flogging resumed when the boy regained consciousness.] It was cruel – cruel![24]

Some of the flogged boys were later released without charge.

Public whippings were the 'kindest method of punishment',[25] the only language Indians really understood, according to Lieutenant-Colonel Frank Johnson in Lahore: '. . . mere imprisonment and mere fines do not act, they do not deter the people.'[26] 'I would sooner have been deprived of the services of 1,000 rifles than the power of inflicting corporal punishment.'[27]

Dyer was also enthusiastic about public floggings, but not because it was kind, as his colleague Johnson argued, but rather because it was a fate worse than death. Those accused of attacking Miss Sherwood deserved nothing less: 'Shooting was, in my opinion, far too mild a punishment and it was for me to show that women must be looked upon as sacred.'[28]

Dyer, who had visited Miss Sherwood in hospital, ordered the street where she had been attacked to be blocked with picquets at either end. Anyone wishing to traverse the street had to do so crawling on all fours. People whose only crime was that they lived in the street found themselves brutalised and humiliated every time they tried to get home.

British soldiers followed his order and augmented it, kicking as the Indians crawled or crushing them into the dirt with their heavy boots. At the point of bayonets they were ordered to crawl on their bellies through the dirt. Some of the soldiers manning the lane enjoyed the experience so much they took photographs of themselves with the prostrate natives making their way along the lane: Lala Megha Mal, a 46-year-old cloth merchant from Kucha Kurichhan, described the effect the crawling order had on the innocent and vulnerable:

On the very first day, soldiers were posted in Kucha Kurichhan. I was stopped by the soldiers, when I was returning home at about 5 p.m., and I was ordered to creep on my belly. I however ran away and kept away till the soldiers had left. That day, I came home at 9 p.m. and found my wife laid up with fever. There was no water in the house to be given to her, and no doctor and no medicine. I had to fetch water myself late in the night. The seven days following, my wife had to be without any treatment, as no doctor would like to creep on his belly.[29]

Lala Gonda Mal, a 66-year-old goldsmith, also lived nearby:

I had with me my four sons, Jaggan Nath, aged about 13 years, Mohan Lal, aged 10, Nand Lal, aged 15, and Nath, aged 23. They ordered us to crawl on our bellies. We sat down but were made to crawl on our bellies. We reached home crawling. They walked with us and struck the butt-ends of their rifles on the ground in order to frighten us . . . This continued for eight days. During that period, no sweeper ever came to clean any house; nor was filth and refuse removed. The water man did not come. Late at night, we used to bring water ourselves. Women and children remained confined in the houses with the doors closed.[30]

Dyer never seemed to understand the fuss his so-called 'Crawling Order' would create. Nor did any of his superiors draw a parallel between that abject humiliation of Indians and the 'Devil's Wind' that had swept the country after the mutiny of 1857. Back then, those who lived in Cawnpore in the area of the Bibighar massacre had been dragged to the site of the bloodbath and ordered to lick the walls and floor clean of gore. They may have had nothing to do with the slaughter, but the British soldiers decided that since they had done nothing to stop it, they deserved punishment. The Raj had once again failed to discriminate between combatants and innocent civilians. It had been blind to the distinction between adults and children, too.

In Lahore, schoolchildren were ordered to parade three times a day for thirty minutes at a time, saluting the British flag as they marched. The order applied to infant classes, too, thus children as young as five marched. In some cases, children were made to repeat the mantra: 'I have committed no offence. I will not commit any offence. I repent, I repent, I repent.'[31] Punjab was in the grip of madness, and everyone, from the very young to the very old, was afraid. They prayed for justice but expected none.

CHAPTER 11

TRAUMAS AND TRUTHS

Amritsar seemed to contract after the massacre, seized by a convulsion of anger and fear. Local politicians were either arrested or went into hiding. The civilian population, rudderless without them, shied away from the streets. The soldiers had their city now and their uniforms represented subjugation, humiliation and summary execution. Many, who just days before had been happy to march in Gandhi's non-violent parades, now vowed to take up arms against the Raj. Ramji Dass Sunami, one of Udham's friends from his father's hometown, described seeing him driven mad with grief and rage shortly after the declaration of martial law: '[He] went to the Golden Temple and immersed himself in the holy pool of nectar [the expanse of water surrounding the Temple] and took a solemn oath to avenge it with the blood of O'Dwyer.'[1]

Another of his friends, Manjit Singh Kassid, was worried that the young man's untrammelled rage would devour him. Udham was talking of vengeance and murder without caring about the consequences.[2] In the days after the massacre, talk alone could have landed him and maybe those who listened to him in jail.

As for Brigadier General Dyer, Udham could barely bring himself to say his name: 'He was deeply moved whenever he talked of the incidents of 13 April 1919. When he talked of General Dyer and his action, his eyes became bloodshot with rage.'[3]

Udham was desperate to act, to spill British blood, but he did not know where to begin. He lurked around the bookshops of Hall bazaar, places where boys had once collected seditious pamphlets and distributed them around the province, hoping to be gathered up by some militant group. Nobody came for him. What made things worse was that Punjabis around him seemed to be conflating the identities of Dyer and O'Dwyer, merging them into one '*rakshas*' or demon. '*Brigadier O'Dwyer*' became a composite villain,[4] as omnipotent and terrifying as the devils in ancient scripture. If his fellow Indians did not recognise their enemies, how would any of them be able to punish them?

Udham Singh was not the only one who would see an atrocity that needed to be avenged. Jallianwala Bagh, after the lifting of martial law on 11 June 1919, became a place of pilgrimage. One of those said to have made the journey was a twelve-year-old boy from Lahore named Bhagat Singh. According to his biographers, young Bhagat travelled the 30 miles between the cities unaccompanied, determined to see for himself what the British had done. Though it may seem implausible that such a young boy could make the journey alone, but Bhagat Singh was no ordinary boy.

His father had been in jail the day he was born on 27 September 1907, serving a sentence along with two of Bhagat's uncles, convicted of organising a peasant revolt against the Land Colonisation Bill.

A much-detested piece of legislation, it forced the transfer of property to the government if a farmer died without a son and heir. The bill gave the British the right to sell this confiscated land to developers, *zamindars*, who were rich, indigenous landowners loyal to the Raj.

Leading the farmers, Bhagat's family pushed back, and as a result found themselves in and out of prison throughout his formative years. Bhagat grew up hating the British occupation of his country as much as the absence of the men he loved. If he did indeed make the apocryphal pilgrimage to the Bagh, the bullet holes in the walls gave the twelve-year-old hundreds more reason to fight them.

Bhagat Singh would grow to become one of India's most wanted men and the most important influence in Udham Singh's life. However, in 1919, when Udham was desperately looking for a mentor, their paths never crossed. Even if they had, what would an angry twelve-year-old boy have been able to do for a chaotic Kamboj orphan?

Within months of the massacre, Udham Singh was out of money, having run through what was left of his army pay. Revenge would have to wait; he needed to eat. Udham desperately needed to find a job – not an easy task in post-war India. The war led to a dramatic increase in defence expenditure, which in turn led to increased tax demands from the masses in British India. Though the economy stagnated, trains still managed to run, and where there were railways, there was work.

The British hired senior staff from their own kind, drivers and engineers from the bi-racial 'Anglo-Indian' community and manual labour from indigenous Indians. Jobs for natives were usually to be found in the ditches or cuttings by the side of the tracks, but some skilled workers found work in the repair sheds – long hours for low pay.

Udham Singh had carpentry skills from his time at the orphanage and a knowledge of engine repairs from his time in the army, but even with these he seemed unable to find work in Amritsar. He was forced to try his luck further afield.

Lahore Junction, John Lawrence's legacy to his compatriots, was still one of the busiest railway stations in all of Asia. It was here that Udham Singh finally found some employment late in 1919, but it was barely enough to keep him from destitution. Things got so bad that, by his own admission, he was forced to sleep by the water tanks outside the station, waking to find casual jobs by day.[5] Such a hand-to-mouth existence would have been depressing and debilitating for any man in the prime of his life. For a man who now felt he had a higher purpose, it must have been unbearable.

Casting his net wider still, Udham moved from city to city, lurching from crisis to crisis, taking jobs that lasted no more than a few weeks at a time.[6] By the end of 1919, found himself back in Lahore, but by that time his enemy, Sir Michael O'Dwyer, was gone, retired and back in England, where he had received a hero's welcome.

Sir Michael was always meant to move on from Punjab in April 1919,[7] and some historians have speculated whether he meant to leave his province in the hands of the army at the end of his tenure. Nigel Collett, in his excellent book on Dyer, *The Butcher of Amritsar*, points out that Sir Michael engaged in a 'bitter and unsuccessful fight' to wrest control of Punjab's administration before he had to leave: 'Inconceivable as it may seem, it really does appear that he thought he could bring down martial law on his province, yet still remain in charge. The viceroy, compliant in all else, would not yield on this.'[8]

The new lieutenant governor of Punjab was Sir Edward Douglas MacLagan, more academic than autocrat. MacLagan had written extensively on the history and people of India, and his work on the census of Punjab, in 1891, betrayed something close to affection for the natives. Punjab's pain seemed to lessen with the new appointment, but Udham's life got no easier. By February 1920 he had sunk to new lows, sleeping rough near the railway station again,[9] relying almost entirely on the charity of a local gurdwara for his meals.[10]

Every Sikh gurdwara has a *langar* (dining hall), where people from every background are welcome to come and sit together as equals, eating meals prepared by volunteers. It is more than likely that while sitting cross-legged on the floor of the *langar* Udham first heard of jobs in Africa. Contract work overseas paid considerably better than the piecemeal labouring work he was getting in Punjab. Companies provided billets for workers, and allowances for food. Some even paid for passage, offset against future earnings.

A man named Andrews ran the office on Lahore's Mall Road and, after asking him a few questions, signed Udham up. He was told to expect 240 rupees per month, if, and only if, he committed to an employment period of no less than three years.[11] His new employer was the British-owned Ugandan Railway Company.[12] With few other options, Udham headed for east Africa.

During the 'Scramble for Africa', a period of rapid imperial expansion between 1881 and 1914, colonial powers carved up the continent. Britain, Belgium, Italy, Portugal, France, Spain and Germany vied with each other for land and resources. By the outbreak of the First World War, European powers controlled 90 per cent of all African territory, with the British taking the lion's share. Imperial domination was due, in large part, to the railways.

India had proved that trains could move great volumes of goods to and from ports, and men and guns to restive regions. In Africa, with such daunting expanses to exploit and control, building the Uganda Railway became a priority for the British Empire.

The Uganda Railway stretched 600 miles from Mombasa (in present-day Kenya), a coastal town in the south, to Kisumu on the eastern shore of Lake Victoria. It was built in just five years – an astonishingly short space of time for such a mammoth undertaking. Fully operational by 1901, the pace of construction came at huge human cost. Almost 2,500 men, predominantly Indians, died while working on the serpentine track.[13]

Demand for Indian labourers increased dramatically thanks to railway expansion, and imported Indian workers, *coolies* to their European masters, were shipped over to Africa in their thousands. The word *coolie* comes from the Hindi for 'one who carries heavy burdens'. Over time it would become a racial pejorative for anybody from the Indian subcontinent, regardless of their employment.

Drawn predominantly from the poorest in Tamil Nadu, 'coolie' workers were given lump-sum loans in exchange for signed contracts committing them to work off the debt. Wages were often so paltry that many lived on the point of starvation. Workers were made dependent on their employers, and since quitting a job would have meant overnight starvation, few could afford to object to conditions or to leave.

Reducing thousands to the status of indentured labour, the

treatment of these Indian workers was often so bad that Christian missionaries compared their employers to slave-drivers. Beaten, starved, kept on subsistence wages, Indian workers were regularly humiliated and abused. Most who signed up to work on the Uganda Railway did so because they had been promised a better life. Just like Udham's time in the army, it must have felt like a brutal betrayal.

Africans called the meandering Uganda Railway the 'iron snake', a reference to an old Kikuyu prophecy: 'An iron snake will cross from the lake of salt to the lands of the Great Lake.'[14] To everyone else it was simply the 'Lunatic Line', presumably because you had to be mad to work on it. Thousands of labourers were carried off by disease; others were attacked by wild animals. The treacherous, remote terrain had little or no medical provision, so in the crowded labour camps malaria and black fever could rampage unchecked for weeks on end.

For a while, Udham worked the line, dutifully sending back wages to his distant relative in Sunam, Subedar Jiwa Singh.[15] Jiwa was respected and trusted by all who knew him. Friends and neighbours often left important documents or money in his care, knowing every penny and page would be returned. Jiwa was a man of honour. Udham's money could be stored in no safer place.

Then, after a few months, without warning, the letters and wages sent back to Jiwa Singh dried up. With a full two years left to serve on his contract, Udham Singh disappeared. Running away mid-contract was a serious act, with potentially grave consequences. Since many of the 'coolies' lived on advances from the Ugandan Railway Company, desertion was treated like theft. Unless workers could quickly pay what they owed, they could find themselves on the run from the law.

Some ditched contracts because they could no longer bear the conditions. Others did so because they were homesick. In Udham's case, it would seem that, while he was working on the Uganda Railway, thousands of miles from home, he finally found what he had been looking for in Punjab. He had somehow stumbled on a group of militant Indian revolutionaries, willing and able to begin the next stage of his transformation.

Sir Michael had all but crushed the Ghadars in Punjab after the war, but, Hydra-like, the organisation had been sprouting heads in the most unlikely places. A man named Sitaram Acharya led the Ghadars in East Africa at the time Udham was working on the line. He was considered so dangerous by the British that three of his cohort had already been shot, two hanged, and eight imprisoned for long and rigorous terms.[16] Mere possession of correspondence from Acharya could lead to a death sentence.[17]

Udham was far too lowly to have been introduced to the likes of Acharya himself, but he appears to have inveigled his way into some mid-level Ghadar cadre while in East Africa. It was probably their idea for him to get himself another passport, one which would not make any mention of his aborted Ugandan employment. With a clean passport he could apply for endorsements to get to America, where he might receive the training and contacts he so desperately sought. The new passport Udham got was in his birth name, Sher Singh.[18] Somehow, perhaps with help from his new friends, he also got an endorsement in Uganda for a visit to the United States.[19] He had never been allowed to do more than give out handbills in India, but the East African Ghadars appeared to see greater potential in him. When they sent him back to India, they endowed him with a new confidence, travel documents, and much more than a bundle of seditious handbills.

SUNAM, AUTUMN 1921

Udham was back in Sunam and acting like some kind of conquering hero. He roared into town on a motorbike nobody could quite believe he could afford.[20] It was not the demeanour one might expect from a contract-breaker. Absconders from East African labour agreements usually kept a low profile, a mixture of shame and fear pushing their heads below the parapet. Yet Udham swaggered back into Jiwa Singh's home as if he had nothing to be embarrassed about. His wages had stopped coming back to Sunam some time before, nevertheless he was apparently flush with cash. Not only did he have an inexplicable fund of money, on the back of his bike was tied a German gramophone,[21] yet another luxury he should not have been able to afford. It was a magnet to Sunam's children.

Though Udham had the means to play music, he possessed only one record. Years later, people still remembered the crackling sound of his 'Vande Mataram' playing over and over and over again. The song, translated into English as 'Praise to the Mother',[22] had been set to music by Nobel Prize-winner Rabindranath Tagore. It was the unofficial anthem for India's nationalist movement.

The British had tried to ban the song as soon as it was released. Not only was it a crime to press the disc, even playing it, or singing 'Vande Mataram' in public,[23] became an offence. An impossible law to enforce, the ban only succeeded in making the song more popular. The closing lines of its first verse showed why the British wanted to stop its spread:

> Mother, I praise thee!
> Rich with thy hurrying streams,
> bright with orchard gleams,
> Cool with thy winds of delight,
> Dark fields waving Mother of might,
> Mother free . . .

Where Udham had once talked only of Jallianwala Bagh and revenge, he now spoke animatedly of revolution. To some he sounded like a dangerous madman. Jiwa Singh was more patient than most and gave Udham a roof over his head, though the old *subedar* never really knew when his young guest might be under it; the boy disappeared for days on end, telling nobody where he was going, what he was doing, or when he would return.

Years later, police would piece together an imperfect picture of these mysterious absences. Speeding off on his bike, it appeared that not only was Udham taking bundles of banned leaflets into the villages, continuing in his attempts to seed a rural revolution, but he also was acting as a money mule for the Ghadars.

There were rumours in Sunam that Udham was procuring and smuggling guns,[24] but those who knew him best found such talk preposterous. All Udham's money was locked in Jiwa's *almari*,* some 1,300 rupees.[25] The boy was a big-talker with a bike, that was all. Why would the Ghadars bother with someone like him? It was ridiculous. He was a nobody. A poor, orphan nobody.

Between mysterious sorties, Udham liked to hold court among the teenagers of the town, telling them they were in the presence of a man destined for much bigger things. He spoke of having friends in America. He would tell them a war was coming that would bring the king of England to his knees. To the most impressionable, Udham seem impossibly, dangerously charismatic. The more they admired him, the more he talked up his part.

Though the young might have lapped up his talk, the elders of Sunam just shook their heads at his *haakna*.† The boy was a demonstrable failure, unable to hold down even the most basic jobs in army or civilian life. Wild, full of unwarranted self-importance – Udham was trouble.

Then one day, out of the blue, Udham Singh asked Jiwa Singh to hand over half his savings.[26] He sold his much-loved motorbike, something that must have hurt him deeply, and left.

When next he would appear in Sunam, nobody accused him of being a fantasist. The scars on his back would be enough to silence them.

---

* A locked wardrobe, which in many homes doubled as a safe.
† A Punjabi word for 'puffed up chatter'.

CHAPTER 12

THE UNTOUCHABLES

Sir Michael's reintroduction to London life at the end of 1919 had been nothing short of spectacular. Newspaper editors clamoured for his thoughts, and he was welcomed as a guest at some of the most important tables in the capital. It was as if the Jallianwala Bagh massacre had not touched him at all.

He became a regular on the British lecture circuit, defending his decisions as lieutenant governor and warning packed houses that the Raj was in dire peril. Engaging, commanding and funny, too, audiences devoured his performances, while he, in turn, lapped up their adulation. Thanks to this new-found popularity, Sir Michael had numerous opportunities to berate the secretary of state for India in public. He had never rated Sir Edwin Samuel Montagu, but since his return to England, antipathy had developed into ferocious loathing.

Deeply unhappy about the massacre and subsequent martial law, Montagu found himself battered by Gandhi while simultaneously being bludgeoned by fellow British MPs. The former wanted justice for the dead and wounded; the latter for him to stay loyal to his men. Though it would end up satisfying neither side, Montagu called for an official inquiry.

The Disorders Inquiry Committee, which held its first session in October 1919, was headed up by Lord William Hunter, a former solicitor-general for Scotland. Under him, four British members and three Indians were charged with producing an accurate report on both the massacre and its aftermath. Together, the Hunter Committee, as it became known, would spend forty-six weeks interrogating witnesses and gathering evidence from as far afield as Ahmedabad, Bombay, Delhi and Lahore.

Before the panel even called its first witness, there were objections to its impartiality. Some questioned the suitability of Hunter himself. The man had no Indian experience, knew not a single word of Hindi, and was described by one of his fellow inquiry members as 'a mild man somewhat dazzled by his entry on a new stage'.[1] Others found fault with the inquisitors. Pandit Jagat Narayan, a lawyer and member of the legislative council; Sardar Sahibzada Sultan Ahmad Khan, a lawyer from Gwalior State; and Sir Chimanlal Harilal Setalvad, an advocate and vice chancellor of Bombay University had been selected, but other, arguably more prominent, Indian jurists had been overlooked.

What caused deeper fury still was that the Indians on the panel were outnumbered by whites. If, as would ultimately come to pass, the committee was divided in opinion on racial lines, the British would have the power to overrule the Indian voices. Ever the lawyer, Gandhi railed against the injustice in the very fabric of the process.

Scepticism notwithstanding, the Hunter Commission was given unprecedented access to witnesses and far-reaching powers of inquiry. However, it was not constituted as a court of law, so members of the panel had no power to compel witnesses to appear or answer their questions. Cross-examination would not take place under oath, therefore any who gave false evidence would never be punished for perjury. Gandhi was so affronted by these shortcomings that he set up an unofficial parallel Congress-led inquiry, which would also gather evidence and interrogate witnesses. If Hunter failed in its duty, he would not fail in his. One way or another, the Raj would have to face what it had done.

Sir Michael hated the Hunter Commission as much as Gandhi,

but for very different reasons. Its mere existence was an affront. The thought of 'clever native lawyers' examining white men in uniform was an abomination to him and his friends.

Of all the Indians on the panel, Sir Chimanlal Setalvad was the most skilful interrogator, and quickly became the main hate figure for those brought before him. Some British officers treated the soft-spoken lawyer with sullen evasion, others with naked aggression. Setalvad pressed on regardless and, despite the relative impotence of his position, the admissions he extracted would prove seismic, particularly where Brigadier General Dyer was concerned.

Dyer's supporters watched in despair as the brigadier general self-immolated. During a full day of questioning, Dyer was asked why he had not issued an order for the Jallianwala Bagh crowds to disperse before opening fire:

> At that time it did not occur to me. I merely felt that my orders had not been obeyed, that martial law was flouted, and that it was my duty to immediately disperse it by rifle fire ... If my orders were not obeyed, I would fire immediately. If I had fired a little, the effect would not be sufficient. If I had fired a little, I should be wrong in firing at all.[2]

Setalvad pursued him on the matter of intent. If the entrance to the garden had been wider, would he really have driven his gun-mounted cars in? Would he have used the machine guns on the crowd? Dyer answered without flinching:

> DYER: I think probably yes.
> SETALVAD: In that case the casualties would have been much higher?
> DYER: Yes.

Setalvad put it to Dyer that innocent men women and children were in the garden. Dyer disagreed. In his view, all those gathered were rebels: 'Therefore, I considered it my duty to fire on them and to fire well.' Setalvad pressed him to elaborate:

DYER: They had come out to fight if they defied me, and I was going to give them a lesson.

SETALVAD: I take it that your idea in taking that action was to strike terror?

DYER: Call it what you like. I was going to punish them. My idea from the military point of view was to make a wide impression.

SETALVAD: To strike terror not only in the city of Amritsar, but throughout the Punjab?

DYER: Yes, throughout the Punjab. I wanted to reduce their moral, the moral [sic] of the rebels.[3]

Quietly pursued by the dogged line of questioning, Dyer made one incendiary comment after another. Why had he fired for so long? 'I thought I would be doing a jolly lot of good and they would realise that they were not to be wicked.'[4]

In Westminster, a Cabinet committee received regular updates from both the Hunter Commission and Gandhi's unofficial parallel inquiry. Attempting to limit the damage Dyer was doing to himself and by extension everybody else who had been in Punjab at that time, Sir Michael asked Montagu to let him address Cabinet directly and in private.

Montagu turned him down flat. When Sir Michael tried to go over Montagu's head, the prime minister also told him to go away. It was a bitter blow:

Had I been like Michael Collins, a successful organiser of rebellion against the British Government, the doors of Downing Street would have flown open before me, but as I had merely come to plead for men who had suffered for assisting me in crushing a rebellion against the British Government, Downing Street was a closed door to me![5]

On 26 May 1920, the Hunter Commission was ready to report, though predictably it failed to do so with one voice. The panel could not agree whether Sir Michael had been justified in assuming Punjab was on the threshold of full-scale rebellion. The British thought he may well have had grounds. The Indians did not. Members also tussled over the army's behaviour during martial law, with the question of proportionality dividing them again.

On one issue, they were broadly in agreement: Reginald Dyer had overstepped the bounds of his authority; he had failed to give the people in the Bagh the chance to disperse; he had shown grave error of judgement allowing his men to fire for as long as they did. He fired on the crowd to produce a 'moral effect', and that motivation was deemed deplorable.

Even though they had broadly reached agreement on Dyer, the Indians on the panel refused to put their name to the final report and denounced it for, among other things, failing to adequately address Sir Michael's role in the affair. Issuing a separate minority report, the Indians wanted to make it known that, as lieutenant governor, he had been utterly wrong to assume that Punjab was on the brink of revolt. His actions, and overreactions, had precipitated the massacre and everything that followed.

As for Dyer, the minority report went much further than Hunter. His drum proclamation had been woefully insufficient. Those within the Bagh had shown no violent intent. They had been shown no mercy. Dyer had shot innocent men, women and children blindly and without discrimination. He had failed to offer any medical assistance to those he had left wounded. In effect, he had left innocent people to die.

If Montagu had hoped to calm the waters with this inquiry, he failed miserably. In India, they were already calling Dyer 'The Butcher of Amritsar'.

On 23 March 1920, three days before the final and contested Hunter Commission report was made public, Dyer was forced to resign from the army. He had been recommended for a CBE for his service in the Third Afghan War, however that recommendation was now withdrawn. It was a catastrophic blow. Dyer's career and his reputation were in tatters. India, the land of his birth, was now closed to him.

Dyer's censure, when it became public, caused a storm. British newspapers were inundated with letters protesting the former brigadier general's treatment. One correspondent to *The Times*, Constance Tuting, a resident of Punjab for over twenty years, wrote: 'Will England stoop to pander to their [Indians'] clamour and endanger her own people by condemning an honourable officer doing his duty?'[6]

The top brass of the Army Council agreed, though they had been asked by Winston Churchill to keep their furious opinions to themselves. Writing privately to a friend, the chief of the Imperial General Staff, Field Marshal Sir Henry Wilson, would express anger and exasperation. He regarded the politicians as effeminately craven:

> Winston made a long speech, prejudging the case and in effect saying that the Cabinet had decided to throw out Dyer, and that it was advisable for the Army Council to agree ... The Frocks have got India (as they have Ireland) into a filthy mess ... On that the soldiers are called in, and act. This is disapproved of by all the disloyal elements, and the soldier is thrown to the winds. All quite simple.[7]

Politicians sought to soothe their Indian colony as best they could by condemning the massacre and subsequent excesses of martial law, much to Sir Michael's disgust. One parliamentary proceeding proved particularly hurtful to him.

On 8 July 1920, a debate was slated: 'The Army Council and General Dyer'. Since he was to be the meat at the feast, Dyer wanted to hear what was said about him with his own ears. Sir Michael had insisted on going with him for moral support, sitting by his side in the public gallery, a show of solidarity to those speaking below. The pair sat stony-faced as their conduct was dissected in the chamber. Montagu was one of the first to wield a scalpel:

MR MONTAGU: Once you are entitled to have regard neither to the intentions nor to the conduct of a particular gathering, and to shoot and to go on shooting, with all the horrors that were here involved, in order to teach somebody else a lesson, you are embarking upon terrorism, to which there is no end. I say, further, that when you pass an order that all Indians, whoever they may be, must crawl past a particular place, when you pass an order to say that all Indians, whoever they may be, must forcibly or voluntarily salaam any officer of His Majesty the King, you are enforcing racial humiliation. I say, thirdly, that when you take selected schoolboys from a school, guilty or innocent, and whip them publicly, when you put up a triangle, where an outrage which we all deplore and which all India deplores has taken place, and whip people who have not been convicted, when you flog a wedding party, you are indulging in frightfulness, and there is no other adequate word which could describe it.

MR PALMER: It saved a mutiny.

MR MONTAGU: Somebody says that 'it saved a mutiny'.

CAPTAIN W. BENN: Do not answer him.

MR MONTAGU: The great objection to terrorism, the great objection to the rule of force, is that you pursue it without regard to the people who suffer from it, and that having once tried it you must go on. Every time an incident happens you are confronted with the increasing animosity of the people who suffer, and there is no end to it until the people in whose name we are governing India, the people of this country, and the national pride and sentiment of the Indian people rise together in protest and terminate your rule in India as being impossible on modern ideas of what an Empire means.[8]

Churchill, usually a stalwart defender of the empire and the army, joined the chorus of disapproval. He described the massacre as: 'An episode ... without precedent or parallel in the modern History of the British Empire ... an extraordinary event, a monstrous event, an event which stands in singular and sinister isolation.'[9]

Former British prime minister Herbert Henry Asquith was equally scathing: 'There has never been such an incident in the whole annals of Anglo-Indian history nor, I believe, in the history of our empire from its very inception down to the present day ... It is one of the worst outrages in the whole of our history.'[10]

To hear such words from a fellow Balliol boy, one he had openly admired in the past, cut Sir Michael to the quick. Benjamin Charles Spoor, a Labour MP, demanded an immediate repeal of all the former lieutenant governor's most draconian laws. He pushed for proper trials and sentences for those named and shamed in the Hunter report. To howls of derision from the packed Conservative benches, Spoor rounded on Sir Michael:

It was Sir Michael O'Dwyer who was primarily responsible for the use of aeroplanes at Gujranwala. In connection with that raid, I believe, bombs were actually dropped into the playground of a school. According to the Congress report, all disorder that had occurred in Gujranwala had actually ceased before the aeroplanes arrived and began their bombardment. I submit that Sir Michael O'Dwyer and those like him typify that kind of Anglo-Indian who is the greatest menace to the security of the empire and the greatest barrier to the progressive realisation of responsible government in India.[11]

The response was deafening, with members on both sides rising to their feet, waving fists and order papers, and roaring at each other. Few could remember such anger in the House or such a split in those for and against the men in the gallery. In his broad Irish brogue, the Unionist MP Sir Edward Carson looked up at Dyer and, holding eye contact, praised him as 'a gallant officer of thirty-four years' service ... without a blemish on his record.'[12]

Turning his gaze on Sir Edwin Montagu, Carson bellowed: 'I say, to break a man under the circumstances of this case is un-English. Un-English!' The words were designed to wound. Montagu was Jewish and had been accused many times of being 'foreign' and 'un-English' purely by virtue of his religion.

Anti-Semitic slurs, far less nuanced than Carson's, flew from the Conservative benches. As Sir William Sutherland, the parliamentary secretary to the prime minister, would later note: 'A strong anti-Jewish sentiment was shown by shouts and excitement among the normally placid Tories of the backbench category ... Altogether it was a very astonishing exhibition of anti-Jewish feeling.'[13] Montagu had heard it all before, but it was beginning to drive him to despair.

Montagu was only the third practising Jew to serve in Cabinet. In many of his colleagues' eyes, this defined him as of a lower caste. Unusually tall, Montagu's dapper dress sense and habitual wearing of a monocle made him stand out even before people judged him for the god he worshipped. Despite often blatant anti-Semitism, Montagu managed to hold a number of important posts under two prime ministers before becoming secretary of state for India in 1917. That the Jallianwala Bagh massacre happened on his watch was a terrible irony. Montagu had done more than any of his predecessors to give Indians a semblance of self-government. It was one of the earliest reasons Sir Michael had to hate him.

Montagu had personally travelled to India in 1919 to meet Lord Chelmsford, the viceroy of India, in order to persuade him of the benefits of 'dyarchy', or limited power-sharing with the native Indians. Although Chelmsford was initially sceptical, Montagu was relentless and got him to agree.

A year after Britain's Representation of the People Act granted the vote to all men over the age of twenty-one and property-owning women over the age of thirty, Montagu announced that Indians in the British Empire would also benefit from greater democracy. The Indian legislation went nowhere as far as the RPA, but it was at least a start. The law, enacted eight months after the massacre on 23 December 1919, granted what moderate nationalists had asked for over a number of decades. It gave Indians some say in their affairs:

> The policy of His Majesty's Government with which the Government of India are in complete accord, is that of increasing the association of Indians in every branch of the administration and the gradual development of self-governing institutions with a view to the progressive realisation of responsible government in India as an integral part of the British Empire.[14]

Just over five million of India's wealthiest citizens would get the right to vote, a tiny proportion of the population. Their ballots would have limited potency; they could elect officials for only a few branches of government. Indians would be able to hold office in the Raj ministries of education, health and public works. It fell far short of what the nationalists had wanted, but it was a start.

Sir Michael protested this limited enfranchisement vigorously, supported by a group of influential 'Die Hards'. They objected to any move that diluted British colonial power. Die Hard attacks on Montagu intensified and grew more personal and bigoted. They openly referred to the secretary of state as 'Monty-Jew',[15] and talked of him as if he were an alien traitor, working in the midst of government to dismantle the empire. The constant onslaught was driving him into a very dark place: 'I have isolated myself from my colleagues and such is the racial bitterness in India that nobody who tries can satisfy either Indian or European. The whole thing looks gloomy . . . I wonder when the sun will ever shine again?'[16]

Montagu was not the only one in the grip of depression.

Grey England, with its long, bone-chillingly damp winters, did not suit Rex Dyer. He missed the intense heat of the plains, galloping his horses, mucking in with his men with his shirtsleeves rolled up over sunburned elbows. Dyer was Indian born and bred, but he could never go 'home' again. The country of his forefathers did not fit him nearly as well as India did. His memories of Britain were almost entirely miserable.

As was the custom in wealthy colonial families, at the age of eleven, Dyer, along with his older brother Walter, had been sent to boarding school in Ireland. The Dyer boys, with their 'Indian ways', were a major curiosity at Middleton College in County Cork. The younger Dyer was particularly unhappy. He had a stammer, which on top of his Indian upbringing set him up as even more of an outsider. Dyer was bullied mercilessly.[17] It took years of hard work to rid himself of his speech impediment, but by the time he enrolled at the Royal Military Academy Sandhurst, he was free of it.[18] The military had been the making of him.

After Hunter, Dyer was a soldier no more. He did not know what he was. While Sir Michael seemed to thrive on the attention, Dyer hated talking about Jallianwala Bagh or anything to do with Punjab. The Die Hards did their best to support him, making stirring speeches about his bravery and nobility, crediting him with saving the Raj single-handedly. However, the mere mention of the incident was difficult for him to bear.

Dyer broke his silence just once, in January 1921, when he penned an article for the *Globe* newspaper headlined 'India's Path to Suicide'. In it, and without ever mentioning the incident with which he was most associated, Dyer gave the Die Hards something of what they craved:

India does not want self-government. She does not understand it ... Our politicians are forcing a growth in pretending to India that she is ready for home rule. It is cruel to pretend that she is now approaching the era of self-government. India will not be desirous or capable of self-government for generations, and when self-government does come, it will not be the leaders of revolt who will rule. The very names of most of the extremists smell in the nostrils of Indian manhood.[19]

Dyer reserved particular bile for Gandhi. No doubt the statements the Mahatma made about him fuelled his hatred. In the wake of the Hunter inquiry, Gandhi had said of Dyer:

> His brutality is unmistakable. His abject and unsoldier-like cowardice is apparent in every line of amazing defence ... Such a man is unworthy of being considered a soldier ... No doubt the shooting was 'frightful', and the loss of innocent life deplorable. But the slow torture, degradation and emasculation that followed was much worse, more calculated, malicious and soul killing.[20]

The accusation of 'cowardice' would have been unbearable. A younger version of himself might have punched back, however Hunter had entirely knocked the fight out of Rex Dyer.

Sir Michael tried his best to rebuild his brigadier general. Together with a British newspaper, the *Morning Post*, he appealed for funds for Dyer and his family. Within weeks the coffers swelled to more than £15,000, with another £3,000 raised in Calcutta. Letters of gratitude poured into the newspapers, including one purporting to be from 679 British women in India demanding the reinstatement of Dyer: 'As Englishwomen who know India, and the risk to the lives and honour of Englishwomen at time of rebellion ... We appeal to you to champion our cause, which is also that of all Europeans in India, with a view to getting it [Hunter's judgment against Dyer, and his subsequent dismissal from the army] revoked.'[21]

Money for Dyer kept rolling in, and by 6 December, when the *Post* finally drew a line under fundraising, an extraordinary £26,317. 1s. 10d. had been raised from all over the world. Dyer refused to collect the cheque in person. Smiling and posing for a photograph seemed beyond him, and a somewhat grumpy *Post* editor was forced to put the cheque in the post, along with a copy of the newspaper. The headline read simply: 'A Debt Acknowledged'.

The collection eased Dyer's concerns over the long-term security of his wife, Annie, and his sons, Ivon and Geoffrey, but it was scant recompense for the unrelenting bad news that seemed to plague him in England. Soon after his arrival, Dyer was diagnosed with arteriosclerosis, a disease of the arteries that greatly increases the threat of heart attack and stroke. The condition is degenerative, and it slowed Dyer down considerably. He was told by physicians to avoid stress and exercise.

Overnight, Dyer turned from feared and fearless warrior into an invalid. To keep his mind calm, Dyer's wife found and bought a small dairy farm for his convalescence, on the outskirts of Ashton Keynes in Wiltshire. Green and peaceful, the farm had a dual purpose. It was a place where the Dyers could shut out Jallianwala Bagh, and it would be an inheritance for his younger son Geoffrey. With Dyer's health deteriorating by the day, the couple were forced to think about what would happen after he was gone.

The eighteenth-century farmhouse gave Dyer exactly what he needed. High trees kept out prying eyes, and they were miles from the nearest village. Dyer even started to write his memoirs, not about India, but his time in East Persia. *Riders of the Sarhad* read like an adventure book for boys where he could cast himself as the hero. Publication called for a publicity tour and, in 1921, after two years in self-imposed purdah, Dyer was forced out into the world again.

He found his public appearances taxing, even though he was invariably greeted by standing ovations. Adoring audiences supported his action in Punjab and wanted him to know it. Such affirmation should have helped to build him up, but every so often something would happen to splinter the fragments of Dyer's already shattered spirit.

In April 1921, an Indian student by the name of Santidas Khushiram Kirpalani was having tea at the Oxford Union with an English friend. He was one of a handful of students granted entry that year to prepare for a role in the Indian Civil Service, a direct beneficiary of Montagu's recent reforms.

Unlike Har Dayal and Kitchlew, Kirpalani loved his time at

Balliol, made friends and fitted in well. He was a self-confessed Anglophile, yet any time Jallianwala Bagh came up, he found his affection sorely tested. That afternoon in Oxford, the massacre had come up in conversation again, and Kirpalani was so engrossed in his own anger that he did not notice a man to his side who seemed to be eavesdropping intently:

A gentleman of soldierly bearing approached and greeted us. He was about five foot eight in height, very fair, with blue eyes, a thick moustache and a medium build. He was reserved and soft-spoken. He asked what we thought of this Jallianwala Bagh affair. It was the burning topic of the day. I tore into the subject. Indian boys generally were boiling over with rage and thought the dismissal of General Dyer was not enough and that he should have been hanged for murder.[22] ... My British friend was also very critical. All of a sudden, this gentleman stood up. His face was sad. He said quietly and distinctly: 'I am that unfortunate man.' Suddenly, recognition dawned on us, for his picture had been in all the papers, except that, unlike in the pictures, he was in mufti. He moved away slowly. To this day, I carry that image in my heart.[23]

Dyer, so sure for so long that he had done his duty, heard himself being described as a monster, both by an Indian and one of his own. He became that same inconsolable boy who had once wept over a small, dying monkey.

In contrast, Sir Michael would justify his actions till his dying day and fight anyone who questioned him. He never lost any sleep over what he had done, nor expressed a single regret.

In November 1921, Reginald Dyer suffered a serious stroke that left him weak and partially paralysed. Annie decided to move her husband to an even quieter location, a small village called Long Ashton, near Bristol. The cottage was more secluded than the dairy farm and would be Dyer's home for the next six years. Save for visits from his family, Dyer stayed in almost total seclusion, venturing out only to tend the flowers in his walled garden. At fifty-seven years of age, with his thick thatch of hair now entirely grey, and without his Indian tan, he looked like a ghost of his former self.

CHAPTER 13

LONDON LIMBO

When Udham tried to get to England for the first time, he had no idea that one of his targets was dying of his own accord, but soon realised the other was rising even further out of his reach. Gandhi, for all his trying, had failed to get justice for Jallianwala Bagh, so Udham, in 1922, had taken it upon himself to hatch his own plan. It was not a very good plan, but after his return from Africa Udham seemed buoyed by a newly discovered belief in himself, one that would be eclipsed by his actual abilities.

The idea of getting to England presented itself during one of his motorbike sorties around Punjab. Udham had met a student from Patiala, a sixteen-year-old by the name of Pritam Singh,[1] and listened to his tale of sadness and frustration.[2] That Udham was even mixing with young Indian students is telling. The Ghadars were always trying to enlist the help of bright young men from colleges around Punjab. Udham, with his ample charm and persuasion, would have made an ideal recruiter.

Pritam was a shy-looking boy, with an angular face and wide, trusting eyes.[3] Clever and ambitious, despite the Montagu–Chelmsford reforms, he saw no future for himself in India. He wanted to study civil engineering in America and start a new life there. Pritam said he knew of a university that might even take him, based in a place called Michigan. However, when he applied for passage to America in Lahore, he had been blocked. The travel documents issued to him would only get him as far as England. From London he would have to fight on, applying for a special endorsement to travel to America, after which he would have to battle even harder to get the Americans to let him in. The United States had been tightening its immigration laws, and Pritam found he was in the middle of a bureaucratic nightmare. Udham saw opportunity in his new young friend's misery.

Though woefully unqualified himself, with no knowledge of English and no experience of the country, Udham offered to escort Pritam to London and help him sort out his problems. It was a ridiculous idea, of course. What help could a semi-literate, failed soldier and former labourer on the Uganda Railway offer? Nevertheless, Pritam, no more than a boy, seemed happy to go along with his plan. He desired companionship and Udham needed a convincing cover story if he was to travel to England unimpeded. Escorting a teenager was a plausible reason to travel to the country.

Udham still had his clean passport from Africa, issued in the name of Sher Singh. If his leafleting and cash drops had come to the attention of the authorities, they would be looking for a rebel called Udham Singh. Sher Singh was an entirely unknown quantity.

Passage as far as Marseilles cost 650 rupees,[4] almost exactly the sum Udham had taken from the *subedar*, so, with his documents and the remainder of his motorbike cash in his pocket, he bought his ticket. The fact that Udham was financing his own trip would suggest that he was travelling entirely on his own initiative. There was no support for him at that time, financial or logistical, from either the Ghadars or any other nationalist group. Though he regarded them as his family, they had yet to recognise him as a worthwhile son.

We do not know exactly when the pair set sail, but we can surmise from Pritam's own account that they must have left sometime in the second half of 1922.[5] They sailed on a ship with around forty other Indians, docked in Marseilles, stayed for two days and left for Paris by rail.[6]

After a mere forty-eight hours in Paris, the pair travelled to Calais and then set sail for Dover,[7] leaving almost immediately from Dover to London. Udham seemed in a mighty hurry to reach the capital, but when the pair finally arrived it did not feel like the triumph he had hoped for. He knew nobody, the city was large and confusing, and Udham had no idea where Dyer or Sir Michael lived. He was entirely wrongfooted by the enormity of his task and by London itself. To add to his troubles, he had a frightened young boy to take care of. Pritam, unlike Udham, was not built for this kind of life. When Udham looked at his charge, with his unruly hair plastered down in a severe side parting, perhaps the haunted and hungry expression of his former self looked back at him.

Indians had grown up hearing about the might and majesty of London, the seat of the empire. What Udham actually would have seen was a city gripped by anxiety and depression. The British Isles were still feeling the reverberations of Bloody Sunday, a catastrophic day of violence that had taken place in Dublin two years before. The day marked a decisive turning point in the military struggle between British forces and the IRA, and it also led to a spree of violence both in Ireland and on the mainland. At the centre of the drama was Michael Collins, an Irish republican.

Early on Bloody Sunday, teams of killers from Collins's 'squad' – a special assassination unit – visited over a dozen private addresses in the south of Dublin. By the time the capital had woken up, fourteen people were dead; eight of them were British agents, two were 'Auxiliaries' from the much-feared paramilitary wing of the Royal Irish Constabulary. The rest were either innocent bystanders or civilian informers. In just a few hours, British intelligence in Ireland had been crippled.

Later that day, members of the Royal Irish Constabulary marched into a Gaelic football ground in Dublin called Croke Park, where thousands of people had gathered to watch a match. Without warning, the troops opened fire and fourteen people, including one player, were shot dead.

Though the British government insisted their men were trying to flush out the IRA, parallels were drawn between the Irish experience and that of India. While Ireland buried its dead, the spectre of Jallianwala Bagh rose again. Reprisals followed, and in June 1922 the IRA caused outrage on the mainland when they gunned down Field Marshal Sir Henry Hughes Wilson, one of the most senior British army staff officers of the First World War, right on his London doorstep.

The fear such audacity caused was augmented by economic depression. Numbers of British unemployed were soaring in 1922 and the coalition government led by David Lloyd George attempted to curb wages to meet post-war bills. In response, the nation's coal miners called a strike. Such was the nation's reliance upon coal that a state of emergency was declared soon after. Udham arrived in a land of coal rationing, jobless men and fear of terrorism. Was this really the land that produced India's rulers?

It was Pritam who managed to find them a place to stay, basic accommodation in the heart of the city especially set aside for Indian students.[8] On the corner of Keppel Street and Gower Street, in the middle of a triangle of London colleges, the YMCA Indian Student Hostel was founded as a centre of Indo-British goodwill. It was supposed to be a place where bright young Indians and Britons could swap ideas and learn about each other, fostering ties of trust. What the founders would have made of an aspiring assassin sleeping under their roof is anyone's guess.

Though Pritam fitted right into the YMCA mix, Udham felt desperately out of place. With his poor education he stood out in the company of young men studying law and engineering in the nearby colleges. Spending just two nights under the Gower Street roof,[9] Udham left Pritam at the YMCA and sought something that fit him better. He found Britain's first Sikh gurdwara, which had opened its doors to men like him since 1913.[10]

The terraced house at 79 Sinclair Road looked like every other house on the street. Located just behind Shepherd's Bush Green, it was built of red brick, three stories high, and had a large bay window at the front. For a boy who had grown up in the shadow of the Golden Temple, the plain building looked as different as could be from the gilded Sikh gurdwaras he had known in India. Nevertheless, this non-descript-looking place became his lifeline in London.

Shepherd's Bush Gurdwara had been founded and funded by the maharajah of Patiala, Bhupinder Singh. A great ally of the British during the war, when some of his subjects raised the difficulty of finding places to pray while stationed on British soil, the maharajah took it upon himself to build somewhere for them. Such was the importance of Indian troops during the war, nobody raised an objection.

The gurdwara became a vital link between England and home, first for Indian soldiers and then for the very early Sikh immigrants. After ten gruelling weeks at sea, they would arrive from India, often with only the address of Sinclair Road scrawled on a piece of paper. The four-bedroom house became an emergency shelter for dozens of men.

Wherever they could find space, men would sleep on the floors, pray, and eat communal meals together. Though crowded and basic, Sinclair Road felt much more like home to Udham than Gower Street ever could, and he ended up staying there for months while Pritam repeatedly tried and failed to get his papers for America.

As time passed and the seasons changed, it became clear to Udham that he entirely lacked the skills needed to find Sir Michael or Dyer, let alone to get close enough to kill them. His English was terrible; he was running out of money; he had no gun and no bullets, and even if he had, his disastrous stint in the army barely gave him the confidence to use them. Not for the first time in his life, Udham felt like a powerless failure.

Over at the YMCA, Pritam was faring no better. He simply could not get the Americans to let him in, no matter how many times he banged on the consul's door. Since his arrival in London, Pritam had been corresponding with a Professor Henry Earle Riggs at the

University of Michigan* and had even been offered a place by him in the civil engineering department.[11] Not that this made any difference to the American authorities, who continued to bar his entry.

Riggs was as dismayed as Pritam at the intransigence of his government, and refused to give up hope of getting his Indian student to Michigan. At sixty-eight years of age, Riggs was a railwayman at heart who hadn't been born with a silver spoon in his mouth. Riggs had relied on his pickaxe to make his way, working on the Nebraskan railroads,[12] tough and icy terrain. He worked on railways, studied railways and, thanks to the railways, ploughed his way into academia. When Pritam first contacted him, Professor Riggs was one of America's foremost experts on industrial railroads.[13] Perhaps Riggs saw something of himself in the struggling Pritam Singh. Whatever their connection, Riggs was not giving up on him.

To the outside world, it looked as if Udham was as dedicated to Pritam's dream as Riggs was in America, though when he came up with his own plan for getting Pritam to Michigan, he was not being entirely altruistic. Over the long and frustrating months that he was not able to enact his revenge, Udham had been busily establishing a network in London – befriending Sikhs who had come over to work and save, gathering as much information as he could. One of them was a man named Gurbux Singh,[14] who had not only spent time in the United States, but also told him the best way to get in. Udham was advised to take Pritam as far as Mexico and reapply for permission to enter there. It was easier to push against a new door than the one that had been so repeatedly slammed in your face.

California, Udham knew, was home to the Ghadar movement.

---

* In his interrogation with Amritsar police in 1927, as reproduced in Sikander Singh's *Udham Singh, alias Ram Mohammed Singh Azad*, p. 91, Udham said Pritam was in correspondence with a 'Professor Riggest at Ann Arbor University'. An exhaustive search of teaching institutions in the area turned up a Professor Henry Earle Riggs at Michigan, who was indeed corresponding with a Pritam Singh who had been barred from the United States. I cannot thank the Bentley Museum enough for helping me to trace the correct professor and uncover the paper trail connecting him to Pritam Singh's case.

Resigned to his limitations as an assassin, Udham was enthusiastic about this new adventure. If he could just get to America, maybe his Ghadar brothers could teach him what he needed to learn. The pair left London close to Udham's birthday in December 1923. He was once again ready to be reborn.

CHAPTER 14

AMERICAN DREAMERS

Punjabis had been trickling into America since the late 1800s. Most landed in Vancouver, a British dominion territory, and stayed in Canada to work the lumber mills. Some travelled south across the border, making their way towards Oregon, Washington and northern California, where the Western Pacific Railroad cried out for cheap labour. For a while, that is where they stayed.

However, by the 1900s, men started to tire of the railroad. Drawn to the warmer climate and more lucrative work offered by southern California, they drifted towards its orange and lemon groves. Many of these early Punjabi émigrés came from farming stock, and fruit picking was work they knew and were good at. They toiled and saved until they could afford land of their own, moving from the margins towards cities like San Francisco and San Jose, where they established 'independent ethnic agrarian communities'.[1]

From 1913, however, any efforts to put down deeper roots fell on stony ground. Groups like the 'Asiatic Exclusion League', a political organisation existing solely to keep Asians out of America and Canada, warned that 'brown men' and 'Hindoos' – their generic term for Indians of the subcontinent – would take jobs, homes and even women from God-fearing Christian folk. Powerful newspapers in both America and Canada further whipped up tension, talking of 'An Asiatic Invasion'.[2]

Though the number of Indians seeking to live in America represented a fraction of the overall melting pot, they were swept up in new and draconian legislation. The California Alien Land Law of 1913, also known as the Webb–Haney Act, prohibited 'aliens ineligible for citizenship' from owning agricultural land or possessing long-term leases over it. Overnight, Indians, Chinese and Japanese migrants were lumped in the same 'alien' bracket and stripped of rights and property.

Hispanics, in contrast, were still allowed to own land, and that, coupled with the difficulty Indians faced in bringing in their own wives and children to America, led to many marriages between Indians and Mexicans. These were relationships born of loneliness, love and simple expediency. Punjabis attempting to circumvent the racist laws bought land and property in the name of their Mexican wives, a risky transaction which, if challenged, could see them lose everything they had ever worked for.

Indian men married young, so these new American marriages could be bigamist in nature. Wives and small children were often left behind in Punjab. Men promised to send pay packets; they promised they would be back soon. If their husbands chose to stay in the New World, it would send the Indian women's existences crashing down around them.

The 'new-wives' in the developing 'Mexican Hindu'[3] demographic were just as vulnerable. If guilt or economic hardship got the better of their Indian husbands, they too could find themselves deserted without warning or recourse. The new laws unleashed a spectrum of human cruelty and women invariably suffered most of all.

Pritam and Udham reached Mexico in January 1924.[4] Their ship finally docked in Tampico, a port in the state of Tamaulipas[5] in Mexico's north-east. Close to their American dream, it must have looked and felt much more like a nightmare. A vast oil terminal sprawled alongside the Panuco river, tankers and refineries smeared land, sky and water.

The air was thick with pollution, but also with intrigue. Thanks to its oil reserves, Tampico had become supremely strategically important; war had taught everyone the fragility of supply lines and as a result the place crawled with foreign agents, each attempting to stake a claim on its natural resources. Alongside the state operators, local Mexican warlords vied for territory and power, too.

Udham, serving in Basra during the war, had seen with his own eyes how brutally men could fight over oil. He would not have been fazed by what he saw in Tampico, but for a boy like Pritam, who had never ventured out of Patiala, it must have been immensely overwhelming. Dragging his wide-eyed ward behind him, Udham made for the place Gurbux Singh had told him about. El Paso would be better. El Paso would get them both into America.

Texas on one side, Mexico on the other, the towns of El Paso and Ciudad Juárez nestled against one another, connected by a bridge. When Udham and Pritam arrived on the Mexican side of the border, the atmosphere was particularly tense. Prohibition was strictly in force in El Paso, yet Juárez was awash with nightclubs, cabarets and dance halls. Smugglers flourished, trafficking drugs and liquor into America while lawmen peppered the air with bullets trying to stop them. The border territory was a place of gunfights and gangsters and the younger of the two men, already stressed by the hostility of this new land, must have been more anxious than ever to get into America.

All Pritam wanted to do was open his books and begin a new chapter in his life; however, he would find himself stuck in El Paso for the next ten months. Days after his arrival, the student was detained by American border guards as he tried, legitimately he thought, to gain entry to America. Clutching his documents of acceptance from Michigan University and supporting letters from Riggs, he was told that not only would he not be allowed into America, he would also be held in one of the burgeoning new detention facilities springing up on the border. There he would have to wait until the Americans were ready to deport him back to India.

Professor Riggs did his best to help Pritam from Ann Arbor,

remonstrating directly and repeatedly with the Department of Labor, begging them to reconsider his student's case, but he found his government immovable on the matter. Congress was in the process of passing the Labor Appropriation Act of 1924, officially establishing the US Border Patrol as an independent law enforcement body. There seemed little appetite to overturn one of their first decisions. As Pritam's plight became progressively more pitiful, Riggs turned to the press, sharing the Indian student's situation with sympathetic reporters. This was no hardened criminal; he was a bright young boy who wanted to learn. Michigan readers would become familiar with 'Pritam's adventures',[6] and the sporadic updates on his case were received with interest and compassion.

One reporter even described Pritam as a stranded 'Indian Prince',[7] an uncharacteristic misrepresentation of the boy, especially since it was so easy to disprove. Udham, on the other hand, would happily claim to be Indian royalty on a number of occasions in the future. If Pritam had, in desperation, temporarily suspended his own judgement and taken Udham's advice to augment his identity, it showed just how much of an influence his mentor was having on him.

Professor Riggs continued to apply pressure and the publicity he drummed up about the government's intransigence finally caused the authorities to reconsider, but only if Pritam could provide a bond of $1,000. The sum was supposed to ensure that he would not simply enter the country and disappear into a sea of undocumented aliens. It was astronomically high for a man of no means.

Pritam might have despaired at the insurmountable hurdle, but Riggs came to the rescue once again, convincing a handful of American businessmen to stump up the cash.[8] Though he had never even met Pritam, Riggs was not about to give up on the boy on the border. In October 1924, the money and paperwork finally secured Pritam's entry. When the border guards in El Paso let Pritam out of detention and into America, they stamped his official papers, noting that the teenager was travelling alone.[9]

Not for the last time, Udham Singh appears to have jettisoned someone who relied on him. There can be no doubt that some level of affection must have developed during the long months they spent together. On Udham's assurance, Pritam had travelled to the other end of the world; yet just when Pritam needed him most, Udham appears to have dumped him and run. These were the actions of a man who would let nobody get in the way of his revenge, not even a young lad he must have felt some responsibility towards.

Bizarrely, Pritam never seemed to bear a grudge against Udham. When he finally arrived in Michigan and came face to face with the reporters who had been covering his story for months, Pritam made no mention of his delinquent guardian. Nor did he criticise the American authorities who had caused him so much misery for so long. Instead, Pritam turned all his built-up frustration on the Raj:

> 'Justice for Indians and Europeans is not equal in India,' said Pritam Singh, Michigan's most recent arrival from India. 'If an Indian kills an Englishman he is hung, but if an Englishman kills an Indian the English judge sitting on the bench fines him £100 or sentences him to one month's imprisonment ... The British government is doing all within its power to maintain its rule in India.'[10]

The voice coming out of Pritam's mouth was unmistakably Udham's. But where was the rest of him?

Pritam had chosen to enter America legally,[11] having no choice but to gain official stamps before the University in Michigan could accept him. Udham had no such compulsion. There was no friendly professor waiting for him, no bond of money, and no promise of work. Pritam had been a means to an end, and when he got himself detained, he lost his value to Udham. If there was no ward, there was no need for a chaperone.

Ghadars had been operating an illicit corridor between Mexico and America for some years. Though it was well known to the British police and secret service, they had been unable to stop even those Indians on their 'wanted list' from getting into the United

States illegally and disappearing into the Ghadar fog. The United States had morphed into a nursery, raising a new breed of anti-colonial hybrid – the Indian Bolshevik.

Sir David Petrie, the director of the Intelligence Bureau in Delhi, described his new enemy as the 'Sikh Comintern', a phrase he himself had coined to describe the worrying alliance between Indian militants and Russian Communists. No matter what Petrie did, or how he tried to get ahead of the problem, Indian insurgents were slipping through his fingers and falling into the arms of the Russians.

These included dangerous Ghadars who had been showing up in Moscow since the early 1920s. British spies could only watch in impotent alarm as the Bolsheviks armed and trained these young disaffected Punjabis and, like a regiment of toy soldiers, wound them up and sent them back to the Raj. Petrie knew it, but could do little to stop it.

Aside from his Sikh Comintern, another line of dangerous traffic was developing: a web connecting Russia, India, Mexico and the United States. A Bengali named M. N. Roy, who had been on a British watch list since the start of the war, had already forged powerful links between himself and Moscow's Communist government.

Based in Mexico in the 1920s, Roy had been invited to the Second World Congress of the Communist International, where he had been received by Lenin himself. It was Roy who founded the Mexican Communist Party, the first such entity to exist outside Soviet Russia. He counted prominent Comintern agents like Mikhail Borodin, an adviser to Lenin and later Mao Zedong, as close personal friends.

Another Indian nationalist, Pandurang Sadashiv Khankhoje, a founding father of the Ghadars, was also using Mexico as his base in the 1920s. Petrie knew of Khankhoje from his involvement in the Hindu–German Conspiracy of 1915, the ultimately doomed Berlin-backed attempt to trigger a mutiny within the ranks of the British Indian Army during the First World War. Khankhoje had slipped through British fingers with frustrating ease, travelling to Russia and consorting with the Bolsheviks at the very highest levels.

Ever since 1919, the year of the Jallianwala Bagh massacre, the

Russians had been telegraphing their interest in provoking an Indian uprising as a means to spreading Communism around the world. Four months after Dyer's actions, Trotsky had presented his Eastern doctrine in a secret memo to the Communist hierarchy:

> There is no doubt at all that our Red Army constitutes an incomparably more powerful force in the Asian terrain of world politics than in the European terrain ... The road to India may prove at the given moment to be more readily passable and shorter than the road to Soviet Hungary. The road to Paris and London lies via the towns of Afghanistan, the Punjab and Bengal.[12]

While Udham sought his way across the border in 1924, Khankhoje was back in Mexico, formulating high-level plans to destabilise the Raj. Others in his orbit took on the more mundane job of human trafficking. A Sikh named Teja Singh regularly smuggled Ghadar sympathisers into America from Mexico, and it is likely he had some hand in Udham's illegal crossing. One year later, Teja Singh would be caught and deported back to India to face trial as one of the masterminds of the Ghadars' people-smuggling operation.[13]

What his route was, we do not know, but once safely on the other side of the border, Udham made his way to Claremont in California. It was a new town, barely older than he was himself.

Carving a route between Chicago and Los Angeles, the Santa Fe Railroad company had gouged Claremont out of Native American land in 1887. There were rumours of gold in the surrounding hills, prompting the railroad to splash out on a rest stop complete with a handsome high-end hotel in the new town. The Claremont Hotel became known locally as 'the castle', and would prove to be a monumental and expensive mistake.

The rocky soil at the foothills of the San Gabriel mountains contained neither treasure nor nutrients for arable farming. For a while, Claremont, like the failing crops around it, withered, until a nearby college stepped in to give the place a new lease of life. A group of

Protestant churchmen wishing to create a University of Oxford on the west coast of America bought up the hotel, repurposed the shell and added to it.

The railroad continued to snake its way into the distance while Pomona College sprouted from Claremont's soil. Other colleges grew around it and very quickly Claremont was reborn as a handsome college town. When Udham arrived in 1924, he would have been able to walk down Oxford Avenue and Cambridge Street, surrounded by new buildings and the buzz of young people, their hopes and ideals.

By the time Udham reached Claremont, it had also started to gain a reputation for fruit. The soil, though useless for cereal crops, was perfect for orange and lemon trees. A cooperative of fruit farmers, who would later become known as 'Sunkist', bought huge tracts of land and brought in bumper harvests. Fruit picking was a labour-intensive affair, and Mexican families came to Claremont in their droves to work in the citrus groves. So too did Punjabi itinerant labourers. Udham would have seen a town of two halves: one white and one brown; one with money, the other with muscle. It was perfect territory for a Ghadar to do his work.

Ghadars had been active in American university towns for almost a decade. Two of the first to report on the phenomena were British intelligence officers F. C. Isemonger and J. Slattery. Their reports had made for uneasy reading: 'On the 10th May there was a series of meetings at Fresno, Upland, Oxnard and Los Angeles. Weekly meetings were also held at Claremont during May at which the audience was exhorted to shed its blood in expelling the British from India.'[14]

Ghadar meetings were also being held in Astoria, Washington, and Portland, Oregon, as well as in Stockton, Jersey, and Elton in California. It was becoming difficult for the British to keep up with the activity. Michigan, where Pritam had finally taken up his place, was also fertile territory. Another Indian student studying for his Master's degree in economics and political science at Michigan

State University reported that the first time he came into contact with Ghadars was when he was a student in America. His name was S. Pratap Singh Kairon, and he would one day become the chief minister of Punjab, in a free India.[15]

Udham, having smuggled himself into the country, was immediately put to work by the Ghadars. He became their driver, ferrying Indians arriving on the Pacific Coast to secret destinations around the United States.[16] When not behind the steering wheel of his car, Udham read Ghadar literature and studied the men around him even more carefully. One of them, Jawand Singh,[17] divided his time between El Paso, Pomona and San Francisco, the very Ghadar corridor that had brought Udham into the United States. Another, Sudagar Singh, had travelled to the United States from Japan in 1921, and spent most of his time in Berkeley, the very epicentre of Ghadar activity.[18]

Part of the American Ghadar brotherhood at last, Udham was now among men who knew nothing of his tragic childhood and cared little that he was Kamboj. He could be anything he wanted to be. In the land of opportunity, all he wanted to be was an assassin.

In Claremont, Udham found the space and opportunity to practise the art of disguise: walking with a straight back in a smart suit in one half of Claremont and disappearing into the brown half in his labourer's clothes. Without meaning to, the university town was giving him the very education he had been craving, but it was also giving him status. One academic has suggested that Udham was something of a minor celebrity in Indian circles when he arrived in the United States: 'It seems likely that Udham Singh was sponsored by the Ghadar Party to visit [numerous cities in America] to give them a first-hand account of the Jallianwala Bagh massacre, to promote the growth of local branches of the party, and to raise funds.'[19]

As for his own income, if he needed money, Sudagar and Jawand gave him what they could,[20] but before long Udham's tastes were outstripping what they were able to provide. Out of the grip of poverty, surrounded by people who had more money than he had ever dreamed of, Udham began to aspire to be more 'American'. He developed a taste for the finer things – nice clothes, good shoes, and better cars.

To supplement his Ghadar pin money, Udham found himself a job as a mechanic in a garage selling Hudson motorcars.[21] The company was young and pushy, trying to force its way into the market between Ford and Chevrolet, giants of the motor industry. Hudson cars were distinctive, flashy, and came in bright colours. Like the cars he worked on, Udham too was becoming more ostentatious, dressing in the high-lapelled, slim-fitting pinstripe suits that were the height of fashion in the 1920s.

He earned $54 a week,[22] a fabulous wage by his previous standards, but, then again, everything seemed better in America. Where Britain had seemed grey and tetchy, America was vibrant and confident. This was the roaring twenties, a time of sustained and unprecedented economic prosperity in the United States. Cities thrummed with jazz music and the place was awash with beautiful women in revealing flapper dresses.

America made everything seem within reach. The pin-up of the era was Babe Ruth, a reform-school boy turned baseball god. He was a hero to the downtrodden and disadvantaged, as well as the Ivy-League educated. America was a place built on shattered caste.

Slowly but surely, Udham was becoming seduced by America. He was a handsome man in his mid-twenties, broad-shouldered, with a thick head of hair and intense dark brown eyes that crinkled at the corners when he smiled, which was often. It was no surprise that he attracted female attention. His friend Jawand Singh was already married to a Mexican woman, Josefina Torres,[23] and it appears that not long after he arrived Udham followed suit, falling in love with a woman eight years his senior. He would describe her as his 'American girl',[24] and we only know her name because he was forced to give it to interrogators, as we shall see. Despite intense questioning, they barely got more than her name from him, but

'Lupe'* is enough to trace her light footsteps through this chapter of Udham's life.

Lupe[25] Singh, as she would become, was, according to Udham, the daughter of 'zimindars', the Punjabi word for landowners. A search of naturalisation, census and birth records shows one single 'Lupe Singh' registered at the time Udham was in America and supposedly falling in love.

Born in Chihuahua, Mexico, Lupe Hernandez spent much of her childhood in El Paso, with her parents Guadalope and Concepcion Hernandez.[26] They owned a little farmland, which would have made them *zimindars* in Udham's mind, and their geographical location would have put Lupe firmly in his orbit as he ferried smuggled Indians from the border for the Ghadars.

Now a married man, in 1925 Udham had to find a better-paying job to support them both. He started working for the Harbour Boatbuilding Company in east San Pedro,[27] which took his wages from $54 to $66 a week.[28] The company provided accommodation, too, and for the first time in his life he seemed to have a stable and happy existence. Udham had a home, a job, friends and a woman who loved him. But then, quite suddenly in late 1926, something changed to shake Udham out of his reverie.

Through his friend Sudagar Singh, Udham met a man in San Pedro whom he would later simply refer to as 'Lallo'.[29] Though Lallo described himself as a longshoreman, Udham suspected he was an informer for the immigration department.[30] Such men were paid by the American authorities to keep track of both illegal immigrants and politicised Punjabis who might be involved in Ghadar activity. Almost as soon as Lallo came into his life, Udham decided it was time to leave. He made Lupe pack up their things, quit his job and moved to Long Beach, more than 50 miles south-west of Claremont on the coast.[31]

---

* They would write 'Loope' in their report, a phonetic rendering of a name they were unfamiliar with in Amritsar.

If lemons and learning defined Claremont, Long Beach was all about commerce and calumny. Long Beach's most famous son was the 300-pound silent movie star Rosco 'Fatty' Arbuckle. At a raucous three-day party five years earlier, a young starlet had died mysteriously in Arbuckle's company. Newspapers had gone wild with the story, alleging that 'Fatty' had killed Virginia Rappe with his weight while savagely raping her. Though he was later acquitted of the crime, the scandal clung to his home town and was regularly trotted out in the newspapers.

When Udham arrived, another Long Beach scandal was dominating the news. A 'local couple's honeymoon' ended abruptly when the bride fell from a cliff to her death. It transpired that her husband was a serial bigamist who had left behind seven wives and a 'climax of death'. Residents pored over the salacious copy, while their home town blossomed around them.

Oil had been recently discovered on nearby Signal Hill and an unprecedented building boom followed. A new commercial harbour was opening just as Udham and Lupe arrived, bringing in money from land and by sea. Streets extended quickly all around the newlyweds and, in anticipation of a deal with Fox Films, a new radio station called KFOX made its debut broadcast, just in time to cover the inaugural flight of a locally engineered aeroplane. 'The Douglas' would be the first plane to circumnavigate the earth. By coming to Long Beach, Udham had moved to one of the most happening cities in the whole of the United States.

Work was abundant in the boomtime, and Udham found a job at the Douglas Aircraft Company.[32] The factory produced civilian planes, torpedo bombers and reconnaissance planes for the US navy. Such was the sensitivity of work, company policy only allowed for the hiring of naturalised Americans. With the help of his new Ghadar friends, Udham, an Indian subject of the Raj and an illegal immigrant to boot, decided to become someone else entirely. Frank Brazil, the Puerto Rican Punjabi, was born.

Udham would not be the first among his countrymen to use the name 'Frank Brazil', but he would be the last. According to naturalisation

documents, a Francisco Jose Brazil, aka Frank Brazil, born on 19
September 1899 in the Portuguese Azores, applied for American
naturalisation in December 1920. His official papers described him
as a heavy man, 5 feet 6 inches and 170 pounds, with dark hair, dark
eyes, a scar on his upper lip and another on the second finger of his
left hand. In the box for his occupation, Frank described himself as
a dairyman[33] and told immigration officials that he wished to make
America his new home. He also wanted to change his profession and
work on the shipping lines.

After an obligatory year of official processing, Frank got his wish
in 1921 when he was officially naturalised. Four of his five children
would be born in Stockton, California, where he would live a long
and happy life with his American-born wife Mary. Stockton also
happened to play host to one of the most active Ghadar hubs in
the whole of North America. The gurdwara there was home to the
Khalsa Diwan, the governing body of all Sikhs in America, and it
regularly hosted incendiary Ghadar speakers who spoke out against
British rule in India. It was to Stockton that the Ghadars summoned
supporters with their now-infamous 'Clarion Call for the Ghadar
Army' in 1914, asking for an army to sign up and fight the British:
'No more petition to the oppressors. Now we have to take our rights
with sword!'[34]

The Ghadars were after men and money:

Come brothers, you have earned plenty of dollars! Take the ship
back to our motherland! Come let us go back to our motherland
and raise the banner of revolt! Come to the gathering in Stockton
and take a vow to go back to Hindustan and fight in the Ghadar!
Just as this call is written in blood in the same fashion the letter
of freedom will be written in ours and the blood of the British on
the soil of Hindustan.[35]

Cash had rolled into Stockton ever since. As fast as it did, seditious
material rolled out, printed under Har Dayal's direction and shipped
all over the world. The real Portuguese Frank Brazil may not have

cared a jot about clarion calls or destroying the Raj, but, for a price, he seemed to be willing to loan out his identity. The Ghadars had money, and Frank Brazil had mouths to feed.

The name Frank Brazil first appeared on a crew manifest for the SS *Leviathan* on 29 June 1925. Ships were required to keep detailed and separate records of the 'aliens employed on vessels as members of crew', and the *Leviathan* was no exception, though she was exceptional. Seized from the Germans in 1917, the SS *Vaterland* had her nationality, name and sex changed by her new American owners, the International Mercantile Marine Company. *Leviathan* was kitted out to become the queen of the fleet, one of the largest and fastest passenger ships in the world. She regularly ferried more than a thousand passengers to and from England in a voyage that took around a week. She would find herself crewed by a variety of Frank Brazils.

The 'Frank Brazil' who arrived in New York from Southampton on the *Leviathan* on 8 June 1925 was described as weighing 157 pounds, much lighter than the naturalised Portuguese man who had arrived five years earlier and applied for the seaman's permit,[36] however he was roughly the same height as the one-time dairyman. The Frank Brazil who arrived in New York on 29 June also seemed to fit the man's description, although he was much thinner. If the crew list and particulars are to be believed, he must have dropped 17 pounds in two weeks. Drastic weight loss is possible, but height changes are not.

The Frank Brazil who sailed into New York from Southampton later that year on 10 August, on the same seaman's licence, was 5 feet 11 inches.[37] Frank Brazil who arrived on 31 August was eight inches shorter and weighed only 127 pounds.[38] Another Frank Brazil arrived on 21 September,[39] was described as Puerto Rican, and he was followed soon after on 19 October by a Frank Brazil who was said to be a 'Native American'.[40]

Putting the height, weight and nationality discrepancies to one side, either Frank Brazil was the hardest-working man in the fleet, or the Ghadars were using his identity to move men from Britain to America illegally. It was a faster, more efficient method than that used by Udham and Pritam. For a while, it worked flawlessly.

While Frank Brazils criss-crossed the Atlantic, Udham Singh's Frank Brazil worked happily on Douglas's noisy machine floor. There he earned a handsome wage of $75 a week,[41] the biggest pay packet he had ever received. He lived in Long Beach with Lupe, and for a while he appears to have done little else than live the life of a contented man. Perhaps America had fulfilled him in a way he never expected. Perhaps happiness had finally filled the space where once only vengeance had existed. He certainly seems to have kept up his Ghadar contacts despite his domestic stability, otherwise why, after some eight months, suddenly and without explanation, would Udham quit his job again and uproot his life? We have no idea what toll this took on Lupe, but such upheaval is never easy.

Udham and his wife travelled across the country from Long Beach to Michigan, where Pritam Singh was now happily ensconced in the civil engineering department of the university. We do not know if the two men met, but we do know that Pritam had become an active part of the 'Hindustan Club' at the university, vocal in its opposition to the Raj.[42]

Udham and Lupe were heading to Detroit, but to get there they had taken the 'Michigan Straits'.[43] It was an unusual route to say the least. The journey was needlessly circuitous, taking them over land and water, and only made sense if Udham was trying to shake off or avoid unwanted attention. Lupe must have been relieved when they finally arrived at their new home. She probably assumed they would stay there for ever.

Detroit, like Long Beach, was booming in the 1920s thanks to its burgeoning automobile industry. Demand for mechanics and engineers rocketed, and unlike the Douglas Aircraft Company, where Udham had been forced to adopt the alias of Frank Brazil, in Detroit he could be himself again. Car manufacturers were none too picky about who they hired. Most employed immigrants from Canada, Greece and Italy, but two companies stood out in their willingness to hire non-white staff.

Ford and Pullman positively welcomed black workers, predominantly from the southern states, although a smattering of Punjabi émigrés also found their way into the workforce. Thanks to a mysterious friend he would later only identify as 'Mather',[44] Udham found a job at Ford with relative ease. New to the concept of the assembly line, he started as a trainee on the factory floor. The salary was a measly $36 a week, less than half what he was making in Long Beach, but Udham had not moved to Detroit to advance his career.

He would later tell police, somewhat evasively, that 'Mather' was a 'steel tester', but that he did not know his first name. The 1920 US Federal census reveals a Prem N. Mathur living in Detroit's Highland Park, a 'metallurgist' by trade who worked for a 'motor company'.[45] Udham would later be forced to admit that he too had lived in Highland Park during his time at Ford, so it seems possible, even likely considering his wage, that Prem Mathur not only got him his job, but also shared his home with Udham and Lupe. It was a magnitude of help one might expect from a Ghadar brother.

Indeed, the British had a 'Prem Singh' listed as a known Ghadar in their intelligence files, believed to be in the United States in 1920.[46] Ghadars frequently used aliases loosely connected to their real names. Hindu converts to Sikhism often dispensed with old family names in favour of the ubiquitous 'Singh' surname that bound them to the religion.

Whether Prem Mathur and Prem Singh were the same person or not, it is unbelievable that Udham would not have known his benefactor's full name. If he withheld it from the police, he must have had good reason. Udham would also never offer any explanation as to why, after just five months in Detroit, he upped sticks and moved again.

Was Udham running away from something? Had he had finally been given the green light to do something he had been longing to do? Whatever the reason, late in 1926, Udham and Lupe were on the move again, and from a brief, almost throwaway comment he would later make to police, it would seem that he and his wife already had one child and another on the way.[47] If true, Udham's decision to disrupt their domestic life would have been unbearable for Lupe. No sooner had she put down roots in a city than her husband was pulling them up again, moving her ever further from her family and all she knew. Udham's need, however, trumped everything else. Whatever he was looking for now, he would find it only in New York.

New York in 1926 was not kind to newcomers, especially ones who looked like Udham Singh. The United States had passed a federal law two years earlier known as the Johnson–Reed Act. It introduced a raft of measures, including the National Origins Act and the Asian Exclusion Act, primarily aimed at decreasing immigration from southern Europe – countries with a Roman Catholic majority – Eastern Europe and Eastern European Jews. It also barred entry to all Arabs, East Indians and Asians; basically all non-white people from overseas. According to the US Department of State Office, the purpose of the act was 'to preserve the ideal of American homogeneity'.[48]

Ellis Island, once a hub of immigration, was now more of a historical curiosity than a thriving port of ingress. Though Lady Liberty still lifted her torch above the harbour, these were dark times for dark-skinned outsiders.

'Emberto Es Pecito'[49] was the name police would eventually wrestle out of Udham when he was later forced to disclose where he had been staying in New York. He claimed that he had worked for the Italian at his workshop on 'No. 322 East 104th Street'[50] for a period of around 'eight or nine months . . . where his pay was fixed at seventy-five dollars a week'.[51] 'Emberto Es Pecito' does not exist in any American records of immigration, naturalisation or census, however, an Umberto Esposito, originally from Naples, did live at 401 East 105th Street,[52] a block away from the workshop where Udham claimed to have been employed.

Umberto lived with his wife, Angelina, and very young family: Raphael, aged eight, Anna, aged seven, Francesco, who was five, and little Rosina, who was just a year old in 1926.[53] He appears to have been a warm family man, and through him Udham met 'several Italians, relations of Pasito'.[54] Though he made no mention of children, either Umberto's or his own, we know Udham was a man who loved the company of small children, 'one of the few adults who would take the time to play, and who never got bored of childish stories'.[55]

So why would an Italian, with a family and business of his own, go out of his way not only to give Udham a job, but also a seat around his kitchen table and an introduction to those he held most dear? There were historic sympathies that existed between Italian and Indian nationalists, with the likes of both Gandhi the pacifist and Vir Savarkar, a militant nationalist dedicated to the violent overthrow of the Raj, both paying homage to the likes of Giuseppe Mazzini and Giuseppe Garibaldi. The two Giuseppes had fought hard in word and deed for the reunification of Italy. Umberto, however, was not a man of letters. It is more likely that at first the Ghadars were somehow compensating him for easing Udham's way in the city. He would certainly become a conduit for large sums of cash.

Umberto might have been paid for rendering a service to the Ghadar brotherhood, but it does appear a warmth developed between the two men. In New York, just as in Long Beach before, Udham found himself with a home, job, family and friends, and perhaps it was enough for a while, because he appears to have lived happily in New York for almost seven months.

It would have been more than understandable for Udham, far from the reach of the Raj, living a life of peace and prosperity, to have swallowed his revenge vow and moved on with his life. But like the fairy-tale pea under a pile of mattresses, no matter how personally happy he might have been, the events of 1919 still haunted him.

The past few years had been about proving himself to the Ghadars, about working his way into their esteem. He would need their connections if he was to go back to England and succeed this time round. More than that, his association with the Ghadar resistance had given him a status he had never known before. He was part of something much bigger than himself, and that was a captivating sensation for one who had been invisible for so much of his life. As 1927 dawned, it seemed as if Udham was detaching from the life he had made for himself. Though Lupe might have hoped for so much more from her husband, his journey to New York was but a stepping stone, getting him closer to his quarry.

Every so often, Sir Michael, the proverbial pea, had been rousing him from his American dream. Finally, it seems that, in 1927, Udham had the opportunity to do something about it.

CHAPTER 15

PATRIOTS

Back in England, living at his smart apartment in London's exclusive Prince of Wales Terrace, Sir Michael had become something of a celebrity. The bruisingly critical debates in the House of Commons had brought powerful allies rallying to his side, and he had been raking over the events of his time in office with enthusiasm ever since, touring the speaking circuit and contributing to a number of newspapers and magazines, including *the Patriot*, a radical right-wing weekly financed by the 8th Duke of Northumberland.

The Patriot promulgated a mix of anti-Communism and anti-Semitism, with a generous helping of fervent colonialism on the side. It was the diet of Die Hards, and Sir Michael was happy to feed their appetite with his dire warnings about the future of the Raj and the dangers posed by men like Gandhi. Sensing the time was right to push his side of the India story, Sir Michael settled down to write his own version of events. *India as I Knew It* would be a look back at his time in office and a look forward to what might befall the Raj if the current policy of 'Indian appeasement', as he described it, continued.

While Udham worked to become the man who might one day murder him, Sir Michael, blissfully unaware, concentrated on putting his thoughts on India down on paper. Work was going well, but then something happened that caused him to put away his pen and ink. In 1923, a former member of the viceroy's executive council, a one-time judge of the Madras High Court called Sir Sankaran Nair, decided to take Sir Michael on, and it just so happened that the former lieutenant governor was more than up for a fight.

Nair, like Sir Michael, had also been working on a book, but his was not a memoir. Instead it was a vicious diatribe against a man Sir Michael also detested: Mohandas Karamchand Gandhi, the leader of India's freedom movement.

Nair's *Gandhi and the Anarchy* turned out to be an eviscerating critique of the Mahatma, in which he savaged him over what he thought was a fallacious and costly strategy of non-cooperation. Nair accused Gandhi of getting too close to Muslims. His desire to woo the religious minority was putting Hindus at risk. The project, Nair insisted, had made him blind to atrocities being perpetrated by 'Mohammedans' against Hindus. 'If [Nair's] book had stopped there,' wrote Sir Michael, 'it would have had my hearty approval, as I had been constantly preaching the same doctrine for three years previously. But for some reason or other Sir Sankaran Nair thought it advisable to go out of his way to attack me.'[1]

Nair took a number of swipes at Sir Michael in his book. As a member of the viceroy's council, he felt he had access to insights that had not been available to the Hunter Committee: 'No one feels for the Punjab more than I do. I doubt if anyone was in a position to know more of it than I was. Even now, with all the enquiries made by the Hunter Commission and the Congress Subcommittee, many deplorable incidents, as bad as any, worse perhaps than any reported, have not been disclosed.'

With the full knowledge of these undisclosed facts, Nair felt fully confident to lay blame directly at Sir Michael's feet: 'Before the Reforms it was in the power of the lieutenant governor, a single individual, to commit the atrocities in the Punjab we know only too well.'[2]

For that statement alone, Sir Michael was prepared to sue, but Nair had so much more to say: 'The Punjab Government under [Sir Michael's] direction was hostile to the educated classes, and was determined to supress not only illegitimate but also legitimate and constitutional political agitation . . . the eulogium passed by the English cabinet on Lord Chelmsford and Sir Michael O'Dwyer was an outrage on Indian public opinion.'[3]

Sir Michael engaged the services of London solicitors Sir William Joynson-Hicks and Co. and demanded a retraction plus £1,000 in damages. He was delighted when Nair refused to settle.

The case came before Mr Justice McCardie in the King's Bench division on 30 April 1924, and would ultimately examine 125 witness and last for five weeks. The jury of nine men and three women included Harold Laski, a left-wing academic from the London School of Economics. Had Sir Michael's powerful legal team looked into his background, they would have weeded Laski out at the first opportunity. Not that they needed to worry. Nair never stood a chance.

Justice McCardie showed signs of outrageous bias from the start, nowhere more so than when the question of General Dyer's actions was brought before the jury. He interrupted the Nair team's line of questioning constantly, jumping in even when Sir Michael's side seemed to have no objection. When one expert witness was called and gave testimony that stated Dyer should have issued an order to disperse before firing, McCardie interjected: 'Warning should have been given even if it were useless?'[4]

When Nair's lawyer attempted to cross-examine Sir Michael, McCardie once again jumped in: 'If General Dyer's force had been surrounded and destroyed, no one with the faintest imagination can doubt that Amritsar would have been delivered over to anarchy. You seem to be ignoring the appalling consequences.'[5]

On the central point of Sir Michael's culpability in the massacre and martial law excesses, the judge mused aloud: 'Can a man be said to be guilty of an atrocity when he is acting with complete integrity?'[6]

On 29 May 1924, the jury in the case of O'Dwyer vs Nair retired for just over three hours. Laski was the lone dissenting voice; the rest of the jury unanimously ruled in favour of Sir Michael. He was, understandably, jubilant: 'The view of eleven of the jury was clearly that of the judge, that Dyer's action was justified and my approval thereof next day was of course doubly justified.'[7]

The verdict came too late for Dyer: 'General Dyer is shattered in health, a broken man,'[8] wrote Sir Michael in his memoirs. Though he had been at the very heart of the case, Reginald Dyer was too sick to appear as a witness for either side.

With the Nair verdict firmly behind him, Sir Michael was now free to finish his book and to include the vindication from the British courts. It went to the printers late in 1925, and by 1926 the former lieutenant governor was energetically promoting *India as I Knew It* across the country. It was greeted by a slew of favourable reviews. Sir Michael's account of the Jallianwala Bagh massacre merited six pages out of a total of 453. His justifications took up many more.

While Sir Michael peddled his version of events in England, across the Atlantic in New York, Udham had been busy amassing a small arsenal. The publication poured petrol on his seven years of smouldering rage. He already owned a 'heavy revolver', an expensive piece he had bought for $44 in California. To that he now added a Colt automatic and electroplated pistol along with 139 cartridges of ammunition.[9] It looked as though he was getting ready for his own private war.

Before Udham could even think of embarking on his mission, however, the Ghadars still had things they needed him to do. According to British surveillance reports, by 1926 the Ghadar Party in California was more active than it had been since the First World War.[10] While Udham was gathering his guns and bullets, one prominent Ghadar from Punjab, Rattan Singh, had travelled to America, 'arranging the travel of Ghadar members to Moscow'.[11]

While Rattan worked on strengthening his 'Sikh Comintern' in America, Udham had somehow procured yet another passport 'from the French counsel'[12] with the express purpose of travelling to Eastern Europe. Why the French would have granted him such papers is baffling. As British intelligence were finding out to their cost, these Soviet-backed Ghadars were in overdrive, and their reach and influence was widespread.

Landing in Le Havre, a port in Normandy, northern France, some-time in late 1926, Udham travelled under an unknown assumed name. He embarked on a whirlwind tour of Europe, travelling to Belgium, Germany, Hungary, Poland, Switzerland and Italy.[13] Tucked into his itinerary was a trip to Vilna in Lithuania, and though the British could never prove it, they suspected that he might have used the city to make his way into Russia. This would have made him one of Rattan's new breed of Indo-Bolshevik soldiers. He also had with him a substantial amount of cash, which he would later claim formed the bulk of his savings in the United States, around $1,000.[14] On the wages he had been getting, it is unlikely that any of this cash was his own or meant for him to spend on him-self. He would later claim that the funds had been wired to him by the ever-obliging Umberto Esposito, suggesting once again that he was acting as a conduit and that the Ghadars had friends in many surprising quarters.[15]

Having spent more than four mysterious months in Eastern Europe, on 3 May 1927 Udham made his way to Casablanca in Morocco. Producing his Frank Brazil seaman's papers once more, and appar-ently having run out of money, he applied for and got a job on a ship called the SS *Sinsinawa* as a carpenter. It would pay him a modest wage and also get him back to the United States. He had been away from his family for months, but finally he was coming home to Lupe.[16] Though she must have been grateful for his return, especially if she had been looking after two small children in his absence, the joy would be short-lived. Udham was not planning on staying for long.

Whatever Udham had been sent to do in Europe, the Ghadars seemed pleased with the result. The sums of money wired to him had been considerable and he had returned to America obviously able to account for every cent. Udham was now a man who could be trusted to do bigger things. Udham barely had time to unpack before he was preparing to leave once again, this time with a large quantity of banned Ghadar propaganda and his personal cache of weapons. Pulling on his Western clothes and Frank Brazil identity once more, he sought employment on another ship, one that would take him to India, for the first time in years. The carpentry skills he learned at the orphanage put him in good stead and he was accepted as part of the crew for a ship called the SS *Jalapa*, bound for Calcutta in the first week of July 1927.[17] The tour of duty, he was told, would last three months.

The SS *Jalapa* was a busy steamship that regularly took passengers and cargo from New York to India, via Taipei, Hong Kong, Manila, Saigon, Bangkok, Singapore and Penang. It was a gruelling voyage for the crew, who faced quick turnarounds in most ports. Lupe may have been counting the days till its scheduled return to New York on 15 October 1927, but when the *Jalapa* did eventually sail back into New York harbour, it did so without her husband.

Frank Brazil's name on the crew manifest had been scored out with a heavy black line. The words 'deserted Calcutta August' were scrawled thickly in the right-hand corner.[18] Lupe would never see her husband again and would eventually return to El Paso, the place where she in all likelihood had first met Udham, and where her parents still lived. She would die in El Paso in 1949 of 'chronic ulcerative colitis', a painful and debilitating inflammation of the gut, exacerbated by stress. Her death certificate described her as 'a housewife', although it made no mention of her husband's name or of her children.[19]

Had Udham's 'Frank Brazil' intended to disappear in such a brutal way, or had circumstances simply changed the course of his life? He was certainly capable of callous indifference, as his abandonment of Pritam Singh had proved, but, thanks to his desertion, he was

Sir John Lawrence, Viceroy of India, 1864–69.

The Indian Mutiny of 1857 hardened the attitude of the Indian Civil Service for decades after.

The Golden Temple, Amritsar, c. 1900. The most holy shrine of the Sikhs.

The Raj at play, *c.* 1910.

Indian servants raising the
children of the Raj, *c.* 1910.

Sir Michael O'Dwyer (back row, second from right), Lady O'Dwyer (front row,
third from right) and Una O'Dwyer (front row, second from right) on a cheetah hunt,
Hyderabad, 1909.

King George V and Queen Mary on the dais at the coronation *durbar*, 1911.

Indian soldiers marching through a French village, 1915. O'Dwyer worked tirelessly to urge Punjabis to volunteer for action.

Court sketch of Madhan Lal Dhingra, tried, found guilty and hanged for the assassination of William Hutt Curzon Wylie, 1909. Afterwards, Special Branch became much more interested in the activities of Indians in the United Kingdom.

Escorted supply lines over the Khyber Pass, *c.* 1910. Ishwar Das grew up nearby in the North-West Frontier Province.

Mohandas Karamchand Gandhi, leader of the Kheda agitation, in 1918 when he demanded the British ceased tax collection after a devastating natural disaster.

The Nihang. Akali Sikh warriors, *c.* 1905.

Kala Bagh surrounded by the dark green foliage which gave it its name 'The Black Garden', c. 1900. Ishwar Das grew up here.

Udham Singh's childhood home in Sunam (now a museum).

Ishwar Das Anand, the author's grandfather, shortly before he died.

Udham Singh (standing) jumping into a formal portrait of Bachan Singh (seated, left) and Manjit Singh Kassid (seated, right), Sunam, 1932.

Sir Michael Francis O'Dwyer, Lieutenant Governor of the Punjab, 1912–1919.

Brigadier General Reginald Dyer, or Rex to his friends, 1864–1927. He was known in India as the 'Butcher of Amritsar'.

The narrow entrance to the Jallianwala Bagh through which Dyer marched his force, 1919.

The firing point inside the Jallianwala Bagh, 1919. From here, soldiers fired without warning.

The gallows erected at Kasur on 3 May and taken down under orders of the commissioner of Lahore.

The cage constructed at Kasur for the detention of suspects.

The Kucha Kurrichhan, the site of the assault on Miss Sherwood, which was closed by the crawling order.

In the aftermath of the massacre, the crawling order was designed to humiliate Amritsaris and it was part of a wave of 'collective punishments'.

News of Gandhi's arrest in 1919 caused widespread unrest.

An Indian tied to a ladder at Kasur railway station being flogged.

Victim of the aerial bombardment of Gujranwala after the massacre in Amritsar.

Dyer arrives back in England to face the Hunter Commission in November 1919.

Dyer's coffin, draped with the Union Jack that had flown over his headquarters in Amritsar, is carried on a field gun and escorted by the Irish Guards.

Har Dayal – one of the founding fathers of the Ghadar movement.

Bhagat Singh, 1907–31, a hero to Udham Singh.

Udham Singh found work in the burgeoning motor industry of the United States in Detroit during the 1920s.

The changing face of Udham Singh after his release from prison on 23 October 1931.

One of the many faces of Udham Singh, *c.* 1935.

ALEXANDER KORDA *re-presents* **"ELEPHANT BOY"** *starring* **SABU**

Based on "Toomai of the Elephants" by RUDYARD KIPLING

Directed by ROBERT FLAHERTY and ZOLTAN KORDA   A LONDON FILM PRODUCTION re-released by BRITISH LION

This copyright advertising material is supplied on the express understanding that it will be used for exhibition purposes only, and not for re-sale. Copyright British Lion Film Corporation, Ltd.   Cert. "U"

Publicity flyer for *Elephant Boy* in which Udham would work as an extra.

Udham Singh making *rotis* for a *langar* at the Shepherd's Bush Gurdwara.

Major-General Sir Vernon Kell, 1873–1942. Founder and first director of MI5.

Justice McCardie who presided over the O'Dwyer vs Nair libel case in April–May 1924.

THE DAILY MAIL, Thursday, March 14, 1940.

Daily Mail

FOR KING AND EMPIRE

NO. 13,693 • THURSDAY, MARCH 14, 1940 ONE PENNY

WILLIAM YOUNGER'S Scotch Ale — That's Better!

BEAR BRAND PURE SILK STOCKINGS

SIR M. O'DWYER MURDERED

Lord Zetland, Lord Lamington and Sir L. Dane Wounded by Shots in Crowded Meeting

OUR FOOD STOCKS GROWING

The Government, writes the "Daily Mail" Political Correspondent, are announcing during the lunar rations from tea, to 4 oz. a week. A full decision will be reached this week-end, when an announcement will be made by Mr. W. S. Morrison, Minister of Food.

SIR SAMUEL HOARE, Lord Privy Seal, stated in the Commons last night that Britain's food supplies are better to-day "in every essential respect" than they were when the war started.

Wheat and flour reserves are greater, stocks of bacon, ham, and butter are very high, and stocks of meat and canned salmon are substantially larger.

There are large stocks of whale oil fused for margarine, and dried and bottled fruits are in abundance.

The vote of credit for £700,000,000 for war purposes was carried by 193 votes to 3.
Full statement in Page FOUR.

LATEST NEWS

THIS exclusive picture of the arrest of Mahomed Singh Azad was taken by a "Daily Mail" photographer who was on the spot as the Indian was led smiling to a "black Maria" police van, handcuffed to a detective. Other dramatic pictures—BACK Page.

Finland to Sign 3-Power Pact

HELSINKI, Wednesday.

A CONFERENCE between Finland, Sweden, and Norway for the conclusion of a treaty of defensive alliance will be opened immediately, said M. Tanner, the Finnish Foreign Minister, at a Press conference here to-night.

He added that the war with Russia had hitherto prevented the investigation of the possibilities of such a pact, which "will secure the frontiers and the independence of these three nations."

It is generally believed in Helsinki that the conclusion of an alliance is imminent.—B.U.P.

M. Gunther, Swedish Foreign Minister, told the Riksdag last night that the nation had lightened its burden, but the war in a worse position, than before the Finnish-peace war.

"We have learned in a manner we shall not soon forget how closely the fate of the northern peoples is bound together," he said.

Closer Ties

"From this we must understand that we must be ready with greater concern than before to direct our common policy to our common interest.

"Because of their experiences the northern people should be in a position to strengthen themselves through closer collaboration."

This was taken as an indication that Sweden is prepared to consider mutual assistance pacts between the Nordic States.

Defending Sweden's attitude to the Finnish war, M. Gunther said:

"A policy of intervention would have thrown us, and probably the whole of Scandinavia, into a great war where we should have been made to play the role of counters in the game of the great Powers, forced to be saved food for interests greater and more powerful than our own vital concerns.

"It ceased to be demanded of the Swedish Government that they should, with open eyes, contribute to starting the war between Europe's Great Powers, including perhaps the entire gravity of the war, to Sweden's borders.

"What they would have been Sweden's and Finland's fate?"

M. Gunther expressed concern at the severity of the Russian peace terms. The terms which Sweden submitted to Finland, he said, were much less severe.

"Peace Treaty Starts the Finnish Nation.—BACK PAGE Hitler Forced Stalin to End the War—Page TWO.

Biggest Liner May be "Called Up"

A hint that the Queen Elizabeth, now in New York, might be called on to do war work for Britain, was given in the House of Commons yesterday by Sir Samuel Hoare, Lord Privy Seal.

Giving some figures of tonnage, he remarked that he had left the Queen Elizabeth out of account. He added: "I would not at all like to say that the Queen Elizabeth will not be useful for several purposes in the war later on."

Sir Michael O'Dwyer.
Moslem friend whispered a prayer in his ear.

[diagram: Caxton Hall seating plan showing SIR M. O'DWYER, L. DANE, LAMINGTON, ZETLAND]

How they were sitting and where the shots were fired from.

WELLES GOES BACK TO ROME TO-DAY

By WILSON BROADBENT, Daily Mail Diplomatic Correspondent

MR. SUMNER WELLES, President Roosevelt's European fact-finder, had his final talk with the Prime Minister at No. 10, Downing-street, last night, which Mr. Chamberlain gave a farewell dinner to the United States envoy.

Mr. Welles will leave London, Paris by aeroplane to-day, and will stay one night train from Paris for Rome, where he is expected to have an important conversation with Signor Mussolini to-morrow.

He will then fly to the Duce, most of all he hopes.

Mr. Welles will be in possession of the views of all belligerents. It can be said that his picture of Europe at war will be complete, though Signor Mussolini may be able to add some finishing touches from his talks with Ribbentrop.

It is believed that Mr. Sumner Welles, Mr. Roosevelt's "peace optimist," departed here to-morrow morning, will have talks with the Duce on the possibilities of peace proposals being barked to Paris, sent an Exchange message from Rome.

200 PEOPLE LOCKED IN BY POLICE

SIR MICHAEL O'DWYER, Lieut.-Governor of the Punjab during the Amritsar riots in 1919, was shot dead last night at the close of a crowded meeting of the East India Association in the Caxton Hall, Westminster. He was 76 years of age.

Three other men, all bearing famous names, were wounded by revolver shots fired from the body of the hall by, it is alleged, an Indian.

They were:—
LORD ZETLAND, aged 63, Secretary of State for India and Burma.
SIR LOUIS DANE, aged 84, a former Under-Secretary to the Governor of the Punjab.
LORD LAMINGTON, aged 79, former Governor of Bombay.

A man has been charged with murder and will appear at Bow-street to-day. His name is given as Mahomed Singh Azad, aged about 37.

He is understood to be an educated Indian who formerly lived in Afghanistan. He came to England about seven months ago.

The members of the association, which exists "to promote the welfare of the inhabitants of India," had just listened to an address by Sir Percy Sykes. Lord Zetland had moved the vote of thanks.

He was sitting down again when a coloured man, who had edged his way from the back of the hall through the crowds thronging the aisle, walked towards the Press table at the foot of the platform.

Six shots followed, the first to the right, in the direction of the speakers who were just preparing to leave.

The final shots were aimed in the direction of the people in the front row of the audience.

Sir Michael O'Dwyer collapsed and lay still. Two bullets had passed through his heart.

Lord Zetland fell from his chair. Two bullets had struck him, one in the arm.

Sir Louis Dane was also hit in the arm. He was sitting in the front row. Lord Lamington was wounded in the hand.

For a moment the 200 people in the hall sat in their seats bewildered, or stood with coats over their arms incredulously towards the platform.

Then there was a shout of "Make room."

A coloured man was trying to force his way through the crowded aisle towards the doors.

Then the tension broke.

Miss Bertha Herring, of Wraysbury, near Staines, a girl of 19, helped to force back the man who had struck the men down.

From a side door the police bundled a prisoner into a van and he was taken to Cannon-row Police Station.

First medical help to reach the platform was a woman—Doctor Grace Mackinnon, a retired missionary doctor who has spent many years in India.

She examined Sir Michael and found him to be almost instantly. Lady O'Dwyer was at his side.

He had been waiting to let Kensington home for her husband.

He sat much by her last breath at "Goodbye, I shall be back in time for Mrs. O'Dwyer arrived a few moments late and was unable to get into the hall.

Another surgery was Dr. Lawrence, brother of "Lawrence of Arabia."

"My Brother"

"It was found afterwards that it was a bullet which had struck him. There are marks on my clothes where it went through, scars of burning to my jacket, shirt, and vest," Lord Lamington said to a reporter.

"My rifle are all bandaged up now, as I do not know whether the bullet actually broke the skin."

Detectives last night interviewed Lord Zetland.

The most dramatic description was given by a member of the audience, Mr. A. Aziz, a former president of the Moslem League and a well-known barrister in this country, who told me:

"I was sitting near Lord Zetland and Sir Louis Dane when the shooting started.

"Lord Zetland, a great friend of mine of many years, rose to his feet, and fell to the ground.

"I rushed him with my continued and pulled for decisions as he went on, and hurried to see the man whom I knew was—"

Turn to BACK Page

History in Daily Mail Pictures

HISTORIC news pictures are to be found in "The Daily Mail" on the BACK.

LAST instead of a U-boat—PAGE FIVE.

NORWEGIAN SHIP TAKEN TO NAZI PORT

YUMA home this Thursday, by Germans and taken to Wesermünde. She was bound for Bergen in ballast.—Reuter.

Life is brighter after GUINNESS

—hence the smile

"I have recommended Guinness for some 20 years," writes a doctor, "especially for those who return home 'dead tired' and disinclined for food."
"Guinness sharpens up the appetite wonderfully," writes another.
Even the taste of Guinness—so clean, fresh and invigorating—helps to bring appetite.
Have a Guinness after work and enjoy your evening meal.

GUINNESS IS GOOD FOR YOU

Press and police outside Caxton Hall on the night of the shootings.

Lord Zetland reporting for work the day after the shooting.

Lord Lamington attending the funeral mass for Sir Michael.

Krishna Menon with Jawaharlal Nehru. Both would initially repudiate Udham's actions.

St John Hutchinson, the barrister who would represent Udham Singh in court. His client would take very little interest in his defence.

The Old Bailey, where jurors would take an hour and five minutes to find Udham Singh guilty of murder.

Pictures of Sir Michael in both Jallianwala Bagh and Delhi are frequently defaced by visitors even today.

Indian postage stamp honouring Udham Singh.

Jallianwala Bagh today where topiary soldiers take aim.

David Cameron laying a wreath at the Jallianwala Bagh memorial in 2013. Many felt his words fell short of the apology they were looking for from the British government.

Preserved bullet holes at Jallianwala Bagh.

This statue of Udham Singh outside Jallianwala Bagh was unveiled in 2018. His outstretched hand is holding the blood-soaked dirt of the garden.

now known to the American authorities, and they would almost certainly have informed the Raj authorities in India. Looking back at the events that led to him jumping ship, it certainly seems as if a degree of his own carelessness forced the issue.

The SS *Jalapa* had dropped anchor in the port of Karachi on 27 July,[20] its first scheduled stop in India. The weather was hot and humid and Karachi was a hectic port. As the *Jalapa* took on much-needed fuel and provisions, Udham would have looked over the side and seen a gratifyingly familiar chaos on the quayside: a sea of brown faces, his own language coming from many mouths. He had been away from all this for five long years.

Karachi was the largest grain-exporting port in the whole of the British Empire, and the dock was a tangle of men, winches and crates. Passengers and crew on the *Jalapa* would have been anxious to disembark, if only to find some cooler sanctuary from the pre-monsoon fug. Usually customs officials at Karachi were just as anxious to get through their work as the passengers were to get on with their lives. There were ships coming and going all the time, and much cargo to inspect. Searches of crews' cabins were usually cursory, however this time round Udham saw them rifling with far more diligence than usual.

This gave him even more reason to sweat than the muggy climate. Udham had brought his guns and bullets aboard the *Jalapa*, and though he was confident he had hidden them well, in a secret compartment in his toolbox,[21] he was not so sure about the Ghadar newspapers he had smuggled on board in his suitcase. They would be regarded as being as dangerous as his guns, strictly prohibited in India. Had the customs men found them, they would have immediately understood his intention to have them reproduced and distributed among his people in India. The propaganda alone could have landed him swiftly in jail.

In the end, it would not be his guns and Ghadar propaganda that would get him into trouble, but instead a large number of what the customs officer described as 'obscene postcards'.[22] The cards were never described in any further detail, but if they had been pornographic, as one might suspect from the use of the word 'obscene', it would not have been so surprising. Widely available in America, these things were extremely rare in conservative India. They would have been valuable currency in certain, less salubrious, circles, a way of sweetening deals or getting things done quickly.

Perhaps his years in America had made him blasé about such things, but Udham had not thought to hide his dirty postcards. He saw his stash confiscated and was forced to pay a fine. The cost of the discovery was higher than the customs official would ever know. Udham was now on the authorities' radar, for a silly and embarrassing mistake. It was enough to make him want to disappear fast.

Though the postcards had linked him neither to the Ghadars nor his true identity, the name 'Frank Brazil' was now flagged for the minor offence. This brought the risk of further inquiry at future ports. Udham knew that his American crewmates and *Jalapa* employers had accepted his claim of being 'Puerto Rican', but he was an Indian in India now. The Raj had more experience of his kind than the Americans who had either blindly or wilfully looked the other way. The next man to check his papers might be more diligent than the postcard confiscator. He could not and would not take the chance.

At the next available opportunity, Udham decided he would jump ship. The *Jalapa* was due a long layover in Calcutta. It was perfect. Nobody would expect him back for days, giving him plenty of time to get away from the port and out of the city. When the *Jalapa* next docked in Bengal, Udham disembarked normally, telling his crewmates that he would see them in ten days. Toolbox and suitcase in hand, he had no intention of coming back.

Instead, Udham went to 'Imperial Hotel near New Market'[23] to lie low, a cheap dive of a place where nobody asked any questions. Only when he was sure that he was not being followed, Udham bought a ticket for the Calcutta Mail, a train that would take him north.[24] Armed to the teeth, with his Ghadar sedition giving weight to his belongings, Udham was going back to Punjab.

CHAPTER 16

THE SUFFERING OF SIMPLE BOYS

Udham was finally going home, but one of the men he wanted to kill had slipped his reach for ever.

The downward spiral for Rex Dyer began on 10 July 1927, on a night when the skies above Long Ashton, his hideaway home in the countryside, were lit up by a dramatic electrical storm.[1] Lightning knocked out the power supply to Dyer's cottage, leaving his family scrambling for candles. When his wife Annie went in to check on him, Dyer was greatly agitated. Nothing she, nor her son Geoff, nor her daughter-in-law Phyllis, said seemed to calm him. His mind seemed entirely filled with thoughts of Jallianwala Bagh. As Phyllis tried her best to reassure him that the darkness, like his ill health, would pass, Rex turned to her and said: 'Thank you but I don't want to get better. So many people who knew the condition of Amritsar say I did right ... but so many others say I did wrong. I only want to die and know from my Maker whether I did right or wrong.'[2]

Later that same night, Dyer suffered a catastrophic stroke that robbed him of speech. His family watched powerless as his condition deteriorated.

On 23 July 1927, Reginald Dyer, 'The Butcher of Amritsar', died in his bed, surrounded by the people who loved him most. His end had been neither quick nor kind, though Annie tried to ease his suffering, holding him till the very end. Dyer's death certificate would say that he died of a cerebral haemorrhage, exacerbated by his arteriosclerosis. His family would always believe that he died of a broken heart.[3]

Reginald Dyer's body was taken to his local church on 27 July for what was supposed to be a small ceremony of remembrance. However, press from around the country got wind of his passing and descended on the quiet village of Long Ashton in numbers. It seemed to reporters as if every resident of the sleepy parish, as well as many from the surrounding area, had turned out to honour their reclusive son.

A line of mourners fell into step behind Dyer's family as they made their way from his home to the pretty little All Saints Church nearby: 'The procession was watched by villagers with bare heads. Scores of motor vehicles using the main Bristol-to-Weston-super-Mare road halted as the cortege passed.'[4]

The vicar of All Saints, Reverend John Varley, seeing the packed pews before him, took the opportunity to take a swipe at those who had criticised Dyer in life: 'Our brother deserved well of this country,' adding: 'We pray that for him there may be granted the three-fold boon of light, refreshment and peace.'[5]

The final boon would have meant the most to Dyer. He had never known a day's peace since the shootings at Jallianwala Bagh, as one in his close circle told a reporter:

'His death is undoubtedly a direct result of the Amritsar affair,' a life-long friend told a press representative yesterday.

He was broken hearted over the Amritsar affair. It played on his mind terribly, and to gain rest from his thoughts he used to read literally all day and night. When his eyes were too tired, his wife, who is devoted to him, would read aloud.

General Dyer's grief was not only at having his career ruined. He was more concerned at having had to be the cause of so many deaths. General Dyer was the most kind-hearted and gentle man alive. He was just a big, simple boy, and hated to see others suffer. Yet he always told me that if he were to re-act the Amritsar case a million times, he would always give the same order to fire. It was the only thing a true soldier could have done in the circumstances.[6]

After the service, the congregation left Dyer's coffin, draped in the union flag, for one last night of quiet solitude before his final journey to London next morning. He had been traduced from the benches of the House of Commons seven years earlier. Though he would never know it, the capital would react very differently now.

When Dyer's coffin reached London, it was taken to the Wellington Barracks, close to Buckingham Palace, where it was placed, reverentially, in the Guards' Chapel. The rain was falling gently as mourners, some of whom had travelled for miles, came to pay their respects. At 1.30 p.m., those assembled watched solemnly as the coffin was carried out by Irish Guardsmen and gently placed on a gun carriage draped with the union flag. Reporters were struck by the presence of so many weeping strangers:

> Two women in deep mourning, who wished to be nameless, stood on the stone steps leading to the Guards' Chapel, Wellington Barracks, where the body of Brigadier General R. E. H. Dyer of Amritsar fame, arrived later yesterday morning. They were women who were residents at Amritsar, during the historic incident and told a representative of the press that they desired to pay tribute to one whom they regarded as 'a very gallant officer'.[7]

The 75th Battery Royal Artillery, a Somerset regiment, provided the guard of honour and, together with the scarlet coats and tall black bearskins of the Irish Guards, they formed a protective wall around the gun carriage bearing Dyer's body. The light rain of the morning had turned into a heavy downpour as the cortege made its way slowly up the Mall, one mile to St Martin-in-the-Fields, just off Trafalgar Square. Despite the rods of rain, a crowd walked behind the coffin cortege. Dyer's widow Annie was veiled and supported by her brother-in-law, Colonel Edward Richards. Dyer's children and the nurse who looked after him until the end followed. Behind them, drenched but determined, a silent army of men and women, soldiers and civilians.

Several hundred were waiting at the church. They included ex-servicemen of the 25th London Regiment, the same body of men who had enforced the crawling order in Amritsar after the massacre. Though they came in civilian dress, their affiliation was clear from the numerous service medals that clanked on their chests as they walked up the stairs to the chapel. One man, who gave his name as P. H. Nicol, spoke for them all when he stopped to address the gathered reporters: 'He was one of the finest officers I have ever served under.' The roads around St Martin-in-the-Fields were closed to accommodate the crowds who had come to say goodbye. These included prominent members of the military, including Sir George Arthur, the private secretary to Lord Kitchener himself.

Conspicuous by his absence was Dyer's greatest champion in life. Sir Michael O'Dwyer, who, according to the press, 'was unable to attend the funeral', and had sent a proxy. No further explanation was given for his lack of attendance. Perhaps none was needed. Sir Michael had spent so many years defending his brigadier, his loyalty was not in question.

In the days leading up to the funeral, Sir Michael had given one of his most bombastic interviews to the Press Association:

'If anyone was a victim of political expediency it was poor Dyer,' said Sir Michael. 'If prompt action had not been taken on the 13th April to reassert British authority in Amritsar, which had been in abeyance since the murders of British civilians on the 10th, I, as head of civil government in the Punjab realising how quickly the rebellion was spreading from Amritsar in all directions would have asked that an officer be put in command who would take drastic action.'

'Everyone in India approved his action, and we had letters and telegrams from all quarters expressing approval – even from the government itself. Everyone was surprised when his action was called in question and he was recalled, for we all recognised that he had saved the situation in the only way possible.'[8]

Each time Sir Michael justified the killings of April 1919, Punjab's barely healed wounds reopened. News of Dyer's epic send-off merely poured salt over already unbearable hurt.

AMRITSAR, 30 AUGUST 1927

Savar Ali Shah first got word that 'a foreigner' was staying at the address of a known local prostitute at around 6 p.m. on the evening of 30 August 1927, but it barely gave the sub-inspector cause to raise his head from his desk at first. There was always so much to do. What did he care how some *angrez* chose to occupy himself behind his *memsahib*'s back? For generations the warren of gullies that made up Katra Sher Singh Bazaar[9] had held seedy secrets. Above and between the hectic fabric shops and whirring tailors' rooms, Madame Nur Jehan and her ilk plied their trade without much interference from the likes of him.

When it became apparent that the prostitute's 'foreigner' had brown skin, it piqued the sub-inspector's interest. Western clothes were worn by well-heeled, educated Indians. For one of them to be roaming the sweaty back streets of Amritsar's red-light district was unusual. For him to be boarding at a house of ill repute, well, that was downright suspicious. The stranger was apparently going by the name of 'Sher Singh', which told Savar Ali nothing at all. It did not appear on any of his lists, either local or from the central bureau, but still, his instinct told him it was worth checking out.[10]

Within an hour of hearing about the mysterious visitor to his city, Savar Ali had assembled and despatched three men to visit Madame Nur Jehan's brothel and find out more about this 'Indian foreigner'.[11] It could be something, it could be nothing – he would only know if he banged on some doors. His men, Savar Ali knew, could bang heads together, too, if needed.

Wearing his American clothes around the bazaar had been foolish, but Udham's vanity often trumped his good sense. Had he even acknowledged the risk, he might have felt it was worth it. A double take from a pretty girl in the market would have meant more to him than money. In their eyes Udham would see what he already felt in his bones. He was a different man. He was a better man. He was a man worthy of attention. No longer the pathetic orphan who cried for his dead family; no longer the failed soldier without a war story; Udham had come back to Amritsar to be a hero to his people – they just did not know it yet.

His city lulled Udham into a false sense of security. Renting a room in the heart of one of Amritsar's oldest bazaars, the smells wafting through his high window – a mixture of spice, dust and piss – were all ones he had known since childhood. The prickling moisture on his skin came from Indian heat, quite different from the summers he had spent in America. It would have felt like a loved one's embrace, familiar, intoxicating, but with jarring reminders of unhappier times, too. Like bony fingers, they prodded at his conscience, even as the city held him tight.

Jallianwala Bagh was just minutes away, and though the orphanage was further, a fragment of his unhappy childhood was pottering around his room in flesh-and-blood form. As Udham carefully folded his American clothes and put them away, Tara Singh watched him and chatted amiably. They had been boys together at the orphanage.

Tara showed Udham what his life might have looked like had he not left India: never straying far from the orphanage and scraping a living using the same carpentry skills he and Udham had learned as children. Now they were men. Tara had a job working at a nearby factory. There is every reason to believe that his was a hand-to-mouth existence, since he seemed perfectly happy to be seen with his friend under the roof of a prostitute. In fact, it had been Tara Singh who suggested Udham might get a cheap room at the brothel. No man living a 'respectable' life would have done that, nor been so comfortable spending time there.

Madame Nur Jehan had given Udham a simple *charpoy* (a rope-strung cot) in the pokey top room of her building, charging him 10 rupees a night for the privilege.[12] It was not much, but Udham was used to worse. He even seemed to get on well with the madame, taking his meals with her, even convincing her to go on drives around the city. It was not a friendship exactly, but it was companionship. That very day, Madame Nur Jehan and Udham had visited the Ram Bagh gardens for a couple of hours.[13] It was the same place Dyer had used as his base on the day of the massacre.

We do not know how much Tara knew of his old friend's Ghadar/Bolshevik transformation, or what he made of Udham's reversion to his birth name, Sher Singh. We do know that just before 7 p.m. on 30 August 1927, Udham left the brothel in his Indian clothes: a white cotton pair of trousers, loose-fitting cotton *kurta* shirt, red coat and *naswari* brown turban. He told Tara and the madame that he was going to the Hall bazaar.

Savar Ali's police raided the brothel just minutes after he left. It is impossible to know whether it was Tara or the madame who ultimately betrayed Udham, but when the police left the brothel shortly after interviewing them both they knew what Udham was wearing, where he was going and that he had a gun in his pocket.

Udham meandered his way towards the Hall bazaar. As far as he was concerned, he was now invisible. Just another Indian wandering the busy market at dusk. At 5 feet 8 inches, however, Udham was taller than most, and when the police emerged from one of the narrow gullies leading to the market, despite the failing light, they found him quite easily.

Udham never saw them coming. All of a sudden a large policeman, Sohne Khan, jumped on his back. Like a bear, he wrapped his arms around Udham from behind, pinning his arms to his side. Udham tried to reach for the gun in his pocket, but could not release his hands. He and the policeman came crashing down together, still in the peculiarly violent embrace, as two other officers piled in to subdue him.[14] The gun in his coat pocket was fully loaded and ready to fire.[15] It was a miracle the thing did not go off in the scuffle.

Having successfully disarmed their suspect, the police hauled Udham back to Savar Ali's station and threw him into a cell, while the sub-inspector started the First Information Report, or FIR, which would eventually lead to prosecution. The next morning, the prisoner would be transferred to a place where more experienced men than Savar Ali Shah could question him. Amritsar police had ways of getting the truth out of men like this. There was so much they did not know about 'Sher Singh'.

Udham was held and questioned for fifteen days straight,[16] during which time he was interrogated morning and evening by two seasoned detectives, who took it in turns. In the 1920s, Indian police were not averse to beating confessions out of a suspect, and between them, Goga Singh and Murad Ali managed to break Udham Singh. When they were finished with him, he had told them almost everything. Almost.

He told them about his parents and the death of his brother. He told them about the orphanage, about his failure in the army and about his ignominious return to India. He told them about his destitution, sleeping under water tanks near the station, scrapping for work. He told them about going to East Africa, working the Lunatic Line and abandoning his contract.

Day after day, the police peeled back the layers of his life, only to find there was so much more to learn. Not only did this man go by the name Sher Singh, he was 'Ude Singh', the orphanage nickname Tara Singh would have used for him. Most tantalisingly, he was apparently Frank Brazil. When they discovered that gora (white man's) alias, the story of his time in America, or a version of it, came pouring out of Udham.

He told them about Pritam, about meeting him in Punjab all those years before and wanting to help him get to the United States. He told them about travelling to England with Pritam, meeting Gurbux Singh and his advice about El Paso. He did not tell them how he had abandoned his young companion at the border, leaving him to rot in detention, nor the names of the Ghadars who had scooped him up and taken him to Claremont.

He did talk about Long Beach, working in the car factories there, about moving to Detroit, and about Mr Mather [*sic*], who had got him a job at Ford. He would not, however, divulge Mather's full name, nor where he came from in India, claiming he did not know. Punjabis are well known for finding out each other's family histories within minutes of meeting each other. The joy of discovering '*pind*' or 'village' connections remains one of the great pleasures of being part of the Punjabi *biradri*.* It is impossible to believe that anyone who had spent weeks in Mr Mather's company, who owed him his job and quite possibly the roof over his head, would not have exchanged such basic intimacies.

Udham told his inquisitors that he had travelled to Europe, visited Germany and Russia, Hungary and Poland, because he wanted to see something of the world. When asked how exactly he had paid for the trip, he claimed he had saved most of the money and 'Pasito' [*sic*], his Italian benefactor, had lent him the rest.[17]

When pushed to account for the vast sums it would have cost for such a trans-European trip, Udham spoke of a New York benefactor named 'Joe Henry',[18] who 'first of all lived in California and had now opened a restaurant [the Marlborough] in New York'. The mysterious Joe had apparently dropped more than $1,000 at Esposito's home for Udham to use as he saw fit. There was never any explanation of why he might do such a thing.

The story, like many of Udham's confessional ramblings, seemed insane. Why would a *gora* of all people spend that much money

---

* Literally translated as 'brotherhood'; it carries a particularly tribal/caste/geographical context when used by Punjabis.

on a Kamboj illegal alien? The story might well have earned Udham a beating.

Four years after the savage interrogation that drew so much from Udham Singh, a 'Joe Henry' would appear in the records of the United States Naturalization Department, though the police never made the connection. On 1 July 1931, one 'Lahorey Singh also known as Joe Henry' put in a petition for American citizenship in New York.[19] He gave his address as 25 South Street, New York, and declared his place of birth to be a village called Hiren, 'in the district of Jullund [sic]' in Punjab.[20] Though Joe Henry's name was now officially American, he was as Sikh as Udham himself. For a man to change his name so drastically was suspicious. For him to have such vast sums of money to funnel into Udham's pockets through a third party, even more so.

There are some things that can be inferred from the interrogation. Udham, it appears, had used Tara Singh as callously as he had once used Pritam Singh. Sometime after his friend had got him the room at the brothel, Udham had convinced Tara to let him store a suitcase at the factory he worked at. The fact that Tara had never been identified as a Ghadar sympathiser in Sher Singh's FIR, though he was mentioned in it, and that the police appear to have let him go after their initial questioning, suggests he was a convenient dupe for Udham. He needed to hide his suitcase, and Tara Singh had a place that would fit his needs, no matter what danger it might put him in.

Police had found a key in one of Udham's pockets after his arrest. They forced him to show them what it unlocked, and that was when they discovered his suitcase in Tara's place of work. Inside, they found more than they could ever have hoped for: two pistols, clearly marked with identifying serial numbers – one empty, the other fully loaded; and further down, in folds of cloth, another distinctly foreign-looking firearm. It was the Colt automatic Udham had recently procured in America, a type of gun rarely seen in India.[21]

There was a substantial amount of ammunition in the case too, '150 cartridges'[22] according to the updated FIR, as well as a few personal items: a black woollen jacket and black wallet, or 'purse', as the police called it, containing six photographs. Most of them were unremarkable, some were of Udham himself, but one intriguingly showed an unknown 'white woman',[23] as the investigators put it. We can assume the picture was of Lupe, and the fact that he still carried her image with him must indicate that he still had feelings for her, even though he had abandoned her for the sake of his mission.

Kotwal officers noted down the rest of the contents of the suitcase: 'some certificates, one card, an empty match-box' and 'one envelope with address in English'.[24] Frustratingly, they never disclosed whose address it was. They also found a pile of printed material, arguably as dangerous as the guns and ammunition that spilled out of Udham's case. There were copies of the banned Ghadar publication *Ghadr-di-duri,* filled with anti-British propaganda, and *Ghadar-di-Goonj* collections of banned poetry, particularly powerful tools for the movement. Seditious verses were far easier to remember, recite and disseminate among those who could neither read nor write.

Udham also had copies of *Gulami-di-Jehar* (*The Poison of Slavery,*) and *Desh Bhagat-di-jaan* (*Lives of the Martyrs*), both considered seditious by the British. It was clear that these, like the Colt automatic gun, had been produced in America.[25] Some of the articles within had even been penned by Sir Michael's old nemesis, Har Dayal.

Udham's suitcase groaned with incriminating material. Caught red-handed, worn down by days of interrogation, Udham now had nothing to lose. He told his interrogators that he had 'come from America to free the country from the British'.[26] He also told them the Russians were 'busy getting India free'.[27] By now, such words were mere icing on the cake. Amritsar police knew they had managed to lay their hands on a real-life Ghadar.

Udham was presented before Amritsar's District Magistrate, a man named S. Bishan Singh, and sentenced to five years' rigorous imprisonment. Had Sir Michael still been in charge, the punishment would likely have been far more severe. To a man like Udham, who had dedicated his life to avenging the suffering of April 1919, the sentence must have been crushing. He had done everything right as far as he was concerned. He had left his country, travelled thousands of miles, proved himself to the Ghadars, won their backing, and now, just when he was within touching distance of his revenge, Dyer was dead, honoured by his countrymen, Sir Michael was still roaming free, unrepentant as ever, and he was going to prison.

Udham had given up everything, including a woman who had loved him, and, if his throwaway remark to the police was true, children too. And for what? So that history could repeat itself? So that two little boys in America would grow up without a father, so that he might once again be labelled a failure, just another faceless non-entity in Punjab's vast and crowded prison system? When the police had finished with him he must have been all but spent, yet just when he should have been at his lowest ebb, Udham managed to find reserves of strength that many of us will never need. He had come so far that something inside him decided that prison would not break him.

CHAPTER 17

LOSING GOD

Multan Jail, Udham's home for the next five years, was a newly built institution 250 miles south-west of Amritsar. A sentence of 'rigorous imprisonment' entailed ten hours of hard labour daily, poor rations, and the strictest of disciplinary regimes. Beatings were frequent. The best way to survive a sentence of RI was to keep one's head down and attract as little attention as possible. That, however, was not Udham's style now.

Prisoner Sher Singh was uncooperative from the start. He preached the Ghadar message to inmates, spoke of the evil of British rule and was thrown into solitary confinement and frequently flogged for his acts of agitation.[1] Released back into the general prison population, he would do the same thing again . . . and again. Multan jailers eventually tired of his antics. Udham was a contagion. He needed to be sent somewhere else.

As Udham himself put it, in the space of those five years he was 'transferred from one prison to another'.[2] There are few prison records that survive from this time, but it is more than likely that one of the prisons that played host to the troublesome inmate from Multan was Mianwali Jail, some 200 miles north-east of Lahore, in the Dera Ismail Khan Division of Punjab province.

Mianwali was one of the most ferocious penal institutions in India, with a regime specially designed to deal with political prisoners. With a population of around 500 in 1927, the accommodation was basic, consisting of clay-lined walls, bucket latrines, straw mats and little else. When the sun went down after a day of hard labour, prisoners were plunged into exhausted darkness with nothing but their thoughts to wrap around themselves, and the prospect of another back-breaking day ahead.

Dysentery, typhoid and lice were constant companions in Mianwali, as were difficult nationalist prisoners. The most notable among them was a young man called Bhagat Singh. He would become one of the most important figures in Udham's life.

Articulate, educated and softly spoken, Bhagat Singh seemed out of place in the harsh environment of Mianwali Jail. While other prisoners collapsed in grateful sleep, Bhagat, a bookish young man of twenty-two, spent his evenings in the dim light of his cell studying the Raj's penal code. He used what he learned against the wardens and higher prison authorities, complaining frequently about conditions, the quality of food and the indignity of tasks he and his fellow prisoners were forced to perform. Objections were polite, succinct and appeared to be written by a lawyer. None of them made his life any easier. Bhagat Singh already knew he was going to die and was resigned to the fact. He just did not want to make it too easy for the authorities while he waited for his execution.

Bhagat Singh, who supposedly made the pilgrimage to Jallianwala Bagh after the massacre in 1919, had murdered a British policeman, Assistant Superintendent John Saunders, and for that he would hang. The intended victim had been another man, a superintendent named James A. Scott; Saunders had just happened to be in the wrong place at the wrong time.

Scott had ordered baton charges against peaceful nationalist protestors in Lahore on 30 October 1928. They had been taking part in a silent march against the Simon Commission, a parliamentary review of the political situation in India that included not one single Indian on its panel. As a result of Scott's lathi charges, 63-year-old Lala Lajpat Rai, a prominent nationalist leader, was so badly beaten he later died of his injuries. Bhagat had loved Lajpat like a father and vowed to avenge him.

On 17 December 1928, Bhagat and his associates lay in wait outside the police district headquarters in Lahore. They had watched the station, knew Scott's movements, and had planned an audacious ambush. To kill a senior police officer right outside his own police station would send a clear message to all British law enforcement: 'If you kill us, you will not be safe anywhere.' However, at the time Scott was expected to leave, Saunders emerged instead. Bhagat and his men opened fire. Saunders was killed instantly.

The gunfire drew a stream of police from the station, but miraculously Bhagat and his gang got away. Later that same evening, with the help of Ghadar sympathisers, Bhagat Singh was spirited out of the city. Others may have lain low after such a narrow escape, but Bhagat chose to spend the days after travelling around the north of India, boasting about what he had done. He took with him a specially designed magic lantern, showing images of British oppression and Indian resistance. While he whipped up support in the countryside, his organisation, the Hindustan Socialist Republican Association, or HSRA, plastered a confession of sorts all over Lahore:

> We are sorry to have killed a man. But this man was a part of [a] cruel and despicable and unjust system and killing him was a necessity. This man has been killed as an employ [sic] of the British Government. This government is the most oppressive government in the world.[3]
> We are sorry for shedding human blood but it becomes necessary to bathe the altar of Revolution with blood. Our aim is to bring about a revolution which would end all exploitation of man by man. Long live Revolution![4]

The murder of Saunders caused a bump in recruitment for the HSRA, but Bhagat was determined to do more. On 8 April 1929, together with a man named Batukeshwar Dutt, Bhagat Singh crept into the gallery above the Central Legislative Assembly in Delhi as members debated. From their high vantage point, the pair threw two bombs into the chamber.

Luckily for those below, the explosives were only smoke bombs, designed to cause maximum pandemonium. Representatives ran in panic and those who could not see their way to the exits crouched under desks in terror. Bhagat Singh had ample time to escape, but instead stood his ground yelling *'Inquilab Zindabad!'* – 'Long Live the Revolution!' – from the public gallery. When the police finally made it up the stairs to detain him, they found him throwing anti-British leaflets at the terrified, upturned faces of politicians below.

It was as he served time for the 'terrorist attack on the Assembly' that the authorities tied Bhagat Singh to the murder of Saunders. He was transferred to Mianwali, where he would wait three years for an inevitable sentence of death by hanging. Though under close watch, Bhagat still managed to smuggle out incendiary tracts to his followers:

> We hold human life sacred beyond words. We are neither per-petrators of dastardly outrages [...] nor are we 'lunatics' as the Tribune of Lahore and some others would have it believed. [...] Force when aggressively applied is 'violence' and is, therefore, morally unjustifiable, but when it is used in the furtherance of a legitimate cause, it has its moral justification.[5]

Bhagat explained why he had made no attempt to run during the bombing of the Assembly: 'We ... deliberately offered ourselves to bear the penalty for what we had done, and to let the Imperialist exploiters know that by crushing individuals they cannot kill ideas. By crushing two insignificant units the nation cannot be crushed.'[6]

Udham Singh was utterly beguiled by Bhagat Singh. Though he was older than him, he took to calling him his *'guru'*, the Hindi word for 'teacher'. He was especially interested in Bhagat's atheism, a startling concept to one who had been saved by devout Sikhs at the Khalsa orphanage. Udham had been raised never to question the existence of God.

Bhagat was facing death, yet he refused to fall back on the prom- ise of reincarnation, or the 'immortal bliss' of *moksha*. From his place on death row he found time to write a long and passionate essay entitled 'Why I am an Atheist':

> If you have no belief in Him, then there is no alternative but to depend upon yourself. It is not child's play to stand firm on your feet amid storms and strong winds . . . I know that will be the end when the rope is tightened around my neck and the rafters move from under my feet. To use more precise religious terminology, that will be the moment of utter annihilation. My soul will come to nothing . . . Without any selfish motive of getting any reward here or in the hereafter, quite disinterestedly have I devoted my life to the cause of freedom. I could not act otherwise.[7]

Bhagat Singh was hanged on 23 March 1931 at 7.30 p.m. When they cut him down from the gallows, no prayers were recited over his body.

Udham lost his belief in God the day his guru died. In the future, whenever anyone asked him what his religion was, he would open his wallet and show a picture of Bhagat Singh, which filled the place where Lupe's image had once lived. 'This is what I believe in now,'[8] he would say, jabbing the picture of Bhagat with barely contained emotion. Something about the way Bhagat had sacrificed himself touched him deeply. The man had committed the ultimate selfless act, stood his ground when he could have run, and done it for the freedom of his nation. He had done it to inspire countless other Indians to rise up for the cause. He had done it to avenge Lala Lajpat Rai. When his own time came, Udham hoped he would be half the man Bhagat Singh had been.

The execution of Bhagat Singh knocked the fight out of Udham for a while. According to British Home Office records, he was released on 23 October 1931, with almost a year of his sentence left to serve – something that would never have happened had he kept up the insolent disruption that marked the beginning of his prison term. For a while after his release, he simply disappeared. Many in his hometown of Sunam assumed he was dead.

SUNAM, SPRING 1932[9]

'What's the matter with you?'[10]

Manjit Singh Kassid was looking over his shoulder at the man behind him, who could not seem to sit still. They had been hunting on the back of Kassid's camel and Udham kept shifting and groaning.

'My back, it still hurts.'

'Why?'

'Why do you think?'[11]

Manjit felt foolish for even asking the question. Udham had already shown him the scars.

Rumour had it that Udham had gone straight to Kashmir after his release to recover his strength, but nobody really knew for sure. Months later, he had turned up at Kassid's door, looking haunted and thin. The British had wrecked his body, leaving him almost unrecognisable. As Kassid wrote sadly in his blue exercise book: 'He was once a strong, very jolly person.'[12] The man who faced him was a ghost of someone he used to know.

Gently Kassid and others in Sunam coaxed Udham back to health. Most avoided the topic of Udham's recent incarceration, but Kassid was one of the few who encouraged him to talk about his time in prison. The answers were more robust than the man delivering them: 'I would incite other prisoners inside, you know, against the treatment they gave out in there . . . I started some strikes, refused to cooperate, got others to refuse too . . . They flogged me at least once a month, with a cane, here.' Udham still winced when he touched his back, even though the beatings had stopped months before.[13]

Though the welts had hardened and turned silver, it soon became clear that under the surface the scars of his rigorous imprisonment were as raw and angry as the day he had got them. Udham was more emotionally volatile than ever before. One day, Kassid remembered taking Udham to see a mutual friend in Sunam. Bhai Hoshiar Singh kept a picture of Maharajah Duleep Singh in his sitting room, the last Sikh monarch of the Punjab. Many homes in the province had the same print: a reproduction of a portrait of Duleep by the court artist Winterhalter, painted at Buckingham Palace, showing a beautiful teenager bedecked in jewels and silks.

Duleep's story was Punjab's humiliation. He had been forced to sign over his kingdom to the British when he was only eleven. His mother had been taken from him and locked in a tower and he in turn had been exiled from his kingdom and all he knew, ending up in Britain. The maharajah's life had ended in penury, and he had died alone and broken on the floor of a Parisian hotel.

A poem was pinned under Hoshiar's picture of young Duleep: 'I have been thrown to the far-flung place, had everything, all that I once cherished, my Kingdoms and my very life taken from me. I am now in a foreign place, so far from my people. So far from my homeland.'[14]

Udham read the poem and stared into Duleep's face for the longest time. Suddenly, and without warning, he broke down, crying inconsolably till his bony body shook with the effort. Manjit could make out only a few words amidst the sobbing: 'To hell with these English ... To hell with them.'[15]

Though he no longer spoke of murdering O'Dwyer with the carelessness he had before, Kassid was in little doubt that the rage which was ignited in him after the massacre burned just as hotly as ever.

'What happened to your hair? Why did you cut it?' Kassid asked Udham one day.

'I didn't. They cut it,' he replied. 'The English were not happy with me. Once I got typhoid, I was sick for forty days. When I got better [my fever broke], my hair had vanished. I thought to myself, well this is God's will, who am I to argue?'[16]

It was a half-truth. The prison may have cut his lice-infested hair, but he had chosen to keep it short almost a year later, a sign that he, like Bhagat Singh, had cut religion out of his life. Sikhs were required to keep their hair long and wear it covered by the turban.

Kassid, an observant Sikh, never discussed Udham's fledgling atheism with him. On the contrary, he often accompanied Kassid to the gurdwara, and though they sang devotional songs together, Kassid was canny enough to notice how superficial Udham's belief was: 'I noticed he ate *Jatka* and halal meat, just as if they were the same,'[17] he remembered years later.

Strict Sikhs were vegetarians. Liberal ones only ate *Jatka*, the name given to meat from animals slaughtered swiftly, with one stroke of a blade. None touched the ceremonially bled *halal* meat eaten by Muslims all over India. It was an early example of Udham becoming whoever his companion needed him to be. Kassid noticed his friend's chameleon tendencies but did not mind.

He was just happy to see Udham becoming stronger and more himself. He got back his appetite and once again took to going missing for days on end, just as he had when he came back from East Africa on his motorbike. It was assumed Udham was doing work for his Ghadar contacts once more, though he no longer held court on the matter.

Kassid pressed him on very little, and bit by bit saw the mischief returning to Udham's eyes. Before he had gone to prison, he had always been something of a joker, and lately Udham had taken to wandering Sunam in disguise. One of his favourites was that of a Hindu holy man in a saffron turban and long orange robes. It was a brightly coloured camouflage that Udham claimed had come in very handy in Kashmir when he thought the police were spying on him after his release from prison.

He also liked to pull his Western wardrobe out from time to time. On one occasion a local sweet-maker in Sunam was shocked to see a smartly dressed 'foreigner' standing by his stall. 'He looked strange, had an English hat, a tie around his neck and coloured goggles [sun glasses].'

'Well, Sardar, don't you recognise me?' the 'foreigner' asked Nand Singh, the *halwai* (sweet-maker). Nand stood up from behind his stall and leant in to take a closer look. Recognising Udham at last, he exclaimed: 'Oi, what have you done to yourself?'

'Give me some sweets and I'll tell you. . .!'

Absentmindedly, Nand shovelled some laddoos onto a piece of paper, remembering they were his favourite, but could not take his eyes off Udham's outfit. Looking him up and down for the umpteenth time, he could hold back no longer: 'What on earth *are* you wearing? What do you think you look like?'

Laughing through the mouthful, Udham told the sweet-maker: 'Lovers of this country have no dress, no face.'[18]

Manjit Singh Kassid would always tell people that Udham's fate was sealed long before he left for England. Towards the end of 1933, he and Udham had gone for a stroll to visit another of Kassid's close friends. Bachan Singh was an important man in the town and had organised a photographer to come and take portraits for him and his close friends: 'At the time Bachan was a *naik* [the equivalent of a corporal in the British army], and you know how it was back then, no Indian soldier could rise higher in the ranks. Most were just sepoys.'[19]

While the men waited for the photographer to set up, a passing Hindu priest offered to read Bachan Singh's palm. Such men usually seek out the most important men in the neighbourhood, hoping that a flattering reading will lead to a healthy 'charitable donation'. The prediction was sufficiently oleaginous: 'You will rise to a high post and retire at the top,' he told the *naik*.[20]

'Don't you want to look at my hand, Pundit-ji?'[21] asked Udham, an impish grin spread over his face. The palm-reader took Udham's hand, turned the palm up and started to look at the lines: 'After a while he told Udham: "Some day you will kill a man with this hand and die as a result. No one will know your name, but eventually, after you are gone, you will be praised for what you did."'[22]

According to Kassid, the comments hung in the air, but an

awkward silence was broken by the bustle of the photographer. The pundit was paid, the photographer set up two chairs, one for Manjit and the other for Bachan, who beckoned over a young boy, a family member who had wandered over to see what was happening. Pulling the child into his lap, Bachan Singh told the photographer to take the picture. Just as he was about to click, Udham leapt into the frame, an early example of a photobomb: 'Hey, and me. You heard what the pundit said, I might do great things one day.'[23]

Perhaps this tale is part of the legend that later attached itself to Udham Singh, but that photograph is very real, and still hangs in Manjit Singh Kassid's family home, blown up now to the size of a film poster. Strangers come to the house to ask to see it. Though Bachan Singh surpassed all expectations and rose to the rank of captain in the army, Kassid became a well-known poet in Sunam, and the child would grow up to become a respected public prosecutor, there is only one man anyone is interested in. Standing at the back with his hand casually on his hip, it is the person who was never meant to be in the picture. Udham, dressed in a long white cotton shirt, a white, loosely tied turban and rough cotton *tehmat,** looks like a Punjabi peasant. He has something of a faraway look in his eyes as he stares into the lens. Perhaps he, like the palm-reader, was looking into his future.

---

* A length of ankle-length material pleated at the front and tied around the waist.

CHAPTER 18

CURIOUS CASE

Kassid did not know it, but at around the same time the photograph was taken, during one of his inexplicable disappearances from Sunam, Udham was trying to get himself out of India. In March 1933,[1] he travelled to Lahore to acquire a new, clean passport, knowing he had no chance of getting to England without one.

Three of his aliases were dead to him now. 'Sher Singh' was a registered Ghadar gun-runner, 'Frank Brazil' was likewise useless – the fake Puerto Rican sailor was known both to the American and British authorities. Luckily for Udham, Tara Singh, his old orphanage friend at the brothel, had only given the police his nickname,'Ude Singh', when they stormed Madame Nur Jehan's in 1927. He now counted on the notion that they did not have 'Udham Singh' on their radar yet. It was a risk: the names were so similar and he did not really know what the police had found out about him in the course of their investigation. If caught making a passport application while attempting to hide such a serious criminal record, he would land himself right back in jail.

His 'born-again' orphanage name 'Udham Singh' had a credible provenance and paper trail behind it. If the consul in Lahore made enquiries about it, they would find a real person, remembered fondly by those who had run the orphanage. Besides, he had little choice. Udham could hardly go to his Ghadar contacts and ask for one of the multiple identities they used to ferry people to and from England, not when there was even the possibility that he was still under surveillance. A known arms smuggler who had expressed his desire to kill British people, Udham certainly merited and believed he had unwanted eyes watching him. The holy man disguise he had used in Kashmir and Sunam had been Udham's attempt to shake off shadows.

Udham's high-stakes risk paid off. Though they would later berate themselves for the laxity of their own checking, the British granted applicant 'Udham Singh' a fresh, clean passport, 'number 52753',[2] on 20 March 1933.[3] He was now free to get to England and hunt down Michael O'Dwyer, just as soon as his body was strong enough.

Not only did Udham need to regain his strength, he needed guns, bullets and money. Cash was his immediate imperative. Without it he would not be able to pay for his passage on a ship bound for Europe. There was also the question of board and lodging when he got to England. Last time, when he washed up on British shores with Pritam Singh, Udham had learned to his cost that a man of no means could end up on the floor of a gurdwara for months. Such a place, with its total lack of privacy, was an impossible operational base for a would-be assassin. Preparation would be everything this time. He might only have one chance. He had to make it count.

The gaps between Udham's visits to Sunam grew wider after he got his passport from Lahore. It is likely that he was arranging for funds through his old Ghadar contacts, though we have no proof. Kassid did not know exactly where his friend was going for weeks at a time, but that was not unusual. It was in Udham's nature to go missing, but Kassid always expected him to come back. Then, one day, Udham left for good. The next time Kassid would hear about Udham Singh, he would be in England. The news, however, would be far from encouraging.

Udham Singh reached London sometime in late 1934,[4] having embarked on a circuitous route that took over four months. It saw him travelling though Italy, Switzerland, Austria and France.[5] When later questioned by police, he never convincingly accounted for how he paid for such a 'grand tour', let alone the car he purported to have been driving. Nor did he say who he was meeting, where he stayed, or what he did.[6] Subsequent travels would suggest a strong possibility that Udham, funded by the Ghadars, may have circled through Russia before making his way to England. He knew the Bolsheviks helped Indian revolutionaries; whether they would help a man with a personal grudge was a different matter. It is also possible that the Ghadars, in exchange for their continuing patronage, had asked him to do some work for them en route to London.

Whoever Udham contacted on his European adventure, he certainly seems to have miraculously arrived in England loaded with cash, enough to pay for rent at a number of locations and a motorbike.

London was just as noisy, hectic and overwhelming as it had been a decade before. But Udham was a very different man compared to Pritam Singh's chaperone in the 1920s. He had local knowledge, a few contacts through the Sikh gurdwara, a more than competent grasp of English, and a suitcase full of Western clothes. He also had money in his pocket and the wherewithal to become anyone he needed to be. Despite his carelessness and arrest for gun-running in 1927, the Ghadars of America would keep faith in him till the very end, even when everyone else cut him off.

Udham had told consular officials that he would be staying in Canterbury, Kent,[7] where he intended to work as a 'sports outfitter'. It was a respectably bland profession and Udham must have appeared appropriately non-descript in his passport interview. However, when he did finally reach England, instead of making his way to Canterbury, Udham went directly to London, and it was here that he first came into contact with Nayyar and Sons, a vast, Indian-owned warehouse based in east London.

In the heart of the capital's rag-trade district, Nayyar and Sons acted as a clothing distributor for a variety of different salesmen, but also something of a neural synapse for a nationwide web of Sikh peddlers. It was a perfect hub for Udham, made up of people who could tell him about the country, where to get the things he needed and, most importantly of all, how to find people. Udham's American adventure had taught him much about the value of networks. Not only did his fellow countrymen support him through lean times in the United States, the more idealistic among them could be converted to his cause. If anything, the Punjabis in London seemed even more receptive.

England in the 1920s and '30s had seen a slow but steady influx of Punjabi men. With low wages and high unemployment in post-war India, they had come looking for jobs, following the slipstream of those who had fought in the war and returned with stories of *Vilayat.** Unlike their soldier brothers, however, these later immigrants were often greeted with overt racism. Irish workers had experienced 'mainland' hostility for decades. Indians who wore their foreignness in their pigmentation were even less welcome.

Early Punjabi migrants tired of having doors slammed in their brown faces. Some returned home dejected, poorer for their failed punt on England. Others applied for pedlars' licences. Self-employed, they could earn money buying cheap stock in bulk from warehouses. They would then spend days on the road, selling door to door. Light, foldable clothing was best as it was non-perishable and easy to store in small, cramped living spaces. Bundles could double as bedding if necessary.

The luckiest pedlars had bicycles, but most relied simply on a sturdy pair of shoes. It was a difficult way to earn a living, and many lived hand-to-mouth existences. Bonds of brotherhood developed between these men, and they often shared addresses, sleeping many to a room, rolling back their bedding to make room for communal meals on the floor.

At a time when Oswald Mosley and his British Union of Fascists were giving voice, and sometimes more aggressive expression, to xenophobia, the risk of violence was never far away. The pedlars

---

* *Vilayat* – the Indian interpretation of the word 'Blighty' used by white members of the Raj to describe their homeland.

bandaged each other up and supported each other financially and emotionally, providing a ready-made pool of assistance and intelligence for someone like Udham Singh to exploit.

He dived headlong into their world, convincing them that he was part of their tribe, inculcating himself into the lives of various groups in different locations. Udham always had a rare gift of making people feel special. Those who struggled most in their lives would always be particularly drawn to him.

Gurbachan Singh had lost his brother and sister in 1903 to the plague in Punjab and, as was the custom among his people, he had been expected to marry his late brother's fiancée. In rural areas of northern India, a 'widowed' woman, even if she had only been engaged, rarely found another family to take her in, and it often fell to a younger brother to take on the responsibilities of his deceased sibling.

Having done his duty, Gurbachan and his wife went on to have five sons and two daughters, too many for a meagre ten acres to support. He struggled to do his best and please his parents, but by 1935, life was getting too difficult. Now in his mid-thirties, for the first time in his life, Gurbachan decided to make choices of his own. England would give him the wage he needed to support his family.

Though his mother begged her only surviving child to stay, Gurbachan's mind was made up. He told his family he would only be gone for a short while, to earn enough to make them proud, enough to give his wife and children the future they deserved. Returning Indian soldiers had made it sound so easy. England was a country of opportunity. Nobody went hungry or died of plague in *Vilayat*. There were factories and jobs.

Like many who had gone before him, when he arrived in London, Gurbachan found the reality impossibly different. 'The English did not give jobs to men who looked like him,'[8] his grandson remembered ruefully years later. 'It was hard and often he was hungry in those early days.'[9]

Out of pocket but undeterred, he looked for other ways to earn money. It was not long before some of his fellow countrymen introduced him to the Nayyar brothers.

The Nayyars gave him a bundle of clothes and advised him to travel to Dover, where there was less competition than in London. For the next year, Gurbachan spent six days a week hawking his wares door to door in the coastal town, and one day a week laying out his things in Dover's open-air market, hoping to make enough sales to get him home with honour.

Life was hard and, though money was coming in, it was not coming in fast enough. Gurbachan had to contend with loneliness as well as disappointment in Dover. The realisation that it might take longer than he first thought to make his fortune dawned on him after a year of hard grafting. He decided to return to the capital, where at least there were people who reminded him of home.

Gurbachan had grown in confidence and ambition during his time in Dover, giving him the self-belief to do things his own way. Refusing to live in one of the crowded pedlar houses, he instead rented a small room in east London's Aldgate, next to the Brooke Bond tea factory. Arthur Brooke's company was the largest tea distributor in the world, taking leaves grown on the slopes of Assam and Darjeeling in India and turning them into Britain's favourite hot beverage. Brooke was a respected employer, whose word was said to be his bond – hence the name of his brand, 'Brooke Bond tea'.

The East End of London was filled with run-down commercial property and slum housing crammed with the working poor. It had always played host to hopeful immigrants: first the Huguenots, escaping from religious persecution in France; then the Irish, who came to escape starvation; and finally the Ashkenazi Jews, fleeing the pogroms in eastern Russia.

From the early 1900s, Indians jostled for space too. Lascars, the Indian seamen who worked on ships carrying cargo from India, first drifted in from the docks, putting down shallow roots in the grime. Many had little choice. Their masters on the shipping lines sometimes refused to pay them, cutting them loose without enough money to get back home. It was a transient, desperate life for many, but others dug in deeper, determined to change their fortunes. The lascars were joined by economic migrants in the 1920s and '30s who formed pocket enclaves, clustered around factories and warehouses where few others wanted to live.

It was here, in the East End, that Gurbachan first met Udham Singh, and an immediate and deep friendship was formed. Gurbachan later told his grandson: 'He was tall and handsome and very funny. Perhaps the funniest bloke he knew in those days.'[10]

As Gurbachan remembered it:

Pedlars from all over London would gather one day a week for a meal at one of our places. We would all make something different and end up creating a feast between us. Udham always came to these get-togethers and he stood out. Partly because of his stories, he had so many stories. Partly because he was so well dressed, and partly because of his hair. The rest of us Sikhs all kept our long hair and wore turbans, but he was the only Sikh I knew who had short hair.

And he had stuff! Stuff we could only dream of. He had a motorbike *and* a car. A car! In those days! It was amazing. The rest of us had so little. I had been there for a whole year, worked hard, done well, and I couldn't afford a bicycle till much later.[11]

Despite the disparity in their finances, Gurbachan and Udham grew close and started to spend time together away from the group:

He used to talk about Bhagat Singh a lot. Used to say he was his hero. He would also say that one day he was going to do something even bigger than Bhagat – something he would be remembered for. One day, when we were talking about the things Bhagat Singh had done he said – 'Friend, Bhagat was great – but he will seem like a *Pind di Billi*, a village cat, when you compare it to what I have planned. I will be *jungle da sher* in comparison, a lion in the jungle ... You just see what I do ... just wait.[12]

Gurbachan let most of what Udham said wash over him. 'He was such a big talker all the time, about everything. He told me once that he had killed a policeman in India. I don't think I believed half of what he said.'[13]

Things seemed to be falling into place nicely for Udham. However, on 5 July 1934 he did something that almost derailed his mission entirely. Just months after his arrival in London, Udham applied for endorsements to his passport which would allow him to visit Germany, Belgium, Poland, Russia and Turkey. It was a route, he claimed, that would get him back to India.[14] Everything about the application should have set off alarm bells. Why would a man who had just come to England, supposedly to set up a business in Canterbury, be leaving so soon? Why would he take one of the least direct routes possible in order to get home? Ships sailed directly for India all the time. The address Udham had provided on his application form was not the same as his declared Canterbury address. Instead, Udham now claimed to be living at 30 Church Lane, east London. If any of the consular staff had cared to check, they would have realised this was in fact the address for the Nayyar Brothers warehouse, not a place fit for habitation.

More importantly, the list of countries Udham provided for endorsement sounded bizarrely reckless. His itinerary contained states already hostile to Britain, and others that were on the verge of becoming enemies.

Turkey still bubbled with anti-British resentment after the collapse of the Ottoman Empire during the war. Soviet Russia, which Britain had only recognised in 1933, had Stalin at the helm, and he was busily encouraging Indian insurgency just as Lenin had before him. Hitler's Germany was the object of a secret report by the British Defence Requirements Committee in which Germany was called the 'ultimate potential enemy'. It called for an expeditionary force of five mechanised divisions and fourteen infantry divisions to remain ready for action against the Reich.[15]

Besides the glaring geo-political tensions, Germany hardly

seemed the kind of place a tourist of Udham's colour should want to visit on a personal level either. The country's *Rassenpolitisches Amt*, or Racial Policy department, had made Herr Hitler's ideas on Aryan supremacy clear to the world earlier that same year. German Jews had been barred from employment and attacks on non-white people, especially Indians in Berlin, were becoming more frequent: 'Indians reported numerous racist attacks by children on the street, such as being pelted with stones or taunted as "Negroes". In the opinion of Indian writers, it was "the present race propaganda in the schools and universities of Germany" that was generating a feeling of hatred towards all Indians.'[16]

The outward hostility to Jews and non-whites was only part of the story. Unknown to any but the security services (or Indians who had secret business with the Germans themselves), the Reich's Foreign Intelligence officials were involved in an internal tussle with colleagues in the Ministry of the Interior. The two branches of German government were trying to reconcile their Führer's racial purity ideas with their own pragmatic need to foster relations with anti-colonial groups undermining the British Empire.

While Udham applied for an endorsement to visit their country, the inward- and outward-looking departments of the German government had just about settled on a form of words allowing the Nazis to remain true to the doctrine of 'lesser races' *and* their attempts to destabilise Britain: 'The application of the principle of race . . . must not lead to despair advantageous foreign-policy results if they stand in no relation to the beneficial domestic result.'[17]

Why exactly did Udham feel the need to risk travelling to these turbulent countries when he was so close to Sir Michael? Could it be that, though desperate to get on with his task, he was running out of cash, and needed to make personal collections from hostile forces on the Continent? It would later transpire that Udham was maintaining multiple addresses around England, all of which required some rental contribution. It is also possible that his friends in the United States expected him to perform certain duties in exchange for their continuing financial support. We know that Indian nationalists like

Chempakaraman Pillai, alias Venkat, part of the so-called Hindu German Conspiracy of 1914, were still using Berlin as their base. The Ghadars would have needed men to deliver and collect messages on their behalf.

Udham, we know, was only too happy to serve the Ghadars, not only because he regarded it as a noble calling, but also because he needed substantial amounts of cash. Not only did he have to pay for his complicated living arrangements, he had become a man who liked to show off to his friends, buy rounds of drinks, turn up to pedlar dinners with meat to cook; as Gurbachan said, Udham was a man 'who had stuff'.

He appears to have been in a desperate hurry to travel to Germany and Russia in 1934. The urgency may in part have been due to the fact that Venkat had died suddenly in Berlin at the end of May and left numerous loose ends to tie up. When Udham turned up for his 'Aliens' interview in London in July, his itinerary, which on paper seemed suspicious, looked certifiably insane. He arrived for the appointment with his arm in a cast, announcing that not only did he still wish to make the journey, but also: 'That he wished to travel by motorcycle.'[18]

In a wonderful example of British understatement, the official noted: 'This was considered peculiar in view of the fact that he had recently broken his arm.'[19]

A one-armed man proposing to motorcycle through seven hostile countries would, one might think, be grounds for referral to the security services, but, in a spectacular lapse of judgement, the consular official would later say: 'As he had not at that time been identified as Ude Singh, it was difficult to raise objections.'[20]

The whole process only fell apart when Udham made contradictory statements about how he was going to pay for his trip and was asked for further supporting documentation. He 'ultimately withdrew his application'.[21] Since no official refusal of his request had been issued, he was able to disappear into the fog again. Manjit Singh Kassid, Udham's old friend in Sunam, would later provide a credible explanation for Udham's battered appearance at his endorsement interview. He recalled a mutual friend living in London, whom he did not name, telling him that Udham was desperately looking for cash in 1934. He said he needed to get to Russia urgently. With Venkat now dead, it would have made sense for the Ghadars to want to shore up their Russian connections: 'To get the money [for the trip] he [Udham] staged an accident of his motorcycle. It was to get an insurance payout, he said.'[22]

The unnamed friend also confided something else to Kassid, which would never make it into any MI5 file:

He [Udham] came to my house after that [motorbike accident], and left a bundle with me, documents he said, which he wanted to pick up when he got back from his trip to Russia ... One day, while I was cleaning my house, I checked the bundle, and it fell open. I was stunned to find a pistol wrapped in paper. I moved the whole lot somewhere safer and waited in fury for Udham to come back. When he did, I really gave it to him, told him he could have got me arrested. I asked him what on earth he had been thinking? He just laughed and made the whole thing a big joke. 'Relax,' he said, 'It cost you nothing, it's not as if my bundle was eating your food while I was away'[23]

Seeing his unabating anger, Udham modulated his tone: 'Do you know what this pistol is going to do?'

Kassid's friend was in no mood to hear anything more from a man who had put him in such danger: 'I told him to shut up – told him I did not want to know. He said, "One day all the world will know what I'm going to do with it. You'll see."'[24]

Sir Michael had spent more than two decades since his return to the United Kingdom cultivating the 'hard and austere' persona of a doomsday preacher. Regularly he warned receptive audiences about the imminent collapse of the British Empire. Fleet Street editors lapped up his fire-and-brimstone observations, regularly giving him column inches from which he could thump his pulpit.

Press barons like Viscount Rothermere, proprietor of the influential *Daily Mail*, went further still. Like Sir Michael, he too despised the idea of power-sharing in India and published whole booklets against the idea.

One, in 1931, had been filled with articles written by Sir Michael O'Dwyer and Rothermere himself. It contained arresting headlines like: 'The Truth About This Indian Trouble', 'Vital Indian Facts and Figures' and 'If We Lose India!' The little blue pamphlet garnered an enormous readership, and in it Sir Michael had been encouraged to give full vent to his theories on racial superiority:[25]

The British Empire in India is the greatest achievement of our race. It has been built up by the blood, the brains and the energy of our ancestors. During 150 years it has given peace, security, increasing well-being and honest administration of a medley of hostile races, conflicting creeds and jarring casts who had never, but for a few brief periods, known those conditions before.[26]

WHAT IS INDIA? Not a Country but a Continent. Not a Nation, but a Noah's ark of races religions and tongues. INDIA NEVER HAD – Unity, security, peace, justice, communications, public health – until the British came.[27]

Sir Michael's time in India had ended in 1919, yet he remained utterly defined by it. In speeches, articles, even the reviews of other people's books, he raked over the events of his time in India and justified his actions in Punjab.

He said the things that Die Hards loved to hear: power-sharing initiatives were dangerous; Indians lacked the racial sophistication, temperament and intelligence to govern themselves; Gandhi was a villain; if India gained its freedom, Britain would lose its empire; Westminster was filled with weaklings.

Sir Michael was such a bastion of the establishment that in the mid-1930s, the *Spectator* magazine argued against the banning of the infamous Mosley Blackshirts, on the grounds that they shared some of the same political beliefs as respected men like Sir Michael:

So far as that [Oswald Mosley's political doctrine] has been defined there seems to be nothing very new or very striking about it. On tariffs Sir Oswald is a Die Hard like Sir Henry Page Croft. On India he is a Die Hard like Sir Michael O'Dwyer. On Empire Free Trade he appears to be a follower of Lord Beaverbrook; on armaments a follower of Lord Rothermere.

There can of course, be no question of banning the fascists as a political organisation. They have as much right to exist as Conservatives or Liberals.[28]

Sir Michael was now a poster boy for the far right, and his name was mentioned in the same breath as some of the most influential people of the day. Popular men were harder to murder. They were rarely alone.

Though Udham never mentioned O'Dwyer by name, he did talk to Gurbachan about the Jallianwala Bagh massacre: 'He would ask me, "Do you know how thirsty a person gets after they've been shot? So ... so ... thirsty ... even if you had the water ... it would never be enough."' He told Gurbachan he had been serving water in the garden that day. 'What happened in Jallianwala Bagh left a real mental scar on him.'[29]

Pedlar get-togethers remained the highlight of the week for Udham and his friends. Years later, Gurbachan would remember nostalgically:

We used to laugh so much, and we all had nicknames for each other. There was one little guy we used to call 'Swaga', you know, after that thick plank of wood that farmers back home pull after their plough and plant, to flatten the earth. Another used to boast about the land he had at home and the well in the middle of it, so we called him 'bottom-of-the-well'. Udham we used to call 'Sadh' [the wise man], or 'Bawa' [the sage]. He used to act like he knew everything ... it was funny but also kind of true.[30]

Udham was fond of his nicknames; not only were they far less mocking than others doled out in his circle, but 'Sadh' was also a shortened version of the name of his dead brother, Sadhu Singh. Perhaps it was comforting.

Undeterred by his previous failure to get travel endorsements to Eastern Europe, in 1936 Udham went back to try his luck again. This time, looking respectable and with two working arms, he applied for and was given endorsements to Holland, Germany, Poland, Austria, Hungary and Italy.

Since Russia and Turkey were now off his list and he seemed to have his finances sorted out, the application looked far less suspicious than before. On 12 May 1936, 'the application was granted'.[31]

Udham must have left England as soon as the ink was dry, because on 16 May, just four days later, he was in Germany, asking the British consulate in Berlin for further endorsements. These would have allowed him to get to where he really needed to be: Russia. The passport official in Berlin was not impressed: 'In view of the fact that he had not asked for these at the time of his application in London ... he was informed that his case would have to be referred, whereupon he withdrew his applications.'[32]

Udham's case was now sufficiently odd to merit an enquiry further up the line. The Berlin passport office raised a question with London. If they came across this man again, what should they do? The memo found its way right to the top of the Indian Political Intelligence (IPI) and the desk of Philip Vickery, the same young Irish policeman who had once guarded the king's bedchamber in India. He sent this advice to his colleagues in Germany: 'I agree that this case has some curious features, but I do not think the endorsements should be refused if the applicant, Udham Singh, applies again.'[33]

Udham never did go back to the consulate in Berlin for his endorsements. He made it to Russia without them.

Travelling on unknown papers, Udham had pushed his luck. Vickery now had him in his sights, and when Udham popped up in

Poland, Latvia and finally Russia, the British knew about it. They did not immediately pick him up, rather they watched and waited to see what he would do. We can assume it was sufficiently 'interesting' for Udham's name and photograph to be circulated to British port authorities. One officer in Dover notified his superiors when Udham came back into the country, from Leningrad. Though he was allowed back into Britain unhindered, he was now a marked man.

British security services would keep a close eye on the 'curious' Udham Singh. They would also spend the next few months excavating his 'true' identity.

CHAPTER 19

SHADOWS

NEW SCOTLAND YARD REPORT
No. 76, Dated 4 November 1936
Udham SINGH

This Indian, to whose arrival from Leningrad reference was made in Report No. 67 (page 5), has been heard to express subversive views and to boast that he has smuggled revolvers into India.

He declared that he was residing at 30, Church Lane E, but subsequent enquiries disclosed that the address is occupied by the firm of C. L. NAYYAR Brothers, merchants and general warehouseman, who supply pedlars (mainly Indians, Arabs, etc.) with underwear and other articles for their packs. Although SINGH has from time to time purchased goods from this firm, he has never resided there and his whereabouts are unknown to the company.

It is believed that he is co-habiting with a white woman somewhere in the West End of London and working at intervals on 'crowd scenes' at film studios.[1]

Udham had well and truly blown his cover. Shortly after his return to England, the IPI had not only uncovered his movements around

Eastern Europe, but also infiltrated his circle of friends. Though they had yet to tie his identity to that of 'Sher Singh', the known Ghadar with the conviction for gun-running, one of his close acquaintances had clearly been pulled in by police because they now knew about him smuggling 'revolvers into India'.

Having discovered his bogus address, Scotland Yard was trying desperately to pin down where he was actually living. It was proving more than a little difficult. Udham seemed to be in so many different places at once. In the months after his return from Leningrad, Udham would claim to be living at 4 Duke Street, Spitalfields,[2] and also at the Manor House in Northolt.[3] The first of these addresses was in east London, the second in Middlesex. The electoral roll would later also have him registered at 4 Crispin Street in London, where he appeared to be living in cramped quarters with thirteen other pedlars. A pedlar at another house in Adler Street, just behind Nayyar's warehouse, believed he lived with them,[4] as did those who lived at 15 Artillery Passage, London WC1, in the heart of the city.

Housemates at these addresses were completely ignorant of Udham's multiple residencies, and put his long absences down to the demands of peddling or the pursuit of pretty girls. Udham had an eye for the ladies, and they reciprocated. Of course, it did not hurt that he was their resident 'movie star'.

Though it would have prudent for a would-be assassin to keep a low profile, the show-off in Udham simply could not help himself. He had been taking roles as an extra in big-budget movies since 1936, brazenly appearing under bright studio lights.

Denham Studios, a hub of British film-making, was not far from one of his residences in Northolt. The studio belonged to Alexander Korda, an award-winning, Hungarian-born film director. Korda ploughed both his fortune and reputation into lavish facilities in Buckinghamshire and promised 'prestige, pomp, magic and madness'.

Towards the end of 1936, Korda's studios started casting for a film set in India. It was to be called *Elephant Boy*, based on Rudyard

Kipling's short story 'Toomai of the Elephants'. The plot revolved around a young Indian mahout who harboured ambitions of becoming a great hunter. A thirteen-year-old Indian child actor named Sabu became the eponymous 'elephant boy' of the film, and the movie would turn out to be a huge success, making Sabu a Hollywood star. The making of *Elephant Boy*, however, had been a nightmare.

Korda's director, Robert J. Flaherty, who made his name in wildlife documentaries, spent hours on location in India filming animals, but hardly any time on his human characters. Blowing the budget on beautiful backgrounds, he left gaping holes in the film's storyline. Back in England, Korda was incandescent when he saw the rushes. Flaherty was fired and it was left to Korda's brother, Zoltan, to shoot the missing material.

With no money or time left to go back to India, the brothers used Denham Studios, dressing it to look like the jungle. They rounded up as many London Indians as they could to play incidental 'natives'. Sabu aside, principal Indian parts had all been filled by white men in blackface.

Wearing a loosely tied turban, Udham Singh can be seen in the background of a couple of scenes: a real Indian in a British studio, pretending to be an Indian jungle-man. Bizarre as this might sound, it was not the most extraordinary thing his friends remembered about him from that time in his life.

Gurbachan recalled that, one day shortly after his return from Russia, Udham did what no other pedlar had ever done before. He brought a pretty white woman with him to one of their Punjabi dinners. Most of the men were already sitting cross-legged on the floor, preparing to eat, when he drifted in with a grin. 'He told us to bow down at this lady's feet because she was "Sadhini" – you know – "a wise woman".'[5]

Gurbachan heard from other pedlars that her name may have been Irene Palmer.[6] It was a name the security services would also discover when they looked into Udham's mysterious 'girlfriend'.

Even though the IPI, MI5 and police would all hear Irene Palmer's name a number of times in relation to their investigation into

Udham Singh, scant detail about her is appended to his files. The
police appear to have made no effort to establish who she was or
what she did. Perhaps it was because MI5 and the IPI knew quite a
lot about the mysterious Ms Palmer already.

Looking into the name decades later, one finds no trace of an Irene
Palmer living in London in the census, electoral record or residential records for that time. There is an Irene Palmer with the correct
age profile listed in Wales, but according to her descendants, one of
whom is an amateur genealogist, she was a troubled soul who never
left the country and certainly never mixed with Indians. Could it be
that 'Irene' Palmer was in fact 'Eileen' Palmer?

If that is the case, it would explain why her name was excluded
from Udham's file after the initial report, and why the police were
pulled from investigating her any further. Too many eyes had
access to the thickening Udham Singh file, and by 1937 there was
growing and not entirely misplaced paranoia that government
departments were being infiltrated by Soviet spies. Knowledge of
Eileen was too precious to leak. She was a link to an even greater
prize than Udham Singh. Eileen was a direct link to a man named
Benjamin Francis Bradley, and that made her invaluable to the
security services.

Bradley was a Communist metalworker from east London who travelled to India promoting militant trade unionism in 1927, the same
year Udham was arrested for gun-running. Bradley had organised
a successful wave of strikes on the Indian Railways and was eventually arrested and jailed in 1929 for his part in the so-called Meerut
Conspiracy, a plot to destabilise the Raj with a workers' uprising
on the behest of the USSR.

He and his co-conspirators were accused of depriving: '[t]he King
Emperor of the sovereignty of British India, and for such purpose
to use the methods and carry out the programme and plan of campaign outlined and ordained by the Communist International.'[7] At
the time, Eileen, an idealistic and passionate young woman, did not

even know Bradley's name. She was in London, busy falling in love with her future husband, a man named Horace Palmer.

Horace was a schoolteacher, sometime antiques dealer, and talented violinist. He was also a marked man. Both MI5 and Special Branch had him under surveillance thanks to his active involvement with the Communist Party of Great Britain (CPGB). Eileen adored Horace but was seduced by his politics even more. She learned everything she could from her husband and, if anything, hardened his commitment to the cause.

In 1935, Eileen travelled to India, ostensibly acting as a secretary for the renowned American birth control activist Margaret Sanger, however she was simultaneously pursuing new communist interests.[8] This is what brought her to the attention of the IPI. They began keeping an eye on Eileen, and when the IPI momentarily lost track of her in December 1936, they seemed desperate to find out where she was: 'IPI – HOW [request for special surveillance] on Horace Palmer, with a view to discovering the whereabouts of his wife, Eileen Palmer, who is travelling in India, probably on a Communist Mission.'[9]

Oblivious to the interest in her, Eileen was in India meeting with one of Bradley's co-accused in the Meerut Conspiracy, a Bengali named Sibnath Banerjee, general secretary of the East Indian Railway Association. Through him Eileen was introduced to the struggle for Indian independence. It would become her lifelong obsession ever after.

Writing to her husband, whose letters were by now being intercepted by the IPI, unsealed at the sorting office, copied, resealed and sent on their way, Eileen wrote of Banerjee: 'He was one of the Meerut people who was acquitted – that means he only spent two and a half years in prison awaiting trial and was let off for two years on bail. He was also in Russia 1921/23 – interesting times.'[10]

Banerjee invited Eileen to address a crowd of almost 1,000 Indian workers, and she found the experience exhilarating and profoundly moving. She begged Horace to think about relocating to India: 'Do seriously consider how much more useful we could be here than in England – it's a social crime for us not to come ... TU [Trade

Union] movement, where it exists, is necessarily more militant here than in England.'[11]

India changed Eileen's life, and when she returned to England, perhaps with Banerjee's endorsement, she started to work for Bradley as his secretary. Thanks to an outcry in the British press over his incarceration in India, Bradley had returned to England after being released early from prison in 1933. Eileen, like Udham in his early Ghadar career, served as a 'mule', carrying money and messages to Bradley's Communist contacts around Great Britain.

She was good at what she did, a true believer. Soon, together with Bradley, Eileen was heading up the CPGB's 'Colonial Information Bureau', a successor to the League Against Imperialism. The LAI had been an international, anti-imperial organisation, regarded as a front for the Soviet Comintern.

Bradley produced fiery pamphlets arguing for direct militancy, rejecting Gandhi's non-violent strategy of non-cooperation:

> The dogma of 'non-violence' should be omitted. The entire emphasis should be placed on the development of the mass struggle, on the work of organisation of the workers and peasants as the primary task in the field of organisation, on the active taking up of the immediate demands of the workers and peasants for their vital needs, and the linking of this struggle with the political anti-imperialist struggle.[12]

Eileen's path crossed with many Indian Communists, especially those, like Udham, who had freshly returned from mystery missions to Russia. Though his name does not appear in her surveillance files, there is the suggestion that she was meeting a number of Indian insurgents and was committed to their cause. Surveillance records on Eileen Palmer would become much more detailed later in her life, as she rose inexorably up the ranks of the CPGB. By 1953, Special Branch would describe her as 'One of the Top-Ranking Communists' in Europe.[13]

Udham's trip to Russia, his aliases, his multiple addresses, his boasts about gun-running, together with his friendship with Irene (possibly Eileen) Palmer, earned him his own surveillance detail towards the end of 1936 and well into 1937. Gurbachan Singh was taken aback in 1937 to see plain-clothes police following him, even though Udham seemed blasé about it: 'Two men were always following him. All the time. He knew it too. Sometimes he would go and speak to them, and say, "You look like a family man. Why don't you go home to your family? Don't waste your time on me. Honestly, I promise I will be a good boy."' Gurbachan laughed as he told his grandson the story. 'He just wasn't afraid of anyone.'[14]

Udham's lack of fear, which had so impressed his friend, bordered on the reckless. Either he did not understand the threat, or he was arrogant enough to think it did not matter. His devil-may-care attitude extended, much to the horror of many of his compatriots, far beyond the police, and to God almighty himself.

Nazir Singh Mattu first noticed Udham Singh while praying at the Shepherd's Bush gurdwara. He had noticed Udham helping himself to cash from the collection plate, an unconscionable sin.

Traditionally at Sikh temples, worshippers arrive and are faced with the Holy Book. It sits in the very centre of the room and is watched over by a *granthi*, or priest, who fans it with the reverence of a man serving an emperor. A collection plate or box is usually placed before the book, where, having knelt down in supplication, Sikhs are expected to donate to the gurdwara and its charitable causes.

'He put in six pence and took a half crown,'[15] remembered Nazir many years later. 'Obviously people were looking at him. He said "It has nothing to do with you. It's between *babaji* and me. I am taking it from *babaji*'s bank."'[16]

Babaji or 'father' was an honorary address for Guru Nanak, the founder of the Sikh faith. According to Nazir, Udham benefited from 'father's' generosity on more than one occasion. 'He was never short of money ... He used to say that people may become short of money but I cannot ... If you need to pay for it, just go and pray for it.'[17]

Nazir found Udham's shamelessness intoxicating. He had been an impressionable nineteen-year-old when he first met the older man, living at a pedlar house 3 miles from one of Udham's multiple addresses, The Manor, in Hayes, Middlesex.

Nazir was not himself a pedlar but worked as a fruit-picker on the nearby market garden farms in Osterley and Hampton. The hours were long, the labour intense, and the house he returned to was grubby and overcrowded. It stood behind one of the area's best-known pubs, The Grapes, a favourite among the men who worked at the Nestle factory some 2 miles away.

The air around Hayes was thick with the smell of chocolate and coffee. Indians added to the aroma with their cooking spices, lovingly brought from home wrapped in brown paper, tied with coarse twine. These spices, an immediate portal to their homes and families, were as valuable as gold to them.

Nazir had only been in England for a few months when Udham Singh wafted into his life. Nazir, like Udham, was the survivor of a challenging childhood. His uncle had lost all his own children to tuberculosis, and when Nazir was just a baby, he asked if he could have one of his brother's children to ease the loss of his wife. Nazir was duly handed over.

Though he did not articulate the effect his father's decision had on him, as an old man he would recall that his main reason for travelling to England was that he might be able to send money to his birth mother, perhaps an attempt to ease their mutual loss. Only much later did he find out that his cash never actually reached her, going into his father's pocket as soon as it arrived.

Nazir, the dutiful, separated son, picked fruit and vegetables in England from morning till dusk, earning £2.50 a day, most of which he sent back home. When a friend formally introduced him to Udham, he was immediately drawn to him, in spite of his blasphemous behaviour in the gurdwara. Young Nazir believed he learned more from Udham than he had from any other man in his life: 'I loved the way he spoke, his arguments, every word he uttered.'[18] The affection seemed intense and reciprocated. The two began to socialise, and within a short space of time Udham left The Manor and moved in with Nazir and his fellow housemates, making them think theirs was his only home.

As with his other 'homes', Udham would go missing for days on end, leaving his housemates to speculate on what he was up to. One day Udham decided to take Nazir into his confidence and offered to take him along for one of his mysterious car journeys: 'He said to me: "Look. Join me and I will take you somewhere." I said: "Where?" He said: "I will show you Canterbury on my own expense," and then he showed me everything.'[19] One day, during one of these long road trips, 'Udham Singh, pointing towards a traffic policeman, said: "Should we finish one *firangi*?"'[20]

Nazir was stunned into silence. After what seemed an interminable silence, Udham laughed: '"I was just checking you. I don't want to kill cats and dogs" – he used to call English [police] cats and dogs – "we have to do other [much bigger] things in life."'[21]

Nazir never did say what those 'bigger things' might be, but he continued to travel up and down the country at Udham's side. They visited Coventry frequently, where Udham seemed to have a special interest in a nascent trade union body called the Indian Workers Association (IWA).

Unlike their London compatriots, many Indians in the Midlands managed to find employment in car plants spread across the region. Though they did the same jobs as British workers, they received less money, were barred from promotion, and were subject to summary dismissal if they raised objections.

Against this background, in the early 1930s a Punjabi Muslim, Akbar Ali Khan, working with a Sikh named Charan Singh Cheema, decided to challenge the status quo by forming the IWA.[22] The association deliberately conducted its business in Hindustani to keep discussions secret from the factory bosses, yet almost from inception these meetings were infiltrated by informants who reported back to the IPI and police.

They described the IWA as a hotbed of Ghadar *and* Communist activity. Though files were opened on many of the ringleaders, spies failed to notice a quiet man who stood at the back. He seemed happy to prod discussions along gently, shifting them from factory business to general discontent about British bosses and British rule whenever he could.[23]

Nazir, his young acolyte, went on to become an active organiser of the IWA, instrumental in founding its London chapter. He was immensely proud of his work with them. Almost as proud as he was of his friendship with Udham.* He would have done anything for either of them.

Udham's popularity among the pedlars was no mystery. He swaggered while they stooped, and though he rarely seemed to do any work, he was never short of cash. He drank in pubs, entertaining *goras*† with tall tales from India; a charming chancer, known to con barmen out of free drinks by pretending to be a member of the Patiala royal family.[24] His 'Punjabi prince' persona, one which he had loaned to Pritam many years before, was a hit with the ladies. Fellow pedlars were in awe of his confidence. He was able to romance exotic women while they remained prisoners of their own broken English.

Like a chameleon, Udham Singh inculcated himself into more educated circles, too. Two of his most loyal friends would be Diwan Singh, a practising medical doctor, and Shiv Singh Johal, an educated businessman. Both served the Shepherd's Bush gurdwara, as president and general secretary respectively. It is doubtful they knew of the unofficial loans their temple was making to Udham, though they would have sympathised with his cause entirely.

---

* In the 1940s, Nazir tried to buy a sub-machine gun to kill some *firangis* and make his mentor proud. He was foiled when it transpired that he was trying to buy his weapon not from the IRA, as he thought, but from undercover police. Nazir escaped arrest and went on to become an upstanding member of his local community. He never stopped loving Udham Singh.

† *Goras* – a slang word for 'whites'.

'We all loved him. He was just great with us kids, really great – he liked children, and genuinely seemed to enjoy our company. I remember he brought laughter into the house.'[25]

Sitting in the House of Lords almost eighty years later, Lord Indarjit Singh, now a peer of the realm in Britain, had only the fondest memories of Udham, whom he had come to know well during his childhood in Birmingham. 'I have vivid memories of him, tall and handsome. A *hasmukh** guy. My parents looked forward to his frequent visits and so did we.'[26]

Indarjit was only five when he first met Udham Singh, and would know him over a period of two years. His father, Dr Diwan Singh, was an observant, turbaned Sikh. His mother, Kundan Kaur, was a firebrand nationalist who had once asked her husband, shortly after they were married, if he would mind her learning how to make bombs to use against the Raj. She never did, but she longed for Indian independence.

Religious Sikhs like Indarjit's parents had grown increasingly disillusioned with the British since the early 1900s. Several of their important places of worship were under the control of *udasi mahants* (clergymen) appointed by the Raj. These *mahants* were regarded as stooges and detested by most of the congregation. One had caused a wave of rage and revulsion when, as *jathedar*, or 'head', of the Golden Temple in 1919, he saw fit to present Brigadier Rex Dyer with a *siropa,* a shawl of honour, after the Jallianwala Bagh massacre. It was, he said, a token of thanks on behalf of all Sikhs for getting Amritsar back under control after the riots.[27]

Like most Amritsari Sikhs, Diwan Singh found the act repugnant. As more allegations of corruption and toadying were levelled at *mahants* in Punjab, orthodox Sikhs formed a new brotherhood of 'true believers'. They called themselves the *Akalis*, or 'immortals', and in 1922, at a religious site some 12 miles away from Amritsar, they chose to make their stand.

---

* Happy-go-lucky

Guru ka Bagh, or the 'Garden of the Gurus', is a complex comprising two ancient gurdwaras and a garden. One of the temples commemorates the visit of Guru Arjan in 1585, the other is associated with a visit from Guru Tegh Bahadur in 1664. It was here that, on 12 September 1922, the *Akali* first challenged the British hold on their places of worship. Dressed in black turbans and white *kurta pyjama,** hundreds advanced slowly on the Bagh. Anticipating violence, they had invited members of the press and observers from the Congress Party to bear witness. Among them was the Christian missionary C. F. Andrews, the same close friend of Gandhi who had collected evidence after the Jallianwala Bagh massacre. It is largely thanks to his eyewitness account that we know what happened that day.

The police had cordoned off the area with a line of men, British officers and Indian sepoys, all carrying lathis. The *Akali* were unarmed and resolved to follow Gandhi's principles of non-violence. No matter how the British beat them, they would not reply in kind. If they fell, they would get up again and march to the Bagh, but never raise a hand in violence. Diwan Singh was a medical student at the time and it was his duty to bandage up the wounded, just enough to get them on their feet and walking again.

C. F. Andrews described what young Dr Diwan Singh saw with his own eyes:

> ... I noticed the extraordinary devotion of the women. Their faces were full of motherly tenderness towards those who were going forward, in the name of their religion, to receive suffering without retaliation.[28]

Sikh men of all ages marched in rows of four, approaching the police with their hands pressed together in prayer. As they came close, the police brought down their lathis on their heads and faces. Andrews

---

* Traditional Punjabi clothes comprising a long white cotton shirt that falls beneath the knees, and white cotton pyjamas.

noticed the sticks used by the British had brass tips. Bleeding heavily, they fell in silence and were dragged away, only to be replaced by four more *Akalis*. The Sikhs bore their beatings stoically but kept coming, and very quickly the police started to lose control of their tempers.

> I saw with my own eyes one of these policemen kick in the stomach of a Sikh who stood helplessly before him. It was a blow so foul that I could hardly restrain myself from crying out loud and rushing forward. But later on I was to see another act which was, if anything, even fouler still. For when one of the *Akali* Sikhs had been hurled to the ground and was lying prostrate a police sepoy stamped with his foot upon him, using his full weight.[29]

Many who fell that day had fought alongside the British during the war: 'They had served in many campaigns in Flanders, in France, in Mesopotamia and in East Africa. Some of them at the risk of their own safety may have saved the lives of Englishmen who had been wounded. Now they were felled to the ground at the hands of English officials serving in the same Government which they themselves had served.'[30]

Covered in his compatriots' blood, what Diwan Singh saw that day turned him irreconcilably against the Raj. His participation in the protest marked him as a troublemaker as far as the British were concerned, rendering him unemployable in India. He was forced to leave, trying his luck in East Africa first and then moving to England in 1931: 'I'm not sure why it occurred to him to come to England,' his son would later muse.

Like many Indians who migrated to Britain, Dr Diwan Singh found it easy to reconcile his hatred of the Raj with his genuine fondness for British people. They were not to blame for the excesses of their empire, a sentiment Udham Singh shared. When the two men met at the gurdwara, they may not have had God in common, but they shared many other political beliefs.

Far from devout, Udham made frequent use of the temple, even pitching in to make the communal food in the kitchens. A fully turbaned Sikh, Diwan Singh, with his education and devotion to his faith, made an unlikely friend for an atheist who had long since cut his hair and shaved his beard. Nevertheless, over time the two men established a warm relationship.

Between 1937 and 1939 while the Metropolitan Police's interest in him was at its most intense, Udham travelled frequently to Birmingham to spend time with Diwan Singh's family. Not only did the trips give him respite from the detectives, it also brought him into contact with two little boys. Perhaps they reminded him of the children he had left behind. Indarjit Singh remembered:

Most of the adults who came to our house, and there were lots of them, only wanted to talk to our father, but Udham was different. He used to look for us, seek us out, and talk to us and play with us. We adored him. When it was time to go, my brother and I used to hide his hat. We didn't want him to go, you see, and he would pretend to be cross and we would jump all over him, and he would roar with laughter. I don't know how many times we did that to him, hid his hat just as he was trying to leave, but he always acted as if it was the first time.[31]

Shiv Singh Johal,[32] the general secretary of the gurdwara, worked under Diwan Singh, looking after the day-to-day running of Shepherd's Bush gurdwara:

'My *papaji* [honoured father] owed the gurdwara everything,' explained his son Ajit many years later. 'It was his home when he first arrived in the country. He stayed on the floor with others and later moved into a flat nearby.'[33]

Shiv Singh Jouhl was an *Akali* Sikh who had already got into trouble with the British for his activism around Jullundur in the late 1920s:

He was arrested a couple of times in India for his part in protests against the British, not long prison sentences, weeks rather than months. It marked him out in the eyes of the police. They made his life difficult, see, so he decided to leave and try his luck elsewhere in the Empire. He needed a clean start. He came to England.

When he arrived in London in 1936, I was only three. He left me and my mother in India, and it was hard for us, but he sent back money.

People say my *papaji* was a man with a fiery temper, generally quiet but very loyal . . . I don't know if *Papaji* followed trouble or trouble followed him, and I'm not sure when he first met Udham Singh, but I do know he liked him a lot. He was quite different to my *papaji*. Udham Singh was a cheery chap, who laughed a lot. My father was serious and very quiet. Whatever tied them together was strong. Whatever happened next, my father never abandoned him.[34]

In the two years after his return from Russia, British surveillance was getting in Udham's way. Though he could slip his shadows for stretches of time, it was impossible to get anywhere near Sir Michael. The authorities' interest in him also succeeded in cutting him off from his Communist benefactors. The last thing their operatives needed was to end up with a police detail thanks to their contact with Udham. 'Irene' Palmer appears to have remained in his life, though they would rarely be seen in public together. 'Sadhini', the wise woman, now only existed in Udham's private sphere.

Cut off from his handlers, running out of cash, life in London would have started to feel as impotent and frustrating as it had when he had come with Pritam Singh almost two decades before. By the end of 1937, Udham appears to have dispensed with his reliance on Russian help, and instead looked to America once again.

He needed money, but peddling jobs or the odd bit-part in a motion picture would not have met his needs. His former Ghadar brothers, Udham felt sure, would give him funds to live off while waiting for the heat to cool. Though the British did not know what his primary objective was, they soon found out that he was trying to get to the United States and successfully stopped him no fewer than three times.[35] It would have driven Udham to distraction.

SECRET 22.11.37

Mr Silver.

I return herewith for your retention, the note on UDHAM SINGH's record, which I sent you with my No. 2868 dated 11.10.37, and which was returned to me.

You will see from this note that UDHAM SINGH spent some seven years in the USA which makes it plain that his present statements are an attempt to deceive us.

Inquiries show that UDHAM SINGH peddles hosiery and lingerie and uses a small car for the purpose: he does not seem to be short of money.

UDHAM SINGH served five years' imprisonment in India in 1927–1931 for having smuggled in two revolvers and ammunition. It was clear at the same time that in so doing, he was infected by Ghadar propaganda as the result of contact with the Ghadar Party when he was in California. There are adequate grounds therefore for maintaining a refusal to give him an endorsement for the USA. I think that in any case he would have considerable difficulty in securing a visa from the United States authorities.

DVW IPI[36]

The distinctive, slanting 'IPI' at the bottom of the memo told Cecil Silver that his boss had already seen the report on this Udham Singh character. Colonel Philip Vickery rarely signed documents with his own initials anymore. He used those of 'Indian Political Intelligence', the department he had helped to build from nothing.

Vickery now occupied one of the most important posts in British, intelligence, and Silver, his latest recruit, was still famil-iarising himself with the job when Udham's file landed on his desk. He had spent most of his adult life working for the India Office, but the world of counterespionage and anti-terrorism was new to him.

Silver had joined the IPI at a time when the fabric of imperial security seemed stretched to ripping point. Increasingly audacious attacks by the IRA, the rise of Hitler in Germany and continuing intrigues from the Soviet Union were forcing his colleagues to work round the clock. Silver was doing his best to darn the holes, but every time he did, new ones opened up.

Back in 1915, when Vickery first travelled to London to nurse his infant IPI, he and his colleague John Wallinger had struggled to win over colleagues in the police and secret service. Funding was always an issue. The India Office, which paid the IPI budget, seemed to do so through a clogged sieve.

When Vickery was told in 1925 that he could move his operation from the fusty India Office in Whitehall to MI5's headquarters in Cromwell Road, he might have thought the tide was turning. However, the space MI5 had seen fit to allocate him soon brought him down to earth. The IPI was given three pokey, windowless cabins in the attic, so suffocating that Vickery was almost driven mad in the hot, perpetual twilight.

The main room, which held the typing pool, secretaries and filing cabinets, was so gloomy it was a challenge to read original documents, let alone the anaemic carbon copies that often arrived in their stead. The offices felt like a tomb, offering 'minimum amount of light and airspace'.[37]

Vickery, despite his seniority, was forced to wage a major paperwork offensive just to requisition 'one extra hanging lamp'.[38] The bickering over who should pay for it went on for months.

More than a decade later, as Silver sat reading Udham's file, the department was in a state of flux once more, moving on the coat-tails of MI5 to the slightly more spacious accommodation offered by Thames House on London's Millbank. This time Silver did at least have a desk and lamp to call his own, and the gloom came instead from the contents of the files.

Each day, trolleys came by and dropped off more reports than any one man could reasonably handle. Behind thick spectacles and an air of a disappointed librarian, Silver did his best, spending hours at his desk making connections between different and sometimes unintelligible intelligence held by departments in far-flung corners of the world. Paperwork was Silver's life. Paperwork had saved his life.

In 1917, when he was a 33-year-old clerk working for the India Office, Britain was launching its latest spring offensive against the Germans on the Western Front. Silver received his call-up papers and a cubicle smelling of disinfectant was all that lay between him and the front line. As the doctor poked and prodded him, declaring him fit for duty, Silver knew the news from Europe was sickeningly bad. The Battle of Arras had begun and thousands of men were dying on both sides.

Hearing of Silver's call-up, a senior bureaucrat from the India Office wrote to the recruiting officer in Croydon, asking him to exempt Silver from duty. He was too short-sighted to be of much use as a soldier, he argued, however Silver was indispensable to the Raj and its running.

The letter had no impact, and just as Silver was packing his kit bag on 14 April, resigned to imminent carnage, the secretary of state for India himself waded in to protect him. The tone of Austen Chamberlain's letter was not to be questioned. Silver wasn't going anywhere:

Sir, I am directed by the Secretary of State for India to address you regarding the case of Mr Cecil Herbert Silver . . . Mr Silver is a member of the staff of this office and has acquired a thorough knowledge of certain confidential branches of its work connected intimately with the conduct of the war . . . he is indispensable for his front duties.[39]

The Battle of Arras would turn out to be one of the bloodiest stale-mates of the entire war, claiming the lives of about 160,000 British troops and 125,000 Germans within the space of a month.

Silver's superiors may have recognised his ability, but colleagues mocked him for his perceived lack of personality. Peter Fleming, the dashing brother of Ian, creator of the fictional spy James Bond, would run a specially trained department for the secret service. His 'Auxiliary Units' employed the best of the best and were involved in missions so dangerous, average life expectancy in the field was just twelve days. Agents were licensed to kill, shoot each other, or use explosives to kill themselves if they fell into enemy hands.[40] Fleming would give one of his most daring and valuable assets the codename 'Silver', an internal joke to amuse his department.

Unlike the flamboyant spy, Silver of the IPI was a grey machine, a bureaucrat to his bone marrow. Yet even the IPI's most capable man allowed Udham Singh to slip through his fingers. It was ironic and uncharacteristic that Silver did not make Udham more of a priority, because at the time the Indian was giving him plenty of reasons to watch him even more closely than before.

Cut off from the Russians and now blocked from the United States, by 1938 Udham was getting desperate. He needed money. He also needed logistical support if he was ever going to get out of his London limbo and work out the best way to kill Michael O'Dwyer. As will become apparent, Udham harboured hopes of getting away with the murder and would need a means of getting out of the country after the deed. It was a most un-Bhagat-Singh-like thing to plan, but Udham had a family waiting for him in America.

Knowing he was on a watch list, on St Valentine's Day 1938, Udham nevertheless presented himself at the passport office and asked for endorsements that would allow him to travel to Czechoslovakia, Greece and Norway. His flagged file caused the passport official to tell him to come back a bit later, presumably by which time the IPI could be informed of Udham's latest request. The increased scrutiny scared Udham off. How he ended up in France just two days later is therefore a complete mystery.

Arriving at the British consulate in Dunkirk on 16 February, Udham once again asked for permission to travel to a list of other countries, this time Holland, Norway, Sweden and the USA. He also asked for a renewal of his passport, which was strange because his old passport had months left on it.

In a spectacular failure, which the British described as 'an oversight',[41] Udham was given stamps to travel to Belgium and America. Most in his position would have considered this a victory, but Udham had to try to push his luck. He asked for a new passport again, presumably because he thought a clean passport would come without the troublesome flags attached to his old papers. He was denied.

Udham was now moving at speed. The very next day, he popped up in Antwerp, yet again asking the British Consulate there for a new passport. He apparently produced a British Legion badge and membership card for the Coventry branch of the Legion as proof of identity. Where he got those items remains a mystery, since the description of the serviceman that went with those cards, 'A fully pensioned Jemadar of the Indian Army', was not one that applied to him.

His request for a new passport was turned down yet again. Though he had an endorsement to travel to the United States, he had yet to get a visa. Just as the IPI had said, it was unlikely that he would get one with his troublesome documents.

It was too risky to try the United States, and his circuitous attempts to reach Russia seemed to have been thwarted too. When he surfaced in surveillance files in the summer of 1938, Udham appeared deranged with desperation. With no Ghadar or Bolshevik funds coming in, his need for money was making him reckless.

On 26 July 1938, Udham, together with a postal worker named Mool Chand, travelled to West Kensington, determined to get their hands on some cash. He demanded money 'with menaces' from Messrs Amir-Ud-Din and Fazal Shah Syed, cloth dealers who lived at one of the pedlar houses he knew well. The pair refused, the situation got messy, and Udham and Mool Chand beat up one of the men.[42]

The police were called, Udham and Mool Chand were arrested, charged and remanded in custody for almost a month. The whole thing was an unmitigated disaster and Udham was personally forced to cough up £229 he did not have to pay for his defence. Ultimately his car, which he had relied upon for his secretive forays around the country, was confiscated.

The case came before a judge on 20 September that same year,[43] but collapsed and had to be retried, amid rumours that associates of Udham Singh had leant on witnesses to keep them from coming forward. During Udham's second trial, in which he tried to change his appearance, turning up in the dock in a full turban and beard, the case against him also crumbled. Udham and Mool Chand were allowed to walk free.

Despite a string of suspicious acts, Silver and his peers allowed Udham to melt back into the shadows. It would be an expensive mistake.

CHAPTER 20

RECKONINGS

Britain was balancing on a precipice when Silver took his eyes off Udham Singh. The atmosphere in which the security services were operating had become febrile in 1938. All eyes looked outwards at the mounting threat of war from the Continent. It explains how the IPI lost sight of the enemy within.

Having annexed Austria, Hitler was pressing his claim on the Sudetenland, an area of Czechoslovakia with a predominantly ethnic German population. Neville Chamberlain, the British prime minister, flew personally to Germany for talks, convincing French and Italian counterparts to let Hitler keep what he had snatched. His appeasement did nothing to dampen the Führer's ambition, and Britain girded itself for war.

Udham knew he had been lucky to walk free from prison, and though he continued to stay in London for the most part, he never slept for more than a few days at any one of his multiple addresses, a clear attempt to shrug off any unwanted police attention. The list of his residences had extended to include two more: 17 Mornington Crescent and 8 Mornington Crescent.[1] The gaze of the security services may have shifted, but he was taking no chances. Udham now faded into the background and made no further attempt to reach Russia, Germany or the United States, even though this cut him off from valuable friends, and even more valuable cash flows.

By January 1939, Hitler was secretly ordering a major build-up of his navy, challenging British supremacy at sea. Three months later, his forces were on the move again, invading the remainder of Czechoslovakia and threatening Poland. Preparing for an imminent outbreak of hostilities, Britain rearmed, installing a highly secret radar early-warning system along its coastline.

Conscription was introduced and assurances given to the Poles that Hitler would not be allowed to take their country as easily as he had taken their neighbour. In the background of this maelstrom, two countries, both historic enemies of Britain, formed an alliance. The German foreign minister Joachim von Ribbentrop and the Soviet leader Joseph Stalin signed the Molotov–Ribbentrop Pact, a non-aggression treaty. The stage was set. On 1 September 1939, Hitler invaded Poland. Two days later, Britain declared war.

As his pedlar friends sat transfixed by their radios, listening to Chamberlain's mournful announcements, Udham was nowhere to be seen. He had already left London and made his way to the south coast, securing a room for himself in Southampton,[2] a coastal town where he had managed to get a job with a major contractor – Sir Robert McAlpine's company was doing extensive works on the docks.[3] In July, after only a month, Udham inexplicably quit his job and took up work with a company based in nearby Hampshire: Messrs Lindsay Parkinson and Co.[4] It had a lucrative contract to work on militia camps mushrooming in the area and urgently needed skilled men. Udham signed up under a fake name, 'Singh Azad'[5] – a dramatic moniker to any who understood Hindi or Urdu. It literally translated as 'The Lion Free'. To those with knowledge of India, it would have sounded immediately suspicious: 'Singh' was a Sikh name and 'Azad' Muslim. Nobody at Lindsay Parkinson and Co. seemed to notice.

For a man who had wanted nothing to do with the army since his ignominious return from Basra, it was a strange choice of employment. Udham hated the very notion of the British army, and supported the country's enemies. To now be involved in helping with the war effort made no sense unless he had an ulterior motive.

His new job gave him access to low-level military sites, where, with his ear to the ground, he could pick up interesting chatter. Southampton, where he continued to live and where some of the Parkinson job sites were located, was of great strategic importance. Apart from hosting one of the busiest docks in Britain, it was also the home of the Supermarine factory, a major manufacturer of Spitfires in Britain.

He had no hope of getting work at Supermarine, but his experience of working with aeronautics in America put him in good stead to understand any technical talk that might slip from loose lips in the local pubs. He would recognise parts being ferried in and out of the plant, would know where and how quickly they were coming in. Testament to Southampton's key role in the British war effort, Hitler would try to bomb it off the map a year later.

One has to imagine the heated atmosphere in Udham's work crew. As well as being unusually warm for that time of year,[6] the international conflict fuelled the urgency of the work of Lindsay Parkinson and Co. It would undoubtedly have raised the temperature of the banter between men. Udham and his fellow labourers worked long hours in the sun, building makeshift barracks at lightning speed in preparation for conscripted men who would soon be expected to fight. After work, the pub was the natural place to decamp, drink and dissect unfolding world events.

Perhaps it was the booze, or maybe it was simply a reaction to the intense patriotism of his fellow workers, but something pushed Udham to have a major outburst just weeks into his Lindsay Parkinson contract. He told a fellow English workman, somewhat threateningly, that he was working for people in India, 'who intended to cause trouble' as soon as India was dragged into the conflict: 'He declared that everything was ready for a rebellion and that arms and ammunition had been supplied by Germany and Russia.'[7]

Udham's words were reported to the police the very next morning, however, when they came to question him, 'Singh Azad' was gone. Perhaps the cold light of day had sobered him up, or at the very least shown him how one emotional explosion threatened to detonate twenty years of effort. It was hard to fathom just how he could have been so very careless.

A contributing factor to Udham's instability at this time might be explained by some recent and devastating news. Har Dayal, the leader of the Ghadars in America, had died unexpectedly, and news was just starting to filter across the ocean. The manner of his passing had rocked an already weakened movement. There were murmurings of murder.

Har Dayal, a perfectly fit and healthy 55-year-old man, had been in Philadelphia at the time. According to one of his fellow Ghadar brothers, Hanumant Sahay, Har Dayal had been re-energised by the war. His movement had been dwindling in power and influence thanks to a corralled leadership in the United States and rifts within its rank and file. Splinter groups had been developing, but Har Dayal had never given up hope of making the Ghadars a unified and feared force once again. He saw the outbreak of the Second World War as an opportunity to reinvent the movement, to once more sow dissent in the ranks of the British Indian army and capitalise on potential help from Russia and Germany.

Har Dayal delivered a barnstorming speech on the night of 4 March and, pleased with the result, retired to his bed. Those who came to rouse him in the morning found him dead. Hanumant Sahay would always insist that Har Dayal, his mentor, had been poisoned,[8] and that somehow the British had managed to get to him in America. News of Har Dayal's death, which took a month to reach India, longer still to reach Britain, would have come as a body blow to Udham, already feeling cut off from the world.

The organisation that had given him his revolutionary life was as fatherless as he was, an unbalancing sensation that appears to have pushed him harder to pursue his own goal. If they could get to Har Dayal, how long would it be before the British would get to him?

It was too late and too difficult to get his hands on a new identity, so Udham was forced to stick with 'Singh Azad'. He was next seen in Bournemouth, where barely two weeks later he managed to get work as a carpenter at the Blandford militia camp. Less strategically significant than Southampton, it did at least bring him closer to his own personal mission. Blandford was just down the coast from south Devon, the location of Michael O'Dwyer's holiday home. Somehow, just weeks after hearing of the Ghadar leader's death, Udham finally managed to get his hands on Sir Michael's address. In the accounts column for 13 June 1939, Udham wrote the following in his diary 'Sir M O'Dwyer, Sunnybank, Thurlestone, South Devon'.[9]

Not only did he write it in his diary, but later he would also note it in an aide-memoire to himself, reminding him of the major epochs in his life. Though he would attempt to destroy that document by ripping it to pieces, police would piece together the fragments and find a timeline of sorts. A few simple lines in Udham's handwriting opened up a complicated set of questions:

> 1938 – Met Moola through Col. Appleby, Cheltenham. Took Moola and . . . to Brighton and Bognor.

> 1939 – Moola's letter arrived and I met . . . Windsor Staines and (?) Calif of England – to go to America . . . he and his son . . . Commissioner – San Francisco, if you are keen on Government service . . . gave me his address and said I shall go to Devon on 13 June.[10]

The police would do their best to transcribe Udham's scrawl, but they were only ever able to make out some of his words. Those that they could read sounded like gibberish. However, with the benefit of hindsight, there is much we can unpack today.

'Moola', it would later transpire, was the same Mool Chand who had been arrested with Udham in 1938, trying to get money 'with menaces' from fellow Indians. He had worked for the postal service, which is perhaps how he managed to get his hands on the letter with Sir Michael's address upon it.

Sir Michael's south Devon hideaway was easy enough to reach, even if it involved a meandering coastal route. Killing him there would be far easier than in central London, where porters manned mansion blocks, police were patrolling in numbers, and streets were always busy.

In the same garbled note-to-self, Udham wrote that 'Moola' had been introduced to him by some mysterious Colonel Appleby. He would refer to 'Col. Appleby' a few times in his private writing, always in cryptic ways, careful to give nothing away of his identity. Remembering the landscape of the days leading up to his revenge, he merely noted places they had met: '[1939] Col. Appleby . . . Glasgow and Blackpool . . . and every evening went for a walk, and Weston-Super-Mare Atlantic Hotel, Cheltenham – Queen's Hotel . . . Mary Hotel – every day. Used to take me for a walk.'[11]

A meeting with 'Col. Appleby' had preceded Udham's decision to up sticks from London and move to the coast. Files on Udham Singh, which have been forced open by Freedom of Information requests, contain no follow-up on 'Col. Appleby', nor any indication of further investigation into him. That seems strange to say the least. It is possible they did not find him of interest, but it is more likely there are other files, top secret in nature, connected to the Udham Singh case which have yet to be identified and opened to scrutiny.

A Colonel Appleby does appear in the army lists of 1939, but he was based in Scotland leading his own regiment. He was not the kind of man who would have had the time, let alone the inclination, to meet an Indian pedlar at mysterious assignations around the country. Therefore it is reasonable to speculate that the name was a cover, but for whom, and why?

In 1939, Appleby was the name for a popular fictional character created by the author Michael Innes. 'Detective Inspector Appleby' and his adventures kept readers enthralled throughout the 1930s, and his character, used by the British government to track down enemies of the state, would go on to become the commissioner of the Metropolitan Police. It would have been a pleasingly playful *nom de guerre* for one working to destabilise the realm, while evading police detection.

Other lines in Udham's scrawling memoir require less

speculation: 'Commissioner – San Francisco, if you are keen on government service.'[12] Sir Michael's son, John Chevalier O'Dwyer, was now successfully working as vice consul in San Francisco. Was Udham encouraging somebody to deal with the son, while he dealt with the father?

Udham was so close, closer than he had ever been, to fulfilling his vow, but as so often happened flaws, in his own character blew him off course once again. His pride had cost him his career in the army; vanity had cost him his freedom in Amritsar; obsession had cost him a wife and family; and his temper had forced him out of Hampshire.

In Basra, Udham had chafed at the orders of white superiors, and now at the Blandford camp he behaved exactly as his teenage self. Gaffers described him as 'bad tempered' and 'quarrelsome'. They also described his work as 'unsatisfactory'. On 11 September, 'Singh Azad' was fired. It was far from ideal. 'Col Appleby' had needed him to gather information, Udham was no longer in a situation to do so. He had done something else though, something much worse: 'It was rumoured . . . that he always carried a loaded revolver. One thing which was noticeable was that he always had a large bulge in his hip pocket. How the rumour originated they [his co-workers] did not know.'[13] These were edgy times, and for the second time in a matter of a few weeks, 'Singh Azad' was reported to the police.

A young officer named Fisher of the Hampshire Constabulary was sent out to speak to the querulous and potentially armed Indian, but once again Udham disappeared by the time police arrived. Sniffing around in his wake, Fisher found he was not the only one asking questions. Police from the neighbouring constabulary of Southampton were also investigating the disappearance of their mysterious Indian carpenter, and from the sound of it, they were acting on orders much higher than Fisher's desk sergeant: 'I understand that in September 1939, enquiries were made concerning AZAD by the Southampton Borough Police on behalf of Major General Sir Vernon Kell, whose reference no. is L/255 (1) B/4a.'[14]

It was such a short entry in the police log, showing that Fisher was clearly entirely oblivious to the significance of what he had written. Kell was not ordinary military brass. The 67-year old was in fact one of the most powerful spymasters in the world.

Kell was both the director of MI5, and its founder. A perpetual look of intense concentration had left him with a vertical furrow above the bridge of his nose. There was little about his appearance that betrayed the burden he shouldered. Refined, quiet and considered in speech, his spectacles and neat side parting gave him the look of a somewhat stressed university don, unthreatening and distinctly unmemorable.

In security circles, Kell was referred to reverentially as 'K', and the MI5 motto, 'Regnum Defende' or 'Defence of the Realm', gave some indication of the scope of his responsibility. Perhaps Kell had taken a special interest in the case of 'Singh Azad' because he recognised the oddness of the name. Unlike many of his colleagues, 'K' knew India well, and he had come across men like Udham before.

During the First World War, Kell's MI5 (g) section had infiltrated groups of Indian revolutionaries in Bengal, Britain and North America. Together with John Wallinger, Vickery's predecessor at the IPI, he had foiled a Ghadar Party plot to assassinate Lord Kitchener, the then secretary of state for war.[15]

That Kell himself had picked up a phone to make inquiries of 'Singh Azad' speaks volumes. It tells us there are almost certainly MI5 files on Udham and his alias that have yet to see the light of day. It also tells us that MI5 was deeply fallible in 1939, because after his initial inquiries, Kell either lost sight of or interest in Udham Singh.

The pedlar/carpenter disappeared from sight again. Udham Singh had by now managed to slip through the fingers of the police, the IPI and MI5, all in the space of a few weeks. What he lacked in personal judgement, he more than made up for in skill or luck. For the next six months Udham would lay low, waiting until he was sure the police were no longer looking for him. The date in his diary had suggested he intended to kill Sir Michael on 13 June 1940, when he would have moved to his Devon address for the summer. As it would turn out, Udham could not wait that long.

LONDON, MARCH 1940

The pedlars settled down to their regular meal, each producing a different dish to share with the group. This dinner was the same as the usual communal meals, but it somehow felt different. Udham was back after a long and unexplained absence. Though he was usually a lively addition to any gathering, on this occasion he seemed to be bouncing off the walls. Nobody could really understand what he had to be so happy about.

The past few months had not been easy. Since his return to London in late 1939, the few who had actually seen Udham found him more restless than ever. He seemed to be living a near vagrant life, never spending more than a few days in the same place. For one who had been so flashy and proud, it appeared to be a miserable fall from grace.

Udham was not working, had no car, his motorbike was gone and there was no glamorous girl on his arm. Someone had even seen him signing on for unemployment benefit. Despite his apparent run of bad luck, Udham turned up for this particular pedlar dinner in a giddy mood. He seemed determined to enjoy himself, and had even brought a box of *laddoos* with him, the traditional Indian sweet usually distributed for the birth of a baby boy. Towards the end of the meal, Udham drew aside his old friend Gurbachan Singh and turned deadly serious for a moment: 'If anyone asks you about me, just say you don't know me, OK?'[16] Gurbachan laughed off the comment. His friend was always so dramatic.

Bidding farewell to his raucous pedlar friends, Udham next went to see a far more solemn man, also based in the East End of London. Surat Ali[17] was a one-man nexus of Indian discontent: a trade union activist; a member of the Indian Workers Association; a member of the Communist Party of Great Britain; and a hero to the lascars.

To the British authorities, Surat Ali was one of the worst kind of agitators, and had been under surveillance for some time, particularly after he organised a series of strikes at London's docks demanding more pay for the Indian seamen. The police who kept watch on Surat Ali would have seen Udham coming to visit him on 11 March. They would have seen him leave, but they would have no idea who he was until much later. Nor would they ever know what actually passed between the two men.

Surat Ali would be hauled in for questioning by police in the days that followed, and though he would admit that he knew Udham, he would deny that he had any knowledge of what he was about to do. He also denied supplying him with a gun.[18]

Banta Singh was one of the last of Udham's friends to see him as a free man. A fellow East End pedlar, Banta and Udham had a unique kind of friendship. Perhaps Banta Singh reminded him of the Khalsa brothers who had run the orphanage, but where his other pedlar friendships were defined by goodhearted tomfoolery, he reserved a near reverential respect for this particular man. Banta Singh's son, Peter, described the dynamic many years later:

> My father used to live first at Adler Street and later at Crispin Street in East London, both pedlar houses ... He had known Udham for about five years in London. They even lived together for a spell. It was a funny friendship because they were so different. Udham Singh was so child-like it was almost like he needed my father to act as his adult.
>
> Father was a very religious man, a fully turbaned Sikh. Udham used to call him 'Bhai-ji' – it meant 'priest' or 'the learned one'. I think it was because father wore a white turban and white clothes and knew all his prayers. Father told me that on 11 March 1940, Udham paid him an unexpected visit sometime in the night. He knew how much Udham Singh hated Michael O'Dwyer. He used

to talk about it all the time. That night, Udham was in a strange
mood and it scared my father.[19]

Unable to settle down, Udham paced the floor and spoke very
quickly:

He told my father to pack his things and leave town that very
night if he could. Because he was planning to do something.[20]
    'What are you going to do, Bawa?' My father asked him, even
though he said he knew deep down.[21]
    'Pack your bags and leave now. You are my friend. I don't want
you to get caught up in whatever will come next,' Udham said.

His relationship with Banta was the kind a Catholic might have with
a confessional priest, and Udham clearly felt he could tell Banta
anything without being betrayed.
    Udham had told Banta of his all-consuming hatred of O'Dwyer.
He had even told him that he would kill him one day. As a religious man, Banta believed judgement and justice lay in the hands
of the maker, not his creation, and had, in the past, attempted to
counsel him out of his rage. Udham must have known his pious
friend would try to talk him out of his plan that night too. He
was right: 'I begged him not to do it,' Banta Singh later told his
son. 'I really begged him. But he was adamant. He had waited
twenty years to punish the man who had killed so many that day
[in Jallianwala Bagh]. I told him again and again that nothing
he could do would bring them back. He just bowed his head and
said, "Bhai-ji, you can ask me to do anything, give you anything
but you cannot ask me this. It has to be this way. He has to die
and I have to do it."'[22]
    Udham was testing his resolve one last time. Having failed to
change his friend's mind, Banta was sufficiently disturbed by what
Udham had said that he left London the very next day, moving as
far away from the capital as he could. Banta Singh would settle in
Cornwall in the West Country. He never returned to the capital.

Though he cared nothing for O'Dwyer, it broke his heart that he had not been able to stop, and by extension save, his friend.

13 MARCH 1940

London awoke to a continuous and gentle snowfall.[23] As Udham took the razor to his face, a layer of powdery white began to cover the streets like a thin shroud. He scraped away the cream and coarse black bristle, pulling his skin taut, looking at his face from every angle. He had to look good today. The world would be watching.

Buttoning up his clean white shirt, Udham pulled a sober yet smart suit out of his wardrobe: slate grey, deeply ordinary. This was no time for his exuberant American checks. He had to be respectably boring today. The kind of man nobody would look at twice. An invisible man. A ghost.

The government had passed a law in September 1939 requiring everyone to carry an identity card. Udham looked at his own with satisfaction before slipping it into the top inside pocket of his jacket. He was: 'Mohamed Singh Azad, 8 Mornington Terrace, Regent's Park'.[24] So perfect. He almost looked forward to them finding it.

The name was an iteration of the one that had piqued Kell's interest. Udham knew 'Singh Azad' was known to the police, but he was not ready to let it go. He had chosen it with such care. His recent brushes with the law had given him cause to reconfigure it, so he had merely added a third to the front. Atheist turned prophet, Udham would be Mohamed today, and hopefully for ever after.

India would understand. For two decades he had worked at becoming the man who could make Sir Michael pay for Jallianwala Bagh, however in the process he believed he had become so much more. It was no longer enough to settle his own score; he now had to unite his people in a full-blown revolution. Hindus, Muslims and Sikhs would come together behind his act. He would avenge the dead. He would inspire the living.

The drop in the mercury made his shave less pleasant than it could have been that morning, but it was hugely helpful to his mission. Everyone would be wearing their heavy winter coats. His had big, deep pockets, and Udham had a lot to carry.

Slipping the lid from the square wooden box on his table, Udham counted the contents. Seventeen rounds, all present and correct.[25] He shut the box and dropped it into his right-hand jacket pocket.[26] It was reassuringly solid against his hip. He then dropped eight loose bullets into his right trouser pocket.[27] These would be easy to reach, jingling pleasingly, like innocent small change.

Into his left jacket pocket, Udham slipped his diary.[28] It is unclear why he felt the need to take it with him that day, unless he meant for the police to find it later. The entry for that very day was as incriminating as the weapons he carried: '3 p.m. Caxton Hall, S.W.1 Meeting.'[29] Elsewhere in the same little book he had written the words: 'Action',[30] 'Only the way to open the door',[31] and 'My last month'.[32] Elsewhere in its pages, he had written Sir Michael's countryside address as well as the home address of the Marquess of Zetland, the present secretary of state for India, and Lord Willingdon, a former viceroy. How he got his hands on those addresses, we do not know.

Udham would have to be careful not to stick his hand too quickly into the left-hand pocket of his coat. In it was a squat, heavy-bladed knife, and if he was hasty, he risked slicing off his own fingers. The sharp blade was curved like a crescent moon,[33] specially designed to cut linoleum. A man simply had to jab and pull to leave a long, neat, deep cut.

When he dropped the Smith and Wesson Mark 2 into his pocket, he felt the stitches strain. A big and heavy gun, it measured ten inches from tip of muzzle to flick of the trigger and when loaded it was more than a kilo in weight. At least this coat, with its thick material, would not betray suspicious bulges like his clothes in Southampton. If he pulled his collar up it would hide the bottom of his face. The brim of his fedora would take care of the top half. He would look like just another Londoner facing the chill air.

Udham took the gun from his overcoat to check it one last time.

The cylinder clicked out from its pin position and he looked through its six chambers, making sure they were clean before he dropped in the bullets. This gun was double action, so there was no need to cock it after every shot. He could get off a number of rounds in quick succession.

The size of the revolver was not ideal. His outstretched arm would have to fight gravity to keep the muzzle from drooping towards the floor. It also kicked like a mule. Every time he fired it felt like a cricket ball had been thrown into his hand by a powerful fast bowler.

He would have to focus after every shot, keeping his arm stiff enough to hold his aim, but not so stiff that the shock of the recoil made him drop his weapon. Udham had practised shooting in the woods, but trees did not move. He had to believe that muscle memory would keep his aim true, even as adrenaline coursed through his body.

Udham had waited twenty years for this, and now the day had finally arrived, it required just a little more patience from him. The assassin found he had a lot of time to kill before he would come face to face with his nemesis, but was so relaxed about what lay ahead, he even considered going to the cinema beforehand. A new Paul Robeson picture had been released that week and everything about it would have appealed to him. Robeson was playing an African American sailor named David Goliath in *The Proud Valley*, who travels to south Wales, where miners hear him sing and invite him to join their male voice choir. They give him a job in the colliery and accept him as one of their own. The workers of the world united.

Robeson in turn fights for their rights, laying down his life while trying to save them from a pit disaster. A dark-skinned hero providing hope to the oppressed. In his mind it was Udham's story too. He would have related to Robeson on many levels. The American actor had made enthusiastically pro-Soviet statements in his career, leading him to be blacklisted in many parts of the industry. There could be no more fitting curtain-raiser to his main event.

Udham never got the chance to spend those final hours with

Paul Robeson. The cinema was closed until later that afternoon. So instead Udham meandered through the cold London air towards the India Office in Whitehall. Sometime between 11.30 and midday, he went in and asked to speak to Sir Hasan Suhrawardy. When later asked why he had needed to see the Oxford-educated Indian diplomat, Udham would tell police he wished to discuss the block on his passport, but that seems somewhat implausible. His travel difficulties were well below the pay-grade of such a man.

Suhrawardy was an establishment figure in 1940, but he had not always been. The IPI had files on him stretching over two decades, dating back to his student days. He had come to the attention of the security services because of his close connections to Russia. Suhrawardy, a brilliant Bengali student, had won a scholarship to study in Moscow in 1914. He liked the country and the people so much that he stayed on to become professor of English at Moscow University and was therefore caught up in the Russian Revolution of 1917. Managing to escape the violence, he went home for a while, only to return to Russia to work with the Moscow Art Theatre between 1926 and 1929. The IPI had only stopped taking an interest in Suhrawardy's Russian connection in 1935.

Could it be that Udham was trying to pass one last message to Russia before the end? We will never know, because when he came to call, Suhrawardy was not in. Udham was told to come back later. Of course, he never did.

'I'll be back for tea at five o'clock.' These were the last words Sir Michael O'Dwyer spoke to his wife Una before he headed out of the door.[34] The snow had cleared by midday and bright light streamed through the high regency windows of his London apartment. Sir Michael's housekeeper made a mental note to put the crockery out in time for his return. She liked things to be ready for him and his particular nature had always allowed servants to function with supreme efficiency. Yet something important that afternoon was making him break his usual routine.

The O'Dwyers usually took in an early evening film on Wednesdays, ensconced in the womb-like darkness of a local cinema.[35] Kensington Picture House was their preferred retreat and *The Old Maid*, starring Bette Davis, was showing that week. The film had received mixed reviews when it debuted first in the United States. Unimpressed by the director, critics had been wowed by Davis's performance: 'It probably is not a good motion picture, in the strict cinematic sense ... dramatically it is vital, engrossing and a little terrifying ... As the old maid, Miss Davis has given a poignant and wise performance, hard and austere of surface, yet communicating through it ... deep tenderness.'[36]

The same description had often been used of Sir Michael. A hard man when it came to his politics, but deeply loyal and loving to friends and family and devoted to his wife. Sir Michael had grown increasingly sentimental with age, especially when it came to his animals. One yappy little Scottie dog called Mackay brought him particular joy. Mackay was the kind of animal most found profoundly irritating, a dark and spirited creature that 'raced up and down the stairs', barking at every knock at the door.[37] Knowing he was going to have to leave the old boy locked up in his apartment most of the day, Sir Michael spent the entire morning of 13 March making it up to Mackay, taking him for an extra-long walk before he had to go out himself. The two of them had the run of the finest parks in the capital thanks to the location of Sir Michael's smart home, situated on Prince of Wales Terrace, close to the Royal Albert Hall.

Hyde Park, Green Park and Kensington Gardens opened out in great spaces around Sir Michael's home. Though the greenery was quintessentially English, on the other side of Sir Michael's front door the nine rooms of his first-floor apartment were redolent of India. He had collected curios from his time in the ICS and liked to have them on display, each an aide memoire to both entertaining anecdotes and important chapters in history.

The engagement keeping him from his cinema commitment to his wife was to take place at Caxton Hall. The building had played host to its fair share of drama over the years. Situated in the shadow of the Houses of Parliament in Westminster, fiery trade union meetings, passionate suffragette gatherings and raucous political debate had filled Caxton Hall's spacious rooms over the years. The Tudor Room was the perfect venue for a meeting of the East India Association and Royal Central Asian Society. Sir Michael would not be giving the lecture that day, but he was extremely keen to hear it. 'Afghanistan, the present position' seemed like an important topic for the time.

The Russians had been using Afghanistan as a staging post for their intrigues for years. After signing the non-aggression pact with Germany, they had pounded the Finns into submission. Between them, Russia and Germany seemed to be carving up the world. It was only a matter of time before they turned their attention east towards the oil fields of Persia, then on to India.

Brigadier General Sir Percy Sykes, the keynote speaker that afternoon, was an expert on Russia, India and Persia. A soldier statesman, Sykes had served in the Indian army with the 2nd Dragoon Guards, and later supported Russian forces at Isfahan in 1915. He had also served with army intelligence, and as consul at Kerman in Persia. He knew the terrain and the temperament of the region. He also happened to be one of Sir Michael's closest friends.

The pair had known each other for decades, and Sir Michael had agreed to say a few words to supplement his friend's thoughts. Men like Sykes could help bring Britain safely out of the chaos, Sir Michael believed, and he was only too happy to do his bit to help.

He was not alone. The Marquess of Zetland, secretary of state for India, had carved a space in his wartime diary to chair the meeting. Raj luminaires like Sir Louis Dane, Sir Michael's predecessor as lieutenant governor of Punjab, and Lord Lamington, the former governor of Bombay, had also agreed to attend.

When the doors finally opened at around 2 p.m., the 130 laid-out seats filled quickly. The audience was peppered with former ICS officers, important military men both retired and serving, and members of the public. Considering the VIP list, it was astonishing that there was barely any security at the door. People filed in without having their bags checked. Many got in without having to show their tickets. One would hardly have believed the country was at war.

Speeches were to begin at 3 p.m., and by 2.30 the room was already heaving. A ticketed affair should not, by rights, have been so over-subscribed, but even when the speakers took their seats, people were still squeezing in, finding standing room wherever they could. Sir Michael's seat had been reserved at the very front, on the right-hand side of the hall. Just a few feet away from where he sat, a slightly raised dais had been arranged for Lord Zetland, the secretary of the East India Association, Sir Frank Brown, and Sir Percy Sykes. The clock ticked towards the hour as stragglers continued to slip in apologetically. Most stood at the back wishing to cause as little disruption as possible. Udham was one of the last to squeeze in.

His hat was pulled low, his overcoat now folded neatly over one arm. Waved in impatiently, to his relief, nobody asked to see Udham's ticket. It was lucky, because he had none to show. Unlike other latecomers, Udham headed for the aisle on the right-hand side of the hall instead of the back, and edged his way forward, stopping just shy of the fourth row. He was just a few feet away from Sir Michael O'Dwyer, who sat with his back to him.[38]

All Udham could see of the former lieutenant governor was his snowy white head bobbing in conversation. This was the man who had dominated his thoughts for decades, who had inspired him to travel thousands of miles, who had pushed him into foreign circles and underground organisations. This white-haired man had brought him to the edges of his endurance and capability. The untouchable O'Dwyer within touching distance of the Kamboj orphan at last. Udham watched as Sir Michael chatted animatedly without a care in the world.

Four strides would bring him face to face with his enemy, but Udham held his position and instead settled his back into the wood panelling. As the first of the speakers rose to his feet, he popped a boiled sweet into his mouth. The very spirit of calm attentiveness.

Most people would later say that they did not even notice Udham standing there. Major Reginald Alfred Slee was one of the few exceptions. A retired army officer with the Duke of Cambridge's Regiment, he had a soldier's eye and had been watching Udham standing a few rows in front of him. It had struck him as odd that this man had pushed his way past people to stand where he was. It was not the most comfortable place to watch proceedings. A fellow would have to twist his body sideways in order to see the dais. Almost unconsciously, Slee noted the man's appearance: 'Dark skinned . . . middle-aged . . . probably about forty to forty-five years of age. He was a heavily built man and was dressed in dark morning dress.'[39]

Claud Wyndham Harry Richie, a retired assistant bank manager, also noticed Udham, mostly because he had brushed past him as he walked down his aisle: 'I had not seen him enter but my attention was drawn to him because I could see that he was not a European. I thought that he was a north Indian or an Afghan . . . He seemed very interested in the meeting.'[40]

Introduced by Frank Brown, Sir Percy spoke for about three quarters of an hour, followed by Lord Zetland, who spoke for fifteen minutes. As time ticked on, Udham's face began to betray his feelings. He was smiling to himself, even though Sykes's speech was far from funny. So close. He was so very close.

When Sir Michael O'Dwyer eventually rose to his feet to turn and address the audience from the floor, Udham saw his face for the first time. Sir Michael was older, but had lost none of his presence or energy. He captivated the room with his lively blue eyes, speaking animatedly about 'the riot in the Punjab after the Great War' and the lessons that could be learned and applied in Afghanistan. It was vintage O'Dwyer: portentous but at the same time humorous and engaging.

It must have taken everything Udham had in him not to reach for his pistol when Sir Michael started talking about Punjab. He inched closer, his back still against the wall. There was only one chance to get this right. Patient . . . He had to be patient.

As Sir Michael sat down, a flutter of activity caused heads to turn, but it had nothing to do with Udham. A middle-aged woman had just been let in and there was some shuffling of feet and bags to accommodate her. Marjorie Usher was a prominent member of the East India Association and had been running horribly late. She had been allowed to enter at 4.25 p.m.,[41] though the doors had been closed to other latecomers. Marjorie looked around the room and her eyes immediately settled on Udham: 'About three yards from the platform, I saw an Indian. His face seemed familiar, and on more than one occasion I saw him looking around the room.'[42]

When Lord Lamington stood to deliver his vote of thanks, Marjorie looked away from the Indian. Lamington spoke in the kind of booming voice typical of the chronically hard of hearing. Marjorie missed Udham's imperceptible shuffle forward.

Bertha Herring, a volunteer ambulance driver,[43] was one of the only people to keep her eyes on Udham despite Lord Lamington's distracting contribution. The dark-skinned man had put her on edge: 'I wondered who this man was and how he came to be there. He appeared to be of very unpleasant appearance.'[44]

To the sound of warm applause, the meeting was brought to a close. The snow of the morning had now turned to sleet and people, Bertha included, began to gather up their things, pulling on coats, buttoning up, reaching under chairs for umbrellas. Sir Michael and the other speakers were out of their seats now, gathered in a distinguished-looking huddle at the front, congratulating each other.

Pushing against the flow heading for the exit, Udham made his move. Sir Michael had turned to speak to Lord Lamington when he first noticed Udham approach him. His hand was extended.

At first Sir Michael must have thought he wanted to shake hands. By the time he saw the gun, it was too late. No time to run, instincts kicked in instead and he turned away from the revolver, hands across his body, protecting his chest. The gun was practically touching his back when it went off for the first time.

Udham's bullet bored a path through Sir Michael's 75-year-old body, shattering his tenth rib and slicing through the base of his lung. It travelled through the right ventricle of his heart before emerging out of his left side.[45] A wisp of white smoke and sulphur filled the space between them as Udham's gun hand reared up towards the ceiling. He brought it down so quickly that Sir Michael didn't even have time to fall when he was hit again.

The second bullet also flew into the old man's back, entering at a slightly lower angle than the first. Udham's firing was precise and deadly. The round followed a path almost parallel to the first: 'The lower [bullet] smashed the twelfth rib, [and] ploughed up the right kidney, passed through the soft issue of the back of the abdomen.'[46]

Sir Michael crumpled and fell to the ground, in an almost foetal position. He rolled onto his back, staring blankly at the ceiling. It is doubtful whether he even heard the Tudor Room erupt around him. Amid the screams, chairs clattered on the wooden floor as people dived for cover. Udham, crouched behind one of the front-row seats, pivoted and very deliberately took aim at the dais. Firing his third shot, he hit Lord Zetland at chest height. Once again, the heavy Smith and Wesson kicked hard against his grip, and once again, Udham wrestled it back into position to let off another round almost immediately. Both bullets found their mark. Lord Zetland, who had turned his body in an attempt to get off the stage, was hit twice in the left side. He slumped in his chair clutching at his chest.

Believing he had delivered fatal wounds, Udham now turned his fire on 79-year-old Lord Lamington, the hard-of-hearing former governor of Bombay, and 83-year-old Sir Louis Dane, Sir Michael O'Dwyer's predecessor in the Punjab.

Dane had been standing next to his old friend Sir Michael. The order in which Udham had selected his victims gave him vital seconds to get away. He had managed to put around six feet between himself and Udham when he too was caught by Udham's fifth bullet. Dane raised his hand in an instinctively protective way and the bullet smashed through, shattering the bones in his forearm. By rights it should have continued its trajectory and embedded itself in his torso, but something was very wrong with Udham's gun. He was firing with precision, but the bullets were not travelling with as much force as they should have been.

Lord Lamington, a frail man, was not so fast on his feet as Dane. He was shot at much closer quarters by Udham's final bullet. It too was destined for his torso, but like Dane, Lamington's outstretched hand took the bullet and all of its force.

Udham should have killed every one of his victims that day. As a lawyer would later put it: 'Every bullet found a billet.'[47] However, only one man would die.

It would take a gun and ballistics expert to later discover that the bullets Udham had used were too small for his gun, .44 calibre instead of the .455 which would have fit the chambers snugly. The loose fit of these smaller 'wrong' bullets had forced propellant gases around the casings, significantly slowing the flight of the bullets as they left their chambers and reducing their impact. Lord Zetland, Louis Dane and Lord Lamington owed their lives to that fact.[48]

The gun was hot in his hand when Udham made a break for the door: 'Make way! Make way!'[49] he screamed, shoving people out of his way. Bertha Herring, still in her seat on the aisle, saw him barrelling towards her and, though most were paralysed with fear, something inside her snapped. Yelling at her sister to stay down, she leaped at Udham as he passed. Bertha was a substantial woman and she body-checked him with all her might, grabbing at his shoulders and toppling him to the floor. Her extraordinary reflex set off a chain reaction.

As he struggled to untangle himself from Bertha and get back on his feet, Claude Wyndham Harry Riches also hurled himself at Udham, bringing him down for a second time:

'I took a step forward and jumped, landing on the man's shoulders. As I landed my coat, which was on my arm, went over his head and unsighted him. He fell on his face to the floor and as he did so, his right hand struck against something and he dropped the revolver about six inches from his hand. I pinned the man's hand to the ground with my right hand and leaning over him, with my left hand I flicked the revolver away.'[50]

Major Slee grabbed the gun, while two serving officers who had been sitting at the back of the hall vaulted over the mess of fallen chairs and crouching people to where Udham was now sprawled on the floor. They pinned him, one with a foot on his outstretched hand.[51]

Realising there was no chance for escape, Udham stopped struggling almost immediately and lay perfectly still. For a few moments, the only thing that seemed to be moving in the Tudor Room was the curling white smoke that had just been discharged from his gun.

Eerie silence descended on all in the blood-spattered Tudor Room, broken only when Marjorie Usher, the latecomer, snapped herself out of her horror-stricken trance and made her way forwards towards Sir Michael. His breathing was shallow and laboured. Marjorie knelt and, not knowing what else to do, gently raised Sir Michael's head onto her lap and fanned him with her programme.

Dr Grace Mackinnon, who had been sitting on the front row, was jarred into action by Marjorie's futile tenderness. She joined her, kneeling by her side, and set about trying to find the bullet wounds, attempting to staunch Sir Michael's bleeding. He was beyond her help: 'I could do nothing for him.'[52]

The women had broken the spell and the Tudor Room reanimated. Another member of the audience, Dr M. R. Lawrence, the brother of T. E Lawrence, or 'Lawrence of Arabia', ran forward. Sir Michael's life was now slipping away fast. Lawrence looked to the others, groaning and writhing around him. He set about trying to calm them, running his hands over their bodies, trying to find entry and exit wounds.

Sobbing, shouting, anger and fear now replaced the stunned silence of the Tudor Room. One woman ran out into the street screaming for a policeman. Perhaps it was a late rush of adrenaline that drove retired medic Colonel Carl Henry Reinhold to throw himself on the pile of bodies pinioning Udham in the aisle: '[I] added my weight on top of them,'[53] he told police proudly later.

It did not take long to realise that he was in fact squeezing the breath out of the servicemen as well as Udham, so he scrambled off the human pyramid and went instead to where Marjorie knelt. Sir Michael was now motionless on her lap and she was whispering words of comfort into his ear. Reinhold realised he was watching him take his last breaths: 'I think he died within a few minutes.'[54]

Shot through the heart,[55] the former lieutenant governor of Punjab bled out surrounded by people who were powerless to help him. It was a macabre echo of the fate of so many at Jallianwala Bagh.

Philip Bloomberg had not been shot, but he was in agony. A journalist with the Press Association (PA) wire service, he had drawn the short straw that night and been sent to cover the Caxton Hall meeting. No other newspaper could be bothered. He was therefore the sole journalist in the room when Udham Singh started shooting.

He witnessed extraordinary scenes, and any editor would have given his eyeteeth for Bloomberg's account. His copy, had he been able to file it, would have had everything: high drama, high-profile victims, an exotic villain. Bloomberg watched as a lady doctor and a male colleague – somebody said he was Lawrence of Arabia's brother – splinted Louis Dane's shattered forearm with a lady's umbrella. It should have been the scoop of his life.

Instead, Philip Bloomberg would live out every journalist's worst nightmare. He was witnessing history but he could tell nobody about it. As soon as Bloomberg managed to gather his wits enough to phone the story in, the police had entered the Tudor Room and were locking down everything and everyone inside.[56] To make matters more excruciating, Bloomberg could see the press table from where he was standing. There was a telephone right there, on top of it, within reach. It might as well have been on the moon.

Every minute, more police arrived, adamant that nobody should move, much less talk to anyone outside till they had been processed. A couple of officers had been stationed in Caxton Hall and had arrived within seconds. Pockets had to be searched, identities and home addresses had to be taken and detailed witness statements had to be recorded and signed. As Philip Bloomberg was herded into an adjoining room, he could see Sir Michael's body lying there, his head resting against the leg of his press table.

Within half an hour, a thick police cordon was being thrown around Caxton Hall. Bloomberg's Fleet Street competitors, who arrived at the scene within the hour, counted around 150 police officers, almost one for every member of the audience still trapped inside.

Popping camera bulbs strobed the descending gloom. Journalists buzzed like hornets over ripe fruit, filling the nearby red telephone boxes and shouting their copy down the line, while their photographers remained rooted to the spot. There was one picture that everyone wanted. They would wait all night if they had too.

Only the news editor of the *Daily Express* thought to send a reporter to Sir Michael's home, where he not only doorstepped the housekeeper, but forced his way inside. The reporter noted that Sir Michael's walls were covered with 'pistols and swords and Indian idols'.[57] Pushing past the poor woman's confusion, he asked her why the cups and plates were laid out on the table. She had been expecting him back, she said. He was meant to be home any minute. The water was still hot in the kettle. Mackay was by the door, wagging his tail, waiting for a master who would never return.

The stunned housekeeper, faced with the reality of events, now found herself babbling to the reporter, little realising that every word she said would be printed in the next day's newspaper. Sir Michael and his wife were planning to spend the summer in their country home in Devon, she said. They always did that. They planned to be there in June, she said. He was coming home for tea. He was coming back. She had the tea things all ready.

CHAPTER 21

MOHAMMED SINGH AZAD

Detective Inspector Deighton was the first senior police officer on the scene. Arriving on his heels came police surgeon Dr Arnold Harbour. The two shook hands and walked over to the body, confirming what everybody knew. Sir Michael was dead and his body lay on the floor exactly where he had fallen. Rolling his body on its side gently, Harbour showed Deighton the scorch marks on the back of Sir Michael's jacket. The gun had been extremely close when it had been fired.

Turning to the dark-skinned suspect who had been watching them work with an air of detachment, Deighton noticed that he was now smiling. Udham had been forced to sit in a chair on the front row, and was handcuffed to an officer:[1] 'Do you understand English?' Deighton asked.

'Yes,' replied Udham.[2]

'You will be detained pending further enquiries.' Deighton said the words slowly and clearly to avoid any doubt.[3]

Udham looked Deighton straight in the eye, his smile unnerving and unwavering: 'It's no use, it is all over.'[4] Nodding his head towards Sir Michael's body, he said slowly and clearly: 'It is there.'[5]

Stretchers began to arrive. Somebody placed a handkerchief over Sir Michael's face. Paramedics rushed Louis Dane to Westminster

Hospital and Lord Zetland to St George's Hospital. Lord Lamington, who lived only ten minutes away in Wilton Place, insisted on being taken home. He wished to be treated by his neighbour, a retired Swiss surgeon. Nobody could talk him out of it. The surgeon would later report that the 75-year-old had sustained 'a multiple fracture of two long bones of the right hand, and had metal chipping embedded in his wound.'[6]

Louis Dane was also being treated for a shattered forearm. The bullet which had gone straight through his bones had been caught in his clothing. It tumbled out onto the hospital floor as the doctors examined him.

When Lord Zetland was wheeled into St George's Hospital, he was clutching his heart, convinced he had taken two bullets to the chest. Doctors described him being in a state of 'great agitation', however when they loosened his shirt they could find no puncture wounds. There was no blood, only a 'moderate amount of swelling in the subcutaneous tissues'[7] about his chest. The bullets had found their mark but failed to pierce his skin. Zetland, who had felt the impact of the shots, could not believe what the doctors were telling him, and to reassure him, a radiographer was called to take images of his torso.

What had been meant to calm the secretary of state did the exact opposite, because when the radiographer held the film up to the light, it clearly showed a bullet lodged in his chest. It made no sense. Perplexed, the radiographer tried to take an image from a different angle; that was when the bullet fell out of Lord Zetland's clothes.[8] It too had been stopped by fabric. While the secretary of state marvelled over his lucky escape, the second bullet that had hit him was being discovered in the Tudor Room.

Still covered in Sir Michael's blood, watching police take photographs and measurements of the body, Marjorie Usher had noticed a handkerchief on the chair upon which Lord Zetland had fallen. It was tightly folded, small enough to sit in his breast pocket. The embroidered letter 'Z' in the corner clearly identified it as Lord Zetland's property. 'I picked it up intending to return it to him. I held the handkerchief for at least half an hour before I discovered a bullet inside the fold and several holes in the handkerchief.'[9] She handed both to the police.

Lord Zetland would always believe he was the intended target of the killer and that he had been the first to be shot. It was a reasonable assumption as secretary of state he was the most important man in the room. The evidence, however, told a different story. Udham's primary target had always been O'Dwyer. The secretary of state had merely been a bonus.

There had been ample opportunity for Udham to walk up to the dais and shoot Zetland at close quarters, but he had saved that intimate proximity for Sir Michael, his first victim. Sir Frank Brown corroborated: '[I] had the impression that Sir Michael O'Dwyer received the first shot.'[10] Sir Percy Sykes was of the same opinion and had a military clarity about events:

> I heard and saw a flash, and I saw my old friend Sir Michael shot
> dead . . . I saw him fall, he fell and turned round facing the corner
> chair in which he had been sitting, I then charged at the flashes,
> there was smoke and I could not see the accused who was evi-
> dently crouched behind Sir Michael's chair . . . one or two bullets
> passed very near my head; I have had that before so I knew what
> it was. Two bullets aimed at Lord Zetland passed very near me,
> then I had to pull up for a second. Everything took place in about
> 20 seconds.[11]

Udham's aim had not let him down. His weapon had.

As police continued their search of the murder scene, Udham was taken to one of the smaller offices on the first floor and placed in the custody of Detective Sergeant Sidney Jones. A solid officer, Jones was attached to the nearby Rochester Row station. He was told to search Udham and inform his superiors of anything of interest.

The first thing he turned out of his suspect's pockets was the identity card in the name of Mohamed Singh Azad. He then found the spare bullets, box of ammunition and diary. Jones had been ordered to sit with Udham until it was time to transfer him to police headquarters at Canon Row. He settled into his chair, facing the seated prisoner, who still wore an expression of mild amusement.

While they sat staring at each other, news rippled round the building that Lady O'Dwyer was on her way. She had been informed of her husband's murder, but police had not expected her to demand to see him immediately. Sensible of the effect the blood-spattered scene might have on her, they had tried to dissuade her, but Una was adamant. She wanted to see her Michael.

When Lady O'Dwyer's car pulled up outside Caxton Hall, Field Marshal Sir Claud Jacob materialised out of the thickening dusk to open her door. Lady O'Dwyer allowed herself to be steered towards the Tudor Room and the ageing soldier propped her up when her legs gave out.[12] It was not clear who had called Jacob or how he had got there so quickly, but the O'Dwyers had always had powerful and well-connected friends.

As her grief filled the Tudor Room, metres down the corridor, Udham Singh asked for a cigarette.[13] Jones noted down the request in his book but did nothing. Usual police procedure dictated that an officer should write contemporaneous notes at a crime scene, and pages in Jones's notebook, a standard issue, rough-grain Metropolitan Police pad with the distinctive crown insignia on the buff-coloured front, certainly suggested that he knew the rules.[14] The rest of it was filled with incidents Jones had attended that week: minor break-ins, street altercations, vagrancy and robbery, scrawl filled with crossings out and notes in the margins.[15]

Jones's Caxton Hall notes started in that same style, however changed dramatically two pages in, suggesting that he stopped taking notes at the scene and filled in the rest later. In place of messy jottings he had written neat, legible words in fully formed sentences. When later questioned about this break with protocol, Jones would only say: 'Something may have happened so that I was not able to write them [his notes] down there and then. I cannot explain why that should be.'[16]

Poor practice aside, Sergeant Jones would swear under oath that his notebook contained an accurate representation of what passed between him and Udham in that room that night. According to him, though Udham appeared docile, solicitous even, he was unable to stay silent. From the moment he opened his mouth, he incriminated himself over and over again.

It all started when Jones was itemising the contents of Udham's pockets. He was examining his curved blade when Udham broke his smiling silence: 'I had the knife with me because I was set about in Camden Town a few nights ago.'[17]

Jones was unsure whether his prisoner understood the police caution read to him earlier meaning anything he said could be used in evidence. He warned him to keep quiet, but Udham seemed in a buoyant and chatty mood: 'I did it because I had a grudge against him. He deserved it.'[18] 'I do not belong to any society or anything else.'[19]

When Jones's boss Detective Inspector Deighton came into the room and dramatically placed four empty cartridge cases on the table before them, Udham's smirking calm slipped for the first time that evening. He seemed angry instead: 'No! No! All the lot. Six,'[20] he said, holding up six fingers.[21]

Deighton picked up the bullets from the table and returned to the Tudor Room, to search for the two remaining bullets. He had no way of knowing that one was still lodged in Sir Michael's body and the other had been confounding a hospital radiographer and a panicking secretary of state.

Alone with Jones again, Udham was now agitated: 'I don't care. I don't mind dying. What is the use of waiting till you get old, that's no good. You want to die when you're young. That is good. That's what I am doing.'[22]

In a climbing state of passion, Udham exclaimed: 'I am dying for my country.'[23]

Looking at Jones's notes today, it feels as if the long periods of silence were too much for Udham to bear. He and the policeman were in that office together for around four hours, during which time Udham asked for a copy of that evening's paper, wanting to see if he had made it into the late edition. Jones ignored the request, passing him a cigarette instead, perhaps to calm them both down. Smoke twisted around a temporary silence. Then, without warning or provocation, Udham started to talk again: 'Is Zetland dead? He ought to be. I put two in him right there.'[24] Udham pointed to his left side. Then fell silent again.

From time to time Udham seemed to forget Jones was even there, giving answers to questions that had not even been asked: 'I bought the revolver from a soldier in a public house at Bournemouth. I bought him some drink, you know ... My parents died when I was four or five.'[25]

It was as if Udham was trotting out some kind of rehearsed dialogue: 'I had property which I sold,' he said apropos of nothing. 'I had over two hundred pounds when I came to England.'[26]

At some point Udham mused aloud: 'Only one dead, eh! I thought I could get some more. I must have been too slow. There was a lot of womans [sic] about, you know.'[27]

At 8.50 p.m., police were finally ready to move Udham. All the witnesses had given their statements and been sent home, even those with the most to say. Bertha Herring had proved a particular hit with the freezing reporters on the pavement outside and had revelled in their attention. Like an intense and excitable version of Margaret Rutherford, she relived her experience for whoever asked her to. As much as the press enjoyed her spirited account, and would use it in their papers next day, there was really one thing they were waiting for.

It was Divisional Detective Inspector John Swain who finally came to collect Udham. Together with Jones, they escorted him down the stairs and towards the exit. He had been entirely compliant throughout the evening. With the lightest of touches to the elbow, he was manoeuvred out of the door towards the bristling press pack.

The sun had long set and it was bitterly cold outside. Police had returned Udham's hat, which he wore tipped back on his head. His overcoat, emptied of its weapons, was nonchalantly slung over his right arm, hiding the handcuff which attached him to Jones. He looked like he was popping out for a stroll with two friends.

The press shouted incomprehensible questions while photographers yelled to get Udham to look their way. Instead of ducking his head and quickening his pace as many do during the so-called 'perp-walk', Udham slowed his pace. Then, without warning, he turned to the bank of flashing cameras and grinned.

A frenzy of popping lit up the night, capturing a series of extraordinary images. With his eyes wide and teeth bared, Udham appeared to be enjoying some kind of ghoulish euphoria. The newspapers had their front page. It had been well worth the wait.

The drive from Caxton Hall to Canon Row Police Station takes only seven minutes, even less if the driver has a clear run of it. In those few minutes something strange happened to Udham Singh.

Though he had been revelling in his execution-style murder of Sir Michael all evening, the 'Mohammed Singh Azad' who presented himself at Canon Row had a very different story to tell. As an exhausted Detective Inspector Swain sat down to write up his confession, his prisoner told him calmly: 'I did not mean to kill him, I just did it to protest. I did not mean to kill anybody.'[28]

Stunned by the dramatic volte-face, Swain processed Udham without comment. He asked his prisoner to sign his short statement, which Udham did in the name of Mohammed Singh Azad.[29] His shoes and belt were removed, and Udham was taken down to the cells.

The hour was late. The paperwork was brief:

13th day of March 1940 To Supt C.I.D 10.50 p.m.

Mohomed [*sic*] Singh Azad aged 37, was charged at this station at 10 p.m. today 13th March 1940, with the murder of Sir Michael Francis O'Dwyer and will appear at Bow Street Police Court at 9.30 a.m., 14th March 1940. The prisoner attended a meeting at Caxton Hall this afternoon (13.3.40) at which Sir Percy Sykes was giving a lecture on Afghanistan. The prisoner fired six shots from a Smith-Wesson revolver killing Sir Michael O'Dwyer and wounding three others. Commissioner and other senior officers were informed and attended D.A.C.I. informed.[30]

Swain was finished for the night, but civil servants, summoned from their homes, were just dragging themselves back into the office. Who was this man? How had this happened? Was this part of a bigger plot? Was there any surveillance chatter that could have averted this debacle? The questions were falling like sleet from on high, and answers were demanded by morning. A secretary of state had been shot, for heaven's sake! In Westminster of all places.

Across the city in Fleet Street, irritable subs ripped up their carefully planned layouts and started all over again. At the printing presses, inky, nicotine-stained fingers reset plates, while in dozens of darkrooms photographers beetled about in the shadows, desperate to find the image they knew was sitting somewhere on their film.

The sinister grin emerged from numerous trays of crimson. Britain would have a face to hate by morning.

That same night, a clipped and understated male voice from the BBC Home Service broke the news in its nine o'clock bulletin:[31]

Sir Michael O'Dwyer, a former governor of the Punjab, was assassinated this afternoon at a meeting in the Caxton Hall, London ... Sir Michael O'Dwyer was seventy-four, and he joined the Indian Civil Service in 1885 ... from 1913 to 1919 he was lieutenant governor of the Punjab. It was during this period, on

13 April 1919, that the Amritsar shooting occurred. A mob had attacked banks and other buildings and Europeans had been killed. At the request of the civil authorities, troops were called out and a number of natives were killed. This shooting raised a great political controversy at the time.[32]

In Berlin, the Nazis leapt on the story. By 9.15 p.m., a German announcer was interrupting usual programming to bring listeners the following:

The Indian freedom moment has now gone over to direct action against the English oppressors of India. This evening Sir Michael O'Dwyer was shot by an Indian at a meeting of the India Society. Lord Zetland, Sir Louis Dane and Lord Lamington were also injured. The shootings occurred towards the end of an over-crowded meeting at Caxton Hall ... The Indian fighter for freedom has been arrested.

Goebbels himself was wading in, and by the time the midnight bulletin came round, the story had been sharpened to do the most damage: 'News of the shooting and killing of Sir Michael O'Dwyer recalls the past misdeeds of British administrators in India.'[33]

'Mohammed Singh Azad' had become at once the most hated man in Britain and a hero to the Third Reich.

'Outrage at London Meeting',[34] 'Sir Michael O'Dwyer Assassinated',[35] 'Hit by two shots',[36] 'A Cowardly Outrage',[37] 'Lord Zetland and Lord Lamington wounded',[38] 'Sir Michael was shot in back',[39] 'Woman Tackles Assassin',[40] 'Assailant seized and Overpowered',[41] 'Disgrace ... We are Ashamed',[42] 'Volley of Shots at London Meeting',[43] 'Senseless Crime'.[44] The headlines screamed out from the morning papers.

For the first time in weeks, the war had been knocked off the front pages. German papers told the same story in a very different way: 'The death of O'Dwyer is likely to arouse a great satisfaction among the Indian population . . . behind his death stands the will of the whole Indian people to avenge their massacred countrymen . . . yesterday's assassination shows that the young generation of a nation whose civilisation is thousands of years old is determined to resist the English terror.'[45]

By evening, Goebbels was encouraging all-out revolt in India:

The active resistance to Britain's Indian policy by the nationalists of the country has recently taken a more concrete form in Sir Michael O'Dwyer's assassination at Caxton Hall by a Punjab nationalist, Mohamed Singh Azad.

Indians apparently have not forgotten that on 13 April 1919, Sir Michael O'Dwyer had 600 defenceless Indians executed in the province of Punjab. Sir Michael O'Dwyer was one of the most ruthless and bloodthirsty of the Punjab's governors. It was he who forced the Punjabis to shed their blood for the benefit of Britain during the last war. The assassination was a vendetta, and a justified one at that. We realise that a widespread revolt is impending in India.[46]

It was clear that the Germans would use the 'avenger' angle to destabilise the Raj. The British secret service had to paint Udham in a very different light, and they had to do it quickly.

CHAPTER 22

NAME IN VAIN

Who is this 'Mohamed Singh Azad'? The question, referred to no fewer than thirty-one different heads of department, yielded nothing. In a space marked 'Former papers for AZAD Mahomed Singh charged with the murder of Sir Michael O'Dwyer', the handwritten comment 'unable to trace'[1] summed up a collective frustration of the government and security services.

'Azad' had been presented at Bow Street Magistrates' Court the morning after his arrest and had smiled throughout the proceedings.[2] Taken directly from the dock to Brixton Prison, he was to be held on remand till his trial for murder. Though he had barely said three words during his own committal, while he was being processed by Brixton Prison guards Udham appeared in a markedly talkative mood. His words were immediately reported to the governor in charge:

> Sir, I respectfully beg to report the following matter to you. About 11.40 on this date [14 March 1940] I was in charge of the above-mentioned prisoner in Reception when he made the following remark to me.
>
> 'At this time yesterday, I was going to the pictures when I think to myself, it is better I go and see this fellow Michael. He has lived a long life. It is twenty years after.'
>
> I am Sir, Your obedient servant[3]

His admission that he sought out 'this fellow Michael' indicated a premeditation which the prosecution might find invaluable if they chose to pursue the death penalty. His comment linking the killing to the Jallianwala Bagh massacre 'twenty years after' was less helpful. Brixton's governor forwarded the incendiary admission to his superiors, little realising that it would provoke a massive cover-up.

Less than twenty-four hours after the shootings, every effort was being made to separate 'Mohamed Singh Azad's' murderous act from the Jallianwala Bagh massacre.[4] The Nazis had already made too much of the link and the British were determined to smother any potential uprising in India.

The IPI was doing most of the heavy lifting, with Vickery and Silver laying the groundwork, characterising Sir Michael's assassin as some lunatic lone wolf even before they knew who he really was. To admit the assassin was part of a bigger organisation or conspiracy made the defence of the realm look weak; far from ideal at a time of war and heightened insecurity.

When it later became apparent that Mohamed Singh Azad was in fact Udham Singh, a Ghadar and Communist, known to Special Branch, MI5 and the IPI, and that each department had missed significant opportunities to bring him in over the years, Vickery and his colleagues had even more reason to control the narrative.

Forty-eight hours after the Caxton Hall shootings, Vickery fired off a note to his colleague, Denys Pilditch, director of the Indian Intelligence Bureau in Delhi. In it, he updated him on the investigation and 'Mohamed Singh Azad's' confession and true identity. The memo also disclosed the undercurrent in Whitehall. The document was marked 'Secret', with good reason:

My dear Pilditch, I have not cabled you about the unfortunate affair at the Caxton Hall, as I understand that the India Office yesterday sent a telegram to the Government of India recording the main facts . . . The assassin, who on his arrest gave the name of Mohamed Singh Azad, has since proved to be UDHAM SINGH alias UDE SINGH, who is, of course, well known to us.

He has since made a highly unconvincing statement to the police, in which he says that he had not intended to kill anybody, but merely to make a gesture of protest. He explains (and this part of his story is probably true) that he went to the India Office on the morning of the crime, to secure a recommendation of an Exit Permit (actually he called there asking to see Sir Hassan Surhawardy [sic], one of the Indian Advisers, who happened to be out), but did not secure any satisfaction. On the way out from the waiting room, he chanced to see on the noticeboard, an announcement of a joint meeting of the East India Association and the Central Asian Society that afternoon. This announcement, he says, gave him the idea of utilising the Caxton Hall meeting to make his protest, for which purpose he took with him a revolver which he says he purchased in Bournemouth (presumably in September last).

Although the first part of UDHAM SINGH'S statement is completely unsatisfactory [that he had not meant to kill anybody in Caxton Hall], the judicial methods in vogue in this country render it improbable that the police will ever get the true story out of him ... The revolver, which is still under expert examination, is said to be an obsolete Service type and could only be fired with accuracy at very close range ... I am doing what I can to ensure that UDHAM SINGH does not make the court room a platform for objectionable political propaganda. There are already indications that that is the line he will take. Although he appears to be mentally unstable the crime was of such a deliberate and premeditated nature, that there can be little doubt that the verdict will be one of 'wilful murder'.[5]

Vickery was desperately trying to clear up a mess that had occurred on his watch – and treading a fine line in doing so. Acknowledgement of any Russian interference or German help would shake Britain's confidence. In creating the 'lone wolf' image, Vickery could not make Udham seem too mad either. If he did, there was every likelihood that he might be deemed unfit to stand trial.

Police searching the address on Udham's fake identity card found a number of items which were proving unhelpful to Vickery's strategy. Udham had roubles hidden in the room. Elsewhere among an assortment of Udham's Western clothes and Indian *kurta pyjamas* they found a French beret[6] and a map, showing the 'International Motor Route from London to Cape Town and Calcutta'.[7] It appeared to have some kind of code scribbled on the back.

A red diary for 1939 was a veritable tangle of intriguing loose ends. It had French addresses written in it: 'Grand Hotel de Nice' and '29 rue Victor Masse Paris ixe'.[8] There were also numerous references to Berlin, which, like the writing on the map, appeared to be in code: 'Delhi SW 4 o'clock SW 3.30 Berlin 1514'[9] and 'H.6 Bill 26. Swiss 19. George 14. H.M 25. Jack 11. F.7 NL 75. Tom 9. Sohm.16. B.33. Tom 13 – 36. 7 S.PS. 7N 5'.[10]

Hassan Surhawady's name and home address appeared, along with the comment 'Re Anglo French Ambulance Unit', and the phrase 'Honor Huld' was written between two addresses, 'Maple St 1 floor' and 'St George Hospital East End'.[11]

No listing exists for a 'Honor Huld' at either of these addresses, or indeed anywhere else in London. Nor does she appear in any census, electoral roll or telephone directory for 1939–40. Though 'Honor Huld' looks like the name of a woman, the words had a German meaning too: 'honour' and 'graciousness'. A German contact perhaps? A coded call to arms? Though some of the writing in the flat needed decryption, one line did not.

Written in the red diary, at the end of an indecipherable series of letters and numbers, was: '4.30 Caxton Hall 13 March 3 p.m. Caxton Hall'.[12] This was the date and almost the exact time of Sir Michael's assassination. They would show Udham's later statements – that he had only happened on the meeting by accident, that he had not known Sir Michael would be there, nor even know who Sir Michael was – for the lies they were.

The apparent codes strewn around his room raised fundamental questions for those protecting Britain from her enemies. Had Udham received his instructions through some kind of cypher? Had he been sent to Caxton Hall to kill these men? Had he taken it upon himself to settle some kind of score? What were the coordinates and place names about? Who, or what, was 'Honor Huld'? If these matters were pursued, we do not know where they led. So many of the papers in the case of Udham Singh were buried by Vickery and his peers. Though thousands of pages have since been excavated, they may be the tip of a very murky iceberg.

Vickery continued to insist that there was no connection between Udham and foreign powers. Even though Udham's past passport applications suggested otherwise, he pressed his argument in internal documents to other government departments: 'There is no evidence to indicate that his action was sponsored by any organisation, association or other person, and I am of the opinion from all the facts that the outrage was the product of his evil mind and brought to successful culmination in the secretive and isolated manner in which he has spent his life.'[13]

At 80 Bandywood Road in Birmingham, seven-year-old Indarjit could not for the life of him understand what was going on in his own house. The adults around him had been acting very oddly for days. Just a few nights before, something his parents had heard on the radio had made them behave as if it was his birthday ... no ... more than that ... as if it was *everybody's* birthday.

Rubbing sleepy eyes, he and his brother came down in their pyjamas to see their mother weeping with joy, vowing to buy sweets for everyone in the street. His father, Dr Diwan Singh, was clatteringly jubilant too. Unable to sit still, he kept leaping up from the kitchen table, joyously repeating the mantra: 'He's gone! That man is gone!' The boys were faintly aware of the crackling voice in the background coming from the wireless. Indarjit worried what their neighbour, the friendly local greengrocer Mr Pandry, might think of all this noise at such a late hour.[14]

When he asked his parents what they were celebrating, Indarjit's mother grabbed him, and held him tight: '*Puttar* [my sweet child] ... A good man ... a good Indian man just punished a bad man for a wicked thing that he did ... a terrible wicked thing.' It was not much of an explanation, but he and his brother were content to dance around the kitchen too, enjoying the *ronak* (exuberant celebration), and the unexpectedly late bedtime.[15]

The next morning, the excitement of the night before seemed like a dream. Padding down to the kitchen for his breakfast, Indarjit saw a new, sombre mood pouring out of the newspaper in his father's hands. It flooded the kitchen, spilled into the rest of the house and into the world. Grown-ups, family friends as well as turbaned strangers washed up nervously at their door throughout the day. His mother ushered them into the house and their whispering filled the kitchen, pushing out the memory of their night-time party: 'It can't be him.' 'It's him, I'm telling you.' 'But look at the name.' 'Look at the picture. Of course it's him.' 'Did he tell you?' '... not a word.'

Every so often, Indarjit thought he heard the name 'Udham' among the whispers. It made him think of his 'uncle'.* He had not seen him in ages. Udham-uncle would have noticed the two little boys hugging their knees on the stairs. He would have taken them to one side, explained what was going on. They could have played the hide-the-hat game.

After the strange night and even stranger morning, life at Bandywood Road appeared to go on as usual, yet everything felt different. Indarjit overheard his parents talking about money with an urgency he did not recognise. He heard his father telling his mother that certain things needed to be done. That she would have to be strong. She told him that she had strength enough for all of them. Indarjit's father said he had created a bank account in her name and was putting all their money into it.[16]

His father's close friendship with Udham Singh had put the

---

* In Indian households, friends of parents are called 'uncle' and 'aunty' even if there is no blood relationship.

family at risk. There was nothing to link him to the Caxton Hall shootings, or any evidence to suggest he had known of Udham's intent, but still, Indarjit's mother and father were tense, waiting for a knock on the door, anticipating a police van which would take him away. Years later, when asked if his father might have known what Udham was planning, Lord Indarjit Singh would simply say: 'I'm pretty sure he did not. If he did . . . I'm not sure he would have talked him out of it. My parents hated O'Dwyer with a passion. In their eyes he was a mass murderer who got away with it.'[17]

'It makes no difference to me whatever. Do what you like but I still say I am Mohamed Singh.'[18]

The meeting between Udham and Detective Inspector John Swain at Brixton Prison was not going well. The smiling man who had sat opposite him in Bow Street Magistrates' Court had been replaced by a man who was both angry and adamant. Swain had gone to visit Udham in prison to inform him that his true identity had been discovered and his name on the charge sheet would be changing to 'Udham Singh' accordingly. To say the news had been badly received was an understatement.

Udham demanded pencil and paper so that he might write a formal letter to Swain's superior. In it, he asked for certain personal items from his flat. The letter simultaneously revealed his belligerence and his lack of formal schooling: 'Will you please send my cigarettes with which I have in my passition [possession] and 1 shirt long-sleeve and 1 Indian Shoe.'[19]

In an implied taunt to the police, suggesting he had been doing a lot of running to keep one step ahead of them all these years, he requested a new pair of shoes from his flat, the old pair having lost their heels because they had been 'left buzy [busy] with your Police'.[20]

Udham also asked if he might have his turban and a pair of cotton trousers from his flat, to wear while he was in prison: 'The hat do not suit me as I am a Indian.'[21]

Taunting over, Udham came to the crux of his letter: the matter of his name and his meeting with Swain: '[I] like to tell you one thing do not try to change my name what so ever I have given to you my name is Mohamed Singh Azad I do not care if any one say any thing let them go to hell But I want to keep my name I have told your man they came to see me . . . do what so ever you like But don't change my name.' Signing the letter, he added a postscript: 'All over the world I am called by Mohamed Singh Azad MSA.'[22]

His request for the charge sheet to remain in the name of Mohamed Singh Azad was flatly refused. As were all his repeated requests for a change of clothes and shoes. An internal letter from Inspector Swain to his superintendent explained the grounds upon which he should be turned down: 'The shoes [at his flat in Mornington Terrace] are of sandal type . . . he also asked for his turban. His object then was to dress up and give the case added political appearance.'[23]

Udham did not know, but herculean efforts were underway to rob him of any connection to his true motive. Even his sandals were contentious.

The police in India and England were rounding up Udham's friends and acquaintances. One pedlar, who had no connection with him at all, was arrested simply for having the word 'Azad' written on his suitcase.[24] Others reported being roughed up and threatened by police. It would have been much easier for men like Dr Diwan Singh, Shiv Singh Johal and Surat Ali to walk away from Udham in the days after the shootings, but they remained fiercely loyal.

Their steadfastness galvanised those who had been afraid immediately after the arrest, and about a week later, pedlars, dock workers and the Indian doctor fraternity started to come out of the shadows. They seemed seized by a collective anger and shame. How could they back away from a man who had done what many of them had dreamed of doing themselves?

Pedlars offered what little money they could for their old friend's defence via the Shepherd's Bush Gurdwara. Surat Ali also started collecting money, mainly from ship workers around the East End.

Udham's old Ghadar friends in California mobilised too, and cash started pouring into the radical Stockton Gurdwara.

With a trial bearing down on them fast, there was building anxiety in the highest echelons of the British government. What if Udham Singh turned his court proceedings into a political spectacle, stirring up Indians in general and Punjabis in particular? In a top-secret memo, never meant to see the light of day, somebody of significance in the security services, perhaps Kell himself, or Vickery of the IPI, sought to discuss strategy with his peers across departments:

> Experience of political-criminal trials in India gives rise to expectations that UDHAM SINGH will do all he can to make political capital out of his crime. There are already some indications that this is his intention. Realising that nothing can save him from the gallows, possibly wanting to pose as a martyr, he may be expected to adopt an air of complete assurance – even insolence – and to indulge in a good deal of bravado, to play up to the gallery and generally to make himself out to be a hero. He is probably hoping that his behaviour in court will receive wide publicity, partly to encourage Indians both in this country and at home to commit similar crimes and partly to impress the English public with the intensity of the popular movement in India for the removal of British rule.

The unsigned note continued:

> A great deal will depend on the counsel engaged to defend him. Their influence, particularly if they are Indian will go far to influence him in his actions in court. If he were being tried in India, he would certainly raise the revolutionary war-cry 'Inquilab Zindabad!' (Long Live Revolution!) on arriving and at leaving the court precincts – a brief cry of defiance hurled at the judge and the whole British Empire. When invited to make a statement he would also spread himself in a political oration – carefully

prepared beforehand – enlarging on the evils of the British system of administration of India.

The next few lines of the memo suggested that pressure might be brought to bear on Udham's defence team. If they were English, it would be easier to persuade them to steer their client away from the political minefield which might blow up the past conduct of the Raj:

> If he is wisely advised by his counsel he will probably refrain from such behaviour in an English court, but the possibility cannot be ignored. To guard against the possibility certain steps should be at once taken. The Director of Public Prosecutions should be warned and asked to explain the situation to the court before the case comes up for hearing. Also measures should be adopted to ensure that undue prominence is not given in the press to any heroics in which UDHAM SINGH may indulge. It is presumably possible to limit the number of press representatives, all of whom should be requested to deny the accused the publicity which he may be seeking. The press censors should be informed of the possibilities and put on their guard. All press messages for India and America in particular should receive careful scrutiny.

These methods, though important, would not guarantee success:

> Should the prisoner indulge in objectionable conduct, a threat to clear the court and hold the proceedings *in camera*, with only two or three press representatives present, might prove very effective.
>
> The court room is certain to be crowded and the most interested spectators will be Indians, who may attempt to display manifestations of their sympathy for the accused man. As the possibility of a further 'spectacular outrage' being committed in court by some disaffected Sikh cannot be altogether overlooked, Scotland Yard will no doubt take such precautions as are possible to scrutinise those securing admission; the precedent afforded by recent IRA trials may prove useful.

Finally, the unsigned memo acknowledged the link between the Jallianwala Bagh massacre and Udham Singh's actions, something that the British government would strenuously deny in public: 'The anniversary of "Jallianwalabagh" [sic] will fall on 13 April and arrangements are in train for the holding of commemoration meetings both in the West End and in east London. It would be advisable to avoid holding the trial on this date.'[25]

Albert Canning, chief constable of police and head of Special Branch, bridled at some of the tactics being suggested: 'I will let you know the name of the counsel briefed to defend Singh as soon as I learn it,' he said, adding:

> The problem of curtailing press activity ... is a difficult one. Any attempt to limit the privileges of press representatives at court is bound to be followed by an outcry, and even if there were only one or two agency reporters allowed in, their reports would be circulated to all the papers. The press and censorship department of the Ministry of Information can, however, control messages regarding the matter sent abroad, but this is a very thorny question.[26]

Canning stood alone. All other branches of the security services agreed with the two-pronged strategy of muting the press and undermining Udham's defence. Philip Vickery and Cecil Silver started making back-channel approaches to editors and encouraging operatives to find out which lawyers Udham's friends were approaching.

Courting the press proved easy. The largest independent news agency in the world, Reuters, which would be providing copy to most newspapers in Britain, agreed not to report anything politically incendiary, nor to connect Udham's act with the freedom struggle in his country or the massacre. A coded telegram from the secretary of state for India to his viceroy confirmed the English press at least had been effectively muzzled: 'Udham Singh's trial. Arrangements have been made with Reuters and we will do what may be possible in conjunction with Censorship Bureau here in regard to messages through other channels. As however we can give no guarantee it is presumed that careful censorship will be exercised at your end in relation to messages from correspondents of Indian newspapers.'[27]

With the press coverage taken care of, it was time to focus more closely on Udham's defence.

CHAPTER 23

TRIAL AND TRIBULATION

All his life Vengalil Krishnan Krishna Menon divided opinion bitterly. A graduate of the London School of Economics, he had studied under Harold Laski, the only dissenting juror in the O'Dwyer vs Nair libel case of 1924. Laski described Menon as the keenest mind he had ever come across.

A trained lawyer, Menon was wiry, dark and dapper. His long, tapering face, strong brow, winged nostrils and widely spaced eyes gave him a lupine look. Everything about Krishna Menon suggested a calculating, intelligent intensity. When he smiled, which in photographs was not very often, he looked more hungry than happy.

In 1940, Menon was one of the best-connected Indians in the United Kingdom, boasting close friendships with Jawaharlal Nehru, the future Prime Minister of India, and many of the top cadre of the Indian National Congress. Thanks to a foray into British publishing in the 1930s, editing the Bodley Head's *Twentieth Century Library* series and founding the Pelican imprint for Penguin, he had also nurtured warm associations with the left-wing cultural and political elite of Great Britain. Bertrand Russell, Aneurin Bevan, Stafford Cripps and Michael Foot were all good friends.

Menon had initially wanted to disassociate himself from Udham's actions. As secretary of the 'India League', an anti-imperial organisation, he repudiated the shootings within hours of the event.

Expressing revulsion, he claimed to speak for all Indians: 'The tragedy at Caxton Hall yesterday will be regretted and condemned universally in India. Indian national opinion abhors such acts of terrorism, which find no apologists or supporters in any section of Indian political opinion. Congress and other nationalist circles have always condemned them. Indians in this country, students and residents and all friends of India feel similarly.'[1]

Jawaharlal Nehru and Mahatma Gandhi were similarly scathing. Gandhi fired off an uncompromising condemnation in his newspaper *Harijan*: 'The news of the death of Sir Michael O'Dwyer and the injuries to Lord Zetland, Lord Lamington and Sir Louis Dane, has caused me deep pain. I regard this act as one of insanity.'[2] Nehru wrote in his newspaper the *National Herald*: '[The] assassination is regretted but it is earnestly hoped that it will not have far-reaching repercussions on [the] political future of India.'[3]

Gandhi and Nehru had been locked in delicate negotiations with the British and wanted desperately to promote a counternarrative to that of the late Sir Michael O'Dwyer. Indians were not violent barbarians. They could be trusted to run their own affairs. The Raj could either negotiate with men like Gandhi and Nehru, or leave India to militants like Udham Singh.

The Gandhi–Nehru condemnation was somewhat compromised by the youth wing of their own party. At the Annual Session of the All India Congress Committee, held weeks after the Caxton Hall shootings, a commemoration was held for the victims of Jallianwala Bagh. Young men and women shouted slogans in support of Udham Singh, declaring him to be a revolutionary hero. Congress representatives in the Punjab Assembly refused to condemn the O'Dwyer murder, defying their own leadership.

When it became clear how much publicity Udham's case was getting, and how much support he had within British Indian circles, Krishna Menon appeared to rethink his own position. If there was to be a trial, it would be a very high-profile affair, and Krishna Menon wanted in.

Thanks to their surveillance of him, the IPI and MI5 got to hear about Menon's Damascene conversion even before Udham's friends did. Menon approached a barrister, with whom he shared chambers, and without any instruction from the prisoner himself, asked him to represent Udham and retain him as junior counsel. Menon had started working on the preliminaries when he heard Surat Ali, the trade union leader, had already engaged a lawyer, supported by funds from the Sikh community.[4]

Krishna Menon was furious. Surat Ali had beaten him to the punch, and instead of offering to help, he decided to wrest the case from Ali's hands. As a result, two enormous egos spent crucial time bickering among themselves, shredding any chance Udham might have had for a coherent defence. The authorities could barely hide their glee at the chaos:

> The present position is that a battle royal is in process of being waged between Menon . . . and Surat Ali with the Sikhs on the other. The Sikhs led by a certain Shiv Singh [Jouhl] have started collecting funds from their compatriots and a sum of nearly £200 is already available. Somewhat unexpectedly Menon's hand has been reinforced by a cable which he has received from Ajmere Singh, secretary of the Sikh Temple in Stockton, California, asking him to telegraph whether Azad was being defended legally. Ajmere Singh is an active member of the Ghadar Party.[5]

With precisely no legal standing in the case, Krishna Menon took it upon himself to send a telegram to the Stockton Temple, informing them that *he* was now running Udham's defence: 'Krishna Menon being barrister unable to communicate you direct. In consultation Krishna Menon. Legal arrangements partly made. Will cable further.'[6]

Menon then used his communications with Stockton to convince Shiv Singh Jouhl to dump Surat Ali and bring the Sikhs over to him.[7] 'It seems clear that Menon is most anxious to be briefed for the defence . . . and will probably seek to procure evidence of insanity.'[8]

Krishna Menon did not care about Udham's motivations or state of mind. He had a two-pronged interest in taking over his trial: firstly, it would confirm his importance in the eyes of the world; secondly, it would allow him to steer proceedings in a direction that best helped his friends Nehru and Gandhi in India. If it did not serve their interest to have Udham's nationalism dragged into court, he could keep it out. On the other hand, if the situation demanded it, there was nobody better than Krishna Menon to create a political grandstand.

Krishna Menon's attitude to Udham was neatly summarised in another of Vickery's secret IPI memos: 'Menon is not interested in Udham Singh or the result of the trial but merely in the opportunity that this offers for making political capital.'[9]

Sowing confusion and distrust among friends, Krishna Menon put all his efforts into taking over the Udham Singh case. Vickery noted: 'The whole affair is subject to so much intrigue that it is difficult to ascertain what are Udham Singh's own views in the matter; the truth is probably he is quite indifferent as to who defends him and thinks that it is pointless collecting funds for that purpose.'[10]

Vickery was right. Sitting in his cell at Brixton Prison, Udham was busy working out how best to kill himself.

CHAPTER 24

LETTERS, BOOKS, CARS AND CODES

Days after the assassination of Sir Michael, the FBI communicated a new threat to Great Britain's interests, from California. They believed they had uncovered a Ghadar plot to murder Sir Michael's only son, Jack O'Dwyer. The cypher telegram, sent by diplomatic staff in San Francisco, was meant for a few select eyes only:

Limited distribution
Decipher. Mr Butler (San Francisco)
22 March 1940

Local police state they have received reports from an Indian informant, who has hitherto proved reliable, which indicates that Indian extremists in California maybe contemplating attempt on the life of Mr O'Dwyer. In view of the criminal record of many Indians in California police consider this report should not be disregarded.

I have requested the police to take protective measures but they maintain it is impossible to guarantee that attack by some fanatic may not take place. I am also consulting FBI. In the meantime all reasonable precautions will be taken.[1]

It was just as Udham had scribbled in his own notes. He would take care of Sir Michael; others were encouraged to deal with his son. Somehow, his Ghadar friends had got the message and were doing their best to hold up their end of the deal.

Sir Michael's son had not made it back for his father's burial, nor the commemorative Mass that followed. Serving as the British vice consul in San Francisco, he remained in California and never commented publicly about his complicated sense of loss. When local press picked up the story of his father's murder, he refused to speak to them: 'J C O'Dwyer, British vice consul in San Francisco, remained in seclusion today, grief stricken over the London assassination of his father, Sir Michael O'Dwyer.'[2]

Back in London, Una, Jack's mother, was broken by her grief, and it was left to his sister to articulate the family's feelings. Editorials linking his violent end with his turbulent time in office triggered outrage. No account had been settled here, she said, and nobody in India was happy about her father's murder: 'My father always stood for the people of India. Now these people are sorrowing with us.'[3]

The police, IPI and MI5 put all their efforts into securing a swift trial. Drawn-out proceedings would only encourage copycat killings, and Udham had dangerous admirers, as the threat to Jack O'Dwyer proved. Udham's demonstrable links to Russia, Germany and the Ghadars would never make it into the public arena. Nor would they be shared with Udham's dysfunctional defence team. Vickery's aim remained simple and clear: Udham was to be painted as a criminal, a maverick murderer, and nothing more. He set about surgically removing any political motive.

Udham had once toyed with the idea that he might just survive his Caxton Hall shootings. All he had to do, he figured, was stay alive long enough for Britain to lose the war. If Germany emerged victorious, he might be freed as a political prisoner. It was almost certainly this notion that led him to make blatantly contradictory statements to the police and courts after his arrest. Where first he had proudly claimed ownership of the murder, he now denied it on numerous occasions. He had not known who Sir Michael was; he was just going to protest about his passport difficulties; he had meant to shoot at the ceiling. It had all been a terrible accident.

The deadly accuracy of his shots and the entries in his diary showed those statements to be lies, but Udham persisted. His hope was built on precedent. In his hidden diary, discovered by police at his London flat, were two faded newspaper cuttings.[4] These have never been examined before, but give a compelling explanation for his oft-misunderstood denials, which others have used to argue that he might have been insane. Udham was perfectly sound of mind and his contradictions and confusing statements were in fact the last Hail Mary of a man who knew he was going to die, but would have preferred to live.

The first article was about a woman named Hannah Ainsworth,[5] an Anglo-Indian who had married a British soldier and was abandoned by him when they came to live in Britain. The desertion, coupled with the racism she had faced, appeared to have driven poor Hannah mad. The press had covered her case with a great deal of sympathy. It did not hurt that she was beautiful:

> Judge and jury were faced with unusual facts when Mrs Hannah Ainsworth, a handsome Indian woman, appeared today at Manchester Assizes, where she was sentenced to twelve months in the second division. She had been committed on a charge of assaulting a police officer. A highly educated woman, she had, it was disclosed, married a private soldier in the British army in India, came with him to live at Bury, and, after a separation had taken place, became obsessed with the idea that certain people were keeping her apart from her husband.

Hannah, during a raving fit, had taken to the streets and fired a pistol at police officers. It was never made clear if she knew they contained blank rounds or not. Despite the seriousness of the act, the judge gave Hannah the most lenient sentence he could. Ainsworth's defence was one that Udham would parrot almost word for word.

She had meant to protest, she said. She was a woman with a griev-ance. Britain had treated her and her fellow Indians badly: '[She] said since she came to this country three years ago she had tolerated great insults about her country and people. I have been slighted, she declared. These people do it, only out of prejudice.'[6] Perhaps Udham hoped that if he sounded like Hannah, he might be treated like her.

The second cutting told the story of two Indians who got away with murder, quite literally. In December 1931, Santi Ghosh and her friend Suniti Choudhury were just fifteen-year-old schoolgirls when they walked into the office of Charles Geoffrey Buckland Stevens, a British bureaucrat and district magistrate in Calcutta. Producing guns from their school uniforms, they shot him dead at point-blank range.

At the trial, the pair used the dock to make incendiary political statements, claiming they would rather receive the death penalty than imprisonment. They had killed Buckland, they said, in retri-bution for the hanging of Udham's hero, Bhagat Singh. Defying the authorities to hang her too, Suniti Choudhury said: 'It is better to die than live in a horse's stable.'[7]

Because the girls were minors, they were spared execution and instead transported for life. Both were released early, in 1938, as part of an amnesty agreement with Gandhi. Perhaps Udham hoped for similar intervention. He could spend time in a British jail, stringing out months between investigation, trial and appeal, he thought.

His plan was wrong on two fundamental levels: there was no desire to string out proceedings, just to string him up; and Gandhi had already washed his hands of him. When he reconciled himself to his reality, Udham decided to take his life on his own terms. In a series of extraordinary letters, written from Brixton Prison, he planned his suicide.

The content of the letters must have sounded bizarre to prison censors. Among the first was a letter to the Sikh Temple in Stockton, California. Though addressed to the gurdwara, it was clearly meant for someone else; the intended recipient was 'Kumari'.

Everything Udham wrote in prison was vetted, censored and copied, with complete facsimiles being sent to Vickery and Silver at the IPI. It was not the first time both had seen that particular recipient's name.

A letter to 'Kumari' had also been discovered at Udham's Mornington Terrace flat. At first glance, it appeared to be a love letter. Most of it was written in English:

> Sat Sri Akal [the traditional Sikh salutation]
>   I am kept of your letter with you have written me from New York. My love this is my last letter to you as I hope to be going back to India soon. You will understand what I meen [sic]. Please write to my friends in India . . .'[8]

The next few lines were written in Urdu: 'Darling, I used to tell you that our next meeting will be impossible . . . and what I had determined to do made my heart a stone. These things have plunged me into a kind of trance.'[9]

The separation of these few lines in Urdu suggested they were private and meant for an intimate acquaintance. The fact that two languages were used suggests Udham meant the letter for multiple sets of eyes. Switching to English again, he wrote:

> I want you to forgive me not to see you any more you will know reason very soon you always have been in my thoughts and best friend have had in my life. Its only thing I am taking with me one ambition I had to see India free so if I don't see freedom of India but peoples of my country will see soon. I have no desire of living I think I had seen enough that nobody had the opportunity of seeing so much and the money in the same bank you sent cash from if you will show this letter written by me I should think you will get about 2,600 dollars and send to my sister.[10]

He had signed the letter 'Yours ever, M. S. Azad' – a cool sign-off compared to the passion of his Urdu lines, again suggesting that the letter had messages for more than one person.

That letter, like the entries in his diary, had all the hallmarks of code. The '$2,600' he said would be released upon the production of his badly written and non-legally attested letter was a colossal amount of money in 1940, more than Udham could ever have laid his hands on. There were other things that made no sense. He talked of sending money to a sister, but Udham's only sibling, a brother, had died in the orphanage.

Was he referring to Lupe? Was he attempting to make arrangements to look after her if the worst came to pass? The name 'Kumari' gave nothing away of the identity of the recipient. In Hindi, the word simply means 'princess'.

Though he knew all his prison correspondence was being vetted, he could not help but try to contact 'Kumari' again. Sending his letter once more via the Stockton Gurdwara in California:

Dear Friend,
    Few week before [word illegible] had letter from you as you said about my friend Kumari is going back home and should meet her in India. I have written her many letters that I am unable to see her ... I said I might be back end of 1940, anyhow if she left America please write to her to my peoples and my sister specifically they should forget all about me. I am not a free man any more to write what I like and go wheresoever I like. The time has changed altogether. And life I am having is short one.[11]

He then brought up the matter of a 'car' which 'Kumari' had to find and sell as a matter of urgency. It was a strange thing for a man charged with a capital crime to worry about. Unless the 'car' was something else. Something important to the struggle:

The car she left in Continent is still there and I am unable to bring with me as we left the car in Milan thought to go back to India by land so please tell if she can do anything. Write to the firm to sell car for her and it is worth to do, and she will get very easy money then of £200 for doing so. So that is all only one more thing to say to remember what I have told her when I first met her in Riga in 1937.[12]

There was no record of Udham travelling to Riga in 1937, and if he had met 'Kumari' where and when he said, then it would have been on a passport the IPI did not know about. Riga was a well-known stopping-off point for people who wished to travel unseen to the Soviet Union. If 'Kumari' was there too, it suggests 'she' also had a familiarity with the illicit Moscow corridor. Udham, in his letter, thought 'Kumari' might be surprised at the recent turn of events, and he held her partly responsible for it: 'She bought me to this hell otherwise I would be somewhere else,' and 'She could not change my mind and whensoever I talk about [it] she call me some big shot.'[13]

Had 'Kumari' sent him to London to do something else? Had she failed to understand his commitment to his revenge? Had she refused to give him approval? Failed to give him the back-up he might need? The letters raise far more questions than answers, but they do confirm Udham's frequent trips to Eastern Europe.

Four days later, Udham wrote to 'Kumari' again, once more directing the letter through the Stockton Temple in California:

Dear Kumari

Sorry not to write to you before. I have lost your address. But last letter I have written to Dr Roy. Hope you will get and write to my sister about me and try to transfer the money I had in Long Beach to her name, and I like you to go personally to see her when you go back and [get] the car. you must write to the firm they will sell for you. It is not good to me any more.[14]

Long Beach was one of the places Udham had lived with Lupe, giving more credence to the notion that when he spoke of his 'sister', he was talking about her. His desertion of Lupe had been cruel. Perhaps he was trying to do right by her now:

I have murder case against me – do believe me. You can see by the paper I am writing on. It is you who brought me to this country. Still I don't blame nobody – it is I myself.

But I know one thing, you will not forget me for a few days' time. It might the time we were together in Continent and the day we nearly drown ourselves in the boat in Warsaw. That time is all over now. I have seen all I could, I think more than anybody else has seen. Remember me some time, you will simply laugh when you have my letter – you will not believe me at all.[15]

The letter then lurched to the present and flushed with passion:

My dear, I am only waiting for trail [sic]. It might be 22nd or 25th April and soon you will be free girl again. Hope you enjoy your best of life and sincerely I am telling you, you must believe me this time, I thought I could see you once again in my life but how we can – you are thousands of miles away.

I might be dead before you get this letter. I know I am getting married very soon with a thick rope and engagement could not be happy one for both of us.

Dear, you will remain in my heart till my end comes. I love you and shall go on loving you for eternity. I now I shall meet you in the next world if the worst happens.[16]

The fact that 'Kumari' might have been a political contact does not preclude the notion that she also had a sexual relationship with Udham. Police had found condoms with the roubles in Udham's room. His pedlar friends knew he liked a pretty girl on his arm. It is entirely possible that he had even grown to love this mysterious 'Kumari'. Having declared passion, Udham returned to business again:

So don't forget what I have told you, write to my peoples, and to Milan, Italy for the motor car, and go to the bank for me so they can transfer the money. I think it is between $2,500 and $5,000.

That is all I want you to do for me because they know you. But
unless you go there and tell them the manager will not believe
you . . . you must go yourself. So cheerio, my love.[17]

Apart from the letters he wrote to 'Kumari', Udham also wrote
several times to his friend Shiv Singh Johal at the Shepherd's Bush
Gurdwara. At first he pretended the two of them were strangers,
perhaps trying to save him from being dragged into the IPI's
orbit. He asked for 'books', never giving specific titles or places
where these 'books' might be found. The urgency of his requests
led the security services to believe that 'books' represented something else. Udham was clear about the books he did *not* want: 'I
don't want your Religious Books as I do not beleve [*sic*] them nor
Mohamedenis . . . I am a Prisoner and writing from Brixton Jail.
I have to stay here. I am having many body guards and I am well
looked after, I hope and wish soon I will be born again when all
of you will be old. Because the case against me is case I waited for
many years.'[18]

The IPI was working hard at deciphering Udham's true meaning, but Shiv Singh Johal took it at face value. He sent a variety of
uplifting and poetic texts. Udham wrote again, attempting to make
his message clearer. He had no interest in religion, he stressed, yet
seemed desperate for one particular copy of the Quran: 'I have given
Quran Sherif in English to some one in the East. If you go that side
please ask I think there is one Library in Poplar where they keep
Indian books. Thank you.'[19]

He assumed Johal would know where in 'the East' he meant
without having to be more specific. To ensure Johal did not take him
literally again, Udham added a postscript which sounded insane.
Nobody asking for the Quran would follow with: 'I have left my
God in India But I hear there is a English God I do not understand
him. And I eat cows and pigs because they are European.'[20]

Pork is forbidden in Islam, beef is forbidden in Hinduism and
Sikhism. Udham was again trying to make clear that when he asked
for religious books, *he did not really want religious books*. Johal

failed to understand yet again. He sent him a copy of the Quran along with some Sikh religious poetry.

It was becoming too much for Udham to bear. Addressing his next letter to 'Mr Jahal Singh', he deliberately misspelled his friend's name. 'Jahal' is the Hindi word for 'idiot'. 'Dear Mr Jahal Singh, I am sending your books back.'[21] Udham also instructed his friend to stop fussing over his legal defence: 'I never care much about dying I am born to die and I must.'[22] 'I do not know who is doing this all lot for me about Soliciter [sic] and Counsel ... I never afraid of dying so soon I will be getting married with execution.'[23]

Udham wanted to be remembered like his idol Bhagat Singh, hanged in Lahore on 23 March 1931: 'I am not sorry as I am a soldier of my country and it is since 10 years when my best friend has left me behind. And I am sure after my death I will see him as he is waiting for me. It was 23rd and I hope they will hang me on the same date as he was.'

Udham signed off again asking for 'Books': 'Plase [sic] do remember to sent the Books soon you have the time. That all I do here. also one (Prayer Book).'[24]

Udham would ask for his 'books' on six separate occasions over the space of three months, and with ever increasing desperation. Shiv Singh never understood what he wanted. Vickery, however, had cracked the code.

In a letter Udham managed to smuggle out under the noses of the censors, thanks to a corrupt warden, he was able to be far more explicit about his needs. Addressing the letter to 'Mr Singh c/o R. Sharman, 20 Cotton Street, Poplar', he gave away more than he could possibly have imagined.

The address had been under surveillance for some time. Udham's post confirmed Vickery's suspicions that the house was a dead-letter drop, an address where communications could be collected and forwarded to other eyes. On his envelope Udham had written: 'This letter is for you, read it.' He had signed it using the nickname only his closest friends knew: 'Bawa'.[25]

The first sixteen lines were in broken English, and clearly meant for the warden who had smuggled his letter out. There were instructions to a friend to pay him for his trouble and to provide a sum of money for luxuries Udham may want in prison.[26] The rest of the letter was in Urdu, a language the prison guard could not understand:

That which is written above is all bunkum! Greetings to all. I am not afraid to die. Still I am duty bound to make an effort. I have excited the cupidity of the man who sent this letter by saying that I am sending for money from outside. If there is to be any fuss, you can say that I don't know this Bawa.

I have no friend but you to whom I can write. You know that now it is a question of life or death. If you have the courage, this is what I want you to do. Get hold of a thick book and in its binding place a saw suitable for cutting iron [a hacksaw blade] about ten inches in length, half an inch in breadth. Can be bought in Woolworth's [a British general store] for 3d or 6d. It should be made into two pieces and very carefully inserted into the binding of the book so as not to be visible. The book should be Hindustani and should appear old. Send it to me in a parcel and do not write the name of the sender. Do not fail in this. Write the name of somebody else. I shall be sincerely grateful to you. If this succeeds my life is saved and I can hope to do other work which remains. But my life is in your hands, it is up to you to save it or destroy it.

If I am successful then these wicked gore* will have good cause to remember us Indians. Now, there is for me one very big job which I alone can do.[27]

He ended with a message to his Ghadar brothers: 'My greetings to all. I fancy that I shall put up a bit of show as I said in America, and I am not afraid to die.'[28] The final message is an important

---

* Pejorative for 'white people'.

one. In the 1920s, when Udham was living and working for the Ghadars in the United States, he had told them that he intended to do something big. He may even have told them what it was he had wanted to do. Even though the group had waned in its strength and influence in the 1930s, they remained vitally important to Udham Singh. He had left America years before, but his Ghadar brothers would never leave him.

A hacksaw blade was indeed sent to Brixton Prison days after his smuggled letter made it out,[29] although Udham Singh would never get to hear about it. It was intercepted in the post room and he was never told. Udham was left feeling increasingly desperate, forgotten and alone. Two weeks later, a police detective from Special Branch contacted Brixton Prison warning that Udham's friends were still trying to help him kill himself:

> A person named [name redacted] is going to try <u>very desperately</u> to get something through to Singh (Capital Charge) so that he (Singh) may end his life. It is not known what form it may take or what method is to be employed. It may be poison or a weapon, and it is possible the attempt will be made at a visit.[30]

The governor increased his watch on Udham, put the post room on notice, and for good measure confiscated Udham's reading spectacles. If he was so determined to kill himself, he might just break one of the lenses and slit his wrists.[31] The governor assured Vickery and Kell that no further letters would be smuggled out of his prison, nor would any blade or poison reach Udham Singh.

With no help forthcoming, Udham decided to die the hard way. He would starve himself to death. His hunger strike would take him right up to his trial. It was at this point that Dr Grierson, the prison medic, ordered a regime of force-feeding.

The trial at the Old Bailey commenced on 4 June 1940 and lasted only two days. Udham Singh was represented by lead barrister Mr St John Hutchinson, with Krishna Menon as junior counsel. Against him was the poetically named Mr Travers Christmas Humphreys and his co-counsel G. B. McClure.

The prosecution called twenty-four witnesses and these included eyewitnesses like Bertha Herring, Harry Wyndham Riches, Percy Sykes and Reginald Alfred Slee. They also called policemen who had interacted with Udham on the night of the shootings and the next day. Ballistics experts explained how the revolver had malfunctioned and how Udham had fired deliberately, accurately and, in Sir Michael's case, at deadly close range.

The select few journalists who had been allowed into the court rehashed the gory details of the case for their readers. A few also took note of the shadow of a man Udham had become: 'For forty-two days while he was awaiting his trial in Brixton prison Singh had been on hunger strike. He lost more than five stones and went almost completely bald.'[32]

Astonishingly, the defence had only one witness on their list, Udham himself. When he was questioned and cross-examined, he stuck to the story he had put in his statement at Canon Row Police Station. He had simply gone to protest. He had not meant to kill anybody. Somebody must have knocked his hand to make the gun go off. The prosecution tore his argument to shreds and he did little to fight back. Udham seemed to take very little interest in his trial at all.

Neither the prosecution nor the defence introduced the Jallianwala Bagh massacre or Udham's political connections with the Ghadars and the Communists. The documents that had shuttled between the IPI, MI5 and Special Branch remained locked away. Krishna Menon hardly spoke at all.

On 5 June, just before 2.30 p.m., the jury retired for an hour and five minutes, before returning with a unanimous verdict. Udham Singh was guilty of murder.

Before passing sentence, the judge asked if he had anything to say. Though the newspapers did not report it, it was at this point that Udham came to life for perhaps the first time in months. Producing a sheaf of handwritten papers from his pocket, he unleashed a torrent of rage that had built up for years:

I am not afraid to die. I am proud to die. I want to help my native land, and I hope when I have gone that in my place will come others of my countrymen to drive the dirty dogs – when I am free of the country. I am standing before an English jury in an English court. You people go to India and when you come back you are given prizes and put into the House of Commons, but when we come to England we are put to death. In any case I do not care anything about it, but when you dirty dogs come to India – the Intellectuals they call themselves, the rulers – they are of bastard blood caste, and they order machine guns to fire on the Indian students without hesitation. I have nothing against the public at all. I have more English friends in England than I have in India. I have nothing against the public. I have great sympathy with the workers of England, but I am against the dirty British Government. Your people are suffering the same as I am suffering through those dirty dogs and mad beasts – killing, mutilating and destroying. We know what is going on in India hundreds of thousands of people being killed by your dirty dogs.

The judge ordered prison officers to drag him from the dock. As he was pulled away, Udham was heard to scream: 'You people are dirty. You don't want to hear from us what you are doing in India. Beasts. Beasts. Beasts ... England, England, down with imperialism, down with the dirty dogs.'

Udham spat at the barristers as he was hauled towards the exit, ripping his papers into dozens of pieces, throwing them into the air.[33] They fell like leaves after a storm. His distant voice was heard to shout: '*Inquilab! Inquilab! Inquilab!*' 'Revolution! Revolution! Revolution!'

When silence descended once again, Justice Atkinson placed the small square of black silk on top of his powdered wig and passed a sentence of death. True to their promise, the press did not report his final words.

After the trial, Udham Singh was taken to Pentonville Prison to await his execution. His defence lodged an appeal, which was rejected on the grounds that there was no new evidence to bring before the court. Shiv Singh Johal started a petition asking for clemency, and though almost 400 Sikhs, Hindus and Muslims signed it, Surat Ali refused to circulate it among his followers in east London, objecting to the fact that they would need to provide their addresses and worrying about police harassment. Krishna Menon did nothing at all.

Reverend Holland, a vicar who visited Udham in prison, wrote to the secretary of state, as did a number of Quakers and some British followers of Gandhi, begging the government to commute the sentence on humanitarian grounds. Holland argued that Udham had told him personally that he had lost loved ones in Jallianwala Bagh and the event had driven him slightly mad.

Even Lord Lamington, one of the men Udham shot that evening at Caxton Hall, wrote to the home secretary wondering whether it might be better to let Udham live. He seemed patently 'insane' after all. They were all thanked for their interest but told firmly that the execution would go ahead as planned.

Udham Singh was hanged at Pentonville Prison at 9 a.m. on 31 July 1940. Any last words he may have spoken before his execution were heard only by his hangmen, Cross and Pierrepoint, who never repeated them. When the last shovel of dirt was thrown on his coffin, the British hoped they had covered up his story with him.

Most papers pertaining to Udham's case were ordered to be sealed for 100 years. Some of them, like Udham himself, were meant to remain buried for ever.

CHAPTER 25

THE RETURN

In 1946, a year after armistice, the Labour government in Britain found itself economically crippled by the cost of war. It neither had the domestic mandate to plough fresh resources into the Raj, nor the loyalty of an increasingly restive native population in India itself. The 'jewel in the crown' was slipping from Britain's grasp, and all that remained was to determine the manner in which it would let go.

Lord Louis Mountbatten, the last viceroy, was cast as midwife both to a post-colonial India and a newly created Pakistan. Liberation from British rule would come at a terrible price, involving the division of three separate provinces – Assam, Bengal and Punjab. The divide, cutting through districts based on their religious majorities, came to be known as the Radcliffe Line, named after Cyril Radcliffe.

Radcliffe, a boundary commissioner who famously had never been east of Paris, was given just five weeks to create two new countries. His line ploughed through cities, towns, villages, friends and families. It left an ocean of blood in its wake. Some fifteen million people were displaced by partition, and two million were killed.

Punjab, the province that had given birth to Udham Singh and which he had hoped to unite as Mohammed Singh Azad, was left with a scar running through its heart. Lahore went to Pakistan, Amritsar remained in India. Punjabis scattered from their ancestral lands in an unprecedented refugee crisis, the like of which has never been seen in the world before or since.

Through it all, and despite the concerted British effort to bury Udham Singh's name and legacy, somehow his story managed to live on. As India began to build its new identity, it found stories of anti-colonial defiance served as a foundation for a new sense of national pride. Punjab had never stopped being proud of the avenger of Jallianwala Bagh, but in the decades following independence, his reputation grew throughout the country. In the 1970s, an Indian mass movement demanded the return of Udham Singh. Eventually, it got its wish.

New Delhi, 19 July 1974

Shravan Amavasya

For Hindus, with their lunar calendar, there are certain moonless nights that belong primarily to the dead. Ancestors are honoured, little clay lamps are lit in their memory, and prayers are said for their souls. One such, the *Shravan Amavasya*, happened to fall on 19 July 1974.

The coincidence was lost on the hordes of bureaucrats sweating anxiously on the tarmac of New Delhi's airport. Religion was far from their minds, though they had performed nothing short of a miracle. Working for months behind the scenes, pushing against initial resistance from their counterparts in Whitehall, Indian civil servants had fulfilled a seemingly impossible brief. They had managed to bring Udham Singh home.

When the wheels of the specially chartered flight carrying Udham's body touched down on Indian soil on 19 July, the roar of the plane's jets was matched by that of the crowds. They had fought so hard and waited so long to bring him home. The chief minister of Punjab, a Congress politician named Giani Zail Singh, along with Shankar Dayal Sharma, the president of the Congress Party, stood on the tarmac to receive his casket, as if they were welcoming a visiting head of state. Heads bowed, the two men, both of whom would go on to become presidents of their country, placed garlands on Udham's coffin. A company of soldiers then gently lifted Udham, shoulder high, and placed him reverentially in a waiting hearse.

A long procession of police and ministerial cars formed an escort around Udham's vehicle as it pulled out of the airport at walking pace, to allow crowds outside to catch a glimpse of the cortege as it went by in the darkness. Undeterred by the heavy monsoon rains, thousands had come. The rain mixed with their tears as they threw flowers at Udham as he passed. A thick carpet of wet petals guided his way to the capital.

Nehru's daughter, Prime Minister Indira Gandhi, was waiting for him, standing at the entrance of Kapurthala House, the former residence of the maharajah of Kapurthala. The distinctive brush of white in her jet-black hair streaked like lightning from her temple to her nape as she stepped forward in the relentless rain to place a large floral wreath on his coffin. In the morning he would start his final journey, an eleven-day tour of the north, but for one night the Kamboj orphan would rest under the roof of a king.

There had been such unprecedented excitement at the prospect of his homecoming that Indira Gandhi had decreed Udham's remains should tour all Punjab, taking in every major city in the state. Udham would finally come to rest in Sunam, the town where he was born. There he could be cremated in the Sikh tradition.

A reporter from the *New York Times*, Bernard Weinraub, had been despatched to follow Udham on his final journey. Weinraub was struck by the depth of feeling that greeted the cortege wherever it went: 'The coffin of Udham Singh, draped in garlands and carnations, moves slowly along the flat, wet roads of the Punjab. Thousands of Sikhs, bearded and turbaned as always, line the road and surge around the van carrying the coffin of their martyr, who was hanged by the British colonial rulers in 1940, on its final pilgrimage through this north-western state. Raising their fists the Sikhs shout in Punjabi: "Udham Singh forever!" and "Long live Udham Singh!"'[1]

Critics of Indira Gandhi accused her of using Udham for her own political ends, to distract from bigger economic problems faced by her people at the time. It was an accusation angrily brushed aside by Zail Singh, her chief minister of Punjab: 'Why have we done it now? ... We felt it was the correct thing ... Udham Singh avenged our national humiliation ... He played a role in our liberation. He vindicated our self-respect and honour.'[2]

Though Udham died an atheist, all religions scrambled to honour him, the Sikhs in particular: '"In some ways Udham Singh was a true Sikh," [Zail Singh] said in Punjabi. "The Sikh gurus taught us to be fearless of death. We don't want to die in bed, but on the battlefield, for the nation. We are patriotic. We are fearless. Sikhs don't hate anyone because of caste or creed or sex. Everyone is equal. Udham Singh was a true Sikh."'[3]

On 31 July 1974, Udham Singh arrived in Sunam and the small town was filled to bursting point: 'My father was part of the welcoming committee and a civic leader in the town,' remembered Gagandeep Singh, who still lives in Sunam today. 'He used to tell me that Sunam sat like a bride, waiting for her groom the day he came back to us. She was decorated with lights and flowers, and the guests came from miles to pay their respects. All Punjab loved him. All Punjab wept for him.'[4]

Giani Zail Singh lit the pyre, and kept watch while it burned. The symbolism was powerful and clear, the orphan Udham was the son of all Punjab. The fire burned out, the embers turned from red to grey, and finally, on 2 August, Udham's ashes were collected and divided into seven separate urns.[5]

In his speech to the court, Udham had talked about a united India and embodied that ideal in the name under which he chose to murder Michael O'Dwyer. To honour his message, it was decided that one urn of his ashes should be sent to Haridwar, an ancient city sacred to the Hindus, where ashes are submerged in the River Ganges; one urn was sent to Kiratpur Sahib, where traditionally Sikhs take the ashes of their dead; and the third urn was sent to Rauza Sharif, the *dargah* or shrine of a Sufi Muslim saint, Ahmad al-Fārūqī al-Sirhindī.

Two urns were kept in the library of the Shaheed Udham Singh Arts College in Sunam, where they were meant to wait for the construction of a memorial museum bearing Udham's name. Forty-five years later, they are waiting there still.

One urn was buried under the foundation of a 27-foot-high minaret constructed in the town in honour of its famous son. The town is also dotted with numerous statues of him and memorial plaques bearing his name. Tehal Singh's humble one-room house has become a place of pilgrimage.

The last of the seven urns was taken to Jallianwala Bagh, the site of the 1919 massacre.[6] In 2018, a statue of Udham Singh was unveiled outside the gardens. It depicts him standing with his arm outstretched, palm up, holding a clod of blood-soaked earth in his hand. A reminder of a promise that took twenty-one years to fulfil.

ACKNOWLEDGEMENTS

There are so many people I need to thank. First among them is Avtar Singh Jouhl, of the Shaheed Udham Singh Welfare Trust in Birmingham. It is thanks to his tireless efforts and relentless Freedom of Information requests that over a thousand papers regarding Udham Singh were released to the public in 1996. Mr Jouhl allowed me unfiltered access to his files. Many of these documents were never meant to see the light of day and were ordered sealed in perpetuity following Udham's execution. Some documents were held back for a further twenty years. I gained access to them in 2016. They revealed details of Udham's botched execution. It is little wonder they had been withheld from the public.

Some of these top-secret documents served as tantalising signposts to Special Branch and MI5 files which remain untraceable. I hope one day they too will be found.

Dr Navtej Singh of Punjab University has been invaluable in helping me navigate my way through a blizzard of paperwork, and I am very grateful. Avtar Singh Jouhl in particular has shown superhuman patience and endless generosity of spirit when it came to sharing what he found, and delighting in what I was unearthing.

Following in Udham's footsteps took me from Britain to India and the Punjab, and to the United States, and I have people to thank in all of these places.

In Punjab I would like to mention the Desh Bhagat Yadgar centre in Jalandar, and particularly thank Dr Raghbir Kaur, the ex-general secretary of the museum, and Balwinder Kaur Bansal, a senior archivist. Their shelves are a repository of valuable Ghadar and nationalist material. Their knowledge and support was almost as valuable to me.

I am profoundly grateful also to the Central Khalsa Orphanage in Putlighar, Amritsar, where staff and boys took me to see a recreation of Udham Singh's room and told me about the ethos of the orphanage, which remains unchanged to this day. The orphanage does great work and should be applauded for giving a future to so many who otherwise may have fallen on stony ground.

In Sunam I was lucky to meet men and women who were generous with their time and knowledge. Chief among them was Gagandeep Singh, whose father was one of the foremost local politicians in Sunam at the time Udham's remains were brought home. Gagandeep and his wife Ranjeet Kaur opened their hearts and home to me, and spent a great deal of time and effort showing me around Sunam and introducing me to relevant people.

Shingara Singh, the curator and guardian of Udham's family home in Sunam, has likewise been unstintingly generous with his time and knowledge.

Historian Rakesh Kumar, whom I visited in Ferozpur in Punjab, has done exemplary work on Udham Singh's story, and I would like to thank him for his time and hospitality. He was very helpful in showing me what happened to Udham's remains after they were cremated in India.

Jewan Depak deserves very special thanks for pointing me to original Punjabi sources, including the unpublished memoir of Manjit Singh Kassid, and helping me to translate these faithfully. His efforts and enthusiasm for this project were beyond helpful.

If there has been one area of frustration in the writing of this book, it has been the difficulty in getting my hands on the original confession of Udham Singh, made in 1927. It has been widely reproduced in the work of Dr Sikander Singh, cited within this book. He told me the document quoted in his work lies in the National Archive in New Delhi, and though the relevant file does show up on the archive database, repeated attempts to locate it over a period of two years failed. On occasion it was suggested that the file might have been misplaced. On others, that it was not and had never been in the collection. Sikander Singh insists it is there.

Unable to see the original with my own eyes, I determined to fact check what had been quoted. To that end I spent over a year and a half cross-referencing names, dates and places against Metropolitan Police files, American census records, immigration documents and the archives of various local and central government institutions in the United States and Great Britain. These are all cited in the endnotes.

It was greatly reassuring to find corroboration in a plethora of official records. The fact that some of the spellings in Sikander Singh's reproduction of the confession were near approximations of what I was finding was comforting rather than concerning. It lent credibility to the idea that the confession was taken down by non-English-speaking police during what must have been a brutal interrogation. To the scribe, these names were entirely foreign.

Believing Udham's confession was real was not the same as believing it was true. It was gratifying to find supporting documents in a number of 1920s and 1930s archives that supported his confession details and suggested he had given a true account of his American adventure. Finding Lupe Singh was an especially rewarding moment.

I am grateful to archivists at the Bentley Library in Michigan who were able to find Professor Riggs ('Riggest' in the Sikander Singh text) in the 1920s faculty records. They provided vital leads which helped me trace the Pritam Singh story in other contemporary sources and the Michigan press.

My thanks to my friend Susie Aboulhawa, who took time out of her own hectic life to trawl New York census, electoral and residential lists to confirm or disprove some of my theories.

Back in England, special thanks is owed to Gary Poole, former governor of Pentonville Prison, and Gagandeep Singh, the serving Sikh chaplain at Pentonville. Together they guided me around the prison, showed me where Udham was held, where he was executed and where his body was buried. It was a sobering and moving experience.

Amandeep Madra of the UK Punjab Heritage Association remains my go-to guy when I need somebody knowledgeable to bounce ideas off. The work he and his colleagues are doing in locating war graves of Indian soldiers and showing how many were recruited from villages and towns in Punjab will add greatly to the historical record.

It was Amandeep who very kindly introduced me to Robert Clark. His help in navigating First World War archives was invaluable. Robert shone such helpful light on the enlistment processes and places Udham Singh would have encountered before his tour of Basra.

Historian Nick Lloyd was extremely helpful in talking through the life and personality of Sir Michael O'Dwyer. I'd like to especially thank Nick for sharing his thoughts on the relationship between Sir Michael and his son. I know he has a book on the former lieutenant governor in the pipeline and I greatly look forward to reading it.

Daniel Brückenhaus, author of an extraordinary book on the surveillance of anti-colonialists in Europe, was both delightful and extremely generous with his time and knowledge. Not only did he share original research from German archives, he helped me to understand the Sikh–German nexus that existed in the run-up to the Second World War.

My thanks to Christiane Baehr, who diligently translated some of these original German documents. We have been friends since school; I stalled after A-level German, and just as in the old days, she helped me with my homework.

Sital Singh of the Punjab restaurant in London was a treasure trove of information. His grandfather, Gurbachan Singh, was one of the Sikh pedlars and close friends of Udham Singh during his time in London. Funny, generous and with an extraordinary recall, Sital Singh brought his grandfather to life.

My sincerest thanks also to Peter Singh, the son of Banta Singh, one of the last people to see Udham as a free man. He has been wonderfully helpful in piecing together the final days before the assassination and giving me an idea of Udham's state of mind on the eve of his revenge.

I have known Lord Indarjit Singh for almost two decades, but I had no idea of his personal connection to the Udham Singh story till I was deeply involved in my research. As the son of Dr Diwan Singh, head of the Shepherds Bush Gurdwara, Lord Singh had his own recollections to share, as well as his father's. The irony of discussing Udham's story in the House of Lords in Westminster, a stone's throw from the assassination, was lost on neither of us.

It is thanks to the brilliant historian and collector Peter Bance that I found the account of Nazir Mattu in Sheffield archives. Peter, you are a star and never let me down. Thank you.

It is clear that Shiv Singh Jouhl was a pivotal figure in Udham's later life in prison. He stood by his friend till the end and took possession of Udham's meagre belongings after he was hanged. I heard that Shiv Singh had a son, Ajit. When I tried to trace him I hit numerous brick walls. Nobody knew where he was. Some said he had emigrated to Canada, others that he lived in America. Some insisted that he had passed away. My journalistic nerves jangled with the need to find out for sure, and after almost two years of searching, I am delighted to say I found Ajit Singh Jouhl alive and well and living in England. He was also a fount of useful information, and I will never forget the afternoon he and his wife, Elaine, spent at my home piecing together an extraordinary mosaic.

Dr Kim Wagner is just the best of the best. While I waded through Udham's life, he was doing magnificent work researching and writing about the Jallianwala Bagh massacre itself. Though we were ploughing overlapping fields, Kim was always an amazing support and generously helpful. In Kim I know I have found a dear friend for life.

Thanks to two wonderful men I have learned more than I thought I ever needed to know about guns and bullets. Chris Cobb-Smith, who became a friend after looking after me on somewhat risky BBC foreign assignments, and Jonathan Ferguson, Keeper of Firearms & Artillery at the National Firearms Centre in Leeds, have together helped me understand what it feels like to hold, conceal and fire the gun Udham used at Caxton Hall. My thanks to the wonderful archivists at the British Library and The National Archives. You have seen far too much of me lately.

Ian Marshall of Simon & Schuster and Rick Horgan of Scribner have been magnificent. When I was drowning in sources and losing sight of my story, they pulled me up for air. Ian in particular has been a patient midwife for *The Patient Assassin*. His counsel has been kind and creative. I thank them both for their faith in me. My thanks also to Frances Jessop for casting a cool and considered eye over my work. I can sometimes get caught up in convolution. Frances invariably set me free. Kaiya Shang, also at Simon & Schuster, has been a veritable angel. A lesser woman may have been driven mad by my constant tweaking, but not Kaiya. Or if I did send her round the twist she never showed it.

Thanks also and always to John Ash and Patrick Walsh at Pew Literary. Patrick is so much more than my literary agent. His guffaw at the end of a phone call is more restorative than a slug of gin ... Speaking of which, without my mates Mel Cochran, Zeta Hade and Claire Solomon, I might have lost my marbles. Thank you, wonderful women, for putting up with my endless moaning, and pouring coffee or cocktails down my craw. Thanks, too, to my long-distance sisters Gullie and Sid. Always at the end of a phone line. Thanks also the wonderful Diana D – you kept the wheels from falling off so many times.

My family have played a huge part in the writing of this book. My father and uncles, the sons of Ishwar Das Anand, have ingrained his story in my mind and heart. Thanks to you, Dad, Lala-ji's memory lives on in the pages of this book. I think you would have been proud.

My father-in-law, Mengha Singh, a wonderful raconteur, whose own father was a pedlar at the same time Udham Singh was pretending to be one, brought that hand-to-mouth world to life. Coming from such humble beginnings, what you and my mother- in-law, Sawaran Kaur, have accomplished is truly awe-inspiring.

And to you, Simon Singh, my husband and my love – thanks so much for your support and for keeping the ship afloat while I disappeared into the sometimes seemingly endless storm of research and writing . . . And to you, my sons, Hari and Ravi, thanks so much for constantly pulling me into the sticky, noisy, wonderful world of the living, even when I was wading through some of the most harrowing accounts of the dead.

NOTES

Chapter 1

1 BBC broadcast, London, 14 July 1940: http://www.churchill-society-london.org.uk/UnknWarr.html.

2 Albert Pierrepoint, *Executioner Pierrepoint: An Autobiography*, Harrap, 1974, p. 125.

3 *Ibid.*

4 *Ibid.*, p. 94.

5 *Ibid.*, p. 126.

6 TNA PCOM 9/872 – Secret memo from Hugh Grierson, Senior Medical Officer, Brixton Prison, 6 June 1940.

7 *Ibid.*

8 Pierrepoint, *Executioner*, op. cit., p. 96.

9 *Ibid.*, p. 126.

10 *Ibid.*

11 *Ibid.*

12 *Ibid.*, p. 127.

13 TNA PCOM 9 /872 – Secret memo undated: The execution of Udham Singh (unsealed 2016).

Chapter 2

1 From 'Obituary of Sir Michael F. O'Dwyer' by Percy Sykes, *Journal of the Royal Central Asian Society*, Vol. 27.2, 1940, p. 139.

2 Sir Michael O'Dwyer, *The O'Dwyers of Kilnamanagh: The History of an Irish Sept*, John Murray, 1933, p. 2.

3 Sir Michael O'Dwyer, *India as I Knew it*, Constable & Company, 1926, p. 1.

4 Sir Michael O'Dwyer, *The History of the O'Dwyers* (originally published as *The O'Dwyers of Kilnamanagh: The History of an Irish Sept*), with foreword by Tom O'Dwyer, Celtic Bookshop, 2000, p. 17.

5 *Ibid.*, p. 8.

6 *Ibid.*

7 *Ibid.*

8 John Beames, *Memoirs of a Bengali Civilian*, Chatto & Windus, 1961, p. 102 (written in 1896).

9 O'Dwyer, *India as I Knew it*, op. cit., p. 19.

10 *Ibid.*, p. 7.
11 *Ibid.*, p. 8.
12 *Ibid.*
13 *Ibid.*
14 Report from the Select Committee on East India Produce: Together with the Minutes of Evidence, 1840, Thomas Cope evidence, 14 July 1840, Parliamentary Papers, p. 451.
15 O'Dwyer, *India as I Knew it*, op. cit., p. 27.
16 *Ibid.*, p. 29.
17 *Ibid.*
18 *Ibid.*, p. 42.
19 *Ibid.*
20 *Ibid.*, p. 78.
21 *Ibid.*, dedication plate.

Chapter 3

1 Mrs Margaretta Catherine Reynolds, *At Home in India: Or Tâza-be-Tâza*, H. Drane, 1903, p. 122.
2 Sayha Sunami, *Sunama Da Itihas*, Sunam, 1982, p. 31 (Punjabi).
3 Udham Singh would use many dates of birth in his life, but 26 December 1899 is celebrated as his official birthday. The date has been corroborated by the historian Navtej Singh (*Challenge to Imperial Hegemony: The Life Story of a Great Indian Patriot Udham Singh*, Publication Bureau, Punjabi University, 1998, p. 33) based on interviews with Bhai Chanchal Singh Kambo (a relative of Udham Singh), Captain Ram Singh and Jamadar Kala Singh, all of whom lived in Sunam.
4 IOR L/P5/12/500, Udham Singh statement to police, collated biography submitted to the assistant chief constable by DD Inspector J. Swain, 19 March 1940.
5 David Arnold, *Colonizing the Body: State Medicine and Epidemic Disease in Nineteenth-Century India*, University of California Press, 1993, p. 200.
6 J. N. Hays, *Epidemics and Pandemics: Their Impacts on Human History*, ABC-CLIO, 2005, p. 345.
7 From an interview by Sikander Singh of Mai Aas Kaur (28 November 1984), cited in Sikander Singh, *Udham Singh, alias Ram Mohammed Singh Azad*, B. Chattar Singh Jiwan Singh, 1998, p. 80.
8 Bharat da Garurav, *Sardar Udham Singh*, Jagan Nath Sandhey, Gurdwara Parbandhak Committee, 1975, p. 2 (Punjabi).
9 Navtej Singh, *Challenge to Imperial Hegemony: The Life Story of a Great Indian Patriot Udham Singh*, Publication Bureau, Punjabi University, 1998, p. 5.
10 *Ibid.*

11   B. S. Maighowalia, *Sardar Udham Singh: A Prince Amongst Patriots of India, the avenger of the massacre of Jallianwala Bagh, Amritsar*, foreword by Krishna Menon, Chhabra Printing Press, 1969, pp. 13–14.

12   Gurcharan Singh, *Shadeed Udham Singh*, Punjabi University, 1995, p. 45.

13   B. S. Maighwallia, *Prince Amongst Patriots* op. cit., pp. 13–14, and Sikander Singh, *Udham Singh*, op. cit., p. 81.

14   Navtej Singh, *Hegemony*, op. cit., p. 36.

15   Diwali, according to the lunar calendar, fell on 5 November that year.

16   Sikander Singh, *Udham Singh* op. cit., p. 81.

17   *Ibid.*

18   Navtej, *Hegemony,* op. cit., p. 37.

19   Navtej *Hegemony,* op. cit., p. 38.

20   Register of admissions, Khalsa Central Orphanage, Putlighar, Amritsar, entries 121 and 122, 28 October 1907.

21   Sikander Singh, *Udham Singh*, op. cit., p. 82.

22   Navtej Singh, *Hegemony*, op. cit., p. 40.

23   Suba Singh, cited by Sikander Singh, *Udham Singh*, op. cit., p. 83.

24   Minute book, *Festival of Empire Minute Book*, Coll. Misc., 459, London School of Economics Archives, London.

25   *Daily Telegraph*, 9 July 1911.

26   Hansard, *Durbar Expenditure*, Vol. 22, 16 March 1911.

27   O'Dwyer, *India as I Knew it*, op. cit., p. 102.

28   *Ibid.*

29   *Ibid.*

30   Jessica Douglas-Home, *A Glimpse of Empire*, Rain Tree, 1988, p. 60.

31   *Ibid.*

32   A. F. Madden and John Darwin (eds), *Select Documents on the Constitutional History of the British Empire and Commonwealth: The dominions and India since 1900*, Greenwood Press, 1993, Vol. 6, p. 660.

33   *Ibid.*

34   *Los Angeles Herald*, 15 November 1909.

35   Jessica Douglas-Home, *Empire*, op. cit., p. 61

36   O'Dwyer, *India as I Knew it*, op. cit., p. 167.

37   *Ibid.*, p. 168.

Chapter 4

1   Shyamaji Krishravarma: Life and Times of an Indian Revolutionary, Lakshmi Publications, Delhi, 1950, p. 123.

2   Daniel Brückenhaus, *Policing Transnational Protest: Liberal Imperialism and the Surveillance of Anticolonialists in Europe, 1905–1945*, Oxford University Press, 2017, p. 15.

3   *Ibid.*

4 Brückenhaus, *Policing* (op. cit.), p. 27; Har Dayal speech cited in Niroda Kumāra Baruwā, *Life and Times of an Indian Anti-Imperialist in Europe*, Oxford University Press, 2004, p. 39.

5 O'Dwyer, *India as I Knew it*, op. cit., p. 162.

6 *Ibid*. p. 170.

7 *Ibid*. *p*. 162.

8 *Ibid*.

9 *Ibid*., p. 125.

10 *Ibid*., p. 157.

11 *Ibid*., p. 413.

12 Santanu Das, 'The Indian Sepoy in the First World War', British Library, 6 February 2014: http://www.bl.uk/world-war-one/articles/the-indian-sepoy-in-the-first-world-war

13 O'Dwyer, *India as I Knew it*, op. cit., p. 216.

14 *Ibid*., p. 213.

15 Heike Liebau (ed.), 'The World in World Wars: Experiences, Perceptions and Perspectives from Africa and Asia', *Studies in Global Social History*, Vol. 5 2010, p. 141.

Chapter 5

1 Still the case today. Author interview with custodians of the Khalsa Orphanage, Amritsar, 2016.

2 *Ibid*.

3 *War Speeches of Sir Michael O'Dwyer*, Superintendent Government Printing, 1918, p. 85.

4 *Ibid*., p. 87.

5 *Ibid*., p. 44.

6 *Ibid*.

7 *Ibid*., p. 55.

8 *Ibid*.

9 Udham Singh alias Sher Singh Amritsar Kotwali statement 1927, cited in Sikander Singh, *Udham Singh*, op. cit., p. 84.

10 *Ibid*.

11 *Ibid*.

12 *Ibid*.

13 *Ibid*.

14 *Ibid*.

15 Paul Ghuman British, *Untouchables: A Study of Dalit Identity and Education*, Ashgate Publishing Limited, 2011, p. ix.

16 Dietrich Jung, 'The "Ottoman–German Jihad": Lessons for the Contemporary "Area Studies" Controversy', *British Journal of Middle Eastern Studies*, Vol. 41.3, 2014, p. 41.

17 'Despatch received by the Secretary of State for War and the Chief of the General Staff', India Second Supplement to the *London Gazette*, 10 July 1917, pp. 1–13.

18 *Ibid.*

19 Udham Singh statement, 1927. Cited in Sikander Singh, *Udham Singh,* op. cit., p. 85.

20 TNA HO 144/21444 CRIMINAL CASES: SINGH, Udham Convicted at Central Criminal Court (CCC) on 5 June 1940 for murder and sentenced to death, early history of Udham Singh, cites his service in Basra. Sikander Singh, *Udham Singh,* op. cit. citing statement of Udham Singh alias Sher Singh Amritsar Kotwali statement 1927.

21 Sikander Singh, *Udham Singh,* op. cit., interview with Bhajan Singh by the author, p. 85.

22 Udham Singh alias Sher Singh Amritsar Kotwali statement 1927, cited in Sikander Singh, *Udham Singh,* op. cit., p. 85.

23 *Ibid.*

24 *Ibid.*

25 *Ibid.*

26 *Ibid.*

Chapter 6

1 Mahatma Gandhi, *Young India*, Vol. 10, Navajivan Publishing House, 1928, p. 338.

2 Mahadev Haribhai Desai, Narahari Dvārakādāsa Parākha (ed.), Hemantkumar Gunabhai Nilkanth (trans.), *Day to day with Gandhi: Secretary's Diary*, Vol. 1, Sarva Seva Sangh Prakashan, 1968, p. 111.

3 Mohandas Karamchand Gandhi, *The Collected Works of Mahatma Gandhi: 26 April 1918 – April 1919 (CWGM)*, Vol. 15, Publications Division, Ministry of Information and Broadcasting, Govt. of India, 1965, digitized 25 July 2011, p. 2.

4 *Ibid.*

5 *CWMG,* op. cit., Vol 14, p. 477.

6 *Ibid.*, pp. 474, 510.

7 *New York Times*, 24 April 1918.

8 *Congress Party Inquiry 1919–1920*, Delhi, 1996, first published 1920, pp. 24–5.

9 Author interview with S. S. Gill, curator of the Udham Singh museum in Sunam: Shadeed Udham Singh Zadi Ghar, Sunam, 2016.

10 O'Dwyer, *India as I Knew it*, op. cit., p. 236.

11 The Amritsar Massacre, Nick Lloyd, op. cit., p. 70.

12 Cited in Nick Lloyd, *The Amritsar Massacre: The Untold Story of One Fateful Day*, I. B. Tauris, 2011, p. 34.

13 *Evidence Taken Before the Disorders Inquiry Committee*, vol. 1,
    Superintendent Government Printing, 1920, p. 125.
14 Gandhi to V. S. Srinivasa Sastri, 9 Feb 1919, *CWMG* op. cit., Vol. 17, p. 280.
15 Descendants of those who knew him in Sunam certainly remember him
    as a smuggler of seditious papers. In author interviews they describe
    him travelling to distant rural areas, drumming up support for the
    Amritsar actions. Since they are passing on what they heard from their
    own, long dead family members, there is no way of cross-examining
    these accounts, although their proliferation suggests veracity. Police
    would certainly arrest him in 1927 for possessing seditious literature
    with the aim of distribution.
16 *Bombay Chronicle* quoted in Nick Lloyd, *The Amritsar Massacre* op. cit., p. 38.
17 *The Tribune*, 12 April 1919.
18 *Ibid.*, 8 April 1919.
19 *Disorders Inquiry Committee*, op. cit., Vol. 4, p. 137.
20 O'Dwyer, *India as I Knew it*, op. cit., p. 269.

Chapter 7

 1 Gandhi, *Young India,* op. cit., p. 378.
 2 *Ibid.*
 3 Report: *Disorders Inquiry Committee 1919–1920*, Committee on Disturbances
    in Bombay, Delhi, and the Punjab, Calcutta, 1920, pp. 12–13.
 4 Lloyd, *The Amritsar Massacre*, op. cit., p. 43.
 5 *Ibid.*
 6 Miles Irving to A. J. W. Kitchin, 8 April 1919, in *Disorders Inquiry
    Committee*, Vol. 6, Punjab Government and Sir Umar Hayat Khan, Calcutta,
    1920, p. 3.
 7 *Ibid.*
 8 Ian Colvin, *The Life of General Dyer*, W. Blackwood & Sons Ltd., 1929, p. 144.
 9 *Congress Punjab Inquiry, Evidence*, p. 15.
10 *Report on the Events of April, 1919*, Indian National Congress, p. 30.
11 *Evidence Taken Before the Disorders Inquiry Committee*, op. cit., Vol. 3,
    p. 43.
12 *Report on the Events of April, 1919*, op.cit., p. 31.
13 *Ibid.*
14 *Ibid.*, p. 30.
15 *Ibid.*
16 O'Dwyer, *India as I Knew it*, op. cit., p. 275.
17 *Punjab Disturbances, April 1919*, compiled from the *Civil and Military
    Gazette*, Vol. 1, p. 26.
18 O'Dwyer, *India as I Knew it*, op. cit., p. 275.
19 Colvin, *Dyer*, op. cit., p. 161.

20 *Ibid.*

21 *Ibid.*

22 *Ibid.*, p. 162.

23 *Ibid.*, p. 163.

24 *Ibid.*, p. 162.

Chapter 8

1 Nigel Collett, *The Butcher of Amritsar: General Reginald Dyer*, Hambledon Continuum, 2005, p. 43.

2 Colvin, *Dyer*, op. cit., p. 3.

3 *Ibid.*, p. 7.

4 *Ibid.*, pp. 5–6.

5 *The Congress Punjab Inquiry 1919–1920*, op. cit., p. 29.

6 In his own memoirs, Sir Michael acknowledges that though the telegraphic and telephonic communications were cut on 10 April, the railway telephone was still operational, and he was receiving reports, albeit 'confused', from the men on the ground. O'Dwyer, *India as I Knew it,* op. cit., p. 274.

7 *Disorders Inquiry Committee*, op. cit., Vol. 3, p. 201.

8 O'Dwyer, *India as I Knew it,* op. cit., p. 282.

9 Conversations with the author's father.

10 The sons of Lala Ishwar Das Anand could not remember the names of the boys. His eldest son, Dharam Swarup Anand, knew details about them, but not what they were called. My own father wondered whether Ishwar Das could not bear to say their names.

Chapter 9

1 *Disorders Inquiry Committee*, op. cit., Vol. 3, p. 212.

2 *Ibid.*

3 *Ibid.*

4 Collett, *Butcher*, op. cit., p. 246, quoting *The Times,* 1924 transcript of the Sir Michael O'Dwyer v Sir C. Sankaran Nair trial, May 1924, evidence of Rup Lala Puri taken on commission in Punjab.

5 *Hunter Report, Evidence*, Vol. 3, pp. 117 and 122. Evidence of Brigadier General Dyer.

6 *Indian National Congress, Punjab Subcommittee*, Vol. 2, pp. 82–3.

7 It has been alleged by some historians that Hans Raj was in league with the local police, particularly since he would later become 'an approver' for the British in a subsequent legal case, i.e. a witness for the prosecution against his own countrymen. I have found no hard evidence to substantiate this claim.

8 *Times Literary Supplement,* 9 April 1964, quoting a letter from a British SNCO

Sergeant Anderson to Rupert Furneaux; Collett, *Butcher*, op. cit., p. 260.

9 Collett, *Butcher*, op. cit., p. 261.

10 *Ibid*.

11 *Report on the Events of April, 1919*, op. cit., p. 86.

12 Kapil Deva Malaviya, *Open Rebellion in the Punjab (with Special Reference to Amritsar)*, Abhudaya Press, 1919, p. 62.

13 Statement of eyewitness Mr Girdhari Lal, who happened to watch the scene from the window of his house overlooking the Jallianwala Bagh. Ref: *Report of Commissioners*, Vols. 1, 2, Bombay, 1920, reprinted 1976, pp. 10–11.

14 *Ibid*.

15 Interview with Bharpur Singh, survivor of the Amritsar massacre. BBC documentary, 'Gandhi – Rise to Fame', November 2009.

16 Evidence of Mohamed Ismail. India National Congress report, Vol. 2, pp. 70–1.

17 Estimates vary widely – the British at first put the number of fatalities at 200 but admitted the number of dead could well have been higher. Congress put the figure nearer 1,000 killed and 1,500 wounded. Pandit Madan Mohan Malaviya collected the information for the party with a view to raising the issue in the Central Legislative Council.

18 Raja Ram, *The Jallianwala Bagh Massacre: A premeditated plan*, Publication Bureau Pujab University, 2002, p. 128. Appendix C: list of persons killed in Jallianwala Bagh on 13 April 1919, File-Pb. Govt. Home-Military – Part B – 1921 – No. 139.

19 Evidence of Ratan Devi from *Report on the Events of April, 1919*, op. cit., pp. 116–18.

20 *Ibid*.

21 *Ibid*.

22 *Ibid*.

23 *Ibid*.

The Legend of Udham Singh

1 Legend has it that a young man was serving water to the crowds that day, a service he performed for the sake of the orphanage that raised him. There is no hard evidence to prove this, but as has been stated, the official lists of dead and wounded are unreliable. What we can say is that though the British had every reason to place him far from the scene and had better access to records than we ever will, they could state their certainty in no better terms than 'We cannot say for certain that he was present.'

2 Author interview with Gurbachan Singh, London, and with family of Manjit Singh Kassid, Sunam. See also Interview with Sh. Ramji Dass Sunami, a close friend of Udham Singh by Sikander Singh, 15 December 1984, quoted in Sikander Singh, *Udham Singh*, op. cit., p. 86.

3 Letter from Reverend W. E. S. Holland to Secretary of State for India Leo

Amery, 11 June 1940.

4 The Ghadar Directory of 1934, Punjab University Library, BK-003681.

5 Such is the pride of Sunam in its most famous son, suggesting he was not actually caught in Dyer's firing is met with such hostility that my source has asked to remain nameless, and I am respecting that request.

Chapter 10

1 O'Dwyer, *India as I Knew it*, op. cit., p. 283.

2 *Ibid.*

3 *Ibid.*

4 *Ibid.*

5 *Ibid.*

6 Months later, on 29 October, the government of India would set up an official panel to consider Dyer's actions and the events of April 1919. 'The Disorders Inquiry Committee of 1919–1920' was headed by Lord William Hunter, a senator of the College of Justice of Scotland. More commonly known as 'The Hunter Commission', the committee was made up of four British members and three Indians, who questioned witnesses and considered evidence over a period of forty-six weeks.

7 *Evidence Taken Before the Disorders Inquiry Committee*, op. cit., Vol. 3, p. 127.

8 O'Dwyer, *India as I Knew it*, op. cit., p. 285.

9 *Ibid.*

10 *Ibid.*, p. 286.

11 *Ibid.*

12 *House of Commons Parliamentary Papers: 1909–1982*, Vol. 14, H. M. Stationery Office, 1920, p. 48.

13 O'Dwyer, *India as I Knew it*, op. cit., p. 287; and *Parliamentary Papers: 1909-1982*, op. cit., p. 48.

14 O'Dwyer, *India as I Knew it*, op. cit., p. 70.

15 Statement of Brigadier General D. H. Drake-Brockman, Commanding Delhi Brigade. *Disorders Inquiry Committee I: Delhi (Calcutta 1920)*, p. 172. Quoted in HoC Debate by B. C. Spoor MP, 8 July 1920, Hansard Vol. 131, cc. 1705-1819.

16 The *Bombay Chronicle* was owned by Pheorzshah Mehta, a wealthy Parsi with strong Nationalist sympathies.

17 Benjamin Guy Horniman, *British Administration and the Amritsar Massacre*, T. F. Unwin Ltd, 1920, p. 146.

18 Horniman, *Massacre*, op. cit., p. 148.

19 Horniman, *Massacre*, op. cit., p. 149.

20 Evidence of Mr Marsden. *Report of the Commissioners Appointed by the Punjab Subcommittee of the Indian National Congress: 1920*, Vol. 1, p. 100.

21 *Ibid.*

22 *Hunter Report,* op. cit., p. 85.

23 *Ibid.*

24 *Indian National Congress. Commissioners Appointed by the Punjab Subcommittee 1920,* p. 177.

25 *Disorders Inquiry Committee,* Vol. 4, p. 6.

26 *Ibid.*

27 *Ibid.,* p. 286.

28 Collett, *Butcher,* op. cit., p. 284.

29 *Punjab Disturbances, 1919–20,* op. cit., Vol. 1, p. 62.

30 *Indian National Congress, Commissioners Appointed by the Punjab Subcommittee 1920,* p. 167.

31 Horniman, *Massacre,* op. cit., p. 160.

Chapter 11

1 Interview with Sh. Ramji Dass Sunami by Sikander Singh, 15 December 1984, quoted in Sikander Singh, *Udham Singh,* op. cit., p. 86.

2 Interview with Jewan Deepak, a nephew of Manjit Singh Kassid.

3 Quoted in J. S. Grewal and H. S. Puri, Letters of Udham Singh, Guru Nanak Dev University, Amnistar, 1974, pp. 97–8; and also Navtej Singh, *Hegemony* op. cit., p. 54.

4 Even today many Indians believe Udham Singh assassinated Dyer. One of the top searches on Google when you enter his name is 'When did Udham Singh kill Dyer'.

5 Statement of Udham Singh alias Sher Singh to Amritsar Kotwal, cited in Sikander Singh, *Udham Singh,* op. cit., p. 87.

6 *Ibid.*

7 O'Dwyer, *India as I Knew it,* op. cit., p. 264.

8 Collett, *Butcher,* op. cit., p. 276.

9 Udham Singh alias Sher Singh statement to Amritsar Kotwali 1927, cited in Sikander Singh, *Udham Singh,* op. cit., p. 88.

10 *Ibid.,* op. cit., p. 89.

11 *Ibid.*

12 *Report on Ude Singh, Udham Singh, Sher Singh, Frank Brazil,* secret file from DIB shared with IPI, 11/10/37, IOP P&J (S) 466/36.

13 Christian Wolmar, *Blood, Iron & Gold: How the Railways Transformed the World,* Atlantic Books, 2009, p. 182.

14 Ronald Hardy, *The Iron Snake,* G. p. Putnam's Sons, 1965, p. 13.

15 Author interview with the family of Jiwa Singh in Sunam, 2016.

16 Nazmi Durrani, *Liberating Minds, Restoring Kenyan History: Anti-Imperialist Resistance by Progressive South Asian Kenyans 1884–1965,* Vita Books, 2017, p. 101.

17 *Ibid.,* p. 102.

18 Udham Singh alias Sher Singh, statement to Amritsar Kotwali 1927, cited in
    Sikander Singh, *Udham Singh*, op. cit., p. 89.
19 *Ibid.*
20 Memories of his motorcycle return. Sikander Singh interviews with Dr
    Bhajan Singh and Ramji Singh of Sunam, cited in Sikander Singh, *Udham
    Singh*, op. cit., p. 90; and Manjit Singh Kassid unpublished memoirs
    Sunam.
21 Udham Singh alias Sher Singh statement to Amritsar Kotwali 1927, cited in
    Sikander Singh, *Udham Singh*, op. cit., p. 90.
22 *Ibid.*
23 Bankimcandra Chatterji, Julius J. Lipner (trans.), *Anandamath, or The
    Sacred Brotherhood*, Oxford University Press, 2005, p. 76.
24 Sikander Singh, *Udham Singh* op. cit., p. 90.
25 *Ibid.*, op. cit., p. 89; Gurcharan Singh, *Shaheed Udham Singh*, op. cit., p. 117.
26 From the statement of Sher Singh alias Ude Singh, 1927, Amritsar Kotwal,
    cited in Sikander Singh, *Udham Singh*, op. cit., p. 90.

Chapter 12

 1 General Barrow, quoted in Collett, *Butcher*, op. cit., p. 333.
 2 Hansard, 5th ser. (Commons), Vol. 131, cols. 1725, 1736.
 3 Amritsar: *Minutes of Evidence taken before the Hunter Committee, 1920*,
    Parliamentary Archives, DAV/123.
 4 *Ibid.*
 5 O'Dwyer, *India as I Knew it*, op. cit., p. 329.
 6 Letters to the Editor, *The Times*, quoted in Savita Narain, *The
    Historiography of the Jallianwala Bagh Massacre, 1919*, Spantech & Lancer,
    1998, p. 45.
 7 Wilson, quoted in Collett, *Butcher*, op. cit., p. 361.
 8 Hansard, Army Council and General Dyer. HC Deb 08, July 1920, vol. 131
    cols. 1705–1819
 9 *Ibid.*
10 *Ibid.*
11 *Ibid.*
12 *Ibid.*
13 Neil James Mitchell, *Democracy's Blameless Leaders: From Dresden to Abu
    Ghraib, how Leaders Evade Accountability for Abuse, Atrocity, and Killing*,
    NYU Press, 2012, p. 62.
14 *Papers Relating to the Application of the Principle of Dyarchy to the Government
    of India: To which are Appended the Report of the Joint Select Committee and
    the Government of India Act, 1919*, Clarendon Press, 1920, p. 326.
15 Patrick French, *Liberty or Death*, Penguin, 2011, p. 35.
16 Sir Sigismund David Waley, *Edwin Montagu: A Memoir and an Account of*

his Visits to India, Asia Publishing House, 1964, p. 230.
17 Colvin, *Dyer*, op. cit., p. 7.
18 *Ibid.*, p. 8.
19 Collet, op.cit, p.407
20 Mahatma Gandhi, *Collected Works*, Publications Division, Ministry of Information, GOI, 1965, Vol. 18, p. 45.
21 Letter to *Pioneer Mail* from 'A. B.', 2 July 1920, *Pioneer Mail and Indian Weekly News*.
22 Santdas Khushiram Kirpalani, *Fifty Years with the British, Memoirs of an Indian Civil Servant*, University of Nevada Press, 1993, p. 63.
23 *ibid.*

Chapter 13

1 *US School Yearbooks, 1880–2012: The Michiganensian Yearbook, Year: 1926* – the entry for Pritam Singh (with picture) says he was born 'in about 1906'.
2 Udham Singh alias Sher Singh, Amritsar Kotwali statement 1927, cited in Sikander Singh, *Udham Singh*, op. cit., p. 90.
3 Photo of Pritam Singh, *US School Yearbooks, 1880–2012*.
4 Udham Singh alias Sher Singh, Amritsar Kotwali statement 1927, cited in Sikanker Singh, *Udham Singh*, op. cit., p. 90.
5 *Michigan Daily*, 18 November 1924.
6 Udham Singh alias Sher Singh, Amritsar Kotwali statement 1927, cited in Sikander Singh, *Udham Singh*, op. cit., p. 90.
7 *Ibid.*
8 *Ibid.*
9 *Ibid.*
10 *Ibid.*, p. 91.
11 The *Michigan Daily*, 18 November 1924.
12 *Henry Earle Riggs papers: 1911–1942*, Bentley Historical Library, Michigan, Call number: 852137 Aa 2.
13 *Ibid.*
14 Udham Singh alias Sher Singh, Amritsar Kotwali statement 1927, cited in Sikander Singh, *Udham Singh*, op. cit., p. 91.

Chapter 14

1 http://immigrationtounitedstates.org/360-asian-indian-immigrants.html.
2 *Vancouver Daily World*, 13 August 1907.
3 Udham Singh alias Sher Singh, Amritsar Kotwali statement 1927, cited in Sikander Singh, *Udham Singh*, op. cit., p. 91.
4 Pritam Singh gave a number of interviews to the *Michigan Daily* in 1924 in which he described being stranded in Mexico for ten months. A record of border

crossings from El Paso into Texas show Pritam was finally allowed in on 10 October 1924. The National Archives and Records Administration; Washington D.C.; *Manifests of Alien Arrivals at Columbus, New Mexico, 1917–1954*; NAI: 2843448; Record Group Title: Records of the Immigration and Naturalization Service, 1787–2004; Record Group Number 85; Microfilm Roll Number 6.

5 In his confession (Sikander Singh, *Udham Singh*, op. cit., p. 90) they 'embarked on a French boat and landed at Tamples'. As with many foreign names in his 1927 confession at Amritsar Kotwal, the police officer taking notes appears to have made a stab at spelling places and names he was unfamiliar with.

6 *Michigan Daily*, 15 October 1924.

7 *Ibid.*

8 'Detroit Business Man offers to go Bond for Indian', *Michigan Daily*, 18 November 1924.

9 *Manifests of Alien Arrivals*, op. cit., Record Group Number: 85; Microfilm Roll Number: 6 – Entry for Pritam Singh.

10 The *Michigan Daily*, 13 December 1924.

11 Though there is clear evidence that Pritam crossed the border from El Paso, and the Riggs letters and Pritam's own account suggest he was languishing at the border, there is also a record of a Pritam Singh arriving in Michigan from India via an ocean crossing on November 1924. Either the student returned briefly to India after gaining entry (which is possible but seems unlikely since he was so short of funds) or somebody was using his identity to get others into the USA). National Archives and Records Administration (NARA), Washington, D.C.; *Manifests of Alien Arrivals at Port Huron, Michigan, February 1902–December 1954*; Record Group 85, Records of the Immigration and Naturalization Service; Microfilm Serial A3441; Microfilm Roll 8.

12 Orlando Figes, *A People's Tragedy: The Russian Revolution, 1891–1924*, Random House, 1997, p. 173.

13 *Ghadar Directory* op. cit.

14 F. C. Isemonger, and J. Slattery, *An account of the Ghadr conspiracy 1913–1915*, 1919, IOR/V/27/262/9.

15 Gurdev Singh Deol, *The role of the Ghadar Party in the National Movement*, Sterling Publishers, 1969, p. 194.

16 Udham Singh alias Sher Singh, Amritsar Kotwali statement 1927 cited in Sikander Singh, Udham Singh, op. cit., p. 92.

17 *ibid.*; Jawand Singh's naturalisation records show that he lived in El Paso and census records show he also lived in Fresno for a time. A search under his wife, Josefina Torres, shows she was living in Pomona. The National Archives at Fort Worth; Fort Worth, Texas; Record Group Title: *Records of District Courts of the United States, 1685–2009*; Record Group Number 21.

18 Udham Singh alias Sher Singh, Amritsar Kotwali statement 1927, cited in Sikander Singh, *Udham Singh*, op. cit., p. 92; Passenger lists for Sudagar Singh

show he travelled from Yokohama to Berkley in 1921. There is no further record of Sudagar on passenger exit lists, border crossing lists, census reports or electoral rolls. It is as if he disappeared. Like Udham, he left a barely perceptible footprint in American bureaucracy. Like Udham, it is likely he changed his name, once, or perhaps multiple times.

19 Navtej Singh, *Hegemony*, op. cit., p. 65.

20 Udham Singh alias Sher Singh, Amritsar Kotwali statement 1927, cited in Sikanker Singh, *Udham Singh*, op. cit., p. 92.

21 *Ibid.*

22 *Ibid.*

23 Josefina Torres married to Jawand Singh. The National Archives at Fort Worth; Fort Worth, Texas; Record Group Title: *Records of District Courts of the United States, 1685–2009*; Record Group Number 21.

24 Udham Singh alias Sher Singh, Amritsar Kotwali statement 1927, cited in Sikander Singh, *Udham Singh*, op. cit., p. 92.

25 *Ibid;* The spelling is 'Lloope' in the confession at Amritsar Kotwal in 1927 produced here, but Lupe is the correct spelling for that Hispanic name. Unfamiliar names to the Indian ear are often variant in this confession.

26 Texas Department of State Health Services; Austin, Texas, USA, *Death Certificates, 1903–1982*.

27 Udham Singh alias Sher Singh, Amritsar Kotwali statement 1927, cited in Sikander Singh, *Udham Singh*, op. cit., p. 93.

28 *Ibid.*

29 *Ibid.*

30 *Ibid.*

31 *Ibid.*

32 In his Kotwali confession he merely called it the Aeroplane Department, however the Douglas plant was the only one fully operational by the mid-1920s.

33 National Archives at San Francisco; San Bruno, California; NAI Number 605504; Record Group Number RG 21; Record Group Title: *Records of District Courts of the United States, 1685–2009*.

34 Ghadar pamphlet, 1914, printed by the Yugantar Ashram, Ghadar headquarters, San Francisco, Desh Bhagat Yaadgar collection Jalandar, Punjab.

35 *Ibid.*

36 *Passenger Lists of Vessels Arriving at New York, New York, 1820–1897*. Microfilm Publication M237, 675 rolls. NAI: 6256867. Records of the US Customs Service, Record Group 36. National Archives at Washington, D.C. - Microfilm Roll: Roll 3665; Line: 12; p. Number: 80.

37 *Ibid.*, Microfilm Roll: Roll 3697; Line 62; p. Number: 87.

38 *Ibid.*, Microfilm Roll: Roll 3710; Line 63; p. Number: 107.

39 *Ibid.*, Microfilm Roll: Roll 3723; Line 9; p. Number: 144.

40 *Ibid.*, Microfilm Roll: Roll 3743; Line 4; p. Number: 108.

41 Udham Singh alias Sher Singh, Amritsar Kotwali statement 1927, cited in
    Sikander Singh, *Udham Singh*, op. cit., p. 93.

42 A photo of Pritam Singh appears in the entry for the Hindustan Club. *The
    Michiganensian Yearbook, Year 1927.*

43 Udham Singh alias Sher Singh, Amritsar Kotwali statement 1927, cited in
    Sikander Singh, *Udham Singh*, op. cit., p. 95.

44 *Ibid.*

45 Year: 1920; Census Place: Highland Park, Wayne, Michigan; Roll T625_801;
    Page 5B; Enumeration District: 705 Pyem N. Mathur appears on the digital
    archive, but examining the document itself, one can see the handwriting of the
    entry below has looped over the name.

46 Entry in the Ghadar Directory for Prem Singh, op. cit.

47 Udham Singh alias Sher Singh, Amritsar Kotwali statement 1927, cited in
    Sikander Singh, *Udham Singh*, op. cit., p. 96; he claimed he 'had got two sons
    from that wife.'

48 https://history.state.gov/milestones/1921-1936/immigration-act

49 Udham Singh alias Sher Singh, Amritsar Kotwali statement 1927, cited in
    Sikanker Singh, *Udham Singh*, op. cit., p. 96.

50 *Ibid.*

51 *Ibid.*

52 Umberto Esposito. The National Archives and Records Administration;
    Washington, D.C.; *Petitions for Naturalization from the US District Court
    for the Southern District of New York, 1897–1944*; Series: M1972; Roll 308.

53 Umberto Esposito, petition number 64266, 1926 entry in the *New York Index
    to Petitions for Naturalization, filed in New York City 1792–1989.*

54 Udham Singh alias Sher Singh, Amritsar Kotwali statement 1927, cited in
    Sikanker Singh, *Udham Singh* op. cit., p. 97.

55 Author interview with Lord Indarjit Singh, who knew Udham Singh as a child
    and has very fond memories of playing with him.

Chapter 15

1 O'Dwyer, *India as I Knew it*, op. cit., p. 332.

2 Sir C. Sankaran Nair, *Gandhi and Anarchy 'Indore'*, Holkar State printing
   press, 1922, p. 47.

3 *Ibid.*

4 TNA J 17/634 – O'Dwyer vs Nair libel case.

5 *Ibid.*

6 *Ibid.*

7 O'Dwyer, *India as I Knew it* op. cit., p. 356.

8 *Ibid.*

9 FIR of Udham Singh, Amritsar 1927, in Navtej Singh and Avtar Singh Jouhl,

(eds), *Emergence of The Image, Redacted Documents of Udham Singh*, National Book Organisation, 2002, pp. 456–7.

10 Seema Sohi, *Echoes of Mutiny: Race, Surveillance, and Indian Anticolonialism in North America*, Oxford University Press USA, 2014.

11 Maia Ramnath, *Haj to Utopia: How the Ghadar Movement Charted Global Radicalism and Attempted to Overthrow the British Empire*, University of California Press, 2011, pp. 140, 152, 203.

12 Udham Singh alias Sher Singh, Amritsar Kotwali statement 1927, cited in Sikander Singh, *Udham Singh*, op. cit., p. 96; also TNA HO 144/21444 – Early History Sher Singh [memo], undated.

13 TNA P J (S) 466/36 – Secret Memo to Silver – notes on Ude Singh, Udham Singh, Frank Brazil 11/10/37.

14 Udham Singh alias Sher Singh, Amritsar Kotwali statement 1927, cited in Sikander Singh, *Udham Singh*, op. cit., p. 96.

15 *Ibid.*

16 Frank Brazil on the manifest of the SS *Sinsinawa*, 18 May 1927, leaving from Casablanca.

17 TNA MEPO 3/1743 – [Secret Memo] Ude Singh, Udham Singh, Sher Singh, Frank Brazil 11/10/37.

18 *Passenger crew lists for the SS* Jalapa *Year: 1927; Arrival: New York, New York*; Microfilm Serial: T715, 1897–1957; Microfilm Roll: Roll 4150; Line 6; p. 232.

19 Lupe Singh death certificate, 6 August 1949, Texas Department of State Health Services; Austin, Texas, USA, *Death Certificates, 1903–1982*. There is a Californian census record for a Lupe Singh, who apparently married a much older man, Harnam Singh. This could be the same woman who, desperate for some stability, married a man twenty years older than her – perhaps out of necessity. Harnam Singh only arrived in America in 1931, so the dates would fit her abandonment. Harnam Singh passenger record 1931: The National Archives at Washington, D.C.; *Passenger Lists of Vessels Arriving at San Francisco, California*; NAI Number 4498993; Record Group Title: Records of the Immigration and Naturalization Service, 1787–2004; Record Group Number 85.

20 TNA MEPO 3/1743 – Secret Memo to Mr Silver. Summary history sheet on Udham Singh 11/10/37.

21 Udham Singh alias Sher Singh, Amritsar Kotwali statement 1927, cited in Sikander Singh, *Udham Singh* op. cit., p. 99.

22 TNA MEPO 3/1743 – Secret Memo to Mr Silver. Summary history sheet on Udham Singh 11/10/37.

23 Udham Singh alias Sher Singh, Amritsar Kotwali statement 1927, cited in Sikander Singh, *Udham Singh*, op. cit., p. 100.

24 *Ibid.*

Chapter 16

1 Collett, *Butcher* (op. cit.), p. 423.
2 Ibid., p. 424.
3 *Ibid.*
4 *Scotsman*, 28 July 1927.
5 *Ibid.*
6 *Yorkshire Post* and *Leeds Intelligencer*, 25 July 1927.
7 *Gloucester Citizen*, 28 July 1927.
8 Press Association interview with Sir Michael O'Dwyer, reproduced in the *Yorkshire Post* and *Leeds Intelligencer*, 25 July 1927
9 From Savar Ali report, Kotwal 327/139 appended to FIR report on Sher Singh, Navtej Singh and Avtar Singh Jouhl, *Emergence,* op. cit., p. 456 (translated from the Urdu).
10 Register of FIRs for 1927 (Urdu) City Kotwali, Amritsar – Nos. 5–24 (1) Kotwal 327/139 – FIR report on Sher Singh (alias Udham Singh), Navtej Singh and Avtar Singh Jouhl, *Emergence*, op. cit., p. 222.
11 *Ibid.*
12 Udham Singh alias Sher Singh, Amritsar Kotwali statement 1927, cited in Sikanker Singh, *Udham Singh*, op. cit., p. 101.
13 Udham Singh alias Sher Singh, Amritsar Kotwali statement 1927, cited in Sikanker Singh, *Udham Singh*, op. cit., p. 101: 'They remained in the Rambagh from 12 till noon that day.'
14 Register of FIRs for 1927 (Urdu) City Kotwali, Amritsar – No 5–24 (1) Kotwal 327/139 – FIR report on Sher Singh (alias Udham Singh), Navtej Singh and Avtar Singh Jouhl, *Emergence*, op. cit., p. 222.
15 *Ibid.*
16 According to the FIR 5–24 (1) addional index, Udham was held and questioned from 30 August to 14 September 1927. Interrogation shifts were identified as 'morning' and 'evening' with Goga Singh and Sub-Inspector Murad Ali named as investigating officers.
17 Udham Singh alias Sher Singh, Amritsar Kotwali statement 1927, cited in Sikanker Singh, *Udham Singh*, op. cit., p. 98.
18 *Ibid.*
19 National Archives and Records Administration; Washington, D.C.; ARC Title: *Index to Petitions for Naturalizations Filed in Federal, State, and Local Courts in New York City, 1792–1906*; NAI Number: 5700802; Record Group Title: Records of District Courts of the United States, 1685–2009; Record Group Number RG 21.
20 *Ibid.*
21 FIR 5–24
22 *Ibid.* Information added after the Challan report – reproduced and translated Navtej Singh and Avtar Singh Jouhl, *Emergence*, op. cit., p. 458.

23 Though she was Mexican, the death certificate of Lupe Singh (op. cit.) noted her race as 'white'.
24 FIR of Udham Singh, 1927, Navtej Singh and Avtar Jouhl, Emergence, op. cit., pp. 457–8.
25 Copies of these publications are held at the Desh Bhagat Yadgar centre in Jallander.
26 Udham Singh alias Sher Singh, Amritsar Kotwali statement 1927, cited in Sikanker Singh, Udham Singh (op. cit.), p. 105.
27 Ibid.

Chapter 17

1   IOR L/P5/12/500 – Particulars of antecedents relative to prisoner Mohammed Singh AZAD Canon Row Police Station, 'A' Division, 13 March 1940.
2   Ibid.
3   HSRA handbill – signed by 'Balraj', 18 December 1928, The Hanging of Bhagat Singh: Complete Judgement and Other Documents, vol. 1, Unistar, 2005, p. 199.
4   Ibid.
5   Bhagat Singh and Bhupendra Hooja, Camana Lāla (ed.),The Jail Notebook and Other Writings, reprint edition, LeftWord Books, 2007, p. 132.
6   Ibid.
7   Ibid.
8   Interview by Sikander Singh with Sh. Ramji Dass, Udham Singh, op. cit., p. 108.
9   The British noted in their file that they believed Udham went back to Sunam in 1933 'for a short time' (Early History of Sher Singh alias Udham Singh – memo to ACC, HO 144/21444), but it seems from Kassid's account that it was much sooner after his release.
10 From the unpublished memoir of Manjit Singh Kasid, a friend of Udham Singh in Sunam. With the kind permission of his family.
11 Ibid.
12 Ibid.
13 Ibid.
14 Ibid.
15 Ibid.
16 Ibid.
17 Ibid.
18 Interview by Sikander Sigh with Dr Bhajan Singh from the town of Sunam, Sikander Singh, Udham Singh, op. cit., p. 108.
19 Manjit Singh memoir, op. cit.
20 Ibid.
21 Ibid.
22 Ibid.

23 Author's interview with Naranjan Kaur, daughter-in-law of Manjit Singh Kasid, Sunam, 2016.

Chapter 18

1 Udham Singh succeeded in getting a new passport from Lahore on 20 March 1933 – Secret memo to Silver 11/10/37 IORL/PJ/12/500.
2 *Particulars of antecedents relative to prisoner Mohamed Singh Azad – to Canon Row Police Station 'A' Division*, 13 March 1940, IORL/PJ/12/500.
3 *Ibid.*
4 IORL/PJ/12/500 –Secret Note on Mohammed Singh Azad Canon Row on 13 March 1940: *Particulars of antecedents relative to prisoner: Mohamed Singh Azad*. Police reported he reached London in 1934.
5 *Ibid.*
6 IORL/PJ/12/500 Udham Singh succeeded in getting a new passport from Lahore on 20 March 1933 – Secret memo to Silver 11/10/37 P & J (S) 466/1936.
7 Udham gave his address as 4 Best Lane, Canterbury, Secret Memo including Exract from New Scotland Yard Report 76, 4 November 1936.
8 Interview with Sital Singh, the grandson of Gurbachan Singh, by the author, 2016.
9 *Ibid.*
10 *Ibid.*
11 *Ibid.*
12 *Ibid.*
13 *Ibid.*
14 *Ibid.*
15 Keith Neilson, Greg Kennedy and David French, *The British Way in Warfare: Power and the International System, 1856–1956: Essays in Honour of David French*, Ashgate, 2010, p. 120.
16 Daniel Brückenhaus, *Policing*, op. cit., p. 177.
17 *Ibid.*
18 IORL/PJ/12/500 – Secret document to Silver IPI – 11/10/37 Summary of Ude Singh, Udham Singh, Sher Singh, Frank Brazil.
19 *Ibid.*
20 *Ibid.*
21 *Ibid.*
22 Manjit Singh Kassid memoir, op. cit.
23 *Ibid.*
24 *Ibid.*
25 *The Daily Mail Blue Book on the Indian Crisis*, April 1931.
26 *Ibid.*, p. 3.
27 *Ibid.*, p. 9.

28 'Should Blackshirts be Banned?', *Spectator*, 15 June 1934, p. 4.
29 Author interview with Sital Singh, grandson of Gurbachan Singh, 2016.
30 *Ibid.*
31 *Ibid.*
32 *Ibid.*
33 Memo from Johnston 28/5/36 – IOR/L/P5/500.

Chapter 19

1 Extract from New Scotland Yard Report No. 76, 4/11/36, IOR/L/P512/500, p. 158.
2 *Ibid.*
3 *Ibid.*
4 Evidence of Banta Singh, resident of Adler Street, given by his son Peter Singh to the author, 2018.
5 *ibid.*
6 Author interview with Sital Singh about his grandfather, Gurbachan Singh, London, 2016.
7 Communist Party of Great Britain Archives, Labour History Archive and Study Centre, CP-IND-BRAD Bradley Papers.
8 TNA KV 2/2507 IPI 6/12/35 – Trace request IPI.
9 TNA KV 2/2507 IPI – H. O. W. request 7/12/36.
10 TNA KV 2/2507 – Letter from MI5 re Eileen Palmer – and intercept of letter from Eileen to Horace 6 and 7 December 1935.
11 *Ibid.*
12 R. Palme Dutt and Ben Bradley, 'Anti-Imperialist People's Front in India', *The Labour Monthly*, Vol. 18.3, 1936, pp. 149–60.
13 TNA KV 2/ 2507 – Detailed Summary of Eileen Palmer's activities from 1933–1953 ref DDG through DB through B1 Mr Thistlethwaite.
14 From the author's interview with Sital Singh, grandson of Gurbachan Singh, 2016.
15 Interview with Nazir Singh Mattu, from the Culture Coventry Sound Archive, 'Coming to Coventry', PA 2671/1/50.
16 *Ibid.*
17 *Ibid.*
18 *Ibid.*
19 *Ibid.*
20 *Ibid.*
21 *Ibid.*
22 IOR L/PJ/12/645, File 273/42 – Indian Workers Union or Association: reports on members and activities.
23 Author interview with Sohan Cheema, Coventry, 2017, historian and archivist for the IWA.

24 Author interview with Sital Singh, grandson of Gurbachan Singh, 2016.

25 Author interview with Lord Indarjit Singh, December 2016.

26 *Ibid.*

27 Aroor Singh's grandson would later publicly atone for his grandfather's actions.

28 *Report of the Civil Disobedience Enquiry Committee Appointed by the All India Congress Committee 1922*, Vol. 1, Indian National Congress, Civil Disobedience Enquiry Committee, p. 157.

29 *Ibid.*

30 *Ibid.*

31 Author interview with Lord Indarjit Singh, December 2016.

32 Shiv Singh would also spell his name 'Jouhl' in later years, but I have chosen to use the spelling used by Udham Singh in 1940.

33 Author interview with Ajit Singh Johal, the son of Shiv Singh Johal, November 2016.

34 *Ibid.*

35 TNA PCOM 9/872 from Sheet C of the papers Udham Singh brought into court with him in 1940 – Letter to Carew-Robinson, 20 June 1940: '1937 India Office for USA, Application refused. 1939 Two more refused.'

36 IOR/L/P5/12/500

37 IOR L/P&J/12/34 IPI Financial Arrangements – and L/P&J/12/38; Vickery to Hirtzel – 13 June 1924.

38 *Ibid.*

39 IOR/L/PJ/6/1439, File 1862: Feb 1916–Apr 1917, IOR L/PJ/6/1439 copy of letter to the Recruitment Office Croydon from the Secretary of State for India, 14/4/17.

40 'The British Resistance: The true story of the secret guerilla army of shopkeepers and farmworkers trained to defy the Nazis in a suicidal last stand', *Daily Mail*, 25 November 2011.

41 IOR/L/PJ/12/500 – Note on Udham Singh, Sher Singh, Frank Brazil and Mohamed Singh Azad attached to 'My Dear Pilditch' Secret letter, 15 March 1940, presumably from Vickery of the IPI to Denys Pilditch.

42 IOR/L/PJ/12/500 – Secret: Extract from New Scotland Yard Report 121 dated 27 July 1938.

43 IOR/L/PJ/12/500 – Secret: Extract from New Scotland Yard Report 126, dated 5 October 1938.

Chapter 20

1 TNA HO 144/21445 – Udham Singh's multiple addresses 1939–1940.

2 TNA HO 144/21445 – 581 Wimborne Street, Bournemouth.

3 TNA HO 144/21445 – The Employment history of Udham Singh aka Sher Singh aka Mohammed Singh Azad.

4   *Ibid.*

5   *Ibid.*

6   Monthly Report of the Meteorological Office M.O 443, Vol. 56, No. 9 – report for September 1939.

7   IOR/L/P5/12/500 – Secret Memo: The particulars of Udham Singh, Sher Singh, Frank Brazil, and Mohamed Singh Azad, appended to a letter from Sir Denys Pilditch, esq. - Superintendent, Indian Police and Director, Intelligence Bureau, India.

8   Dr 'Krant' and M. L. Verma, *Swadhinta Sangram Ke Krantikari Sahitya Ka Itihas*, Vol. 2, Praveen Prakashan, p. 453.

9   TNA HO 144/21445 – Exhibit 20 in the trial of Udham Singh, also statement on oath of Richard Deighton, Detective Inspector, Trial date: 1 April 1940.

10 TNA PCOM 9/872 from Sheet C of the papers Udham Singh brought into court with him in 1940 – Letter to Carew-Robinson, 20 June 1940.

11 *Ibid.*

12 *Ibid.*

13 TNA MEPO 3/1743 – Memo from Dorset Constabulary Blandford, Wimborne, 21 March 1940.

14 TNA MEPO 3/1743 – Report from D. I. Fisher Bournemouth Division, Hants Constabulary, 23 March 1940.

15 Richard Popplewell, *Intelligence and Imperial Defence: British Intelligence and the Defence of the Indian Empire, 1904–1924*, Psychology Press, 1995, p. 224.

16 Author interview with Sital Singh, the grandson of Gurbachan Singh. Also cited by B. S Maighowalia, who interviewed Gurbachan Singh himself for his book: *Sardar Udham Singh: A Prince Amongst Patriots of India, the Avenger of the Massacre of Jallianwala Bagh, Amritsar.*

17 Also known as Surat Alley.

18 IOL/PJ/12/500 – Metropolitan Police Special Branch report, 15 March 1940.

19 Interview with Peter Singh, son of Banta Singh, by the author, February 2017.

20 *Ibid.*

21 *Ibid.*

22 Interview with Peter Singh, son of Banta Singh, by the author, February 2017.

23 Meterological Office report for 13 March 1940, National Meterological Library and Archive DWR 1940–43.

24 TNA HO 144/21445 – Evidence of Detective Inspector Richard Deighton 1 April 1940, also MEPO 3/1743 List of Property belonging to Mohammed Singh Azad.

25 TNA MEPO 3/1743 – Statement of Robert Churchill, 19 March 1940, expert witness on gun and ballistics.

26 TNA MEPO 3/1743 – Statement of John McWilliam, Police Sergeant 51 'A' Division attached to Rochester Row Station, 13 March 1940.

27 *Ibid.*

28 *Ibid.*

29 TNA MEPO 3/1743 – Metropolitan Police Summary of Caxton Hall Shooting, Canon Row Police Station 'A' Division, 16 March 1940, 'To Superintendent'.

30 *Ibid.*

31 *Ibid.*

32 *Ibid.*

33 *Ibid.*

34 Interview with Sir Michael O'Dwyer's housekeeper in the *Daily Express*, 14 March 1940.

35 *Ibid.*

36 Review in the *New York Times* by Frank S. Nugentaug, December 1939.

37 *Daily Express*, 14 March 1940.

38 HO/144/21444 – Secret Summary on Udham Singh.

39 TNA MEPO 3/1743 – Statement of Reginald Alfred Slee, Major (retired), Canon Row Police Station 'A' Division, 13 March 1940.

40 *Ibid.*

41 TNA MEPO 3/1743 – Statement of Marjory Usher, Canon Row Police Station, 13 March 1940.

42 *Ibid.*

43 Susan Farrington and Hugh Leach, *Strolling About on the Roof of the World: The First Hundred Years of the Royal Society of Asian Affairs*, Routledge Curzon, 2003.

44 TNA MEPO – 3/1743 Statement of Bertha Herring, Canon Row Police Station 'A' Division, 13 March 1940.

45 TNA MEPO – 3/1743 Note on Westminster Coroner's Court findings, Horseferry Road, SW1, touching on the death of Sir Michael Francis O'Dwyer, p. 13 in original indexing.

46 *Ibid.*

47 TNA DPP2/761+728 from the trial notes of McClure – summary of his case strategy. Released 2016.

48 TNA MEPO 3/1743 – Murder of Sir Michael Francis O'Dwyer by Udham Singh at Caxton Hall, Westminster, on 13 March, 1940 Ballistics report of E. J. Churchill, gunmaker, Orange Street London, EC2.

49 TNA MEPO/3/1743 – Bertha Herring statement taken by Detective Sergeant Bempton at Canon Row Police Station, 'A' Division, 13 March 1940.

50 TNA MEPO/3/1743 – Statement of Claud Wyndham Harry Riches, taken by Detective Inspector A. Philpot, Canon Row Police Station, 'A' Division, 13 March 1940.

51 *Ibid.*

52 Dr Grace Mackinnon speaking to the *Daily Express*, 14 March 1940.

53 TNA MEPO/3/1743 – Statement of Colonel Carl Henry Reinhold, taken by Detective Sergeant Carl Hagen, New Scotland Yard.

54 *Ibid.*

55 *Ibid.*

56 Philip Bloomberg's telephoned report, carried in the *Manchester Guardian*, 14 March 1940.
57 *Ibid.*

Chapter 21

1 TNA MEPO 3/1743 – Metropolitan Police Summary of Caxton Hall Shooting, Canon Row Police Station 'A' Division, 16 March 1940, 'To Superintendent'.
2 *Ibid.*
3 *Ibid.*
4 *Ibid.*
5 *Ibid.*
6 TNA MEPO 3/1743 – Statement of Jerrard Philip Kenny, M.D M.R.C.S Physician Surgeon, 17 March 1940.
7 TNA MEPO 3/1743 – Statement of Michael Redmond Hayes, I.R.C.P, M.R.C.S, St George's Hospital, 16 March 1940.
8 TNA MEPO 3/1743 – Statement of Margaret Shepherd Jones, witnessed by Police Sergeant William Baldwin, CID.
9 TNA MEPO 3/1743 – Statement of Marjorie Usher, witnessed by Detective Sergeant William Bray, 'A' Division.
10 TNA HO/144/21445 – Statements of Crown Prosecution Witnesses on Oath, Sir Frank Brown under cross-examination by the prosecution.
11 TNA HO/144/21445 – Sir Percy Sykes evidence at the trial of Udham Singh – under oath – cross-examination by Mr McClure of the prosecution.
12 *The Times*, 14 March 1940.
13 TNA MEPO 3/1743 – Statement of Detective Sergeant Sidney Jones, Canon Row Police Station, 16 March 1940.
14 TNA MEPO 3/1743 – Sidney Jones notebook.
15 *Ibid.*
16 IOR Mss Eur C826 – Copy of transcript of proceedings in the trial, on 4 June 1940, of Udham Singh for the murder of Sir Michael Francis O'Dwyer (1864–1940), Lieutenant Governor of the Punjab 1913–19.
17 TNA MEPO 3/1743 – Statement of Detective Sergeant Sidney Jones, Canon Row Police Station, 16 March 1940.
18 *Ibid.*
19 *Ibid.*
20 *Ibid.*
21 *Ibid.*
22 *Ibid.*
23 *Ibid.*
24 *Ibid.*
25 *Ibid.*

26 *Ibid.*

27 *Ibid.*

28 *Ibid.*

29 *Ibid.*

30 TNA MEPO 3/1743 – Metropolitan Police Telegram: 13 March 1940 – distributed 14 March 1940 – From Supt AD – notification of the charging of Udham Singh.

31 IOR/L/PJ/12/500 – Reactions to the Caxton Hall Outrage, Secret Letter, 29 March 1940.

32 Script of BBC news bulletin, from Roger Perkins, *Amritsar Legacy: Golden Temple to Caxton Hall – The Story of a Killing*, Picton, 1989, pp. 15–17.

33 Script of German 9.15 breaking news and midnight bulletin from Perkins, *Amritsar Legacy*, op. cit., pp. 17–19.

34 *The Times*, 14 March 1940.

35 *Daily Telegraph*, 14 March 1940.

36 *Ibid.*

37 *Daily Express*, 14 March 1940.

38 *Ibid.*

39 *Daily Mail*, 15 March 1940.

40 *Daily Telegraph*, March 1940.

41 *The Times*, 14 March 1940.

42 *Daily Mail*, 15 March 1940.

43 *Manchester Guardian*, 14 March 1940.

44 *Sheffield Telegraph*, 14 March 1940.

45 Script of German a.m. news bulletin, from Roger Perkins, *Amritsar Legacy* op. cit., pp. 19–22.

46 Perkins, *Amritsar Legacy* op. cit., pp. 17–19.

Chapter 22

1 MEPO 3/1743 G. R. number 201/MR/1911 – Memo for General Registry of Crime.

2 *Daily Telegraph*, 15 March 1940.

3 TNA PCOM 9/872 – SINGH UDHAM: convicted at Central Criminal Court (CCC) 5 June of murder and sentenced to death – letter from p. L. Dunham to the governor of HM Prison Brixton, 14 March 1940, internal document No. 1012B.

4 TNA PCOM/872 – Memo from Prison Commission to Undersecretary of State 18/3/40, internal ref p.30623/2.

5 IOR/L/PJ/12/500, 15 March 1940 – Memo to Denys Pilditch containing Police and Special Branch summary on Udham Singh.

6 TNA MEPO 3/1743 – List of Property belonging to Mohamed Singh Azad.

7 IOR/L/PJ/12/500 – Metropolitan Police Special Branch, 15 March 1940

(enclosure in memo to Silver), signed by Inspector Whitehead and G. Gill for Superintendent.

8 *Ibid.*

9 *Ibid.*

10 *Ibid.*

11 *Ibid.*

12 *Ibid.*

13 *Ibid.*

14 Author interview with Lord Indarjit Singh, December 2016.

15 *Ibid.*

16 *Ibid.*

17 *Ibid.*

18 TNA HO 144/21445 – Letter to the Superintendent from J. Swain DD Inspector 'A' Division Canon Row Police Station, 16 March 1940.

19 TNA MEPO 3/1743 – Letter from Mohammed Singh Azad to Supt Sands from Brixton Prison, 16 March 1940.

20 *Ibid.*

21 *Ibid.*

22 *Ibid.*

23 TNA MEPO 3/1743 – Letter from Inspector J. Swain to Superintendent [Sands], 11 April 1940.

24 Author interview with Jaswant Singh, the nephew of Rattan Singh Azad, an East End salesman who was picked up in Whitechapel the day after the killing.

25 IOR/L/PJ/12/500 – Secret memo 18/3/40.

26 Secret memo from Chief Constable Albert Canning, Special Branch, New Scotland Yard, London SW1, 19 March 1940.

27 IOR/L/P5/12/500 – Secret document – copy of telegram from Secretary of State to Gov. of India, Home Department, no. 1827, 17 April 1940.

Chapter 23

1 'The India League tragedy "regretted and condemned"', *Manchester Guardian*, 15 March 1940.

2 'An Insane Act', *Harijan*, Vol. 8.7, 23 March 1940, p. 56.

3 *National Herald*, 15 March 1940.

4 *Ibid.*

5 *Ibid.*

6 *Ibid.*

7 *Ibid.*

8 *Ibid.*

9 IOR/L/PJ/12/500 – Secret Memo dated 8 April 1940 – Udham Singh's defence – Vickey IPI to Silver.

10 *Ibid.*

Chapter 24

1   TNA F0371/24205 – Secret Telegram RE: J. C. O'Dwyer, 28 March 1940.
2   *Fresno Bee*, 14 March 1940.
3   'Sir Michael was Shot in Back', *Daily Mail*, 15 March 1940.
4   IOR L/P5/12/500, 15 March 1940 – Memo to Silver containing Police and Special Branch summary.
5   'Woman with a Grievance', *Gloucestershire Echo*, 11 May 1939.
6   'Pistol Charge', *Manchester Evening News*, 11 May 1939.
7   'INDIA: I & My Government', *Time*, 2 August 1932; also *Calcutta Telegraph*, 10 March 1913.
8   TNA HO 144/ 21445 – Letter of Udham Singh to Kumari (11 February or March 1940).
9   *Ibid.*
10 *Ibid.*
11 TNA HO 144/21445 – Letter from M. S. Azad, Brixton Prison, 20 March 1940; also Grewal and Puri, op. cit., pp. 36–41.
12 *Ibid.*
13 *Ibid.*
14 TNA HO 144/21445 – Letter from Udham Singh to Kumari via Stockton Gurdwara, 26 March 1940 (signed M. S. A.).
15 *Ibid.*
16 *Ibid.*
17 *Ibid.*
18 TNA HO/144/21445, Letter from M. S. A., Brixton prison, 30 March 1940; also Grewal and Puri, op. cit., p. 42.
19 *Ibid.*
20 *Ibid.*
21 *Ibid.*
22 *Ibid.*
23 *Ibid.*
24 *Ibid.*
25 IOR/L/PJ/12/500 – Smuggled letter from 'Bawa' to Mr Singh c/o R. Sharman, 20 Cotton Street, Poplar, postmark 3 April 1940.
26 *Ibid.*
27 *Ibid.*
28 *Ibid.*
29 TNA PCOM 9/872 – Handwritten Memo to Lamb,18 April 1940.
30 TNA PCOM 9/872 – Memo from prison officer Geoff Watson to the governor of Brixton prison, 23 April 1940.
31 TNA HO 144/21444 – Minutes from Brixton Prison to prison commissioners for observation, 15 June 1940.
32 *Daily Express*, 6 June 1940.

33 The police later pieced together the ripped fragments, revealing a long incendiary speech Udham had wanted to give in court. Among his papers they also found a diary of sorts. They can be found in TNA PCOM 9/872.

Chapter 25

1 'Sikhs Hail Return of 1940 Martyr's Remains to Punjab', *New York Times*, 5 August 1974.
2 *Ibid.*
3 *Ibid.*
4 Gagandeep Singh speaking about his father, S. Kulbir Singh, president of the Sunam Municipal Council. Interview with the author, December 2016.
5 Rakesh Kumar, local historian whose work on Udham Singh revealed the fate of his remains. Interview with the author, December 2016.
6 *Ibid.*

BIBLIOGRAPHY

Source Material from Archives

London: The National Archives (TNA); The British Library: India Office Records (IOR); Culture Coverntry Sound Archive (PA)

TNA: MEPO 3/1743: Murder of Sir Michael Francis O'Dwyer by Udham Singh at Caxton Hall, Westminster, on 13 March 1940

TNA: PCOM 9/872: SINGH UDHAM: convicted at Central Criminal Court (CCC) 5 June of murder and sentenced to death

TNA: HO 144/21444: CRIMINAL CASES: SINGH, Udham convicted at Central Criminal Court (CCC) on 5 June 1940 for murder and sentenced to death (1940)

TNA: HO 144/21445: CRIMINAL CASES: SINGH, Udham convicted at Central Criminal Court (CCC) on 5 June 1940 for murder and sentenced to death (1940) part II

TNA: DPP 2/761: UDHAM, Singh: Murder appeal (1940)

TNA: DPP 2/728: UDHAM SINGH: Murder (1940)

TNA: FO 371/24205/165: Indian sedition in the United States: The plot against Sir Michael's son

TNA: CRIM 1/113/5: The murder of Sir Curzon Wyllie by an Indian student, Madan Lal Dhingra (1909)

TNA: J17/634 O'Dwyer vs Nair libel case

TNA: KV2/2507 Files on Eileen Palmer

IOR: L/PJ/12/500: Udham or Uday Singh: activities outside India; assassination of Sir Michael O'Dwyer; trial, appeal and execution in London

IOR: Mss Eur C826: 1940: Udham Singh papers

IOR: L/PJ/7/1775: The grant of passport endorsements in error by the Vice-Consulate at Dunkirk to Udham Singh who is on the passport stop list

IOR: V/27/262/9: F. C. Isemonger, and J. Slattery, An account of the Ghadr conspiracy 1913–1915 (1919)

IOR: L/P&J 12/34 IPI Financial Arrangements

IOR: L/PJ/12/645 Indian Workers Union or Association : reports on
members and activities

PA: 2671/1/50 Nazir Singh Mattu

New Delhi

National Archives of India – File No. 77, 1940, HOME Department,
Political (Secret) Government of India

Home – Political B – January 1915, Nos. 278–282, Activities of the Ghadar
Party

Home – Political Deposit – September 1919, No. 31, Total Number of
Casualties at the Jallianwala Bagh

Home – Political Deposit – April 1919, No. 49, Fortnightly Report March
1919

Home – Political B – June 1919, Nos. 408–431, Daily reports of Punjab
Government in connection with the disturbances

Home – Political Deposit – October 1919, No. 31, Total number of
casualties at the Jallianwala Bagh

Home – Political – 1924, File No. 200/2: O'Dwyer versus Nair

Parliamentary Papers and Government Publications UK and India

War Speeches of Sir Michael O'Dwyer, Superintendent Government
Printing, 1918

Report of the Committee appointed in the Government of India to
investigate the disturbances in the Punjab, etc. [and evidence taken
before the Disorders Inquiry Committee] (see also Command 681) –
London H. M. Stationery Office, 1920

Minority report – see above (pp. 87–140) signed: Jagat Narayan, C. H.
Setalvad, Sultan Ahmed

Hansard (online) – Official record of Parliamentary debates and
proceedings

Parliamentary Papers (Westminster) Command 534: Reports on the Punjab
Disturbances

The Collected Works of Mahatma Gandhi (CWMG), MK Gandhi:
26 April 1918–April 1919, Publications Division, Ministry of
Information and Broadcasting, Government of India, 1965, digitised
25 July 2011

Printed Material

Ahmed, Rehana and Sumita Mukherjee (eds), *South Asian Resistances in Britain 1858–1947*, Continuum International Publishing Group, 2012

Aijazuddin, F. S., *Lahore, Illustrated Views of the 19th Century*, Mapin Publishing Ltd, 2004

Aijazuddin, F. S., *Lahore Recollected*, Sang-e-Meel, 2004

Arnold, David, *Colonizing the Body: State Medicine and Epidemic Disease in Nineteenth-Century India*, University of California Press, 1993

Bance, Peter, *Sikhs in Britain*, Sutton Publishing, 2007

Beames, John, *Memoirs of a Bengali Civilian*, Chatto & Windus, 1961

Brückenhaus, Daniel, *Policing Transnational Protest: Liberal Imperialism and the Surveillance of Anticolonialists in Europe, 1905–1945*, Oxford University Press, 2017

Chatterji, Bankimcandra (trans. Julius J. Lipner), *Anandamath, The Sacred Brotherhood*, Oxford University Press, 2005

Collett, Nigel, *The Butcher of Amritsar*, Hambledon and London, 2005

Colvin, Ian, *The Life of General Dyer*, William Blackwood and Sons Ltd, 1929

Da Gaurav, Bhartia, *Sardar Udham Singh*, J. N. Sandhey, 1975

Dalrymple, William, *The Last Mughal*, Bloomsbury, 2009

Datta, V. N. and S. Settar, *Jallianwala Bagh Massacre*, Pragati Publications, 2000

Deol, Gurdev Singh, *The Role of the Ghadar Party in the National Movement*, Sterling Publishers, 1969

Desai, Mahadev Haribhai (ed. Narahari Dvārakādāsa Parīkha, trans. Hemantkumar Gunabhai Nilkanth), *Day to Day with Gandhi: Secretary's Diary*, Sarva Seva Sangh Prakashan, 1968

Douglas-Home, Jessica, *A Glimpse of Empire*, Rain Tree, 2012

Draper, Alfred, *Amritsar: The Massacre that Ended the Raj*, Cassell, 1981

Draper, Alfred, *The Amritsar Massacre: Twilight of the Raj*, Buchan & Enright, 1985

Duncan, R. S., *Peerless Priceless Pentonville, 160 Years of History*, R. S. Duncan, 2000

Durrani, Nazmi, *Liberating Minds, Restoring Kenyan History: Anti-Imperialist Resistance by Progressive South Asian Kenyans, 1884–1965*, Vita Books, 2017

Farrington, Susan and Hugh Leach, *Strolling About on the Roof of the World: The First Hundred Years of the Royal Society of Asian Affairs*, Routledge Curzon, 2003

French, Patrick, *Liberty or Death: India's Journey to Independence and Division*, Harper Collins, 1997

Gandhi, Mahatma, *Young India*, Navajivan Publishing House, 1928

Gandhi, Mahatma (ed. Louis Fischer), *The Essential Gandhi: An Anthology of his Writings on his Life, Work and Ideas*, Vintage Books, 1962

Ghuman, Paul, *British Untouchables: A Study of Dalit Identity and Education*, Ashgate, 2011

Giani, Bhajan Singh, *Sade Shaheed*, Jullundhur (Punjabi)

Giani, Tirlok Singh, *Shaheed Udham Singh Sunam te Jallianwala Bagh*, Amritsar, 1979 (Punjabi)

Gill, M. S., 'Udham Singh, The Patriot who Avenged the Jallianwala Bagh Massacre', *The Illustrated Weekly of India*, 30 January 1972

Goebel, Michael, *Anti-Imperial Metropolis*, Cambridge University, 2017

Ghosh, Durba, *Gentlemanly Terrorists, Political Violence and the Colonial State in India, 1919–1947*, Cambridge University Press, 2017

Greenberger, Allen J., *The British Image of India: A Study in the Literature of Imperialism 1880–1960*, Oxford University Press, 1969

Grewal, J. S., *The Sikhs of the Punjab*, Foundation Books, 1995

Grewal, J. S. and H. K. Puri (eds), *Letters of Udham Singh*, Guru Nanak Dev University Amritsar, 1974

Gupta, Shiv Kumar, *Jallianwala Bagh and the Raj*, Jallianwala Bagh Commemoration Volume, 1997

Hays, J. N., *Epidemics and Pandemics: Their Impacts on Human History*, ABC-CLIO, 2005

Horniman, B. G., *British Administration and the Amritsar Massacre*, Mittal Publications, 1984

Inqulabhi Yodha Udham Singh, Khalsa Sikh Orphanage, 1974

Jeevani Shaheed Udjham Singh, Patiala, 1988 (Punjabi)

Johnston, Hugh, *The Voyage of the Komagatu Maru: The Sikh Challenge to Canada's Colour Bar*, Oxford University Press, 1979

Josh, Sohan Singh, *Hindustan Ghadar Party: A Short History*, Desh Bhagat Yadgar Committee, 2007

Judd, Denis, *The British Raj*, Wayland Publishers, 1972

Kaul, Chandrika, *Reporting the Raj: The British Press and India*, Manchester University Press, 2003

Khan, Yasmin, *The Raj at War*, Vintage Books, 2016

Khullar, K. K., *India's Freedom Fighters: Udham Singh*, Nasik, 1983

Kumar, Rakesh, *Udham Singh: KrantiKari Shaheed Udham Singh*, Sangam Publications, 2015 (Punjabi)

Lal, Shereen, *Imperial Violence and the Path to Independence*, I. B. Tauris, 2016

Liebau, Heike *et al* (eds), *The World in World Wars: Experiences, Perceptions and Perspectives from Africa and Asia*, BRILL, 2010

Lloyd, Nick, *The Amritsar Massacre: The Untold Story of One Fateful Day*, I. B. Tauris, 2011

Madden, A. F. and John Darwin (eds), *Select Documents on the Constitutional History of the British Empire and Commonwealth: The Dominions and India since 1900*, Greenwood Press, 1993

Maigowalia, B. S., *Sardar Udham Singh*, Hoshiarpore, 1969

Massey, Eithne, *Legendary Ireland: Myths and Legends of Ireland*, The O'Brien Press, 2013

Neilson, Keith and Greg Kennedy (eds), *The British Way in Warfare: Power and the International System, 1856–1956: Essays in Honour of David French*, Ashgate, 2010

O'Dwyer, Sir Michael, *War Speeches*, Superintendent Government Printing, 1918

O'Dwyer, Sir Michael, *India as I Knew it 1885–1925*, Constable & Company Ltd, 1926

O'Dwyer, Sir Michael (with preface and biographical profile by Tom O'Dwyer), *The History of the O'Dwyers*, (originally published as *The O'Dwyers of Kilnamanagh: The History of an Irish Sept*) Colour Books, 2000

Perkins, Roger, *The Amritsar Legacy*, Picton Publishing, 1989

Pierrepoint, Albert, *Executioner: An Autobiography*, Eric Dobby Publishing Ltd, 2017

Popplewell, Richard, *Intelligence and Imperial Defence: British Intelligence and the Defence of the Indian Empire, 1904–1924*, Psychology Press, 1995

Ram, Raja, *Jallianwala Bagh Massacre: A Pre-Meditated Plan*, Punjab University, 1969

Ramnath, Maia, *Haj to Utopia*, University of California Press, 2011

Reynolds, Mrs Margaretta Catherine, *At Home in India: Or Tâza-be-Tâza*, H. Drane, 1903

Sankaran Nair, Sir C., *Gandhi and Anarchy 'Indore'*, Holkar State Printing Press, 1922

Singh, Dr Fauja, *Eminent Freedom Fighters of Punjab*, Punjabi University, 1972

Singh, Dr Gurcharana, *Sunam Da Surma, Sardar Udham Singh*, Jullundur, 1982

Singh, Dr Gurcharana, *Babbar Akali Movement*, Aman Publications, 1993

Singh, Kesar, *Shaheed Udham Singh*, National Press of India, 1973

Singh, Navtej, *Challenge to Imperial Hegemony: The Life Story of a Great Indian Patriot*, Punjabi University, 1998

Singh, Navtej and Avtar Singh Jouhl (eds), *Emergence of the Image: Redact Documents of Udham Singh*, National Book Organisation, 2002

Singh, Sikander, 'How Udham Singh Avenged the Jallianwala Bagh Massacre', *Research Journal, Arts*, Vol. 2.2, 1987

Singh, Sikander, 'Jallianwala Bagh Massacre and its Impact on Udham Singh', *Proceedings of Punjab History Conference, 21st session*, Punjab University Patiala, 1987

Singh, Sikander, *Udham Singh, alias Ram Mohammed Singh Azad*, B. Chattar Singh Jiwan Singh, 1998

Singh, Sikander, *Udham Singh: A Saga of the Freedom Movement and Jallianwala Bagh*, B. Chattar Singh Jiwan Singh, 2017

Sohi, Seema, *Echoes of Mutiny: Race, Surveillance, and Indian Anticolonialism in North America*, Oxford University Press, 2014

Sunami, Sayha, *Sunama Da Itihas*, Sunam, 1982

Talbot, Ian and Tahir Kamran, *Lahore in the Time of the Raj*, Viking, 2016

Tickell, Alex, *Terrorism, Insurgency and Indian–English Literature 1830–1947*, Routledge, 2012

Vashishat, K. C., *Shaheed Udham Singh alias Ram Mohammad Singh Azad*, 1974

Visram, Rozina, *Ayahs, Lascars and Princes,* Pluto Press, 1986

Wagner Kim, '"Calculated to Strike Terror": The Amritsar Massacre and the Spectacle of Colonial Violence', *Past & Present*, Vol. 233.1, 2016, pp. 185–225

Wagner, Kim, *The Amritsar Massacre: India and the Crisis of Empire 1919*, Yale University Press, 2018

Wagner, Kim, 'Savage Warfare: Violence and the Rule of Colonial Difference in Early British Counterinsurgency', *History Workshop Journal*, Vol. 85.1, 2018, pp. 217–37

Walton, Calder, *Empire of Secrets*, Harper Press, 2013

Waraich, Malwinder Jit Singh, *Ghadr Movement Original Documents Judgements*, Vol. 3, Unistar, 2012

Wolmar, Christian, *Blood, Iron & Gold: How the Railways Transformed the World*, Atlantic Books, 2009

Wolpert, Stanley, *Massacre at Jallianwala Bagh*, Penguin, 1988

Woodruff, Philip, *The Men Who Ruled India, The Guardians,* Jonathan
    Cape, 1954
Wylie, J. A., *India at the Parting of the Ways,* Lincoln Williams Ltd, 1934

FURTHER READING

Brar, Harpal, *Inquilab Zindabad: India's Liberation Struggle,* Harpal
    Brar, 2014
Condos, Mark, *The Insecurity State: Punjab and the Making of Colonial
    Power in British India,* Cambridge University Press, 2017
Dorril, Stephen, *Blackshirt Sir Oswald Mosley and British Fascism,*
    Penguin, 2007
Evans, Colin, *Murder 2: The Second Casebook of Forensic Detection,*
    Wiley, 2004
Gilmour, Julie F., *Trouble on Main Street: Mackenzie King, Reason, Race
    and the 1907 Vancouver Riots,* Allen Lane, 2014
Gwyn, Major General Sir Charles W., *Imperial Policing,* Macmillan & Co.
    Ltd, 1936
Lahiri, Shompa, *Indians in Britain: Anglo-Indian Encounters, Race and
    Identity, 1880–1930,* Cass, 2000
Madra, Amandeep Singh and Parmjit Singh (eds), *Warrior Saints: Four
    Centuries of Sikh Military History,* Vol. 1, Kashi House, 2013
Mount, Ferdinand, *The Tears of the Rajas: Mutiny, Money and Marriage
    in India 1805,* Simon & Schuster, 2015
Mukherjee, Janam, *Hungry Bengal, War Famine and the End of Empire,*
    Hurst & Company, 2015
Nasta, Susheila with Florian Stadler, *Asian Britain, A Photographic
    History,* The Westbourne Press, 2013
O'Halpin, Eunan, *Spying on Ireland,* Oxford University Press, 2008
O'Malley, Kate, *Ireland, India and Empire: Indo–Irish Radical
    Connections, 1919–64,* Manchester University Press, 2009
Page, Ra (ed.), *Protest: Stories of Resistance,* Comma Press, 2018
Reid, Walter, *Keeping the Jewel in the Crown: The British Betrayal of
    India,* Birlinn Ltd, 2016
Sharma, Shalini, *Radical Politics in Colonial Punjab: Governance and
    Sedition,* Routledge, 2010
Swinson, Arthur, *Six Minutes to Midnight: The Story of General Dyer and
    the Amritsar Affair,* Peter Davis Publishing, 1964
Ter Minassian, Taline, *Most Secret Agent of Empire: Reginald Teague-Jones,
    Master Spy of the Great Game,* Hurst & Company Publishers, 2012

Tharoor, Shashi, *An Era of Darkness: The British Empire in India*, Aleph, 2016

Visram, Rozina, *Asians in Britain: 400 Years of History*, Pluto Press, 2002

Wagner, Kim, *The Great Fear of 1857: Rumours, Conspiracies and the Making of the Indian Uprising*, Dev Publishers & Distributors, 2014

Wagner, Kim, *The Skull of Amum Bheg: The Life and Death of a Rebel of 1857*, Hurst & Company, 2017

Walter, Dierk, *Colonial Violence – European Empires and the Use of Force*, Hurst & Company, 2017

Wariach, Malwinder Jit Singh, *Bhagat Singh's Jail Note Book*, Unistar, 2016

Williams, Stephanie, *Running the Show*, Penguin Books, 2012

Wilson, Jon, *India Conquered*, Simon & Schuster, 2016

INDEX

National Origins Act, 174
Nayyar and Sons, 209–10
Nazir Singh Mattu, 228–31
New Delhi, 309
New Scotland Yard, report of,
    222–3
New York Times, 68, 311
Nicol, p. H., 188
Nikmu Mal Girdhari, 107
Nilowal, 33
nizams, 38

O'Dwyer, Eunice Jr, 38
O'Dwyer, Eunice Sr, 28–9, 38, 257,
    271, 295
O'Dwyer, Geoffrey, 148
O'Dwyer, Ivon, 148
O'Dwyer, Jack, 39, 111, 249, 294–5
O'Dwyer, John Chevalier, see
    O'Dwyer, Jack
O'Dwyer, John Snr, 19–20, 111
    stroke and death suffered by, 22,
        149–50
O'Dwyer, Margaret, 19
O'Dwyer, Sir Michael, 177–81, 208,
    215 (see also Udham Singh)
    ACS passing among, 22
    among brothers and sisters
        siblings, 19
    ancestral roots of, 18
    and angry missives to London
        from, 67
    and Basanta, 51
    BBC report on, 275–6
    becomes viceroy of India, 21
    birth of, 18
    and boundary dispute, 38
    and building of gallows, 120
    burial of, 295

    celebrity status of, 177
    Commission hated by, 137–8
    critics of, 121
    and debt of gratitude, 66
    and Defence of India Act, 63
    dogged critics of, 121
    Dyer needs support from, 117
    and Dyer's funeral, 188–9
    early school of, 20
    editors attract, 217–18
    executions on watch of, 70
    and family hunger, lack of, 19
    fastidious habits of, 51–2
    first assignment of, 27
    giving no game away by, 43
    goes missing from home, 257–8
    home fired into, 22
    ICS passed by, 21
    and immediate post-death, 263–7
    and India articles, 218
    and Indian extremists in
        California, 294
    'Irish to the backbone', 18
    knighted, 49
    leaves for India for, 23
    leaves India temporarily, and
        returns, 28–9
    and martial law, 120
    memoirs of, 85, 118
    in Montgomery, 56
    and mutiny, 76, 118
    new lieutenant governor, 43, 44
    news reaches, 115
    nickname of, 4
    office extension for, 22
    plans made by, 118
    post-to-post moves by, 28
    praise from, 1
    prepared to sue, 178–9
    and Punjab, 77